Women's Voices on FIRE

Feminist International Radio Endeavour

María Suárez Toro

on behalf of the FIRE collectives from 1991 to 1999

Anomaly Press
(Center for the Study of the Gift Economy)
P.O. Box 3138 • Austin, Texas 78764

Anomaly Press
P.O. Box 3138
Austin, TX 78764

Tune in to FIRE on the Internet at www.fire.or.cr

Cover art by
Liliana Wilson

Edited by
Dalya F. Massachi, Debra Cedeño, Nancy Meredith

Suárez Toro, María
  Women's Voices on Fire: The Feminist International Radio Endeavour / by María Suárez Toro. Edited by Dalya F. Massachi, Debra Cedeño, Nancy Meredith. Cover design by Liliana Wilson.

    p.   cm.
ISBN 0-9672912-0-8

  1. Women in radio broadcasting. 2. Radio and women. I. Title. II. Title: The Feminist International Radio Endeavour.
PN 1991 W6 S80   DDN 302.23 Su   LC 00-131387

Many of the quotes, letters, and e-mail messages in this book were originally in Spanish and translated into English by the staff of FIRE. Many testimonies and names of women on the air have been transcribed from audiotapes.

Printed in the United States of America
at Morgan Printing in Austin, Texas

Dedication and Acknowledgments

On behalf of the FIRE collective, I want to dedicate this book to the many FIRE collectives that have made Feminist International Radio Endeavour possible. Sometimes the collective has been composed of two; other times of four; very often, as in our broadcasts from conferences and events, of hundreds of women.

It has always included Genevieve Vaughan, who founded and has sponsored FIRE since the start.

The collective has also at times included women in agencies that have helped to fund FIRE. These women believed in FIRE and worked to get their agencies to contribute to our endeavor.

The FIRE collective for the publication of this book also includes Dalya Massachi, Debra Cedeño, and Nancy Meredith, who have edited a book written by a Spanish-speaking woman... no easy task! It also includes Adilia Caravaca, and Engracia Gómez who translated the Spanish version, which will also be published.

This book is dedicated to the voices on FIRE, the thousands of women who have come on the air to share their wealth of knowledge with us and with the rest of the world. Their voices are a gift that cannot be measured in time and space, but that keep resounding, just like the airwaves. One could trace their origin, but they are never ending as they expand though the atmosphere and cyberspace, and as they keep coming back to us in our memories. These voices reach the most unexpected places and ears; their trajectories cannot be controlled!

This book is also dedicated to the men who, as listeners and supporters, have given themselves the opportunity to vindicate the loss of a right denied to them by patriarchy: the right to listen to women's profound voices on all issues. We also dedicate this book to those men who have helped FIRE staff learn the technical skills of radio production without taking over the controls!

Personally, as the writer of the book, I want to dedicate this book to four special women in my life in FIRE, women who have been critical in my own development as a feminist communicator, and in the contribution I have made to the development of FIRE.

One of them is *Genevieve Vaughan*. Her special combination of political and economic generosity with Third World women is almost beyond belief, but we can attest to it: I can put my hands in the fire. Thank you!

Another is *Katerina Anfossi Gómez*, compañera co-producer of FIRE since its beginning, and still strongly with it into FIRE's next millennium. Aside from all of the characteristics that make her a very special woman and communicator (and the true sound engineer at FIRE), she has a skill that has made it possible for us to build FIRE to be what it has become: her willingness to always go one step beyond what is really possible for us to do!

In the most critical moment for FIRE in 1998, she also taught me the sense of entitlement of women to own their creations! Thanks for following me sometimes, for pushing me other times, and for walking together with me always.

The third is *Margaret Thompson*, my journalist compañera who has, among other things, taught me to appreciate the way in which FIRE has contributed to the democratization of media by letting women frame their own stories. She has also taught me that I can frame my own life in the midst of our collective struggle to try to change the world!

Finally, I want to thank my mother, *Maribel Toro de Suárez*, as she likes to call herself. She was the first woman who taught me, at age six, to listen to myself and to others as if we were on the radio. It was the lesson I drew from when I became a FIRE producer.

When I was a little girl, I used to cuss a lot. My mother tried all of the usual methods to try to get me to stop. Nothing worked until one day, when I was about six or seven years old, she decided to try a more civilized method. She sat me down on a table in front of her, face to face, woman to woman, and proceeded to explain "Okay, my dear daughter, I am going to teach you to listen to yourself when you say those horrible words."

She proceeded to do so, by taking one hand of mine with hers, and putting it softly over one of my ears. Then she gave me directions: "Okay dear, now yell the ten worst words you know. I promise I will not punish you, because this is an experiment."

I was fascinated with the possibility of yelling all the forbidden words in front of her, right in her face without being reprimanded, so I did. "Coñooooo, Caraaaaaaaaajo, Mieeeeeerda..." I finished with a sigh of relief from getting them out. "Ahhhhhhhh!"

"Did you listen to yourself?" my mother asked.

"Of course," I answered.

"What did you hear?" she continued.

"My anger, Mami, my anger, because I am not allowed to be myself."

Of course I continued cussing, but I think my mother had a new understanding as to the origins of my bad language, an understanding that stemmed from her having listened to me listening to myself!

I also developed a very deep insight that I later recalled when I began producing FIRE: Doing feminist radio is having one ear covered, in order to listen to what's inside, and the other ear open, to listen to others. That is what feminist radio is all about! And this is what this book is all about!

—*María Suárez Toro*

Women on FIRE

Please keep encouraging women to do what you are doing. We have been silent for so long, and that's why we have been suppressed and our needs and aspirations silenced. It is high time that women have institutions and networks where they can be heard. FIRE has given women a voice, so please keep up the good work.

—Bene Madunagu, Coordinator of the Coalition of
Nigerian NGOs on Health, Population and
Development, and member of DAWN

I want to say that FIRE has an important role in the history of the international women's movement because you make it possible for us to dialogue with people we never meet. It was never so important as it is now for women to talk to each other. It is not easy to understand each other when we come from so many different cultural and social realities. The world is too big. A radio program like FIRE makes it smaller and makes the world easier for us, because it allows for a dialogue toward solidarity.

—Rosiska Darcy d'Oliveira, organizer of Planeta
Femmea, women's tent at UNCED

FIRE is that: warmth and light, and dancing energy and power. It is the politics of the airwaves—invisible, everywhere, able to go beyond the walls of tyranny—like feminism.

—Robin Morgan, U.S. journalist and
former editor of *Ms* magazine

FIRE has really lit a fire all around the world to enhance women's under-standing that we need not only a new environment as such, but also a new environment that deals with human justice, economic rights, peace, equality, and a new kind of vision that women have.... Your radio net-work has been very significant in reflecting those views. Our relationship has been wonderful and we will continue working together always.

—Bella Abzug, Director of WEDO

FIRE is a valuable instrument at international conferences in the way you use the interviews to lobby the toughest state delegates so they clarify their positions with transparency and women know where they stand. Also, your putting women's voices on the air, especially for those who cannot come to conferences, provides a link that connects women all over the world.

—Amparo Claro, Coordinator, Latin American and
Caribbean Women's Health Network

The women in Black Against War from Belgrade, Serbia, want to support you in continuing a very important political work with the FIRE radio pro-gram. FIRE is one of the rare radio programs around the world that cares about injustices women in Black from Belgrade have had an opportunity to work with FIRE during the UN World Conference on Human Rights in Vienna, in 1993. It was a pleasure to work with women who are committed and who are supportive of the small non-violent acts that are intended to promote women's human rights and peace.As pease and feminist activists ourselves, we are strongly supporting FIRE and the work that we trust and that aims to end all the discrimination of women, men and children.

—Stasa Zajovic and Lepa Mladhenovic
Women in Black

Fire has given voice to women all over the world. I will never forget the daily broadcasts made during the Vienna Conference on Human Rights uniting women worldwide and keeping their agenda alive in the midst of the tensions of the inter-governmental negotiations. warm wishes to you once more.

—Shanti Dairiam, Kuala Lumpur, Maylasia

Contents

Introduction

Traditionally, at least for the last five thousand years, while men speak, women keep the fire burning....

Feminist International Radio Endeavour is a FIRE that will keep burning as long as we women speak for ourselves.

The evolution of FIRE began well before its first broadcast on shortwave radio on May 1, 1991, and it is continuing beyond the first Internet radio broadcast on August 25, 1998. This book tells the story of FIRE in international women's media through the voices of the many women and men who helped FIRE begin, grow, and continue to blaze.

I have written this book because the story of the first ongoing feminist endeavor in the world of international radio communications needs to be told. Those of us who were involved in the building of FIRE want to document our development and the important role FIRE has played in the global feminist movement. By sharing our story with others, we hope to contribute some insights regarding women in media.

The staff of FIRE have been invited by women's organizations all over the world to tell about their activities, conferences, successes, and struggles. We are more than objective observers of these events; we are integral participants. The story of FIRE is interwoven with the history of the global women's movement in the decade of the 1990s.

Giving Voice to Women's Perspectives on All Issues

From tiny villages in rural areas of the Third World to United Nations conferences of tens of thousands of people, FIRE has given voice to women's words.

The UN Decade for Women—1975 to 1985—revealed to the world the existence of an emerging women's movement in all of its diversity. It crossed lines of class, race, ethnicity, nationality, sexual orientation, age, different abilities, North and South, East and West. Together, women were demanding to be heard in the international political arena. Coming to the forefront was the urgency of incorporating a gender perspective and recognition of women's human rights in the framework of all issues debated.

The decade that followed was characterized by the capacity of that movement to articulate a women's perspective and spread it throughout the world. I gave this explanation of FIRE's philosophy on the air in 1996:

> ...feminism today is more than women's rights; it is beyond women's rights. It is also and mainly a perspective, a gender perspective on all the issues in the world. And this is part of FIRE's philosophy: feminism is not only about "women's issues," it is not only about women's rights (although it includes them strongly), but mainly it is a perspective that feminists bring to all issues.
>
> A gender perspective recognizes that the differences attributed to men and women—with the exception of those that are biological—are socially and historically constructed to position women in a subordinate place. Feminism is thus a political stance to promote equality and diversity, and to give visibility to the perspective that women—in that different position—have about peace, social justice,

the environment, women's rights (of course), people's rights to self-determination, and social and economic rights.

International, Regional, National, and Local Advocacy

As we circle the globe—both electronically and physically—FIRE has accompanied women's movements on many levels. Significantly, FIRE is perhaps the only women's radio program located in the South that is truly global in scope. We address not only issues particularly affecting women in our region, but we help women from both "developed" and "developing" nations to exchange perspectives and experiences.

International Impact

FIRE has been instrumental in international conferences the world over. Since 1991, FIRE has covered numerous international women's conferences live, including the 1995 UN Fourth World Conference on Women, the UN Social Development Summit in 1994, the UN Conference on Population and Development in Cairo in 1994, the UN World Conference on Human Rights in Vienna in 1993, and the UN Earth Summit in 1992. We have provided international live coverage of women's voices at these and many other events while most globalized mainstream media either ignored or broadcast distorted coverage of women's contributions in these events.

Our international reach goes both ways. We do not just report on events. We also involve ourselves in regional, national, and local struggles.

Latin American Regional Impact

In February 1996 the indigenous Zapatista movement, based in Chiapas, Mexico, was heavily attacked by the Mexican Army. The surprise attack was so massive that for a few days the Zapatistas were separated and isolated, not knowing each other's fate after the military invasion.

In an effort to find out what was happening in Chiapas, Comandante Marcos, who was hiding in the woods with two other Zapatista leaders, pulled his shortwave radio out of his backpack (he had only a gun and the radio). He wanted to try to listen to international media coverage about what had happened in Chiapas, assuming that, as had often been the case, the local Mexican media would publicize only the Army's press releases about the results of the combat operation.

In scanning the shortwave band, Marcos came across a frequency on which a woman was talking in Spanish about "Las Zapatistas." He stayed with the program for the next half hour and listened to this woman with a Mexican accent talking at length about the historical struggle of women in the political movements in Latin America, their exclusion from decision-making, and also about their political participation in building up the very same movements that excluded them.

Marcos and his compañeros also heard her speak about how in patriarchy there can really be no revolution. "Unless gender is taken into account in the agenda of social transformation and women are included in decision-making," she said, "there can be no real advancement in any process." Frustrated when it was over because they had missed the first half of the program and didn't hear the woman's name, they tuned in to the same frequency the next day for a repeat broadcast of the program, but a half hour earlier.

The next day Marcos learned that the program they were listening to was FIRE, broadcasting from Costa Rica with a talk by Marcela Lagarde, a Mexican feminist whose ideas were well known throughout the region for her reconceptualization of gender in social transformation. Lagarde's talk had been recorded by FIRE six months earlier at the National University of Costa Rica in Heredia, but it was being replayed as part of FIRE's coverage of the latest assault on the Zapatistas.

A few months later, after the situation had been stabilized for the Zapatistas, they asked Marcela Lagarde to come to the Selva Lacandona for a special meeting, the purpose of which was unknown to her beforehand. At the meeting, Lagarde was asked by Comandante Marcos of the FZLN to become the "gender advisor" to the Zapatista movement. She accepted.

Afterwards, Marcos told her how he had learned about her from the FIRE broadcast and how he had realized the importance of bringing gender issues into the Zapatista agenda.

This is but one example of the role FIRE has played in bringing women's voices to influence politics. Accounts of our coverage of, and contributions to, other regional events in the Americas and the global South can be found throughout this book.

National Impact

On the national level, we covered the Costa Rica teachers' strike in July of 1995. What began as a teachers' protest against the government's 1995 legislation to reduce their pension plan became a national protest against structural adjustment policies and the political pact between two main political leaders to implement neoliberal policies.

Teachers and others wanted the government to talk with the people, not only with the political opposition. They demanded a repeal of the new pension law and respect for the social guarantees and rights won since the 1948 liberal revolution in Costa Rica.

Women represented eighty percent of the teachers in Costa Rica. They headed the practical struggle, yet they were not represented in the National Civic Committee of the strike nor in the three teachers' unions. They had little or no voice in their own struggle.

FIRE's Nancy Vargas organized live broadcasts throughout the conflict, sometimes from public phones in the streets of San José while people marched in protest. Other times it was from teachers' homes while they planned their actions. Often, the teachers came to the radio station to speak on FIRE about their struggle.

Sixta Raventos, a Costa Rican teacher and organizer of the strike, spoke to FIRE about the issues at stake in the struggle, live from her house:

There are a lot of accumulated grievances in Costa Rica because inflation is high. There is an erosion of people's income and an erosion of people's participation in public life.... I feel that this has manifested itself mainly in the support of the majority of the population, of the teachers' movement. This is even despite the campaigning of government to turn other people against the strike.... In most opinion polls, people support the teachers.... The quality of education in Costa Rica is at stake, because the pension plan is one of the incentives people have to become teachers.... There is also a general erosion of the

15

educational system in Costa Rica, and the pension plan is only a part of it. We are faced with a lack of books, with bad buildings, and other problems.

Asked about the role of the media, she said:

The media have been closed to expressing the different opinions of the different sectors involved. It seems that there has been an explicit decision—I do not know if it has been organized or not—but an explicit decision to exclude most of the news about this movement from the press, TV, and radio. Last week there was a huge demonstration, one of the biggest ones in the country's history. The way in which the press reported about it made it seem that only a relatively small group of people had gone to the streets. There was a clear distortion by the images on TV because the camera captured only the scenes where people were dispersed.

The teachers from Ciudad Colón and Puriscal—neighbor towns of the radio station—came to FIRE to talk live on the air. Adelaida Mata spoke about her concerns:

The main purpose of our struggle is the defense of rights, not only of teachers, but of people in general.... Ours is a peaceful movement. We want to be heard! Yet the response of the government has been to bring military forces. At the march last July 26, our peaceful mobilization was faced with heavily armed police forces.... We love to work as teachers, but our job is not only to transfer knowledge, it is to shape human beings for the future of our country—human beings who are able to think and to control the destiny of their country instead of kneeling down before economic power.... We want to teach children to struggle for their rights and self-determination, not to yield to the structural adjustment policies that are so prevalent today.

Ana Ligia Matamoros, a special education teacher in Puriscal, said:

The Costa Rican government has given teachers the responsibility to teach democracy, but it does not allow us to exercise it! Women are eighty percent of the teaching force in this country. We are thinking beings. We are capable. Curiously there is a law of equal opportunities, yet there are few women in decision-making positions in the Ministry of Education and elsewhere. We are being denied our rights.

Teachers went back to school after a month-long strike and "negotiation" in which most teachers were not satisfied with the settlement. They rechallenged each other to create new ways of leading and organizing. After the strike, the teachers from Ciudad Colón and Puriscal came back to the radio to thank FIRE for our support:

We go back to school with a bitter lesson: the government will not even listen, and the Comité Civico [negotiating committee] of the strike surrendered at nothing. In class, I will teach students that we all have to organize differently because this is not over; it might get worse.... Now that the strike is over, we will need the radio more than ever.

Local Community Impact

In February 1994, the year before the teachers' strike, FIRE found out about the plans of the Costa Rican government to dump all of the garbage from the capital city of San José in the last forest reserve of its kind, El Rodeo Reserve. The reserve is only a few miles away from the shortwave radio station that broadcast FIRE at the time.

A radio ecotour was one of FIRE's contributions to the struggle undertaken by the communities of El Rodeo, Cordel de Mora, and Ciudad Colón to save the forest and their own health by opposing the creation of the landfill. The community demanded that the government establish a decentralized policy whereby every community and each subregion of the city would have a landfill for its garbage, would recycle, and would reuse garbage. That way, each community, rural and urban, would be responsible for its own waste, and no rural community would have to carry the burden of all of the city dwellers' garbage. Indeed, this became the policy adopted by the government in 1998.

On horseback, we took our listeners through the forest as we broadcast live though walkie-talkies. An international audience in more than 100 countries, including the rest of Costa Rica, was brought to the reserve through radio. They heard the sounds of nature (including our horses), listened to our description of whatever came in front of us along the way, and tuned in to the voices of the villagers by the roadside who were tending their animals, farming, and even leaving their kitchens and children for a minute to speak out about the landfill.

> *My ancestors have lived here for ages, ever since my great grandparents came to El Rodeo. The government has never taken us into account. Why, I ask, are they taking us into account now when they need a new site for the garbage? It has been said that there is obscure business going on over the dump site. It is not obscure. It is very clear to me: they are selling out our health, our environment, and our peaceful living.*

> —Elder Doña Elida Quirós

We met a mountain bike rider along the way who, almost breathless from the four-mile ride uphill from the nearest village of Ciudad Colón, stopped to talk to us. He said that the president of Costa Rica, after having named himself the "ecological president," should put his hand on his heart and answer the question, "How can one of the arteries of the last lung left to the city of San José be destroyed with such a road for garbage trucks?"

We ended the ecotour by getting off the horses and running back to the studio to finish the broadcast. We brought in the sounds of the bulldozers as they mixed with the screams of the crickets and other species, which we had recorded the week before when the machines began their destructive work.

This unique use of radio found its way onto the airwaves of the British Broadcasting Company (BBC) later that week. According to Glenn Housser's World of Radio Monitoring, it had been featured as the "perhaps first ever radio ecotour on horseback."

Four days later FIRE was broadcasting live again, this time from a car parked along a side street of the municipal building where local government delegates of the nearby city of Ciudad Colón were discussing their position in light of the fact that the people of the city were protesting the landfill. One after the other the marchers came to the car and spoke again through the globalized walkie-talkie. Here is the appeal of an eleven year-old girl:

This has got to stop. The government keeps telling us through the school system that we have to be responsible for the protection of the environment. We are a peaceful people. This march of protest is an act of responsibility on my part toward the environment. What are they [pointing at the place where the local government officials were meeting] going to do to take responsibility for our future?

Yielding to the pressure of the marchers and the multiple activities of the week, consisting of petition campaigns, reports in the newspapers, and meetings with the municipality, the government delegates came out of the building after three hours of deliberation to announce that they would oppose the use of the road for the garbage trucks. They then left the site immediately. The protesters were in an uproar because they did not have an opportunity to speak with the official delegates after they reported their position to the people.

Early the next morning FIRE's programming opened with a commentary by Melba Jimenez from Ciudad Colón:

We are not happy. They dealt with only part of the issue. They did not make a commitment to stop construction of the landfill for all of the garbage of the city in the area near the reserve. The road is not the only issue! We want a decentralized policy for the country so that no community has to carry all the burden.

FIRE then asked the audience to call in with their opinions. The telephone began ringing within two seconds. One after the other, seventeen calls came from the people of Ciudad Colón. The nature of the messages from the callers could best be characterized as "amplified rage," but we were also a channel through which they could articulate the challenges ahead.

A highlight of the call-in shows occurred when we opened for calls the next day, and a call came in from Indiana in the United States:

My name is Virginia. I am Costa Rican but have lived in the United States for many years now. I have been listening to my people on your

19

shortwave today. Please tell me how to get to El Rodeo. I am going back to live in Costa Rica and I've decided that's where I want to live. I am with you and will be with you in this struggle.

Another caller from the United States, Tim Hendel, said that upon listening to the dwellers of the area on the shortwave program he was able to grasp the issue through the direct voices of those most affected by it.

A few months later, the community celebrated the fact that the government of Costa Rica had changed its plans to build the dump site even close to the forest. The Constitutional Court had declared the project unconstitutional.

Tribunals: Women Bridging the Artificial Gap Between Private and Public

Tribunals of women telling of their own experiences have been significant in the activities that FIRE has catalyzed and recorded. Starting in 1991 at the World Women's Congress for a Healthy Planet, hundreds of women have used our microphones to testify against violations against them in many areas of life. Throughout the years since that first tribunal covered by FIRE, we have participated in and organized local, regional, and international tribunals on violations of women's human rights—in Vienna during the NGO Forum of the Fourth World Conference on Women, in El Salvador during the Latin American and Caribbean Feminist Encuentro, and in Costa Rica on November 25, the International Day Against Violence Towards Women.

FIRE is committed to continuing this process of women publicly telling and hearing their own stories. Katerina Anfossi Gómez, key organizer of FIRE's radio tribunals, talked about the role that these tribunals have played:

Disseminating the spoken words of women—broadcasting the individual and collective testimonies of women—has been an important achievement in FIRE's international communications strategy because it has fostered the recognition that women's words constitute a political analysis of reality. With the emphasis on women's oral language, FIRE has given to women's words the value they deserve, and when brought together, the array of women's individual testimonies can be seen as links in the chain of oppression.

Alda Facio has been an organizer, judge, and participant in three different tribunals for FIRE. She wrote about why she believes in them:

For me, tribunals are not a space where women feel "weak," or like "victims" or "objects" of history, as some critics have argued... nor do I consider the events that occur in a tribunal to be something that feminists should have transcended, as argued by women who say that we shouldn't keep speaking of ourselves as victims, but rather as agents of our own history.

For me, a tribunal is a space where all participants can feel the enormous strength of women—in spite of so many violations, so many centuries of having our humanity denied us. Here we are, denouncing, organizing, judging, and above all else, saying "no more violence." In a tribunal we become protagonists, because it's a space that we who have suffered the violence create, a space built with our shared imagination, force, and pain.

For me, a tribunal is a space where we feel and analyze our complicity in many forms of gender violence through our silence, by which we reinforce the patriarchy and weaken ourselves.... A tribunal provides an ideal moment for us to become aware of our active participation in maintaining this patriarchal system... participation expressed in the ways we discriminate against each other for our differences: whites against blacks; blacks against lesbians; prostitutes against housewives; housewives against professionals... ad infinitum and in endless combinations.

A tribunal... expresses the pain of a woman who suffers gender violence day by day, perhaps in her own family, in her factory or office, in her community, or her very own body....

A tribunal is a formidable thing... due to the anger that drives it, the fears relived through it, the guilt it generates. But women have always confronted the formidable with bravery. We've always lived in spite of our fears, and we've always carried our guilt. Perhaps what's new is the fury, the anger that this experience gives us. But it's time to honor our fury and to give it free reign....

—FIRE book on El Salvador Tribunal, 1992

FIRE Responds to the Backlash

The first few years of FIRE did not generate much organized backlash. In the hundreds of letters we received from listeners around the world, only two were "hate mail." But on April 19, 1995, our "on the air" mourning of the victims of the bombing of the Murray Building in Oklahoma City in the United States triggered a direct verbal attack on us.

The terrorism had brought death to many men, women, and children and had affected millions of hearts and minds. All evidence indicated that those responsible were angry white male U.S. citizens.

Radio for Peace International—the shortwave radio station in Costa Rica that hosted FIRE's paid air time between 1991 and 1998—in its Far Right Radio Review (FRRR) had warned the international and U.S. audiences that the far right meant business. Throughout the previous year, RFPI had exposed, with ample evidence, what the far right militias were up to and how they used shortwave radio to promote hatred, racism, and violence.

It was not long after the bombing that the far-right shortwave programs beaming out of the U.S. began attacking FIRE. A phone call came through during the FRRR on May 2:

Yes, my name is Bill, and I am calling from Michigan. I have been listening to shortwave for thirty years now, and I am a ham radio operator. I am going to play devil's advocate here. During the last couple of weeks you have been talking about the "far right" and the "right wing" or whatever you call them, and you have said that the hosts of those programs are responsible for the violence that took place in Oklahoma. Let's take this a step further: what about RFPI and its program? I have heard FIRE. One night there were two women talking about abortion as a sacrament!

FIRE's Jeanne Carstensen immediately affirmed that FIRE has defended and will always defend women's health rights. Although it was false to say that two women on FIRE talked about abortion as a sacrament, two women belonging to the organization Catholics for Free Choice had paraphrased a U.S. feminist of the 1960s to say, "If the Pope could give birth, abortion would probably be a sacrament!"

FIRE won a first-degree burn soon after that incident: an "Honorary Mention" in one of the far right's most renowned magazines: *Media Bypass* (vol. 3, No. 7, July 1995). In an article entitled, "Alternative Airwaves" (in quotations in the article itself), author Lawrence W. Myers listed the top ten radio broadcast programs that are, according to him, "liberal/socialist/communist programming." FIRE was rated number one on the list!

Awards

In the midst of the backlash from the far right, FIRE was granted numerous and diverse awards on a yearly basis from 1994 to 1997.

In 1994, FIRE was given the Katherine Davenport Women's International News Gathering Service (WINGS) award for "the coverage of the UN Conference on Population and Development" in Cairo, Egypt.

The following two years, 1995 and 1996, the Peacepower Foundation, based in Florida USA, granted FIRE its Amigas Award for "FIRE's constant work and deep commitment toward the empowerment of women."

Also in 1995, UNESCO granted FIRE two awards for the best women's radio productions related to the Fourth UN World Conference on Women in China. The two productions were History of Gender in Central America, and Tribunals of Violations of Women's Human Rights.

Earth Communications in the United States and Radio for Peace International in Costa Rica gave FIRE their 1996 award for "the excellent live coverage of the Fourth UN Conference on Women, China, 1995."

In 1997, Earth Communications and Radio for Peace International presented another award to FIRE permanent staff members for "loyalty to the development of the radio station."

How This Book Is Organized

This book is organized along broad thematic lines while maintaining the sequential flow of events. However, all of the themes FIRE addresses are integrally related and cannot be totally separated. The FIRE story must be read as a developing whole, for all of its different threads weave a multicolored tapestry.

- Chapter 1 explores the beginnings of FIRE from its inspiration in 1985 through the end of its first eight months on the air in December of 1991.

- Chapter 2 looks at the philosophies, goals, and values behind FIRE and its role in international women's media.

- Chapters 3 through 7 tell the story of FIRE's activities in global conferences convened by the United Nations during the first half of the 1990s. They also tell about FIRE's role in meetings called by feminist organizations and networks around the world.

  The issues addressed can best be traced as they came to the forefront of the international feminist agenda, but our experiences at each conference built upon the ones that had come before. All of the themes continued to be addressed by feminists well beyond their "day in the sun," and FIRE's actions reflect that reality.

  - *Chapter 3, 1992, Rio de Janeiro, Brazil*—Environment and Development (Earth Summit). This was also the year of the commemoration of 500 years of resistance by the indigenous peoples of the Americas.

  - *Chapter 4, 1993, Vienna, Austria*—Conference on Human Rights, in which women's rights were recognized as human rights.

  - *Chapter 5, 1994, Cairo, Egypt*—International Conference on Population and Development, where women's health and empowerment, including reproductive and sexual rights, were addressed.

  - *Chapter 6, March 1995, Copenhagen, Denmark*—Social Development Summit, where our focus was women's right to socioeconomic development.

  - *Chapter 7, September 1995, Beijing, China*—The Fourth World Conference on Women, for which we helped shape a broad platform on women's rights and equality.

- Chapter 8 describes how, after nearly seven years of being on the air, we started shaping FIRE for the future.

- Chapter 9 describes the major changes undergone by FIRE in 1998 when it adopted a legal status in Costa Rica. In August 1998, FIRE's sparks lit up cyberspace when we brought women's voices to the Internet in the first-ever women's Internet radio station.

- Chapter 10 outlines our particular focus on traditionally invisible or voiceless groups of women.

- Chapter 11 provides an in-depth and somewhat technical look at how FIRE operated throughout its first years, both from our studios in Costa Rica and in remote locations.

- Chapter 12 is a compilation of our activities and listeners' voices during our celebrations of FIRE's anniversaries.

- Chapter 13 presents the result of the unique Reception Report Study of FIRE's letters from its shortwave radio program listeners from 1996 to 1997.

- The appendices provide additional information about FIRE's coverage of international conferences and other events.

- At the end of the book is a glossary of terms and acronyms.

We Want Your Input

Throughout this book, you will find the voices of women and men who have been involved with FIRE—either on the air or behind the scenes. FIRE is what it is mainly because of the strong voices and support of women, but most of our written feedback came from men during the first years—perhaps because they are the majority of shortwave listeners worldwide, and it is said that men tend to write more. Throughout the years we have noticed that they often write about how FIRE has opened their ears to feminist voices, which perhaps attests to the fact that the intimacy of radio plays a role in allowing men to listen to women without feeling threatened.

The global network of FIRE's producers, listeners, and supporters is using today's information technology to harness the enormous potential for human development and empowerment. We are facilitators of a new, truly participatory, international reality.

We hope this book will put readers in touch with FIRE's far-reaching international network of women activists. By opening our minds and hearts to the experiences of others, we ourselves become stronger and more fulfilled.

We look forward to receiving your comments and questions about women in international radio. We do not want to be the only ones out there on the international airwaves! We encourage other (current and future) radio women to learn about our experiences, expand on them, and work with us to build a world where all women and men can hear each other's distinct voices and create a more compassionate, equal, and participatory global society.

CHAPTER 1

Igniting the FIRE: Beginnings

Welcome, you are listening to FIRE—Feminist International Radio Endeavour—broadcasting for the first time at Radio for Peace International, a shortwave radio station dedicated to peace, social justice, human rights, the environment, and women's rights. FIRE has been made possible by you and the sponsorship of the Foundation for a Compassionate Society, which is devoted to validating women's values as instrumental in achieving peace and justice for all....

—FIRE's Intro spot

In Costa Rica on May 1, 1991, a unique radio program found its way into the world of shortwave. FIRE became the only daily feminist program on the international airwaves that bounce off the ionosphere and skip around the planet, bringing to the world a gender perspective on all issues.

Lighting the Spark

The beginning of FIRE goes back to 1985—at the Nongovernmental Organizations' Forum of the UN Third World Conference on Women in Nairobi, Kenya, 16,000 women gathered to discuss and share experiences and ideas with each other. They lobbied the official state delegates who approved the historical UN document that came out of the conference, *The Nairobi Forward Looking Strategies for the Advancement of Women.* All member states of the UN agreed to implement and evaluate the results ten years later at the 1995 Fourth World Conference on Women to be held in Beijing, China.

During the fifteen days of the conference, a Women's Peace Tent provided a venue for women from countries in conflict to come together. Women from the then Soviet Union talked for the first time with women from the United States, and women from Palestine had their first discourse with women from Israel. During the times when there was no dialogue, there was singing, dancing, and displays of artwork, all of which promoted the commonalities and needs for networking among women and, of course, the need for women to have an international voice.

After sharing their perspectives on peace, women reaffirmed the need to consolidate their own communication networks on an ongoing basis to confront the new world order of information technology.

Feminist author, activist and funder, Genevieve Vaughan, sponsored the Peace Tent and the group of international women who "womanned" it, a small group which was called the Feminist International for Peace and Food. Created in collaboration with WILPF and other groups, the Peace Tent was a place where the truth could be told by women to women, a venue for communication. Genevieve was a visionary who understood the need for women to have a permanent international voice. She also sponsored a workshop on women and international radio which was attended by some sixty conference participants.

One of the special visions of Genevieve Vaughan has been to give long-term funding to feminist projects from their birth to their maturity. This has been the case for FIRE.

In 1999, she spoke on FIRE's Internet broadcast about her experience of starting the feminist radio venue:

I began back in the early '80s wondering how to create social change and talking to other women about what might be done. At the time we were in Rome where I used to live and a woman there started talking to me about doing an international women's radio station, and I just didn't think it was possible when I first heard about it, but then as I was spending my day there in Rome, I turned on the radio and heard Radio Vatican, and there was the mass being played in all different languages, and so I thought, "Well, women could do that. Women could do the programs, and they could be in different languages." And so I thought, we could also have relay stations all over the world, a place where women's voices could be heard, voices that really haven't been heard throughout the history of patriarchy.

I had several meetings at women's gatherings, such as an Association of Women in Development meeting that was in Washington, DC, and then, especially, in Nairobi, at the UN Decade for Women final conference. We had a meeting of women there who were interested in a women's radio station, which was a very inspiring thing, but I realized as I went on that it would take lots of money to put up a women's radio station with its own antenna. I was thinking of something along the lines of the religious radio stations that have a wide outreach, and I would like to see women's voices reaching out that far, but it seemed like too much of a project for me to put together on my own.

And so years passed, and then I heard someone talk about how they sent information about Radio for Peace through the Internet. I realized that there was this shortwave radio station in Costa Rica, and I thought that might be a venue where I could put at least a women's radio program, if not the radio station itself. This could be a beginning, a start, a first step. And so I thought about it and I thought about it, and then finally, before the Gulf War started, some feminists from New York had invited me to an evening where we were talking over what we could do to stop the war, and I started talking once again about women's radio, and one of the women there said "Well, Gen, you're always talking about this women's radio, but you don't ever do it."

So I decided I had to do it right away, and I got in touch with the Radio for Peace people and said I wanted to buy the radio time on the air. We had conference calls every week or so for about six months, and we found the women who were going to be able to do this radio program. First of all, I wanted somebody from the South, not a woman from the U.S. because I had envisioned this as a multicultural women's radio program with the voices that weren't being heard, the voices of the women who were being affected by U.S. government and business policies, telling us, "Look, Sisters, this is what's happening— what you're part of—and what it is doing to us." I wanted those voices to be on the air and to be heard because women's voices have been covered up by patriarchy for centuries.

Women's voices are the voices of peace, the voices that are telling the truth and that have a vision for peace and that want to live in a peaceful world for their children and for each other. I thought it was really important to have that happen, so when I heard that María Suárez was interested in doing the program, for some reason or other that really rang a bell, and I said, "Let's get María to do it," and that was the beginning of FIRE. I invented the name, Feminist International Radio Endeavour, because it is like a spark that goes on and lights other fires.

Also, fire is something that's a gift. You can give fire to somebody else and you don't lose it. Your stick keeps burning when you light somebody else's stick. So it's not something that anybody can really grab and take as their own. It's something that goes on and on, and that is what communication is like. Those fires light each other and go on and on. So that's what I hope women's voices will do—that they will continue to burn in people's consciousness so we know what is happening and we know what our responsibilities are to try to change the things that are wrong and to follow women's lead toward the things that are right.

The Foundation for a Compassionate Society

Genevieve Vaughan founded the Foundation for a Compassionate Society in an attempt to practice what she calls the "gift economy," a philosophy particularly well-suited for creating FIRE. Her recent book *For-Giving, A Feminist Criticism of Exchange* (Plain View Press, Austin, Texas, 1997) explains that philosophy. In a 1994 Foundation brochure she wrote:

When women's values are validated, we will gain the confidence which will allow us, together with the men whom we inspire, to stop rewarding oppression and to help create a peaceful and abundant world for Mother Earth and all her children.

The Foundation for a Compassionate Society was composed of two entities, a Donation Fund and a Private Operating Foundation which was made up of some twenty-five multicultural women activists managing and implementing projects for social change. The scope of the Foundation was international, with projects in many countries, although the activities were based in Austin, Texas. Begun in 1987, the Foundation gathered together some of the projects Genevieve had already started, created new ones, and was joined by other projects that had begun independently. The Foundation had a lifespan of more than a decade—from 1987–1998 when it closed its doors due to lack of funds, though some of the projects remain. Some of the Foundation's activities are recounted in the last chapter of *For-Giving*.

One of the most outstanding features of Genevieve's work is that for many years she made it her priority to support and sometimes create original women's initiatives that many other funders and funding agencies ignored. In doing so she was breaking new ground. She created long-term projects with physical space for women and mixed peace groups to use—retreat centers and resource centers. She also felt it was important for women from different areas to meet with each other face to face.

From the beginning, our activities have included funding the trips of women from different parts of the world to meet and network with each other and to tell each other about the realities of their countries. Women from Africa, Latin America, the Caribbean, India, and Europe have come to the United States, and women from here have gone to their countries. We have also funded development projects—beginning with a women's farming collective in Mozambique in 1983, continuing with soup kitchens in Chile in 1986-1990, and with ongoing contributions to the women's movement and peace movement in El Salvador....

One major success was the creation of the Peace Tent at the UN Decade for Women final conference in Nairobi in 1985.... The foundation also supplied RVs to women after the Nairobi conference so they could travel through the country, stopping in towns to talk about peace from women's perspectives. The European Caravan traveled through Eastern Europe to Moscow and back to Germany, talking to women along the way....

Most recently we have sponsored trips for women of color from the USA and Europe to go to South America and the Caribbean to meet with their counterparts who have immigrated there from Africa and Asia.... We have also helped sponsor two conferences in the Mediterranean region... a delegation of women to the UN Human Rights Conference in Vienna and one to Zagreb in former Yugoslavia.

—Foundation for a Compassionate Society, 1994

The foundation has also sponsored a women's radio news service based in the United States since 1987—Women's International News Gathering Service (WINGS). The producer, Frieda Werden, helped light our FIRE and continues to work with us on an ongoing basis.

On April 31, 1998, the Foundation for a Compassionate Society officially closed its doors. Genevieve Vaughan continued supporting FIRE, however, and she formally gave the name "FIRE," which she had created, to the women's movement through the station's permanent staff of producers, María Suárez Toro and Katerina Anfossi Gómez.

Radio for Peace International

For seven and a half years after May 1, 1991, FIRE was broadcast at Radio for Peace International (RFPI).

Radio for Peace began in September 1987 on the campus of the University for Peace in Costa Rica, inspired by the need for a voice for the peace movement in the United States. It began as the product of an agreement by two universities: the University of Global Communication (formerly the World Peace University) in Oregon, USA, and the University for Peace in Costa Rica, created by a resolution of the United Nations.

Eventually Radio for Peace became a program of the University for Peace.

Debra and James Latham from the USA and Maximilian Loffler from Germany moved to Costa Rica to build the station. They began broadcasting with a single frequency and a low-power transmitter. Later the station grew to have five transmitters and a 30-kilowatt capacity acquired through a contribution by Genevieve Vaughan in 1992, a contribution motivated by FIRE's presence in RFPI broadcasts.

Genevieve paid RFPI for FIRE's air time, making FIRE the highest source of income of any of RFPI's paid radio programs from 1991 to 1998, and thus the most profitable program at the station.

Genevieve also paid FIRE's salaries and basic operation expenses through RFPI's administrative system until 1998. On the eighth of March 1998, FIRE became part of a nongovernmental organization in Costa Rica: the Asociación de Comunicaciones Feminist Interactive Radio Endeavour (AC FIRE), which was created by the staff of FIRE.

Throughout the years, FIRE staff requested funds for special projects from other funding sources as needed, and FIRE's program and team of women were autonomous within the radio station, a unique position for women in the media. According to a 1995 study by UNESCO:

Women's overall share of jobs in media is low. In Africa, Asia and Latin America the female average is below 25 per cent for broadcasting and press.

The UNESCO thirty-country study showed that only seven media organizations are headed by women. This study obviously did not include everyone involved in media (such as FIRE), but it is part of a larger body of literature that points to the leadership of FIRE within the world of shortwave radio—programming headed by and produced by women.

RFPI had been broadcasting women's programs since its beginning, and accepting Genevieve's proposal for the creation of FIRE's own space was a continuation of RFPI's commitment to promoting women's rights.

One of the most significant things for me has been sharing the dream and the vision with Genevieve from the Foundation for a Compassionate Society, and making it a reality. RFPI had a long history of interest in women's concerns and issues and having women's voices heard. We had even written several proposals, so when the support

e foundation came about, it was just incredible for us that the
ould be fulfilled. The commitment of RFPI has been to con-
...ing women's voices through RFPI programming and provide
a separate, special space with special objectives and goals. Whenever
you try to create something new and different, in a different struc-
ture, and break away from standard ways of doing things, you are in
uncharted territory....

—Debra Latham, General Manager of Radio for Peace
International, live on FIRE, 1992

Putting FIRE on the Air

On that first day on the air, Genevieve Vaughan, Sissy Farenthold, and Cecilia Bustamante from the foundation spoke with Debra about their expectations regarding FIRE. They outlined the guiding principle behind FIRE—that women need an international voice to promote the chance for peace.

During that month, in order to prepare the way for FIRE at RFPI, the foundation sent Debra as a participant to the International Women's Conference, Who Calls the Shots, held in Manila, Philippines. As general manager of RFPI she spoke on the topic, Shortwave: Alternative and Option, and announced the news to the women there that FIRE was on the air.

It became clear during the course of the conference that, although mainstream commercial media is generally closed to change, women must continue the struggle to do as much as possible to get air time and coverage of feminist perspectives. Mainstream public media needs our support because it is being threatened by commercial media.

Women must make maximum use of all alternatives available, and we must train women to work both inside the mainstream, as well as in alternative ways and at the grassroots level. Finally, what is important is not just the number of women in media; the critical factor is the perspective and consciousness of women in the media.

—Debra Latham, article in
Vista, RFPI's bulletin

FIRE was preparing to do just that. It was to become a women's radio program by and about women for all, going on the air two hours a day: one hour in English and one hour in Spanish. Eventually there would be programming in other languages. FIRE sought to...

...create a communications channel on shortwave where women's voices, in all their diversity, are heard by the international community, crossing barriers of nationality, culture, race, geography, and language.
—FIRE's brochure

FIRE was open to all women. We broadcast programs sent to us by women who do local radio, as well as on-the-air visits to the station, long-distance phone calls, coverage of women's actions through our participation in international, regional, local, and grassroots conferences, and integration of written information sent by women's groups.

We insisted on placing feminist radio right where women's actions were developing in order to promote women's presence everywhere. FIRE's producers danced within the movement's rhythms and gave those rhythms a sound on shortwave. We voiced activities and news about women that might not be considered newsworthy by mainstream media.

We cover every topic of interest to women, therefore all issues. I have yet to think of one that women are not interested in.
—María Suárez Toro in FIRE video

All over the world, the spark to ignite FIRE has been glowing in the broad movement of women doing local radio programs: in the South and North, in the East and West, and on commercial and women-owned radio. Since the beginning, women in the media have responded eagerly to FIRE's call. Tapes have arrived from Women on the Line (Australia); Voces Nuestras (Our Voices, Costa Rica); Women's International News Gathering Service (WINGS, USA); Agenda de Hoy (Today's Agenda, Puerto Rico); Y Ahora Yo Tengo la Palabra (And Now I Have the Word, Nicaragua); Pacifica Radio (USA); and Felipa Domestica (Argentina).

In addition, Sally Jacques, an Asian American performance artist, became FIRE's first correspondent and carried out many interviews with women from projects sponsored by the Foundation for a Compassionate Society.

Selection of FIRE's Producers and Other Staff

Requirements for permanent staff, as agreed to by RFPI and as proposed by the Foundation for a Compassionate Society, were that they be:

1. Third-world women, especially from the region where the program would be located;

2. Feminists linked to the women's movement; women from different disciplines, not necessarily journalists;

3. Speakers of both Spanish and English.

The directors of the World Peace University in Oregon and of the University for Peace in Costa Rica accepted the staff proposals and gave the staff accreditation.

Katerina Anfossi Gómez and I were the first hired and began to shape FIRE's personality both in the production of programs and strategies of development in shortwave radio. Monica Saenz, a professional journalist, joined us for three months.

I am a Puerto Rican and had lived in Central America for more than fifteen years, have been a bilingual education teacher for children in New York, and had taught education at the graduate level, both at Albany State University in New York and at the University of Costa Rica. I also had worked on literacy programs for adults in Central America, especially women-to-women literacy projects. Directly before coming to FIRE, I had been the co-director of CODEHUCA (the Central American Human Rights Commission) and coordinator of the Human Rights Education Secretarial, a position resulting from my work as a human rights popular education teacher. I had been an activist in all seven Central American countries before I was hired to build FIRE.

In an interview for RFPI, I talked about what coming to FIRE meant to me:

The uniqueness of FIRE also has an expression in my personal life, and I believe that the personal is political. You see, when I was hired to work on FIRE, it was the first time in my life I was given a job because of who I am and not despite who I am. Let me explain: I was hired because I am a woman, a Latin American, because I am bilingual, and because I am a feminist. Now, that's quite a combination for a Puerto Rican who has lived and worked in Puerto Rico, in the United States, and in Central America.

As a woman I have had to struggle to have a profession and to practice it. It would have been harder if it were not for the strong women's movement demanding our rights in the late sixties and seventies, but it was hard nonetheless. Men have had first choice no matter what. I have worked in schools, universities, and mixed nongovernmental organizations and movements, always knowing that I was second choice. But FIRE's staff was to be only women. We had our own place at last.

At the same time, I had experienced, as a Puerto Rican woman in the United States where I had studied and worked for eight years, that being a Latina is like a curse. Because of the isolation of Puerto Rico and its colonial status, it is hard for many Latins on the continent to understand and accept that we are also Latin. Usually I was hired because I was a trained teacher. At FIRE I was hired because of who I am, not even because of my profession, as I had never worked in radio before.

Being bilingual has had the same disadvantage: in the U.S. we are repressed for speaking Spanish, and in Latin America we are repressed for speaking English! Here, at last, I was hired because I am bilingual. Finally, when you bring in the issue of being a feminist... well if I started telling you the stories of harassment, being discredited, and isolation, both in the progressive movement and in institutions, it would be a very lonjg story. But it ended in FIRE. I was hired because I am a feminist!

Paraphrasing the words of an African American I put on the air, I can say that FIRE saved my life because it has given me a voice, a place, a space where I can live and grow and be all that I am, and speak to the world in my own voice and through the voices of so many other women I get to know through radio and its links to the women's movement. It has saved me from political suicide, gender suicide, cultural suicide, language suicide... and what I mean by that is that the threat of homogenization of all of us by dominant powers can kill all that we are.

Feminism and women's media definitely are making a contribution to counteract that, and it does it at all levels. Do you know what I mean? In feminist media we each have a life of our own to share with all.

Less than two months after the beginning of the English program, FIRE grew to include Katerina Anfossi as founding staff member of the Spanish program.

Katerina, a Chilean feminist lawyer and journalism student, hosted the Spanish program since day one. She has lived in Costa Rica for the last eighteen years and has supported women and women's groups involved in legal conflicts related to domestic violence.
—Vista, 1991

When I was told that there was a place on FIRE and that FIRE was a space for women in radio to promote women, I felt it was such an important project that I came to see if I could work in it. I was hired, and it provided a new possibility of continuity for what I was already doing: promoting women's needs and interests, especially the least protected. I am a lawyer who was working with women subjected to domestic violence.

Women are the most marginalized, unprotected, and discriminated against sector of society, and at the same time there is a new consciousness of the role that women can play. Women are working to change the world. Broadcasting this program is a constant challenge; the communication with women and men who are listening is a great responsibility that I take very seriously.

For us it has been very important to create this space for women, because throughout history women's expression and experiences have been denied. It is a space by and about women, for the world to hear. Women have a culture of listening to radio, and now FIRE is an international place for women to communicate their experiences.
—Katerina Anfossi, FIRE producer, at RFPI's
International Board of Advisors meeting
and for New Dimensions Radio, 1991

Neither Katerina nor I had any previous radio experience before we came to FIRE. Through direct and live hands-on experience from the first day of broadcast, we learned from Debra Latham, director of RFPI, to do the technical work. Katerina recalled those early days:

Having the power to do the technical work ourselves and a voice to the world on a daily basis really felt empowering to me, when you think that most people, especially women, are only allowed to do part of what radio entails. For example, they only write scripts, only broadcast, only write research reports, only manage the technical controls, or only do administrative work—and here we are doing the whole process. It felt like running an orchestra, while also being a part of it.

That first year, Katerina and I were invited to a workshop sponsored by the Inter-American Institute for Agricultural Science of the Organization of American States, where eighteen women from grassroots organizations were to be trained in radio and other media skills. They also were to learn how to express a gender perspective in media. The two-week workshop was enriching in many respects. The contact with other women in radio, as well as the training on the use of editing formats, confirmed that radio—in the hands of women—acquires a personality, style, energy, and vision that is often absent in formal and academic training.

This usually happens because professional journalists are trained to be "objective," which translates into hiding one's own perceptions, emotions, and positions. FIRE believes that journalism is not objective, although it claims to be. Subjectivity comes out in the media, and journalists should be ethical enough to state explicitly their positions and perspectives.

Continuing to Build the FIRE Team

FIRE's second year, 1992, brought two new members to the Feminist International Radio Endeavour team. First was Nancy Vargas, a Costa Rican student of journalism who had worked on the staff of the University of Costa Rica newspaper and at the UCR radio station. She became FIRE's third permanent staff member.

The motivations to work here are many, but the main one is that I am a woman. Independently of our race, class, nationality, culture, and ethnicity, we are discriminated against because we are women. The feminist perspective has changed my life. I was looking for my rights, for a way for my perspective, my life, to have a place in the world. I was hired by FIRE, not because of my professional skills as a journalist, but because I am a woman, because of my sensitivity to our issues and needs. This is a project that can fulfill my expectations, which are the same as those of other women. When I first came, I was told that this is the space for voices of women around the world. I learned quickly that this is our space, my space to speak to the world.

—Nancy Vargas, interview for RFPI

Jeanne Carstensen from the United States, an editor for five years at the magazine *Whole Earth Review* in California, joined FIRE on a temporary basis. She was the first occupant of the "fourth rotating position" for women from around the world of different cultures, ethnic identities, ages, and abilities who came to FIRE to share their experiences and perspectives. She stayed with FIRE from 1992 to 1994. The fourth rotating position has also been occupied by Firuseh Shokoo, a Puerto Rican-Iranian feminist, and Olga Reyes, a feminist from Spain.

Volunteers have been Rebecca Armstrong, Evelyn Azultany, Amber Sharik, Jasmin Edding, Ana Sisnet, Dalya Massachi, Debra Cedeño, and others.

Bringing in Other Experiences

The staff drew on Third-World strategies of "popularization," putting instruments in the hands of people's movements. Katerina's legal and activist work empowering women to face violence against them, and my experience as a women's human rights activist and adult literacy teacher in Central America served us well in this work.

FIRE organized its first conference with *Fempress*, a major Latin American and Caribbean magazine. The meeting brought together some of the women in regional media with whom FIRE had begun to work. It was aimed at sharing experiences and developing strategies to support each other's efforts in women's media.

40

Fifteen women met September 25 - 27, 1991, at the University for Peace in Costa Rica, site of RFPI, where we shared our experiences and challenges and developed a proposal to organize ourselves in a permanent workshop to share and produce material.

Following are brief summaries of what some of the women at the workshop said about their work:

- Norma Valle referred to the way she introduced news about women in a daily news program she produced at the University of Puerto Rico. She developed a wide variety of different formats that can be used to talk about women's issues.

- Ana Elena Badilla from Fundación Arias, an NGO founded by former Costa Rican president and Nobel Peace Prize winner Oscar Arias Sánchez to continue his ideas of a peace plan for Central America, explained that they are interested in reporting about the Ley de Igualdad Real. This Costa Rican law guarantees equality for women, but it is not specific enough in some areas.

- From Voces Nuestras, Liliana Zuniga, Rosario Leon, and Fresia Camacho explained that, along with other staff members, they are teaching women in the Costa Rican countryside how to produce radio programs for their local radio stations. They are connected, through AMARC, with 300 other stations throughout Latin America.

- Alda Facio, correspondent for *Fempress* in Costa Rica and a feminist lawyer, talked about her work in media as a nonjournalist by profession.

- Ileana Ramirez from the Defensoria de la Mujer, a program of the Costa Rican Ministry of Justice, told us that with her voluntary work and that of other women, they have designed a communication project especially to educate the public on the need to end violence against women.

- Servicio Especial de la Mujer (SEM) for Latin America was represented by Thais Aguilar from Costa Rica, who is the Regional Coordinator for the Women's Feature Service in Spanish for Latin America and the Caribbean.

- The Pancha Carrazco Collective in Costa Rica was represented by Milagros Rojas, one of the women who works on the collective's communications project. Mila shared their interest in video and radio to expand women's links to worldwide communication networks.

- Cora Ferro, a feminist theologian who is part of the team designing the Master's program in Women's Studies at the National University in Heredia and the University of Costa Rica. She also works with grassroots women in Costa Rica and the rest of Central America, explained about research that she's doing on the subordinate role of women in the Catholic Church and another one on women's role in politics in Costa Rica.

- The Foundation for a Compassionate Society was represented by Sally Jacques, who talked about her experience as an interviewer for FIRE and the importance of the use of intuition in radio.

- Radio for Peace International was represented by Jennifer Latham. She said that, according to the reception reports she read on RFPI, there isn't much of an opportunity for women to have their voices heard on shortwave. "FIRE is changing that," she added.

- From FIRE, Katerina Anfossi, Monica Saenz, and I explained our perspectives and experiences regarding the beginning of FIRE.

The conference participants identified the following five urgent needs: (1) sharing information with and about women around the world; and (2) giving it back to women through different media; (3) validating women's perspectives in communication; (4) sharing our productions with other media; and (5) questioning the absence of women's perspectives in media worldwide.

Also in 1991, FIRE participated in its first international meeting: the UNEP Global Assembly on Women and the Environment and the World Women's Congress for a Healthy Planet. That meeting included a global tribunal of women's stories about their experiences with environmental destruction.

Besides organizing with other media women to cover panels, interviews, and the tribunal itself, FIRE promoted the drafting of a resolution to bring attention to what women's media could do to multiply women's voices.

All the women in panels, workshops, and activities have been talking about the importance and the necessity of breaking through the media, to be able to educate others on women's perspectives on all issues related to the environment and peoples of the world. We women in media will remain invisible too, if we do not work together with all of you. One thousand women have heard you here. Millions will hear you on our airwaves. We want to let you know that FIRE and WINGS are here to allow that to happen. But we also need your support in letting women know it, because we, too, are invisibilized by mainstream media.

—Statement by FIRE and WINGS at the Women's
Congress for a Healthy Planet, 1991

This conference, which was held in preparation for the 1992 UN World Conference on Environment and Development to be convened in Rio de Janeiro, was the first of many global women's gatherings that we would attend from then on.

Covering the voices of women to bring them back to the station and then sending their voices out to the world was not enough for FIRE. Since that first experience, FIRE has seen its role as networker and promoter of women's awareness about the power of media, and their involvement in it. Along with WINGS, we presented a proposal for dissemination of the proceedings of the World Women's Congress for a Healthy Planet:

Each woman testifying at the World Women's Congress for a Healthy Planet was heard by 1,500 people. Her voice then amplified by radio can be heard by millions. We radio reporters from FIRE and WINGS who attended the Congress have outlets for the stories and programs about the proceedings within our existing programs, and we believe that the entire proceedings should be aired as widely and as often as possible. Radio is the most inexpensive of all the media for the numbers it can reach....

In December, FIRE embarked on yet another vehicle for getting the word out about our work. Liz Canner and Julia Meltzer, two feminists from the United States came to Costa Rica and were invited to come on the air live to talk with us about their visit. On the show, FIRE discovered that they had just graduated in video production from Brown University in the USA and that they had been offered a grant to make a video about women in Latin America. They were free to choose the subject of the video, and they selected FIRE as their topic.

They stayed in Costa Rica for three months and produced *Catch Fire with Us*, a fifteen-minute video documentary in Spanish and in English that portrays the beginnings of FIRE. This documentary also describes the program and encourages women to have their voices heard internationally by sending tapes to FIRE to be played on the air.

By the end of 1991, after our first eight months on the air, we had affirmed that FIRE represented the coming together of women's perspectives in international shortwave communications; the coming together of the international women's movement that expressed itself in Nairobi; the coming together of women in radio, breaking through communications barriers; and the coming together of women's voices in international communications.

In addition to face-to-face chat, body language, street theater, and telephone, radio is a medium of communication that is particularly attractive to women. Women worldwide are increasingly aware of this and have taken a larger role in radio during the last decade.

Since 1991, FIRE found its place in this mosaic and has contributed much to the development of women's media by giving women an international voice and also by recreating the ways in which media can be used in the hands of women, such as the following:

- Live broadcasting with simple technology and amateur producers trained on the spot;
- Using radio production as a lobbying instrument in UN conferences.
- Organizing activities of the women's movement that have to do with radio and its role in linking women's actions with women's voices and an international audience around the world;
- Inspiring young upcoming women radio activists;
- Motivating women to participate in radio, even if they have had no formal training in it;
- Persisting in opening new venues for women's communications and motivating other women to open new doors.

Why Women's Radio?

Studies published in the Latin American magazine *Dialogue for Communications* have cited the most recent research about radio and television reception. Women are the audience, even though they have been marginalized from ownership and production in radio and television.

Radio is "women's media," not so much because women are illiterate, but because radio can be women's company in daily life. They can tune into it while doing the thousands of tasks women are often expected to do.

Women, although not represented proportionately in the production of television and written media, have a broader presence in radio. Radio is also the most inexpensive medium of communication and is largely ignored by media conglomerates for the time being. Therefore, it has become the experimental site for women in media. Likewise, women call the radio, and they feel that it listens to them; they feel that they are participants in it—something that does not happen in television or print media. Radio is a space that women have owned intuitively. In addition, women journalists are hired in radio because salaries are lower. As a result the female/male ratio is greater than it is in television or newspapers.

Shortwave radio is perhaps the least expensive oral means of global communications today. While satellite radio or television broadcasting are more modern, shortwave remains available for those with few resources—both audience and producers.

> *Shortwave radio provides a good alternative to mainstream media sources.... The purpose of the media should be to keep people informed and aware of worldly activities. Yet when only a few gigantic companies have complete control of what will be said, there is no way the news will broadcast an array of opinions and truths.*
>
> —Emily White, student, USA

Our commitment has always been to place ourselves in the middle of the women's movement. The highest priority is to place FIRE where women are struggling to have a place in the international, regional, and local agendas, without favoring any one particular organization. We give a voice to all, especially the voiceless among the voiceless in mainstream media. Women know that even when they do not have a voice at official panels and workshops, they will have a place on FIRE. In international conferences anywhere in the world, in the midst of lobbying, negotiations, and panel presentations where many participants interact, women have also found and held their own voice on FIRE.

Women started opening space in radio even before the women's movement discovered it. We have to use it, and the movement has to change its content. We must speak in the language that women want to listen to, a language that conveys our own thoughts, feelings, and experiences. This is the language of our particular gender perspectives because we have lived experiences as women who have been discriminated against and cast in subordinate roles.

> *We have to develop strategies to transform radio in the hands of women. One of the worst limitations that women have had is self-censorship. We have to overcome that, penetrating media with our hearts.*
> —Norma Valle, *Fempress* journalist and radio producer at Radio Universidad de Puerto Rico, 1991

Reception studies have shown that some of the best ways to reach women are through the testimonies of other women and dialogues among women on health issues related to our bodies, domestic violence, or anything else that opens our minds to new information and perspectives.

FIRE's use of inexpensive and simple technology has been an important factor in inspiring women to participate in radio. Sophisticated technology too often reduces, rather that multiplies, the diverse voices and perspectives. This type of broadcasting:

> *...can be done anywhere there's a telephone line, in a village in Nicaragua or at the heart of an international event. After the initial cost of purchasing the equipment—which includes a mixer, phone interface, several microphones, and various cables, about $800—the only additional cost is for the phone call to Costa Rica for it to be broadcast on RFPI, or to a local community radio station.*
> *As we are all very aware, the world information order is becoming more centralized each day... it is increasingly difficult for the South to*

tell its history in the media. As we all know, women's access to the media, in the North and the South, is extremely limited. For all these reasons, it's quite a good feeling to be able to march into a UN event, for example, hook up our equipment to a telephone and begin talking with grassroots, NGO, and government delegates about the issues, and know that the interview is being broadcast in over sixty countries around the world. Not only are we giving extensive coverage to something mainstream media might cover only in a one-minute "women's angle" piece, but we're doing it from a women's perspective.
—Jeanne Carstensen, 1993

Genevieve Vaughan

CHAPTER 2

FIRE in the World of Women's Media

Over time women have begun to raise their voices in anger, in sad-ness, and in hope. As they continue to do so, they are not only rede-fining media at a global level but also discovering their resources of expression and communication. Whatever barriers women find themselves facing, it is a crucial time for women's voices to be heard.
—Samantha Calamari, U.S.
student in Costa Rica

We have taken our microphones around the world as we share what we have experienced and learn from other women working in the media. Our work has been enriched by these exchanges, as media have become powerful tools for the empowerment of women.

FIRE Around the World in 1992

In 1992, FIRE was heard around the world in live broadcasts from the United States and Mexico.

The United States

In July of 1992, I was FIRE's representative at the Second Feminist Media Pool sponsored by the Foundation for a Compassionate Society in Stonehaven, Texas. The meeting gathered thirty-eight women, mainly in the area of video production, to share experiences and work on building networks to expand the strength of women in video and other media such as radio. Most of the group consisted of African American and Latin American women.

> *I wanted to help these women in video become aware that FIRE is an international venue to help with the dissemination and distribution of their videos—the biggest obstacle mentioned since the first day....*
> *One of the interesting things is that most of them had come into video from radio and told me they wanted to go back to it. Having come from local radio experiences, and all of them being "minorities," they were fascinated that Third-World women had made it onto short-wave.*
>
> —María Suárez on FIRE, 1992

On the second day, FIRE arranged to do a live broadcast through the telephone line—perhaps their first one. Five women came on the air with me:

- Trella Laughlin, chair of the Feminist Media Pool and Let the People Speak, a program on public television;

- Ana Romero, a Winnebago Native American woman from the USA and associate producer of In the White Man's Image, a documentary aired on National Public Broadcasting on *The American Experience Series*;

- African American Ann Bennet, who organized the yearly International Women's Day Video Festival on TV out of Boston;

- Debby Zimmerman, founder of Women Make Movies in New York;
- Isis, an African American woman from the Ozarks who made a video on the National Lesbian Conference in the USA.

The excitement of being on the air was shared by all other participants at the meeting who stopped by the workshop to listen in, as well as by Katerina Anfossi, Nancy Vargas, and Jeanne Carstensen, who were at the controls at the station in Costa Rica.

That night, at the time of FIRE's repeat broadcast, we all sat around a swimming pool and listened to ourselves and each other. It was magical....

—María Suárez

Mexico

Beginning in 1992, FIRE worked closely with the World Association of Community Radio (AMARC). The association's 1992 biennial conference took place in August in Oaxtepec, Mexico. Of the more than 400 participants, 130 were women, and two of them were Nancy Vargas and Jeanne Carstensen from FIRE. Taking part in this conference was perhaps the biggest opportunity up to that time for FIRE to link and network with women in radio. It was also our opportunity to help build a strong women's radio network within AMARC.

The result of intensive lobbying, organizing, and caucusing was AMARC's creation of a women's vice presidency—first occupied by María Victoria Polanco—and also the creation of a Women's Network within AMARC.

Community radio needs to open itself up to the voices of women—voices that speak from their own gender perspective, with their own tone, with their own rhythm and music, their own rationality and sensitivity, and their own way of thinking, of dreaming and of re-creating the world. It is not an easy task, but we have decided to undertake it.

—María Victoria Polanco, *Interadio*, no. 1, 1993

FIRE undertook the challenge of a live broadcast once again in the middle of intense actions to open space for women in AMARC. On the third day of the meeting, Jeanne and Nancy arranged a call from Mexico to Costa Rica, in which Edda Sanga, Libby Lloyd, Ana Leah Saravia, Margaretta D'Arcy, and Dorothy Kidd came on the air on the English program. Rosa Palomino and Gabi Sebasco from the Peruvian Feminist Radio Collective and Elsa Salazar and Viki Quevedo from Radio Tierra in Chile were on the Spanish broadcast.

- Libby Lloyd, associate editor of the South African *Speak Magazine* explained that they were training women for radio because in their country the only programs "are state broadcasts, which are propaganda. We want to change that. When you allow women to speak, they get power. This is neglected in mainstream media."

- Another participant was Edda Sanga, director of the Tanzania Women's Media Collective, and a trainer in broadcasting, who said, "Women in media were very few in my country. We entered media in the '80s to make a difference, and we were inspired by the women's conference that closed the UN Decade for Women in Nairobi."

- Ana Leah Saravia, director of the Women's Media Circle and Radyo Woman Watch in the Philippines, said, "As a producer of radio, beginning on a volunteer basis and with no experience, we wanted to give women a voice. Now we are even on television."

- Margaretta D'Arcy has a radio station in her bedroom in Ireland, with an outreach of almost two miles around her house. "Everyone should have their own radio station at home," she said. "I have it in my bedroom because it is the most intimate place in the house. The magic of this kind of radio is that women want to talk, but they don't want anyone to hear. The intimacy of radio, and in your room, makes women think it is just that."

- Dorothy Kidd from Canada's Co-op Radio in Vancouver said that they were planning to produce a video on women in radio.

A low-power FM station was set up at the AMARC conference, where many of the participants who went on the air could be heard by the local community of Oaxtepec, Mexico. One day Nancy Vargas and Jeanne Carstensen went on the air to talk about FIRE's philosophy, objectives, and experiences. Nancy said that FIRE's emphasis was on the women who have the least chance in life, and she talked about women who had been on the air. That afternoon, a blind woman came to the conference searching for Nancy. Jasmin Mojica from Morelos, Mexico, wanted to meet the women whose voices she had connected to through her radio receiver. She explained that she had heard Nancy say, "All of us form fundamental parts of a puzzle, equally important for the whole to build a better world."

After tears and embraces with Jeanne and Nancy, Jasmin went on the air on AMARC's station and spoke with Nancy about the impact of having felt that she was represented at the conference:

> *I am blind, and it is hard for me to find out what the state of the world is, because commercial radio does not portray the truth. Community radio colors my vision about the world. It puts an end to it being a gray vision. FIRE is so dedicated to helping women be heard. I am very interested in working with you in that struggle. All women should struggle, so that no one decides for us.*

AMARC reported that "Radio Hearts" was opened that day. Reporter Arturo Enriquez Bazurto from Mexico said that to have someone—especially a person who is blind—leave her house to look for a broadcaster she had heard on the air is a turning point in anyone's professional life. Nancy agreed:

> *This experience changed my life. It showed me that one works with an ideal that one thinks might or might not be shared. When you find someone who shares it and goes out of her way to let you know, it means that we are on the right path.*

Fire Around the World in 1993

We continued our work with media women around the world in 1993. FIRE did more live broadcasts from Nicaragua and at conferences in Costa Rica, El Salvador, and the United States. This was also the year of FIRE's first European live broadcast, from The Hague, Netherlands.

Nicaragua

In 1993, The Colectivo de Mujeres de Matagalpa in Nicaragua asked FIRE to do an exchange with them to share experiences and training with the women in their collective who produce the radio program, Ahora Tenemos la Palabra. Their weekly program is broadcast on a commercial radio station in the northern region of Nicaragua. Jeanne Carstensen spent four weeks with them and also had the chance to interview many women's groups in the country.

Argentina, the woman who produced the program in Matagalpa, came to FIRE especially to learn how to run a radio station that could go on shortwave. RFPI staff shared with her the process and technical knowhow about building a radio station with appropriate technology. Bonds were strengthened between the two groups: FIRE and the Colectivo de Matagalpa.

Costa Rica

In our work at conferences around the world, we learned that even after very little training, women are ready to let their voices be heard on radio through live broadcasts. One such instance was at the Fifth International Interdisciplinary Congress on Women in San José, Costa Rica, which gathered more than 1,500 women from around the world. One day the live program was broadcast without any of the four FIRE producers present. Guiselle Mills and Ana Sisnet from the Black Women's Network organized and ran the entire two-hour broadcast in both English and Spanish. In those two hours they had some twenty black women on the air who had come from all over the world to participate in two UNIFEM-organized panels on black women's identity and livelihood. Jeanne Carstensen summed up FIRE's reaction:

We all felt that day that FIRE had reached a new level. As we looked at each other nervously in a workshop during the hours when "our" program was going on without us, it seemed that FIRE really was being used by women, as their medium, and there was also the message that all women can do it.

El Salvador

At the Sixth Latin American and Caribbean Feminist Encounter (Encuentro) in 1993 in El Salvador, there was a meeting of more than forty-eight feminists who worked in radio throughout the region. Katerina, Nancy, and I were among them. The conclusions of this working group on women in radio included the following:

- Communication is a process of encounter and dialogue with an audience; therefore, feminists are building participatory and alternative radio.

VOCES INQUEBRANTABLES

Análisis del Tribunal Latinoamericano y Caribeño de Violaciones a los Derechos Humanos de las Mujeres

Programa Radio Internacional Feminista

Flyer announces FIRE's radio tribunal on violations of women's human rights at the Sixth Latin American and Caribbean Feminist Encuentro in El Salvador, 1993.

- The presence of feminists in radio is stronger and broader in our region.
- We will continue to work to give women back their voices, to ensure that women have access to media at all levels, and to counteract the discriminatory images of women in the media, and we will continue to work toward the recognition and respect of women's human rights.

In addition to strengthening our bonds and commitment toward the democratization of our societies and all communications, FIRE staff organized an on-the-spot radio station with an amplifier set up in the middle of the lobby of the hotel were the encuentro was taking place.

Women on the Air, as we called it, broadcast two or three times a day, whenever large groups gathered to rest or wait for other activities to begin. The broadcasts produced at the encuentro by AMARC and FIRE started with the statement, "Women's words have been taken away. We want them alive, and we want them now. Welcome to Women on the Air."

The United States

In New York, a workshop on women's human rights was organized by the International Women's Tribune Center under the UN Development Program's Training for Broadcasters and Journalists from developing countries. Marjorie Thorp from UNIFEM called for women in media to:

...focus on eliminating attitudes and beliefs that legitimize violence and male control of women. Improving women's access to power is also key. We have to develop alternative strategies to combat the gender ideology that keeps women trapped. Women in media should become advocates.

Under the title FIRE-ing Up Women—We Will No Longer Be Silent, Jeanne Carstensen presented FIRE's perspectives on communications:

Our live broadcasts, done with very simple equipment and installed in the middle of women's activism, give women the opportunity to

55

have direct access to media. They give women a political tool to do their political work.

Netherlands

Also in 1993, the Calling for Change Conference in The Hague, Netherlands, helped clarify the need for powerful media that portray women and their struggles accurately. Shanti Dairiam from Malaysia, Director of International Women's Rights Action Watch—Asia Pacific, explained that once the public campaign to end violence against women was in progress in her country, the media became interested. She said that this was welcomed by women's groups, as it was believed that media attention would greatly enhance their outreach capacity.

So women were working with journalists, using the media to speak out against violence. The media however, were focusing on rape—not wife abuse—especially individual incidents of rape, the more horrendous, the better. Public consciousness was turned to public outcry, and public attention was drawn to these unrelated incidents of rape.... The media are motivated by profit and work to sell themselves. They have no noble or ideological stand in favor of women. Traditionally, the media thrive on sensational events. This is called news.

Fatoumata Sire Diakite from the Association for Progress and the Defense of Women's Rights in Mali, West Africa, described how in her region she witnessed the beginnings of a new form of violence against women as a result of the influx of pornographic movies and nude magazines. However, she pointed out the need for women to transform media.

Nonetheless, the media is a useful, if not essential, tool to raise public awareness, to build public pressure, and to educate society about the causes and consequences of violence against women.

I called attention to the challenge that women have in relation to international media:

They make it seem that violence against women is a problem that women have in the South, and that women from the North have the strategies and the answers to it. They also make it seem that it is an issue placed on the international agenda by the women from the North. We have the challenge... to change that focus. Women from the South and from the North have the problem—violence against women is not an exclusive issue of the South. On the other hand, women from the North and the South also have experience, strategies, and answers to the problem. It must be understood that violence against women was placed on the international agenda by women from the South. It happened during the Decade for Women.

FIRE Around the World in 1994

The year 1994 took FIRE's microphones further abroad—to Thailand, Ecuador, and Argentina.

Thailand

In February of 1994, women communicators from around the world met in Bangkok, Thailand. FIRE's Nancy Vargas was keynote speaker at the conference entitled Women Empowering Communications, coordinated by the World Association for Christian Communication in London (WACC), ISIS International in the Philippines, and the International Women's Tribune Center in New York. Debra Latham and I were also there, along with 500 women from Latin America and the Caribbean, Europe, India, Africa, Asia, and North America.

On the theme Women, Communication, and Power, Nancy's talk dealt with the accumulated experiences of the FIRE team:

FIRE is a philosophy of life: empowering women by raising our voices, by giving back to women our voices to speak from our experiences, our lives, our sufferings and joys... the source of collective and individual power that is in us to move beyond where we are and who we are, to move beyond the world we inherited. That means that media should allow us to inform, know, transform, face obstacles, search for strategies and answers, that is… empower us with a communication created from our roots and identities. Women are very sure of the kind of communication we want, because we have always worked for the ability to confront the communication system and to change the power structures that are present not only in the communication institutions, but also in other institutions in society.

Nancy explained FIRE's vision about empowerment—not only women empowering communication, but also communication empowering women:

We believe in communication as channels that flow and mingle ideas, knowledge, experiences, and feelings expressed by ourselves as protagonists of life, and in which different lines meet to create places where we can agree on answers to our problems. Our commitment to women in radio communications is not only to feminize radio, but to the adoption of a whole new philosophy of transformation and empowerment in our lives.

She also talked about FIRE's views on formats:

We decided not to put too much emphasis on formats where "objectivity" hinders women's work in communication. We try to show… that we women have ideas, feelings, values, identities, dreams, a history—that we have had to learn to survive and become subjects in our lives. That is why, for us, objectivity in communications does not exist. Our language is clear and we cannot, nor do we wish to, stop using it, as we were told by traditional media.

In what other way can we express with all our feelings everything that has happened—and that continues to happen—to us? It is unacceptable and immoral that we women, the poorest of the poor, have to bear the burden of neoliberal policies and structural adjustment policies. In what other words can we tell the world about the violations and atrocities that we are subjected to, if it is not with terms such as "unacceptable" and "immoral," adjectives that are not objective but very subjective and very true?

We have found that women use personal testimony as the most valuable means of describing our lives from our own points of view, without being chopped up by traditional or predetermined formats. In this way we get closer to ensuring that the audience... can identify with particular situations and can show that the violence suffered by women is universal. Another tack used in the program is "commented news and information," which allows us to have more fluid and participatory communication, and to take up themes we want to talk about, valuing women's ability to analyze and think.

One of the most difficult aspects of communication that we women are involved in has been the use and empowerment of language. In this sense we have had to make great efforts to include ourselves in the grammar of language as well as in radio communication, in order also to be included in the grammar of life and in radio language. I have taken some of these words from the great Mexican linguist and feminist, Lillian Levi.

This point can be understood clearly in the example of the Spanish language and other languages where it is very common to say "grandfathers," "fathers," and "men" (abuelos, padres, y hombres) with the assumption that the reference also includes grandmothers, mothers, and women, respectively.

She added that we do not go by the conventional wisdom of not improvising on radio because we know that:

...in the continual struggle that we women have to survive, we have to make a thousand and one improvisations outside of the established disorder that is imposed upon us.

Nancy reported on the results and resolutions of the conference. She pointed out the topics that came out in an addendum to the accepted resolutions. There had been no consensus on those topics, but they were the ones that had elicited passionate discussions among the participants.

The addendum to the resolution addresses the rise of fundamentalism, violence against women, and women taking control of their own sexuality, including the need for lesbianism as a sexual orientation to be made more visible in the media. This same addendum also makes an urgent call to governments to free journalists and writers being held as political prisoners and expresses deep concern over the exploitation of women and girls in the sex industry.

Nancy also reported on the official document from the conference, which includes the goal of creating a new, just, and sustainable world order to meet the needs of women and men—not of institutions. It also promotes all forms of communication that challenge the patriarchal culture of the media, and democratize and decentralize it. Communications should respond to women's and peoples' needs, treating them as subjects of the media, not as objects.

Since the UN Third World Conference on Women in Nairobi in 1985, women's organizations and networks have continued to grow, as have actions on local, national, and international levels. However, participants also noted that powerful negative tendencies still prevail. The document calls for concrete strategies to change these negative tendencies, including:

- Gender perspective training and respect for cultural diversity, which promotes the preservation of oral culture, such as stories, dance, song, theater arts, and others customs and traditions as effective means of communication.

- Integral approaches to the environment and sustainable development.

- Increased media training and increased access to information, including research and documents.

- Strengthening and extending of networks and interchange.

- Guaranteed distribution of information from the United Nations that affects women's lives, including training for utilizing the information. Women's participation in the UN meetings must be guaranteed.

- Wide coverage of the Fourth World Conference on Women (Beijing, China, 1995) and the parallel NGO Forum, for one day of the conference to focus on communications by and for women, and for 1996 to be declared the International Year of Women Communicating.

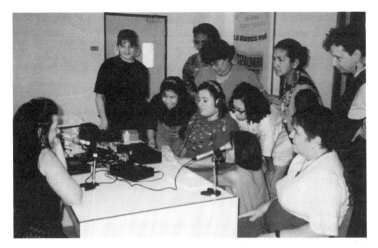

Nancy Vargas (with headphones) leads hands-on radio
workshop in Bangkok, Thailand.

มาเรีย ซัวเรสกับคลื่นวิทยุเพื่อสตรี

María Suárez (top) and Nancy Vargas (with María, bottom) are
featured in the Bangkok press. Nancy was keynote speaker at the
February 1994 conference, Women Empowering Communications.

But talking about communications and communicating was not the only thing that took place at the conference. Debra and Nancy also organized and facilitated a radio training workshop as part of the hands-on activities there.

We were thrilled to be asked by the Tribune Center to organize such an activity. It was to be our first systematic experience in training women from different parts of the world to edit and do live broadcast.
— Nancy Vargas

The objectives of the two-day activity were to contribute to the empowerment of women through the use of technology for recording, editing, and broadcasting. At the same time, it was to be a collective experience that would allow the group to get to know each other through interviews.

There were seven participants the first day, but on the next day we had twelve! They shared editing, interviewing techniques, and the basics of live broadcasting. We could not do an actual broadcast because the office with the international telephone line was closed, but the women spoke, mixed music, and shared in many languages: Thai, Togole, English, and Spanish.
— Debra Latham

Each woman interviewed another and mixed music to accompany her piece, learning the use of the tape recorder, the telephone interface, and the editing board. Some had many years of radio experience but had never "controlled" the controls. This was the case of Petit Peredo from the Philippines, who joined the second day, after hearing that the workshop was hands-on. "I have been doing radio for so many years," she said, "but I never had the chance to use the equipment."

Others were coming to radio for the first time. A Thai woman remarked, "After this FIRE workshop, I think my next step is going to be to work in radio in my country."

A new venue was opened for FIRE. After three years of women's radio, the time was ripe to share, not only the voices but also the skills acquired in the process. From then on, FIRE received requests from women in Latin America and South Africa to do the kind of training that took place at the conference.

Ecuador

On the ninth and tenth of April 1994, Quito, Ecuador, was the site of a Latin American and Caribbean Women Communicators Meeting convened by ALAI (Agencia Informativa Latinoamericana de Información) and AMARC. The aim of the meeting was to reflect on the role of gender communications in society and of consolidating common processes designed to carry out joint actions and formulate strategies for participation in the Fourth World Conference on Women. Katerina Anfossi represented FIRE at the meeting, which drafted the following declaration:

> *In today's world, communications and information exert an increasingly decisive influence on the social, political, and cultural orientation of our societies. The increasing monopolistic concentration of communications media limits the exercise of the right of citizens to free expression and access to information, particularly in the case of socially marginalized segments of the population. Moreover, without information, there cannot be participation of citizens in decisions of common concern. In particular, there exists systematic discrimination against women, whose actions, interests and movements are not taken into account. In this context, it is essential to promote the democratization of communications and to affirm the role of gender-sensitive communications as an indispensable element in the consolidation of democratic practices. We affirm that gender-sensitive communications, as a theme and practice, are a strategic element in the advancement of women and their causes.*

The twenty participants represented various communications organizations, networks, and groups. They agreed to promote the creation of a Permanent Gender Communications Forum coordinated by ALAI, AMARC, ISIS, *Fempress,* and the APC Women's Program. This group constituted a media pool to cover activities related to the Fourth World Conference on Women, to formulate proposals about gender communications, to make claims of women from the South more visible, and to promote the proposal for a year of gender communications.

Argentina

Later in 1994, the Latin American and Caribbean Regional Preparatory Meeting for Beijing was held in Mar del Plata, Argentina. Once again, FIRE and AMARC worked to broadcast Women on the Air. This time AMARC had contacted a local community radio station, and the radio women went every night to broadcast to a local audience who knew there was a women's meeting in town but who might not have otherwise found out what was going on there.

Perhaps one of the highlights of these local broadcasts was the night nine radio women were on the air telling the audience about our experiences. One of them was the Chinese woman who had been on the air on FIRE that morning. After many of us spoke about our audiences of 20,000 or so, someone asked her what her audience was. "Five hundred million people," she said. "I work on China's National Radio." Silence in the recording room... we all looked at each other, flabbergasted... and finally someone asked her: "Do you think we can do a half hour of Women on the Air when we go to China next year? You know, a community radio program for almost one fourth of the world's population!" Finally we all burst out laughing. She did, too. Then she said she would look into it.
—María Suárez, telling stories on FIRE, 1994

The Latin American and Caribbean communicators and journalists there organized the media pool that had been envisioned only a few months before at the communications meeting in Quito, Ecuador. Working together as a team, all the journalists and communicators multiplied our capacities. We drafted articles together, laughed together, did radio as a team, shared the difficulties of getting our work recognized at the meeting, and even drafted our own resolutions.

FIRE'S "Voices without Brackets" live broadcasts in Mar del Plata, Argentina—Ana Duarte reports from the Latin American and Caribbean Regional Preparatory Meeting for Beijing, September 1994.

Another joke came out of that experience. One night we were having dinner together, and we started arguing about the lack of awareness in the movement about the "super-important" work we do. In between our complaints, we also talked about what we had covered that day: the indigenous women's visibility in the NGO Forum, the Black Latin American and Caribbean women who were so outspoken, the lesbians out of the closet, the disabled women, and more. Then we went right back to the complaints about the lack of recognition of our "super-important" work.

"Hey," someone yelled, "there has emerged a new category of invisibilized women: Us!"

Ever since that night, we started making ourselves very visible by moving from workshop to workshop as a group, raising the issues of communications in every discussion, and we were successful. Women communicators and journalists had begun using this opportunity at the Regional Preparatory Meeting to bring our issues into the agenda for the Beijing conference.

Both the Regional Women's NGO Forum and the Official Regional Meeting received proposals by women in media. They had been drafted through a previous series of meetings and workshops on Latin American and Caribbean women in media (ALAI, April 1994) and during Mar del Plata (Colectivo Radial Feminista del Perú, September 1994). The following is a statement presented by women in media at the Nongovernmental Women's Organizations Forum, which took place four days before the official regional meeting:

> *There will be no substantial human development, nor a construct of democracy and citizenship, without an adequate democratizing use of information technology and systems of communications.*
>
> *We affirm the necessity to democratize information and private and public communications as a fundamental human right. We believe that these can become central spaces and agents of the transformation of the condition and position of women that we are promoting.*
>
> *The women's movement, as part of civil society, aims at monitoring public policies in this area and also being vigilant in holding these power systems and their national and international monopolies accountable.*
>
> *We will negotiate a code of ethics, and special emphasis will be given by us to extend and strengthen the alternative, autonomous, and public (communal, national, regional, and international) channels of information and communications that cannot exist and work within the market framework that operates globally.*
>
> *We challenge the power of national and transnational television and its convergence, based mainly on the logic of the market and consumption, and whose activities take place outside of a regulatory code of ethics. Some of the reasons why we challenge it are the following: it intervenes in politics, omitting and fragmenting information, and it conceals cultural diversities and social sectors, extends violence, and privatizes the public and symbolic space.*

The issues and mechanisms proposed had as a basis the issue of power:

The democratic use of information technologies and systems of communications determine today the possibilities of sustainable human development, and also the construct of citizenship. This is why we understand the exercise of communication as a fundamental human right of women and peoples in general.

We also presented proposals to:

1. Guarantee available and public interest space that allows women and all of civil society to have a voice in media.

   Mechanisms: Promote organizations where women and all of civil society participate, pressure, and monitor media.

2. Draft a Convention on Communications based on women's perspectives of society, establishing a code of ethics.

3. Promote and reinforce the experiences of alternative communications proven to be strategic toward development. *Mechanisms:* Legal actions should be undertaken to guarantee the continuity and existence of alternative experiences. *Resources:* International cooperation agencies, civil society, and states should consider this a priority in development strategies, assigning resources to it.

4. Promote and ensure access of women communicators in actions and decision-making at all levels in media.

   Mechanisms: Establish commissions for equal opportunities in media. These commissions should ensure women's participation; promote training workshops in gender perspective for all communicators in state and private media; and prioritize research in communication and its relation to the status of women.

The official Latin American and Caribbean Regional Preparatory Meeting later adopted some of these proposals on a provisional basis.

In Area VII of the official draft entitled Acknowledging the Cultural Plurality in the Region, the following obstacles concerning women and media are recognized:

- Persisting exclusive cultural models that silence or distort the identity and knowledge of women in all areas of social life; these models are present within the family, the educational system, mass media, and the arts.

- The persisting discrimination in media that limits the presence of women in decision-making positions.

At the same time the draft document recognized achievements, such as the growing participation of women in the creation of alternative media, organizations, and networks in the area of culture and communications. It also picked up the proposals presented by women in media. This draft is significant in that it forced the Fourth UN Conference on Women to include the idea of a gender perspective in relation to its concrete proposals about the issue of media. Following are the relevant guidelines adopted in the official text:

- Develop communication strategies to overcome the portrayal of stereotyped images of women and men, stimulating messages that reflect the diversity of roles, living conditions, needs, and points of view of women.

- Ensure a model of equal value of genders, and of cultural diversity in formal and nonformal spheres, changing the models and stereotypes that are perpetuated in education and in mass media.

- Stimulate the formation of a pluralistic and nondiscriminatory social image of women in culture and communications.

- Portray a realistic and plural image of women through messages and campaigns promoted by governments and organizations in civil society through social communications media.

- Stimulate the participation of women with their own voices in all public issues.

- Facilitate women's access to new technologies and to telecommunications and information systems, and train them in their use.

- Favor participation of women in the development of innovative initiatives in social communication media, especially those that integrate new communication technologies.

- Strengthen participation of women in the decision-making levels of media.

- Implement a permanent and systematic awareness among entrepreneurs and professionals in social communications about nondiscrimination.

FIRE Around the World in 1995

FIRE celebrated another innovation in 1995 with a simultaneous live broadcast in Chile and Costa Rica. This was followed by broadcasts from Senegal, China, Germany, and Sweden.

Chile and Costa Rica

A unique live broadcast took place on January 25, 1995. CODEHUCA's Ana Virginia Duarte, a radio woman with FIRE at the Regional Preparatory Conference for Beijing in Mar del Plata, organized a simultaneous live broadcast on FIRE and Radio Tierra in Chile. Radio Tierra, which began in 1991, was the first woman-owned and woman-managed radio station in the world.

On the program, host Carolina Rossetti presented Violeta Menjivar from El Salvador, who was an alternate legislator representing the FMLN in the parliament of her country. She highlighted the role of women in the peace process of El Salvador. From the Dominican Republic, Carmen Criss stressed the economic crisis due to structural adjustment policies there and the role of women in combating them. Another guest was Silvia Narvaez from Nicaragua who talked about the crisis within the Sandinista Party.

All of these women pointed to the responsibility of globalization of the market economy by powerful countries, and the imposition of market trends on poor nations. They suggested strategies to overcome these trends: solidarity and alliances based on the recognition of identities and rooted in specific realities.

Once again, the use of inexpensive technology in women's hands, a lot of creativity, and women getting together to speak out became the spark and fuel of an innovation that might transform the relationship between community radio and shortwave radio. Both can go on at once! Ana Virginia, our new radio woman, has already re-created the technique of live broadcast on FIRE.

Radio Tierra and FIRE had developed a new friendship.

Senegal

Also in January, AMARC's radio women organized a live broadcast of FIRE from Senegal. While the World Association of Community Broadcasters (AMARC) held its sixth conference in that African country, women from Latin America and the Caribbean called FIRE live, giving reports about the Women's Caucus work session held the day before the opening of the conference.

Tachi Arriola from Perú reported that the Women's Network had designed a strategy for global outreach with their radio work from Beijing the following September. FIRE talked to them about the idea of doing shortwave broadcasts from China during the conference. AMARC immediately released the following call to women.

Subject: Radio workers in Beijing

Following the mandate given to us at the Sixth World Conference of Community Radio Broadcasters, AMARC's women's network is currently preparing for its participation in the World Conference on Women that will take place in September in China.

We want and need that women's voices will be heard and that the theme of Gender Communication, Women and Radio will have a space on the Beijing agenda.

In order to plan our participation, we need to know of any radio stations or allied organizations that will be attending the meeting and the names of the delegates. If you know of any women radio workers who will be attending the conference, please let us know.

Thanks in advance for your cooperation.

María Victoria Polanco
AMARC vice president representing
the Women's Network

China

FIRE played a role in the preparations and actions concerning media coverage at the 1995 UN Fourth World Conference on Women in Beijing, China. Together with other women in media, we also contributed to the work of making women's communications visible and integral in the conference's agenda. The story of FIRE at the Beijing conference is told in full in Chapter 7.

Germany

When Interkonexiones, a European-based alternative radio network, invited FIRE and some of the women from the Women's Network of AMARC to take part in their event entitled With New Eyes and New Ears: International Communications, Nancy Vargas knew there had to be another live broadcast. The city of Freiburg, Germany, gathered twenty-five women from Latin America and Europe—all radio women.

These women broadcast live on FIRE, and Women on the Air took shape once again as they spoke of the need to demand the right of women to survive, to sing, to dream, and to struggle to make their dreams come true.

Latin American and Caribbean women living in Germany, did one of the live broadcasts from the Interkonexiones event in Freiburg. They presented the pains and strengths of the Latina migrant women. Two of them were Tania and Beatriz, Uruguayan women who arrived in Germany for different reasons. However, they share their common experience of being migrants in Europe.

Beatriz went to Germany with personal motives. At the time of the live broadcast on FIRE, she was working at the International Family Center.

I have been here for twenty-three years, and it is still hard to get used to the cold weather, and also the coldness of many of the people.... In my job I find help for women who have come in worse shape than I did.... Although I have a university diploma, it is not recognized here, but the ones that come in this decade are worse off.... Migration is more massive now because of the conditions in

Latin America, and at the age of fifty and fifty-five, many women who come here are already destroyed. Since Germany, itself, is in economic crisis, these people have to work for many more years without getting a pension... plus, the laws today state that when there is a job, Germans can get it first, then other Europeans, and we come last!

Tanya came in 1972, just before the coup d'état in Uruguay. She had been forced to leave her country because she was an activist.

All of a sudden I had to leave and was literally transplanted into Germany. I always thought I would return soon, but that was not possible. Daily life was so hard, that Europe was demystified for me very quickly. This is a developed country, but migrants do not have the money to enjoy the development.

Talking about their survival strategies, Tanya said:

We first got together with people who spoke our language. It was mostly other Latins and also people from Spain. With this we re-created the families we had left behind. That was the first and foremost strategy. We created associations and solidarity groups. We were young, so the groups did not last beyond that stage of life. Today, groups are organized on the basis of nationality. It was not like that before; we were Latin Americans. Earlier we had been able to talk about the problems in the region where we were from and the situation of our people here. Today, the social and economic problems here in Germany are so grave that people are not receptive to hearing about problems of other countries. The isolation is terrible.

Because they knew they were on an international broadcast, Tanya and Beatriz used FIRE as an opportunity to address women listeners back in Latin America:

We want to tell you that this is not paradise; that it is not easy to live or to work here. Many of the women who come end up in prostitution, and this might not be what you want to come for.

Other Latina women from Uruguay, Argentina, and Chile spoke of the pains of their lives as immigrants in Europe, and of the xenophobia that had been exacerbated more recently in places like Germany. They spoke of their struggles to use radio to build bridges among peoples of different countries.

International communications were strengthened with this experience. Nancy Vargas came back from Germany with dozens of tapes and many new connections.

Sweden

From October 9 to 27, 1995, a group of nineteen women journalists met in Kalmar, Sweden, for a Women in Journalism course convened by FOJO—the Institute for Further Education of Journalists. FIRE had been invited as a speaker for the course. On October 19, I presented a talk about FIRE and alternative women's media and, more important, we did a live broadcast. Marianne Englund, a Swedish journalist and observer of the broadcast, wrote about it the next day, describing the significance and setting of the course in the words of some of the participants:

This is Radio FIRE

With broadcasting equipment no bigger than a freestyle, María Suárez from Costa Rica steered the voices from women journalists out in the black cold night of Kalmar, Sweden, and further out to listeners all over the world.

One of the voices belonged to Kishali Adhikari from Sri Lanka. Speaking to all the women in the world and especially to women of her own country, she said: "I would like to ask you to think about who we really are and what we really want from life. I would like you to break the barriers of tradition that surround us and to think about ourselves as individuals. Each one of us is special. We have lives of our own and ideas which we should fulfill. Let us work, individually and as a group, to make things better for all of us. Be brave! Stand up and speak for our rights! Dare to be different!"

Some of the women told the listeners about their situation as journalists: "It is very difficult to be a woman journalist in Kenya," says

Sylvia Mudasia and describes a dangerous situation with journalists being constantly harassed by police and the authorities.

Another example is given by the participant from Algeria. "I wish I could tell you about women in a normal situation, but this is not possible. Men and women in Algeria share the same fear because of the political situation; fifty-two journalists were assassinated recently and the list is not closed yet. We are now fighting to be alive."

The women who took part in the course in Kalmar are now setting up a network to help and support each other.

—Marianne Englund, SIDA

Following the course, Agne Eklund submitted a personal account of her experience working with the female journalists who had participated:

Hello, all of the world!!!

My name is Agne Eklund, and I am a Swedish freelance journalist, aged 35. I have had the opportunity to visit Kalmar this week in October and to meet so many fantastic and struggling female journalists from nineteen countries....

My thoughts about this chance to talk on women's radio are few, but huge.... Maybe, if male individuals could handle their aggressive instincts, there would be no wars, no AIDS, no pollution, and no sexual violence.... History shows that we do not learn anything from it, and that is the great sadness about it all....

As long as the ruling class are men and the circle of Yin and Yang and Father Sun and Mother Earth doesn't work, I can only agree with one of my favorites. His name was John Lennon and he said, "Woman is the nigger of the world." What more is there to say?

—Agne Eklund, Borlange

The night before one of the women's live broadcasts, all of the women journalists sat around the television set to watch CNN. It was the fiftieth anniversary of the creation of the United Nations, and the journalists did not want to miss the reporting from the UN headquarters in New York. Just in the middle of it, a fiftieth anniversary commemoration spot was shown regarding women. The dismay and outrage of the journalists about the spot was so loudly expressed in the room that others came to see what was happening.

The spot presented images of African women carrying wood, water, and baskets on their heads. A voice came in saying that for centuries, women have used their heads to carry objects. At a certain point the images and the message changed: African women appeared on the new scene, receiving academic degrees and doing different intellectual jobs. The voice came in to say, "...and now they are using what's inside their heads."

The feminist communicators present agreed that this spot violated our rights, not only in regard to a fair portrayal in the media, but it included other violations of women's human rights, such as violence against women. One of the African women expressed her dismay to FIRE:

> *I ask myself: Is it not violence against women to portray that before the UN came, women used their heads simply to carry things on them, and that with the advent of the UN they learned to use their heads to think?*
>
> *Doesn't the UN realize that women have had to carry burdens that should not be only ours, and that we have had to think of every way to preserve even the existence of humankind and nature itself? Do they not know that we will not take one step back?*
>
> *The United Nations and its member states should know that the women's movement, NGOs, and civil society are already heading the struggle for the [FWCW] commitments to become a reality, and have undertaken many other actions on behalf of our rights.*

The day after the CNN broadcast, the issues regarding concerns about the spot were broadcast on FIRE. Soon after that, a strong protest was sent to the Secretary General of the UN. That letter of protest is reprinted on the following two pages.

FIRE Around the World in 1996

FIRE continued its international live broadcasts in 1996, starting with a workshop in its home country of Costa Rica and traveling to Canada and again to conferences in the United States and Sweden.

To:
The Secretary General
Boutrous Boutrous-Ghali
United Nations
UN Plaza
New York, NY 10017
USA

From:
Delegates to Women in
    Media Seminar
FOJO, Box 622
S-391 26 Kalmar
Sweden

WE PROTEST

We the undersigned women journalists gathered at FOJO, Kalmar, in Sweden, strongly protest against the advertisement commemorating 50 years of the United Nations aired on public television.

The advertisement begins with African drum music and images of African women carrying loads of wood, water and baskets on their heads. A woman's voice then comes on to say that for years African women have used their heads to carry goods. The images then change and we see an African woman in a graduation cap passing from college and later in intellectual work situations. The same voice goes on to say that African women are now using what is inside their heads.

We are outraged by this portrayal of African women for the following reasons:

1) The advertisement shows the African woman as being devoid of intelligence until the United Nations intervened. The UN should remember that it takes a brain to know the best way to carry goods is on the head! It should also bear in mind that when it portrays a situation common to women worldwide, such as unwaged work, it is stereotyping women in general and not just one group of women.

2) The advertisement gives a higher value to intellectual work, at a time when the UN itself has adopted a platform of action at the Fourth World Conference on Women in Beijing in September 1995. The platform calls for the recognition of women's unwaged labor in the gross national statistics. It should also remember that the same conference made a strong call for an end to all stereotypes of women in the media.

We therefore demand the following:

1) The immediate withdrawal of the advertisement in question.

2) Substitution of the advertisement with a newly constructed gender-sensitive and ethno-sensitive advertisement.

3) Equal air time and distribution to be allotted to the new advertisement. We are willing to be consultants on the production of the new advertisement, along with the CSW, CEDAW and other organizations.

Copies of this protest letter are being distributed to the media and other organizations as part of the responsibility in building consciousness.

NAME	COUNTRY
Sylvia Mudasia	Kenya
Zorodzai Machekanyanga	Zimbabwe
Yaa Oforoiwhk Aequah	Ghana
Tina	Ghana
Nabeela Aslam	Pakistan
Li Shu	China
Doreen Limbizi	South Africa
Sandhya Rao	India
Alicia Diaz	Perú
Helena Salem	Brazil
Kishali Adhikari	Sri Lanka
Ratiba	Algeria
Gladys Khoza	Malawi
Meriam Hamimaz	Morocco
Gina Porcena	Haiti
Delta Passingen	Papua New Guinea
Rajshree Shrestha	Nepal
Natsag	Mongolia
Roushan	Bangladesh
Helena	Middle East

Costa Rica

On the twenty-sixth of February, 1996, the University for Peace convened a workshop of women journalists and communicators in Costa Rica. Cynthia Flores, a journalist of the University for Peace, coordinated the activity entitled Towards Media Work with a Gender Perspective. The objective of the activity was to sensitize a group of journalists to presenting information through a gender lens.

A roundtable discussion about the way in which media treats women had as participants the following women:

- Livia Cordero, who presented her personal case of her imprisonment without due process. She told of how media used a sensationalist focus when she was imprisoned under the accusation of being a terrorist, but gave the coverage of her acquittal much less space.

- Sayra Zalazar, coordinator of the Women's Police Station, emphasized the need for a re-education of the press "so that it not only portrays women as victims, but will also highlight the problem of impunity, which facilitates violence."

- Laura Queralt, collaborator of *Fempress*, who talked about the fact that most of the Costa Rican press does not reprint the feminist articles that appear in *Fempress*. She asked why, to which women in mainstream media suggested she contact the editors directly, instead of the directors of their papers.

- Marlen Bermudez, an academic of the University of Costa Rica, talked about the fact that there is a quantitative change in the portrayal of women in media, but hardly any qualitative change.

- Yolanda Bertozzi, an advisor at the University for Peace, spoke about a historical and theological perspective on the issue.

Another roundtable was convened, entitled Communication with a Gender Perspective. Vilma Ibarra of Radio Monumental chaired the discussion, and Costa Ricans Katerina Anfossi of FIRE; Thais Aguilar of Women's Feature Service; Monica Perea, a journalist; Ana Duarte of CODEHUCA; Lorena Fernandez of Voces Nuestras; and Ana Isabel Garcia, director of the Center for Women and Family of the Costa

Rican government spoke to the more than fifty journalists and communicators present at the workshop.

Katerina Anfossi spoke about FIRE's belief that women themselves should be the ones to speak, think, and portray the issues that affect their identity. "In media, this means that we should validate women's experience as a legitimate experience," she said. She also emphasized that this does not mean that women talk only about "women's issues," but about their perspective on all issues and their impact on women's lives:

> *We believe that feminism and its analysis from a gender perspective include the diverse conditions of gender, class, race, ethnicity, age, and abilities that make everyone experience things differently.*

Katerina also talked about the need to hold on to feminist communication spaces so that women can have their own voice:

> *We are concerned about globalization of information, the reductions of alternative media, the little access that women have in media to speak from their own perspective, and the lack of importance given by most media to women's actions and gatherings, and this is why we organized the FIREPLACE in China.*

The FIREPLACE in Beijing, China, was the place where FIRE broadcast their live shortwave program for four hours a day, throughout the entire Fourth World Conference on Women in 1995. Chapter 7 is a detailed description of FIRE's role in this conference.

Lorena Miranda of Voces Nuestras, and director of the radio program En la Misma Onda on Radio Sonora, shared the experience of bringing inclusive gender language into commercial radio programs:

> *A good balance not only has to do with mentioning men and women, but also in having a balance of guests, in giving visibility to people with disabilities, indigenous peoples, and others who are seldom heard.*

Ana Virginia Duarte of CODEHUCA shared the experience of working with FIRE in Beijing, although she wasn't a journalist, and the importance of having FIRE train her to do the monitoring and reporting during the Beijing conference.

Thais Aguilar talked about the need to move beyond roles assigned through socialization, "as it works against democracy and peace."

Ana Isabel Garcia spoke about the issue of media in the Platform for Action of the Fourth World Conference on Women, saying, "The government has a special responsibility to promote equality."

The discussion ended with a proposal and commitment by participants to hold a second meeting where journalists and communicators would design strategies to implement the Platform for Action in a joint effort between women in alternative and mainstream media.

For FIRE, this articulation with other women in media is of utmost importance, because, as Nancy Vargas said in *Vista* just after Beijing: "A very long road stands from the words to the action... but women will not take any step back."

On March 6, staff members of Voces Nuestras visited FIRE for a live show. Katerina Anfossi reminded them that FIRE's audience knows them well, as they hear Voces Nuestras on FIRE very often through the programs sent to FIRE for broadcast. Our guests talked about their community radio experience and their initiation into commercial radio in Costa Rica during 1995.

Voces Nuestras was born in 1989, and it has been a training and production radio center with a gender perspective. We have produced micro programs about many issues, and have trained many rural women in radio production. It comprises three areas: production of the program, In the Same Wavelength, in commercial radio; another, Women and Radio, which is the training area; and a third one, Gender and Development, to empower women in productive projects in relation to radio. At the present there are three rural women's radio programs in Costa Rica that are the product of our training. This is quite an achievement: Their lives as household women have changed; they share their experiences with the public.

Katerina asked them what they felt about the importance of radio in the transformation of women's lives. Lorena Fernandez said that as women become opinion makers in radio, they also change the stereotypes of women.

Katalina Calderon mentioned that the experience in radio has been that it has allowed her to grow and to become aware that she has things to say. "It has expanded my horizons as a young woman, and the voices of other women that I hear have inspired me," she explained.

Lorena said that the idea for participating in commercial radio came out of the need to have an outlet for their cassette productions. Aired at Radio Sonora in Costa Rica during 1995, the half-hour-a-day radio program taught them new lessons:

It takes a grand effort to bring a gender perspective to commercial radio—most of it has very exclusive language, male language to talk about everything. On the other hand, you know that both men and women are listening to you, and sometimes you have to say what men do to women, for example in relationship to domestic violence. We have to really be convincing about what we are doing and saying.

Katerina asked them about the way in which they, as women producers, relate to the issues that women talk to them about on the air. Lorena shared one of their most painful and revealing stories:

For Father's Day this year, we decided to do a radio contest on the air, asking women to call in and honor their fathers by telling the nice things they remembered about them. I myself cannot honor my father, because he was not good to me, but we had decided to promote good images of women with their fathers. Well, calls started coming in, with women saying the horrible things their fathers had done to them, one after the other. All of a sudden a woman called, choking, to state emphatically that she could not honor her father by any means. She could not finish saying what her father had done to her, because she began crying. I remained speechless because her story was my own story too. But I was able to comfort her after a while of creating together on the air, because I have processed my experience. We really have to be convinced about what we are doing. It is in our own lives where we have the experiences to respond to other women!

Katerina responded:

Women need to get involved not only because of what has happened to them personally, but because as women, we all suffer discrimination, and that is enough of a reason to do radio for, by, and about women.

After a music break with songs by Mercedes Sosa, the radio women continued the exchange.

Rosa Chen said, "I do radio because I have something to say, and I want to share it. That's enough of a reason to do radio."

Lorena added:

We all have the potential to participate in radio. We have been socialized to feel that others have to speak, but not women. Yet in women's radio, we realize that women have a lot to say, and in radio, women have a say.

The commercial radio program of Voces Nuestras was suspended in 1996, mostly because of lack of funding. All three women expressed that they felt sad when they had to close it down, and that they kept receiving calls from their audience, some even suggesting how to self-finance it because they wanted it back on the air.

Also during the month of March, FIRE supported a new feminist radio effort in Costa Rica. Three young students of journalism at one of the universities came to do a live show with us. Ana Ines Bolaños, Andrea Fonseca, and Ivania Arias were planning to open a women's radio program at a local commercial radio station. Ivania described their goal:

We have set out to build a radio program with a gender perspective to show the world that Costa Rican women have a lot to struggle for, so we cannot remain silent.

Andrea stated that through the feminist radio program they wanted to give women an instrument for the development of women, and to provide a means for the feminist force in the country to be felt.

Katerina asked them how they came up with the idea. Ana Ines told the audience that the idea began when they discussed what they could do to contribute to the advancement of women:

...and that is when we decided it had to be radio! We will have a cultural section, a health section, and a social section in the program. For example radio reaches places where health programs do not. We will bring in specialists who can give advice to women.

Upon graduation, they became journalists in mainstram radio in Costa Rica. Everytime they come across FIRE staff, they remind us what their experience has meant to them in or for their present work.

The United States

From Expo '96, a large feminist gathering in Washington, DC, FIRE did a live bilingual broadcast featuring (among many others) media women Carla Mancilla, Barbara Kraus, Charlotte Hernandez, and Dawn Gifford. They represented Off Our Backs, a collective that publishes a monthly feminist news journal for and about women that began in the 1970s. They spoke about their publication as a medium for women's communication.

"You are welcome to send news articles," said Barbara in English, after which Carla translated:

The journal is truly made by women's hands: we do everything by hand and do a hand layout. Some of the issues we have covered have been the Beijing Women's Conference, Building a Jewish Women's Culture, and Family Planning Centers in Romania. A section entitled Chicken Lady— in rebellion to being called chicks—features events of interest. We also print announcements. The articles come primarily from the readers.

The group talked about why and how they joined the collective. Barbara said, "I joined the collective in 1991. I was new to feminism. I came to find out about it, and after being a volunteer, I joined."

Carla started her feminist activism in the battered women's movement. She joined the collective in order to "reach more women and help them develop a better understanding about their lives, instead of just the times they happen to get beat up and are in a shelter."

Charlotte, a university student, said, "It has been interesting to live the experience of learning to work in a collective and learning to make decisions by consensus. We work very hard."

Dawn came on the air to say:

I joined the collective in 1994. I started as an intern when I was in my last year in Women's Studies in Maryland. The environment in the collective was contrary to the mainstream, and I wanted to be subversive, working with the grassroots.

These women's experiences showcase another angle of the importance of women-owned media: the opportunity for women to create their own environment, to participate in decision-making about media work, and to have a safe place to experiment, based on their own experiences, knowhow, and perspectives.

Canada

In November 1996, FIRE broadcast live from Vancouver, British Columbia at an alternative women's activist meeting. This meeting was held

parallel to the Asian Free Trade Agreement Summit of businessmen and heads of states. (See Chapter 8 for a detailed description of FIRE's broadcasts from this summit.)

Sweden

In 1996 and 1997, FIRE did four live broadcasts with forty women journalists from Asia, Africa, and Latin America at the Institute for Further Education of Journalists in Sweden. In turn, journalists from Cuba, Mozambique, Algeria, South Africa, and the Philippines featured FIRE on radio programs in their countries.

FIRE Around the World in 1997

In addition to the continuing broadcasts from Sweden, FIRE aired other live broadcasts in 1997 from Brazil, Spain, El Salvador, and the United States.

Brazil

FIRE broadcast daily live coverage of the Seventh International Women's Health Conference held in Rio de Janeiro Brazil in March 1997, giving priority to the voices of women of color present at the conference, and also to Brazilian domestic workers and elder political activists. (See Chapter 8 for a detailed description of FIRE's broadcasts from this conference.)

Spain

In July 1997, FIRE broadcast live from the Intercontinental Conference for Humanity and Against Neoliberalism held in Spain. (See Chapter 8 for a detailed description of FIRE's broadcasts from this conference.)

El Salvador

Also in July, FIRE attended and broadcast from AMARC's First Central American Regional Community Radio Conference, held in El Salvador.

The United States

On November 25, the International Day Against Violence Towards Women, FIRE broadcast live from Spanish Harlem in New York City. The broadcast featured adolescent students from the Escuela Mirabal, who talked about the petition campaign they are circulating to get the U.S. Administration to sign the CEDAW Convention.

FIRE Around the World in 1998

In August 1998, FIRE was invited by the AMARC Women's Network to take part in the Twenty-Fifth AMARC Conference in Milan,

Italy. The network asked FIRE to organize its two daily one-hour broadcasts on an all-day Internet radio station, Planeta Tierra, which was organized by the conference.

FIRE's air time was full of celebration in many languages: Spanish, French, German, Swahili, English, and Italian. (See Chapter 9 for details about FIRE's participation in this conference.)

Since its beginning in 1991, FIRE has put radio in the hands of women. What feminist journalists and communicators are demonstrating is that having a voice is part of having a say in society; that it is part of having a place in politics; that it is part of having rights; that it is part of having an identity and of having a stake in the future.

Our vision has taken us throughout the world—from kitchen tables to dusty villages to international conferences—where we have been making a case for putting radio in the hands of women so our place, our voices, and our perspectives in media will contribute to the reshaping of the world.

CHAPTER 3

FIRE, Native Women, and the Environment

In Guatemala we use firewood to cook. You cannot build a fire with one or two pieces of wood. It will never catch. But if you have a whole pile of wood, it will catch fire and burn to give life.

—Petrona, a Mayan Guatemalan woman
in a FIRE interview, May 1991

The year 1992 was the first full year of FIRE on the air. Perhaps not by chance, it was also the year of commemoration of the 500 years of indigenous resistance to colonization of our American continent. In addition, 1992 was the year of the first United Nations conference to be covered by FIRE—the Conference on Environment and Development in Rio de Janeiro, Brazil (also known as the Earth Summit).

FIRE and Native Women's Rights

FIRE found great inspiration in native peoples' commemoration of 500 years of struggle against colonization of the Americas. Throughout this period of intense activism, we listened to the voices of native women in many on-the-air interviews.

In this year of 1992, we have to move from resistance to affirmation of our rights as indigenous peoples. As native peoples on this continent, we have our own perspective on the significance of this year. While the Church celebrated "evangelization," Spain celebrated "colonization," and governments celebrated the "meeting" of two cultures, we remembered the invasion of our continent and its peoples and celebrated the 500 years of resistance. To this day, we can say that there was really no evangelization, no colonization, and no meeting. We resisted, because what our grandmothers and grandparents had to go through was a massacre. Yet we have survived as a people. This year, we have celebrated the fact that we have an identity. It is still threatened today. For example, even though Rigoberta Menchú has been granted the Nobel Peace Prize, Guatemala is still at war.

—Juanita Batzibal, a Mayan Guatemalan woman, on FIRE's broadcast

Rigoberta Menchú visited Costa Rica as an Ambassador of Goodwill a short time later, as part of a Central American Tour for the UN International Indigenous Peoples' Year (1993). There she spoke of the need for Peace Prize laureates to work for the creation of a light that illuminates and works for peace on a regional and global level.

FIRE's Katerina Anfossi and Jeanne Carstensen had interviewed Rigoberta in February 1992 as she was being considered for the prestigious prize, which she later received.

It is not easy to occupy a place as a woman, to maintain our values and at the same time learn new ones. For the peoples of Guatemala, it would be important that I get the Nobel Peace Prize. It would also be important for women: the victims, the widows, the jobless mothers of many children, silenced by society. How many weavers might there be on this continent who have not had the opportunity to sow their struggles? Many of us women have not had the opportunity to speak up because we were always silenced. They listened to us as testimony, but not as force defying the critical moments....

About the search for unity in the women's movement, I have to say that there are different experiences in every country, and also very concrete experiences. In that sense, unity has to begin by recognizing diversity. There is no place in the world where women have already achieved emancipation, liberty, and full participation in the destiny of their lives, their peoples, and the world. It would bring about a substantial change, but our struggles as women are related to national and global struggles... we [must] learn to build alliances, common interests, and common actions without interference in the natural historical struggles, be it in Africa, here in the continent, or elsewhere in the world.

Women's struggles and indigenous peoples' struggles are inseparable allies because both are oppressed and are an expression of struggle and resistance. If we were to understand each other, we would find many commonalties.

—Rigoberta Menchú in an interview on FIRE

Like Juanita Batzibal, Petrona—another Mayan Guatemalan woman—had used the phrase "from resistance to affirmation" to describe her struggle. In May of 1991 she visited Costa Rica as a member of CONAVIGUA, the National Committee of Widows of Guatemala, which also includes single female heads of households.

I come from Solola, Guatemala, and my culture in Cachiquel. My life as an Indian woman has been very hard, precisely because I am an abandoned woman and mother. There are men who do not understand us. We have to separate, and the separation creates more abuse. Discrimination hurts, whether it is as an Indian, or an Indian woman. We do not have the same rights as men, even though women do double the amount of work that men do. Since the invasion we have been submitted to poverty and misery, so men fight with women. Before, in the time of our ancestors, women were respected more as bearers of life, yet we are abused by men now.

We deserve respect and love because we have resisted and kept our culture. We even have all the responsibility for the subsistence of all.

Garifona women, Indian women, and black and white women have to unite. The lack of unity among women has not been our fault; we never had the opportunity to know each other, but it is happening now, because we all need it. Our unity has to be strengthened. We have suffered violence and marginalization for centuries, and we have not organized ourselves as women. But never again.

One woman alone can't do anything. Let me give you an example: in Guatemala we use firewood to cook. You cannot build a fire with one or two pieces of wood, it will never catch. But if you have a whole pile of wood, it will catch fire and burn to give life.

—Petrona in an interview on FIRE

In March 1992, I attended the symposium, Peace and the Planet: Native Wisdom, Native Rights and Mother Earth, held in Eugene, Oregon. The indigenous women present were interviewed for FIRE about their lives and issues as indigenous women. These testimonies became a tribute to native women in their 500 years of resistance, and the celebration of affirmation of rights and perspectives of indigenous women everywhere.

In the story of humanity in these last five thousand years, women appear shattered and fragmented, divided and disempowered in the midst of gigantic patriarchal efforts to make us invisible in his-story. But there is also a her-story. It is the story of bringing together the shattered pieces, gathering the fragments with enough strength to create something different, not only for her, but for the sake of all peoples. Over twenty-five indigenous women from nations of the North and the South of the Americas spoke on FIRE: Navajo, Lakota, Cherokee, Shoshaw, Haida, Blackfoot, Maya, Gitch'in from Alaska, Aymara from Bolivia, Maori from New Zealand, and native Hawaiian women.

When our grandmothers came as slaves, the first thing that the slave holders did was separate us from our drums. You see, in the African culture, there is a drum and its beat, one for the shoulders, one for the hips, and another for the feet. Exploiters soon learned that and only allowed each group or community of slaves to keep and use one drum.

This fragmented us and split our bodies and souls. Our lives ever since have been an effort to recover the synthesis of all the drums, to affirm our integrity of mind, culture and body.

—Kayilin Sullivan Twotrees, an African
Lakota, in a FIRE interview

Moanikeala Akaka from Hawaii told FIRE one of the most beautiful legends about the Goddess and Volcano Pele in her culture. FIRE played the legend as poetry:

The story of Pele in Hawaiian oral tradition is quite a lesson on the power of women, their role as the first ancestor. Pele is seen as the earth, the first ancestor, the grandmother. And she has a sister—Ilaca, who is the goddess of the forest.

So you can imagine these twin symbols of feminine creativity, you can imagine the wetness, the rich fertility, the heat. All of these things have very sexual connotations, because the earth is having sex, it is birthing. You know, if you look at a crack on the earth, where lava is coming out... it looks like a vagina. And if you see where the land is spilled out, the lava is steaming, it looks destructive, but what follows is Ilaca, spreading the seeds in the fields. The density, the richness... in the olden days women's sexual organs were heaven; they were sacred and were celebrated. That's why we oppose the destruction of Hawaii through the geothermal experiments on the Goddess Pele. That volcano is undergoing an operation of her bosom that is not necessary.

The experimenting companies are looking for geothermal energy, and they know that she is too hot to handle. There have been blasts. It is a desecration of her and of the lowland forests. When we talk to these companies about what Pele means to us, they say she does not exist. Tell me that anyone has proven that Jesus Christ exists; yet many people use him as a reference all the time.

The links with the indigenous women from the continents of North and South America also solidified as Katerina Anfossi attended the International Seminar of Indigenous Women of the Americas held in Bolivia in June of 1992.

Meeting there were approximately thirty indigenous women—representatives of different native peoples. Their objective was to reflect on the situation that they and their communities face today, as well as the role and participation of indigenous women in the movement for revindication of indigenous peoples and original cultures.

They created a network of indigenous women of the Americas with the objective of promoting joint actions in the rescue of their cultures and identities, and to make visible the protagonist actions of indigenous women in the 500 years of resistance.

> *Before the European invaders came to the land of Abya Yala [Cuna name for the American continent], according to our elders, our people lived in peace and happiness. There was an abundance of food, no one went hungry, there was little illness, and women had very important political roles.... This allowed women our own political and social place in life, although it did not mean total equality.*
>
> *Five hundred years have gone by since our grandmothers were raped and assassinated, and even whole peoples have disappeared. Today the people of the same country persecute us and have tried to impose on us their language, culture, and economic models, which have not served to meet the basic needs of the people. Indigenous women are discriminated against, marginalized, and thrice exploited in comparison to men: because we are indigenous, because we are women, and because we are poor. It is urgent to find solutions to the problems that affect us. It is not easy, but it is achievable.*
>
> —Cuna indigenous women from Panama

FIRE also recorded the gesture of our sponsor, Genevieve Vaughan, who spoke about her plans to buy land that had belonged to the Shoshone, and give it back to their original owners. A few months later, when it actually happened, she was interviewed by Jeanne Carstensen. Genevieve read on FIRE what she had said at the ceremony where the land was given back:

> *In this time of commemoration of the 500 years of resistance, I, Genevieve Vaughan, with the participation of my daughters, hereby return twenty-five acres of land in Nevada to the Shoshone peoples to*

own, hold, and keep according to your traditional ways.... We honor
your wisdom and ability as custodians of Mother Earth.
—Genevieve Vaughan, Cactus Springs, Nevada, USA

But the struggle of indigenous peoples for their land rights continued. Three years later, in January 1995, FIRE received a phone call from
Paulina Diaz Navas. Death threats by police in her community had made
the native Costa Rican call FIRE to denounce that the police wanted to
take her inherited ancestral land away from her. The Bribri—Cabagras
indigenous peoples—had migrated from Talamanca on the Atlantic
Coast when colonization pushed them out of the coastal lands and into
the inner mountains of Costa Rica. "This is Paulina Navas calling FIRE
from Buenos Aires, Puntarenas. I want to go live on the air on FIRE,
because I have received a death threat," she told us.

We gave her story the title, Mine Is a Voice that Will Not Be Silenced, and we put her live on the air to tell it. A Bribri native woman,
she narrated the story of seventy years of resistance of her family to
keep their land. Her father and brother, both dead now, left her the
land, which she manages as a single woman. José Joaquin Tensio Alfaro,
one of the local police, had threatened her with a gun. When she tried
to denounce her attacker in the local court in December 1994, José intimidated Paulina's neighbors, trying to make them sign to testify against
her. She described the situation as follows:

Nowadays my land is surrounded by land belonging to big owners.
Because my land belongs to me, a single woman, they feel I am vul-
nerable enough to have it taken away by them. My father died only
two years ago.

When I was twelve years old, my father was put in jail through
blackmail, so that in the meantime, the land could be taken away
from us. He was a Bribri who did not even speak Spanish. It did not
work, and now that he is dead, they are after me.

Paulina also said that she has received the support of the women in
her town, but now her female neighbors had been subjected to sexual
harassment as a means of intimidation, so "they are afraid to leave their
houses or to testify. I want the case to be known beyond our community."

Paulina said she called FIRE because two years before, in 1993, she had been on a live broadcast of FIRE and she had seen how the word had spread very quickly.

In addition to a live broadcast of her story, FIRE took a tape of the program to the Ombudsperson's Office in Costa Rica and asked women's groups and human rights organizations to write to both Paulina and the Costa Rican authorities, expressing solidarity with her struggle.

A year after the first call, FIRE contacted Paulina Diaz Navas again, to follow up on her case. This is what she told FIRE on February 24, 1996:

Those were very difficult and hard times a year ago.... I was fighting for our land rights and for the rights of indigenous women. We now have a legacy for the next generation: the story of how we defended our lands.... For three years I had been subject to sexual harassment by a police officer because he hated my parents. He persecuted me and harassed me verbally. Today, I can affirm that he is no longer a policeman, and we did it! The transit police who threatened my life last year—I can tell you today that he is in prison.

Today, my ownership of the land I inherited from my family is mine and is respected! We indigenous women have to be respected, our right to our lands and our indigenous women's right to work the land has to be respected.

There were women's organizations that listened to me on your program. I am satisfied today, because the tears at the time [last year] have brought forth something good.... It was thanks to the denouncement of the police last year on your program that the Minister of Security, Juan Diego Castro, responded. He sent me the letters that were sent to him by international women's organizations on behalf of my rights. He sent a colonel to investigate the case, and they saw that I was right to fight for my land. He sent orders to the local police, telling them that they had to protect my land rights.

I am thankful to those organizations because they accompanied me, and a little path to justice was opened for me to tell people what I was going through. Today I am respected in my land rights, and no police can harass me. Mine is a voice that, so long as I am alive, no one will silence from denouncing this and other violations of our rights.

FIRE recommended Paulina's name for one of the 1996 International Rural Women's Creativity Awards, which were granted to ten women by the Women's World Summit Foundation in Geneva, which she later received. Letters from our listeners in support of the nominations came from Cuba, Guatemala, Panama, the United States, and Canada. She was granted the award, and travelled to Geneva, Switzerland to receive it.

Native peoples were joined by others around the world in their concern about local, national, and international issues of land and the environment. As these concerns came to the forefront of international attention in late 1991 and 1992, FIRE was on the scene.

Preparing for the Earth Summit

What is really happening is that women around the world are campaigning for an equal say when the decisions about the fate of the planet are made at the biggest United Nations Environment and Development Conference in Brazil in June of this year. We discovered that women's invisibility was being continued in the preparations of the conference. Women decided to have an impact so our views would be taken into account, so we could use the opportunity to empower women and to strengthen the networks that women have built.

—Bella Abzug, live through a telephone call
on FIRE with Debra Latham, 1992

Beginning in 1991, FIRE started planning for its coverage of the Rio Summit from a feminist perspective. First, however, FIRE was to get some help from the international women's movement. One of our partners was Mim Kebler of the Women's Environment and Development Organization (WEDO). They were organizing the World Women's Congress for a Healthy Planet in preparation for women's NGO participation at the Earth Summit.

Mim talked with FIRE, the foundation, and WINGS about the way WEDO was envisioning press work at the meetings. She also offered to line up special interviews for FIRE:

[We] will bring together 1,500 women from all parts of the planet to draft our own agenda about the issue. There will be a Global Hearing

with testimonies about the damage done to women and to the environment, and the links between the two. You should get in touch with these women for special interviews. WEDO will organize that with FIRE.

The World Women's Congress for a Healthy Planet created a global Women's Action Agenda 21 for the next century. Its introduction reads:

We come together to pledge our commitment to the empowerment of women, the central powerful force in the search for equity between and among the peoples of the earth and for balance between them and the life support systems which sustain us all. We undertake our action agenda on behalf of our families and future generations. We appeal to all women and men to join this call for profound and immediate transformation in human values and activities.

FIRE covered the results of the hearing, which expressed women's concerns and demands related to development and the environment. Some women talked about their political experiences:

It is now ten million trees later, not yet quite where we started.... I have criticized the political leadership and I have been portrayed as subversive, so it is very difficult for me not to feel constrained. But I have the energy, and I want to do exactly what they spend hours talking about at the United Nations. But when you really want to take action, you are not allowed because the political system is not tolerant.

—Wangari Mathaii of Kenya, founder
of the Green Belt Movement

Marilyn Carr, from the United Kingdom and senior officer of UNIFEM, called it as she saw it:

When environmental protection work becomes an income-generating activity, the men take over from the women.

—FIRE's series on the Tribunal at the World
Women's Congress for a Healthy Planet, 1991

Meena Renan of Malaysia added:

While the inappropriate development models of the South have to be altered, it is even more important to change the northern economic model, which dominates the global economy and degrades nature. Unless production and consumption patterns change, especially in the North, there cannot be a solution to the current crisis.

Other women addressed specific environmental issues that had both local and global dimensions:

As we enter the last decade of the 20th century... the hopelessness of millions of people around the world has become perhaps the most striking characteristic of our reality.... In 1946, a Navy official came from the U.S. to Bikini Island. He came and told the chief, Juda, "We are testing these bombs for the good of mankind and to end all world wars."

When the Navy officials came, it was too late. There were already thousands of soldiers and scientists on the atoll and hundreds of airplanes and ships in the Bikini Lagoon. They were ready to conduct their tests. The Bikinians had no choice but to leave the islands, and they have never returned. The Navy official did not tell the chief that the Bikinians would not see their home again. Today Bikini is off limits for 30,000 years....

　　　　　　　　　　　　　—Magda Renner, Global Homelessness, Brazil

While WEDO's congress took place in November of 1991 in Miami, Florida, so did the UN Environment Program's Global Assembly of Women and the Environment. The assembly addressed issues of water, waste, energy, and environmentally friendly systems.

Two hundred eighteen success stories were presented, all concerned with these issues. Women from Latin America and the Caribbean, women from Africa, women from Asia and the Pacific, European women, and North American women listened and shared with each other. They were all working on ways of sustaining and healing the earth's resources. Together, they demonstrated that the global resolution of environmental problems and the advancement of environmental management require the involvement of women. Their previously

Katerina Anfossi (left) broadcasts from the 1991 World
Women's Congress for a Healthy Planet in Miami, Florida.

Katerina Anfossi (standing) covers the Twenty-Fifth Congress of the
Women's International League of Peace and Freedom in Santa Cruz,
Bolivia, July 1992.

ignored perspectives, ideas, and energy are all necessary in our collective struggle to heal our planet.

The Global Assembly recommended that the findings be brought to the attention of the Fourth Preparatory Committee of the UN Conference on Environment and Development, the Governing Council of UNEP, and the World Bank and other financial organizations.

UNEP also convened the Global Youth Forum. I attended as 2,000 children from all over the world gathered to testify in favor of protecting the environment. Girls, boys, young women, and young men shared stories of their work to help meet environmental challenges in their local communities. Together, they issued a strong statement:

> *Give youth greater access to the decision-making process at all levels. If we are really going to make a difference, you must allow us positions where we can make a difference. If you are leaving the future to us, then please leave us the present as well. We can't hold one without the other.*
> —Draft Resolution, UNEP Youth Forum, 1992;
> taken from a report on FIRE

After the Youth Forum, I traveled to the Turtle Island Bioregional Conference in Texas. The bioregional vision has become widespread in some cultures in the USA. Although the movement still works to clarify its vision, its emphasis is on creating critical patterns of life in each local place, each region of the biosphere. The movement recognizes that it is indigenous people who are the ones who have lived lightly on the land and who live in harmony with other species, and the mostly middle-class proponents of this movement also want to learn such ways.

What struck me most at the bioregional conference was the circle of women. In this circle, a woman shared the most amazing story of her sexual abuse as a child and how she remained autistic from the time she was gang-raped at the age of three until she was sixteen.

> *When the rape occurred, her mother and grandmother were so affected that they left her to the care of her grandfather. She told us that the only communication she had was with animals because she was so scared and had been abandoned by humans. "I can tell you"—she said to me looking into my eyes—"that worms living in the bark of*

trees sing and communicate. It was the wonderful song of welcoming that I heard every day as I went and lay by the tree in my house. They were so friendly and cheerful, and they were my only friends." She then asked me if I still wanted to ask her why she had joined the bioregional movement. Needless to say, I could not even respond... and she knew my silence was the answer.

—María Suárez on FIRE after the conference

At the time Sissy Farenthold, a Texas-based women's rights and human rights lawyer who was twice a candidate for governor in that state, was researching a case about the recent oil spill in the Mississippi River by the Hollywood Marine Barge Oil Company in Houston. It seemed to Sissy that no information had come out about the spill because of the connections between the company, government officials, and others. She was interviewed for FIRE about her findings regarding other possible international links, including the war in Iraq.

Thank you for giving me a space for the information which no other media have mentioned. Freedom of speech is not a fact right now around this issue. There are two issues involved in this story. One is environmental. The other is corruption and private government, a merging of public and private. The Houston Port, for example, played a role in the war against Iraq, yet we cannot have access to the information. The people who work on the barges have information; research is taking place. Bush made investments.... [Dan] Quayle's Deregulation Commission to make business more competitive is really giving business and companies a license to do anything, and to do it through influence in high places. Hollywood Marine is just an example, but one that will show those and other links.

In October 1991 FIRE's Katerina Anfossi organized the first panel, live on the air, on the social environment, a key issue in Central America. Women from Cuba, El Salvador, Panama, and Nicaragua came together on the air in Costa Rica to talk about their pressing issues concerning the social environment.

For Cuba, the pressing issue was the embargo. El Salvador's theme was the struggle to achieve peace with social justice as an end to the war against peoples and their environment. Panama's issue was the devastating effects of the invasion on city dwellers who were living on the streets. Nicaragua's topic was the increase in the number of street children and women due to the U.S.-supported contra war which prevented Nicaraguans from concentrating on production. "We do not know what will happen with the newly elected government, but the funding offers by the U.S. Administration seem demagogic," said the woman from that country.

FIRE in Rio de Janeiro

June 1992 finally came, and Debra Latham and I traveled to Brazil to attend the United Nations Conference on Environment and Development (UNCED).

María and I stayed with Sueli Garcia while we attended UNCED. She is vice president of the Villa del Parque Association.... Villa del Parque is a poor community of seventy families living along the Tijuca Lagoon and protecting the last mangroves in Rio de Janeiro. Sueli has a house there but is afraid to live in it because she has been threatened. The municipality came and bulldozed three houses. A man and a woman were killed. The community has been accused of polluting the lagoon. The pollution, however, comes from the highrise buildings and the shopping centers around it, which sweep their waste into the lagoon.

Real estate speculation companies and a construction company want to get the people out of Villa del Parque so they can build more skyscrapers. The people are the ones protecting the mangroves through the organization headed by the women of the community.

—Debra Latham in *Vista*

Parallel to the official conference, an NGO Forum was organized some twenty-five miles away. There the women's tent, Planeta Femmea, was the one place where *all* the issues were being openly and clearly discussed and debated. Militarism, which was not even touched on at the official UNCED meetings, was dealt with in the women's truth tent as were issues of biodiversity, debt and trade, population, development, information, education, and power issues.

Rosiska Darcy d'Oliveira, in Memories of Planeta Femmea, describes in words almost like poetry, the perspective of the tent:

It fell to Rio de Janeiro, our place in the world, to host a gathering of the powerful—but also of the dispossessed—who congregated here on the pretext of what was called the Earth Summit, a conference of planetary afflictions. That is how the millennium is ending, on the shores of Guanabara Bay, and on its sands came the realization of an immense fiasco, the failure not just of a regime, nor of any society in particular, but of a whole project of civilization.

This failure can be seen in global imbalances, in the disruption of the seasons, in the dust that pollutes the wild, in the desolation of amputated forests, and in the drifting of the poles. We suffer it as disharmony of the peoples, as the isolation of forgotten continents, the humiliation of human beings treated as expendable, in the ruthlessness of the Market, the silence of meaning. It is as tangible as life thrown off course, the forced sterilization of women, the delirium of science, the exile of ethics.

Now, to celebrate the new millennium, history has prepared new crossroads. Coming from the whole world over, slogging their way across male territory, women have begun little by little to set foot in forbidden halls of knowledge and power, bringing creative disorder into the order of failure....

Peggy Antrobus of DAWN described her view of the situation:

In relation to the environment, women are expected to clean up the mess and save the planet. If they are to do so, they have a right to challenge the people and institutions that create the problem. The primary task of women must be to formulate an analysis of the causes of the problem. Current economic models link development with economic growth at the expense of human well being. Alternatives to the present growth model must be found.... the women's movement and the environmental movement are revolutionary movements.

Among the tent's activities, FIRE took part in a panel entitled The Change Makers: Women and Media, which was convened by the New

York-based International Women's Tribune Center. During FIRE's presentation about what radio can do to support women's struggles to save the environment, Sueli Garcia gave testimony on how a few months prior to UNCED the community of Villa del Parque received a tape through the mail, produced by FIRE, about their issues. Receipt of the tape gave them cause to celebrate that they were not alone in their struggle. Their feeling of isolation had ended because the news of their efforts had come out on shortwave. The tape they received through the mail had become a companion in their struggle. The community even used it to pressure local authorities to take them seriously.

While the agreement made at UNCED had taken into account Women's Action Agenda 21, it left many concerns unaddressed. It did not make concrete commitments to stop global warming or to protect biodiversity. The governments of the North did not make any commitments to reduce consumption and production patterns that are harmful to the environment. The official Action Plan did not take up the recommendation by women to have forty percent representation in decision-making, nor did it take into account women's needs and interests in relation to social policies about reproductive and sexual rights and health issues.

The women's movement came out of Rio de Janeiro knowing that the challenges still lay ahead. Perhaps the largest among them was dealing with the invisible powers that do not have a seat at UN conferences, yet influence them greatly.

Local Brazilian women told us that all of Rio de Janeiro used to be one huge mangrove, but it had been dried up by big tourist businesses for the sake of development. Twenty-five miles of land that had undergone such forced sterilization separated the women's tent at the NGO Forum from the decisionmakers at the official conference.

Halfway into those twenty-five miles stood the community of Favela Rosina, known in Latin American and Caribbean popular oral history as the biggest slum on the continent. It is so big a mountainside, so poor a people, so marginalized an area, that Favela Rosina really looks like a piece of cake that starving people have eaten up by snatching what they could, piece by piece. They then settled on the leftovers by placing a few pieces of cardboard on the barren land so that they could have a roof over their heads.

During the fifteen days of the UNCED meeting, the bottom of the mountain slope where the Favela meets the public main road was filled with military tanks permanently pointing their heavy-duty machine guns toward the Favela. According to one of the women living there, this was done "...so we don't come down to go to the conference."

I tried to visit the infamous Favela, but the women advised against it, warning me, "Drug dealers have made it clear that no journalist can go in during the conference, and if they did, they would not come out alive."

Three miles away from Favela Rosina stood Villa del Parque in the Tijuca Lagoon, the last piece of mangrove left. It was threatened by pressure from big business to dry it up and turn it into a huge commercial center. Two residents of Villa del Parque had already been mysteriously killed. Three invisible powers were holding the fort: corporate business, the military, and the drug Mafia!

Another outcome of the official meeting was the United Nations decision that recognized women "as active and equal participants" in worldwide efforts to maintain a healthy planet. This recognition was declared a significant first step by the Women's Environment and Development Organization (WEDO). However, Bella Abzug, a founder of WEDO, cautioned:

This decision on women's participation must be more than just rhetoric. Women are going to have to act locally and advocate globally to make sure it actually produces what it promises.

Beginning with UNCED, FIRE's links with the global women's movement started to forge connections. Some of the network material that FIRE put on the air came from ISIS International, ISIS Chile, *Fempress*, Womanet, *Ms* magazine, WIN News, the Tribune, Center for Human Rights, UNEP, UNIFEM, Aquelarre, Women in Action, Human Rights Watch, ALAI, Catholics for Free Choice, Puntos de Encuentro, La Red, Nuestra Voz, SEM, Brecha y las Humanas, Las Entendidas, and Haiti Information.

The experiences, recordings of the presentations and discussions in the tent, the Women's Agenda 21, and the pounds of material brought back from Rio de Janeiro formed the basis for many of FIRE's programs.

We also broadcast many testimonies, position papers, articles, and recorded panels with women's perspectives on the issues of women's needs and interests related to the environment and to women's struggles to save the planet. After the UN conference, FIRE started receiving tapes, newsletters, and magazines from many, many parts of the world.

FIRE continued to build on the connections it had begun to make with native peoples, as well as with women in the environmental movement. Through addressing such truly global issues, we were establishing ourselves in the international arena.

CHAPTER 4

Women's Human Rights

The most insidious myth about women's rights is that they are trivial or secondary to the concerns of life and death. Nothing could be further from the truth. Sexism kills.

—Charlotte Bunch, FIRE, 1993

Ever since the beginning of FIRE, producers and listeners alike have been active concerning the interwoven issues of violence against women and women's human rights. We have given voice to the international women's movement to further awareness, legislation, and action about these concerns.

Twenty-eight women's organizations around the planet started a petition campaign in 1992 to get women's rights officially considered as basic human rights, and FIRE has supported this effort since we first went on the air. By linking with networks, the movement, the issue, and each woman involved, we have given a broad international voice to this campaign on our airwaves. Almost one million people around the world signed the petition.

Mobilizing Against Violence and Harassment in the Early 1990s

Rhonda Copelon was FIRE's first on-the-air guest in 1991. She shared late-breaking news about the first draft of an Inter-American Treaty to Prevent, Punish and Eradicate Violence Against Women. Rhonda, a Jewish feminist human rights lawyer from the USA, came on the air a few days after an expert group convened by the Commission of Women of the Organization of American States (OAS) finished drafting the proposal. She had been part of the expert group. It was with great pride that day that the news of the draft treaty came out first on FIRE as we announced, "No international agreement thus far explicitly requires states to protect women from violence. The OAS convention could be the first instrument to fulfill that purpose." Rhonda told the story on the air:

> We were a group of experts from eight countries of the region who met in Caracas, Venezuela, in early August to decide what approach the OAS should take concerning violence against women.
>
> Immediately we decided that what was needed was an Inter-American treaty. We drafted a convention stating that violence against women is a violation of human rights, that it is wrong, and that it must be eradicated. It further says that states have a responsibility to end impunity of both state and private perpetrators and to take broader measures to change the societal, economic, and cultural conditions that produce gender violence.
>
> The draft treaty still has to undergo consultation, and unless women organize, lobby, and demand that it remain unchanged, the treaty can be watered down. Women should organize and lobby their governments so the draft becomes a reality for us in our lifetimes.

Three years later, on the sixth of June, 1994, the General Assembly of the OAS approved the convention. During the three years between that first news in 1991 and the approval in 1994, FIRE provided continual updates on the progress of the convention and accompanied women from the continent who mobilized, lobbied, and took to the streets. FIRE was there with them in their meetings, conferences, and marches, broadcasting these events. Women from organizations such as ILSA, CLADEM, ILANUD, CIM, IIDH, Colectiva 25 de Noviembre CEFEMINA, ISIS Chile, the Black Women's Network, CODEHUCA, CEPIA in Brazil, and especially individual grassroots women, came to FIRE to give testimonies about their lives in relation to all sorts of abuse and their efforts to end gender violence.

FIRE also covered the grassroots work being done by women activists who had drafted methodologies toward popularization of women's human rights. They were frequently on the air talking about the issues, the actions, and the strategies.

We wanted to develop a methodology that we call popularization of women's human rights, which would emphasize the construction of human rights out of our lives, as opposed to the victimization of women. It would transcend recognition of the international and national legislation on human rights and analyze instead the expression of rights in our daily lives as a starting point, reference, and target in the process of reconceptualization of human rights as women's rights and reconstruction of our lives within and for the transformation of our societies.

In other words, we wanted to contribute to the goal of women recognizing ourselves as human beings. This is one of the main objectives of our efforts to get national and international law to recognize women's rights as human rights, precisely because this battle is an empty and formal one if we women don't empower ourselves to challenge the whole patriarchal system that tells us every day and in every way that we are not deserving of rights. Unless this happens, women will look at human rights as something beyond us and not necessarily for us. And what is worse, we will never see ourselves as human.
—Roxana Arroyo, CODEHUCA

FIRE's first live phone call, also in 1991, was with Patricia Williams, an African American feminist, law professor, and activist scholar who was then at the University of Wisconsin. We called her on the air about the controversial nomination of Judge Clarence Thomas to the Supreme Court of the United States. The African American community in the USA was split about the nomination even before Anita Hill's testimony opened the issue of sexual harassment and drove deeper wedges between the two sides. Issues such as the way in which race, law, legitimacy, and gender interact were involved in the debates.

Having read some excerpts of Pat's brilliant book *The Alchemy of Race and Rights* on the air a few weeks earlier, I felt that Pat was the woman to interview about the issue.

She talked to FIRE about the need to analyze the relationship between race and gender and about her experience testifying before the U.S. Senate Committee against Thomas' nomination, based on his open hostility to racial and sexual equity. Only a few weeks later, Anita Hill went to Congress to denounce him for sexual harassment.

Just as intense was FIRE's first experience covering women's actions in the streets. This was the march of the twenty-fifth of November in Costa Rica in 1991. The twenty-fifth of November is the International Day Against Violence Towards Women, in commemoration of the 1960s assassination of the Mirabal sisters in the Dominican Republic ordered by the dictator Trujillo. In honor of their resistance, the Latin American and Caribbean Feminist Encuentro in Colombia in 1980 declared the day of their death as the Day Against Violence Towards Women. Since then, it has come to be celebrated in many parts of the world, thus becoming International Day Against Violence Towards Women since 1992.

Although many activities and community marches had been organized in previous years in Costa Rica, this was to be the first time that all the women's groups united to take back the streets of San José, the capital of Costa Rica. The march has been announced previously, but hardly any media believed that it would be significant. To their surprise, 1,500 people marched through the streets, accompanied by FIRE's microphones.

In 1992, November 25 opened the campaign known throughout the world as The 16 Days of Activism against Gender Violence. Initiated by a coalition of organizations at a leadership institute by the Center for Women's Global Leadership, the sixteen days ran from that day until the tenth of December (International Human Rights Day). The activities held by women in all parts of the planet had as an objective to get the UN Human Rights Conference to be held in Vienna in 1993 to recognize that women's rights are human rights, and that violence against women is a violation of human rights.

As part of that campaign, women in Costa Rica organized the International Arts Festival of Women for Our Human Rights, which gathered women artists from all of the Americas in San José. Jeanne Carstensen wrote about the festival in her memoirs of the event:

> *What is art against gender violence? The mothers and grandmothers of Plaza de Mayo in Argentina say that there can be no healing until there is absolute truth.... Women's art is about not accepting lies, saying our truth and the belief in life. I believe that a will to heal must be inherent in women's expressions, even if darkly; otherwise why would we bother to speak out under the weight of so much pain?*

In addition to listening to others' voices, FIRE became part of the international movement to redefine women's rights as human rights. At one of the first radio training sessions FIRE's producers attended, the 1991 workshop sponsored by the Inter-American Institute for Agricultural Science of the Organization of American States, Katerina Anfossi received honorary mention for a piece she produced about the concept:

> *NARRATOR: Mary grabbed her child in her arms, she picked up her bag, and in silence, said good-bye.*
>
> *How many Marías leave their homes and their towns in search for a shelter?*
>
> *How many Marys change their place of origin, their community of friends; have to change their whole lives. How many change their world in search for protection, which they seldom find!*
>
> *Aren't those Marías immigrants?*
>
> *How many of them have had to seek another place to give them shelter, after finally running away from a battered life?*
>
> *Are not these Marías refugees?*

> *Control: Music.*

> *NARRATOR: How many of us have been or will be physically, emotionally, or sexually abused? Be it by the police, a companion, a brother, a husband, a son, or any other man. Is this not a form of torture?*

How many remain isolated, enclosed within the walls of a place called home. Is this not being disappeared?

Refuge, torture, disappearance, immigration... aren't these human rights violations?

Control: Music.

NARRATOR: Freedom, equality and fraternity. Three strong rights born from the French revolution in 1789, included in the first declaration, called then, the Rights of Men and Citizens. I ask myself then, what about all the women who died for that freedom? A freedom that, in the end, did not belong to them.

What about those women who gave their lives to the struggle for equality, an equality that did not include them.

What about those who fought for a fraternity that became legitimate only for the "frater," while women's participation in that revolution was shattered!

Control: Music.

NARRATOR: I now remember Olympia de Gouche, anonymous hero of that revolution. She received the guillotine when she dared to draft the first Declaration of Women and Female Citizens, after the Revolution. She was charged; she paid with her own life. Yet few of us know about that Declaration and those women's lives.

Control: Music.

NARRATOR: So I have to ask myself: Why, if women are included in the actions, such as revolutions, where people are willing to die, are they not included in the right to life?

I wonder, and I think of human rights. Where are women's rights in all of that?

Covering Women's Imprisonment

In 1992, FIRE received its first phone call from a political prisoner. It was from El Buen Pastor (The Good Shepherd), the women's jail in Costa Rica:

111

Hello, I am calling from prison. Other prisoners have told me that they hear your feminist program on Radio for Peace; that you might report about my case. I am Livia Cordero, a political prisoner in Costa Rica. I need your help.

Livia Cordero, Costa Rican human rights and peace activist, was put in jail in February 1990 on terrorism charges, along with fourteen other popular movement organizers who later were released on bail. A member of the Costa Rican Human Rights Commission, the Central American Human Rights Commission and Women's League for Peace and Freedom, Livia Cordero had been denouncing Costa Rica militarism related to the U.S.-supported Nicaraguan Contras.

She called us after two years and five months of imprisonment without an acceptable trial. She had decided to intensify the campaign to call attention to her case, demanding due process under the law. The Women's League for Peace and Freedom had been campaigning for her release for more than two years, and they needed attention in the press.

FIRE decided to visit Livia immediately, to interview her there in person. The task was not easy. No tape recorders were allowed in the prison, and visits were allowed only on visitation day (too far in the future, given her pressing need to get the word out). The following description of our interview is taken from a letter I wrote to my mother about our experience.

We called a Congressman's assistant to have him get the permission for us to go in and interview Livia. But when we went to pick up the permission slip, we found that he had forgotten to request it. We decided to go to the prison anyway, letting Livia know that we were not authorized to do so. With two tape recorders and plenty of blank tapes, we headed for the women's jail. Guards appeared at the big gate as we came in through a smaller door.

We saw a busload of children coming back to the prison after a regular school day. "Who are they?" we asked the guard.

"The sons and daughters of the prisoners," he answered. "They live here with their mothers because there is no place to leave them while their mothers are in prison. We send them to school and they are well fed here."

We wondered if the same thing would happen if the thousands of women working in the maquilas and free zone parks took their kids to work every day because there is no place for them to leave their children.

We explained to the guard what we were up to, and that the permission was not granted because of an oversight. He made three telephone calls: one each to Congress, his boss, and the Ministry of Justice. "You can go in," he said, "but I am afraid I have to keep your tape recorder and cassettes."

We gave him the visible one, the one hanging from Nancy's neck, and the many blank tapes—except the one we had in one of our pockets. After getting a receipt that detailed all of what he kept, in we went to meet Livia.

Once we were inside the prison, FIRE's microphones registered Livia's story.

They have said that they will take me to trial soon. But that's a policy to stop the movement for due and just process that has been intensified by WILPF this week. The other fourteen who were imprisoned with me are out on bail and are appealing their case. The whole accusation is illegal, and so is my imprisonment. Media attention will help me get out, as will the campaign throughout the world. Women need not only to help each other, but to love and care for each other as women. Justice and peace, respect for human rights—that's what we have to strive for.

—Livia Cordero in Jeanne Carstensen's presentation
on FIRE the day after our visit

Less that two months later, Livia was out of prison. She waited for trial until 1994, when her case was dismissed. When Livia came to testify live on FIRE, we asked her if she felt free of imprisonment. "Not until all human rights, and human rights of all are respected. I cannot get a job, and discrimination against women is still going on," she responded.

FIRE has covered the stories of several other women in prisons. Nancy Vargas' 1992 script for a special series about women's human rights is an example:

TESTIFIER: My name is Yolanda Patricia de Jesus. Battered, beaten up, lacerated. I was born in the San Juan de Dios Hospital in Costa Rica. I have been forced into the Psychiatric Hospital more than three times in my short life.

Control: Music.

TESTIFIER: Do not be afraid. Go visit the women's jail, where I actually live as a common prisoner, and you'll see what true violations of women's human rights are.

Control: Music.

TESTIFIER: My story and my pain is the pain of thousands of women. I am not saying that mine is not my own. All I am saying is that mine is connected to the pain of all women. We are in pain. That's why it is not by chance that we have become women's human rights activists. [Ana Virginia Duarte, coordinator of the Women's Human rights Project at CODEHUCA]

Control: Music.

NARRATOR: How can anyone, after listening to these testimonies, deny that there are violations of women's human rights? The question is: Why are these facts denied in human rights? The answer is not hard to find: for centuries, androcentric and patriarchal views have denied the existence of women, have relegated women to the world of the nonexistent. Despite that, our voices and bodies have not stopped claiming our universal rights, both in the public and private sphere. Women's rights are human rights!

Another imprisonment was exposed in a 1993 testimony for FIRE. Martha, a woman belonging to the Ethiopian Oromo tribe and persecuted by other more powerful ethnic groups, said that she had been a journalist in radio, doing a program in the Oromo language:

The moment our program started catching fire among the Oromo population, the government took over the radio station and transferred all of us to different newspapers. I became a women's columnist in a paper. Only a few years later, at twenty-three years of age, I was imprisoned for ten years because I was trying to tell the truth in that paper. But my imprisonment really began years earlier, when my radio program was closed. The journalist in me died, because through radio I could reach my people.

A conversation with a colleague taught FIRE that women's experiences with imprisonment go beyond our imagination.

I have an impediment that placed me in a wheelchair. When I was very young, my father took me from South America to a hospital in Houston, Texas, to be cured. I spent more than half of my childhood in that hospital for tests, treatments, exercises.

Then I was taken to a Central American country for more of the same treatment, because medical care in the U.S. was too expensive. My whole family moved there with me. After all these efforts, when I was twelve, I was placed in a home, and my family left me there and went back to South America.

I could not even start telling you what hell that home was. To this day, more than twenty-five years later, even though I have been taken out of the home, have a profession, and move around in a wheelchair, it hurts to remember that horrible prison.

Working Our Way Toward Vienna

The theme of the Second United Nations Conference on Human Rights, to take place in Vienna, Austria in June 1993, was Human Rights: Know Them, Defend Them, Promote Them. But women around the world added a new dimension that had to be placed on the agenda of the UN Conference: "Yes, know them, defend them, and promote them, but also reconceptualize them to include women's rights as human rights, and women's perspectives on all human rights."

One of the important stepping stones on the way to Vienna was the conference entitled Linking Hands for Changing Law, Women's Rights as Human Rights Around the World. The meeting, convened by the North-South Institute, gathered more than 100 women's human rights activists and specialists in Toronto, Canada, in September 1992. At Linking Hands, networks began taking shape to give a global

dimension to many of the national and regional perspectives that women have been developing throughout the past decades.
The participants' task was to:

...look at the inadequacy of the present human rights model to guarantee women's human rights.... Genuine improvement of the daily lives of women requires substantial reform on many fronts.
—Johanna Kerr, North-South Institute, 1992

I was concerned that the upcoming UN conference did not have a set agenda or dates. In order for women to work with some concrete details, I interviewed Christina Cerna of the UN Center for Human Rights. In that conversation, I learned about a special provision where NGOs could develop their own independent gathering and register it at the United Nations as a Satellite Meeting. This would make their participation official and guarantee them input to the conference's preparatory documentation.

This exact information sparked the organization of the Latin American and Caribbean La Nuestra (That Which Is Ours) Conference, in November of 1992, and FIRE was there every step of the way. During the meeting, FIRE broadcast live, bringing to the international audience the fact that women were determined to make the UN recognize our needs and interests in their agenda for human rights. We drafted a proposal on women's human rights to take to the UN Regional Preparatory Meeting to be held in January 1993 in Costa Rica.

At that preparatory meeting, we made our first daily live broadcasts at a big event from the Salon las Azaleas at the hotel where the meeting was taking place. The Salon las Azaleas was also the women's action room where all collective actions and strategies initiated.

Equipped with appropriate technology—a telephone interface, a mixer, and three or four microphones—FIRE did high-level broadcasting for the cost of a telephone call. When word got around that the women were doing that, some men from the NGOs and from the hotel came looking for the portable radio station.

One of the experiences that has had the biggest impact on our use of radio as a means of communication and shortwave as an international linkage, has been the live broadcasts at the Latin American and Caribbean Regional Meeting in San José held in January 1993, parallel to the official conference. We brought the radio to where the action was, and women were able to speak from their hearts and their lives, while at the official conference "rational" and "intellectual" evasion of states' responsibilities seemed to be the tone.

—María Suárez, *Vista*

Jeanne later wrote about one of FIRE's most outstanding experiences at the conference:

Noeli Pocatera, an indigenous woman leader from Venezuela, after having delivered her speech on the plenary floor of the Latin American Human Rights Preparatory Conference, came to speak on our live broadcast. She began to tell us about the indigenous rights demands she made in her speech and then suddenly began to pray in Quechua. I stopped translating and we just listened. When Noeli stood up María and I followed her automatically. A few seconds later I realized we were broadcasting live and that we had abandoned the microphones far below on the table. Noeli kept praying and the whole women's action room was silent listening to her. When she finished we all sat down and María and I explained what had happened to the audience. The show went on.

This is an example of something that Margaretta D'Arcy of Radio Pirate Woman—she broadcasts out of her bedroom in Galway, Ireland—once told me: "Don't ever let the women think that the equipment is more important than they are." We could have told Noeli not to stand up, not to move away from the precious microphone, but instead we followed her. She knew what she had to do. This effort of making the experience of doing radio as important as broadcasting is something FIRE is always involved in..

—Jeanne Carstensen, Amplifying
Women's Voices, 1993

Nancy Vargas corroborated these thoughts in an article in *Vista*:

It's important to point out how women of diverse realities, cultures, and ethnic groups have made this communication medium their own.

Through FIRE, they have shared their experiences in search of a more dignified world where women's rights are considered human rights. An example of this was the participation of Laura Bonaparte of the Argentinian group Madres de la Plaza de Mayo who said "…as long as our wombs aren't free, we can't speak of democracy in the world," making reference to military terrorism. Various authorities from the Latin American and Caribbean Human Rights Preparatory Conference emphasized the organizational work of women's groups in the region.

As part of that effort, the final document from that conference contains Point 14 on the theme of women, even though this declaration doesn't include resolutions: "We reaffirm that governments must emphasize the development of actions destined to recognize women's rights and women's participation in national life with equal opportunity and to eradicate all forms of hidden or evident discrimination for reasons of sex, race, social condition, and especially, to eliminate gender violence as well as all forms of sexual discrimination."

On that last night of the meeting, while women were celebrating their achievements, a woman who lives in the nearby mountains of San José found her way into the gathering place. Excitedly, she exclaimed:

I had to come down tonight to see this place before you all go. I've been here all week with you, I know what this place looks like, who you are, and what happened here all week because I listened to FIRE broadcasting from here every day. I had to come see the place in person and share the results with all of you.

The following month, the Center for Women's Global Leadership at Douglas College, part of Rutgers University, convened a Strategic Planning Institute. They brought together twenty-five women from around the world who were engaged in campaigns in their regions to get the United Nations to recognize women's rights as human rights. They drafted strategies and actions toward the Vienna conference and agreed to organize a Global Tribunal on Violations of Women's Human Rights to influence both the Vienna conference and the mainstream media to pick up the issues involved in the women's platform. The

International Women's Tribune Center, based in New York, was instrumental in proposing a tribunal.

A global hearing was held that week in front of the United Nations headquarters in New York, where twenty-three women testified about violations of women's human rights throughout the world. I presented the following testimony on behalf of Latin American and Caribbean women:

> *I come to give testimony on the protagonistic role of women in our region. Women in Latin America and the Caribbean have been at the forefront of traditional human rights movements in the last three decades, with the hope that the transformations we promoted would include us as women. Today we come to state that those movements did not include our rights as women. Thus, we have undertaken them ourselves and are building a movement that will make the UN, the states, and society recognize that women's rights are human rights.*

Commentators Bella Abzug from WEDO and Missouri Sherman, Ambassador from Barbados to the UN, agreed that there was no way in which the UN could avoid the issue at its next conference. "A movement such as the one that expresses itself here cannot be ignored any longer," they said.

Another live adventure took place when the FIRE team broadcast from the Fifth International Interdisciplinary Congress on Women held at the University of Costa Rica, February 22-26, 1993.

FIRE set up a tent in the main plaza of the University of Costa Rica. Most people thought it was the information center; they taped their posters and announcements on the walls and were constantly asking us for conference schedules and workshop times. It's true, we had set up an information center, but not the sort that people imagined; what we were doing in that tent was broadcasting women's voices live to over sixty countries around the world.

More than 1,500 women from different countries participated in this congress, and more than 800 papers were presented. Its principal objective was to bring together women with practical and academic experience related to women in diverse disciplines and areas of knowledge in order to share results and perceptions and to analyze themes of

FIRE sets up their live broadcast tent in Costa Rica, February 1993.

importance to women around the world. The theme of the congress spoke of the need to search for new alternatives for participation at all levels for a better society.

A massive and very international march—Women's Rights Are Human Rights—closed the congress. We all marched through the streets of San José to the Plaza de la Democracia where women celebrated the ongoing struggle to get our issues into the international agenda. FIRE was asked to sit at the *tumbacoco*, the traditional car in every march that has a loudspeaker and accompanies the march in front, conducting the chanting and slogans. Some men in cars or standing on side streets started taunting the marchers as we passed peacefully along. FIRE used the loudspeaker to alter the tone of the situation by thanking the men for standing around "in such support," and thanked the ones in cars for beeping their horns in "solidarity" with our cause. The women cheered, and the atmosphere changed for the rest of the march.

The celebrations for International Women's Day that eighth of March were marked by women's human rights issues throughout the world. I was invited to take part in events that took place in the Dominican Republic and Puerto Rico. At both of them, the women's movement had organized panels and forums where I was keynote speaker, along with local activists.

We do not want mere Declarations out of Vienna. We want concrete mechanisms such as a Special Rapporteur, a UN Declaration against Violence, a Special Protocol to CEDAW so that women can present cases, and the OAS Convention Against Violence. The experience in Central America has shown that there can be no peace until there is an end to gender violence.
—Press release, AFP, Dominican Republic, 1993

Another special effort was organized by Katerina Anfossi on FIRE's Spanish program: a radio tribunal in which incest, gender violence, and political persecution were the topics of the testimonies by Ana Virginia Duarte, Sara Patricia Portuguez, and Livia Cordero.

In addition to myself, commentators about the testimonies were Roxana Arroyo from CODEHUCA and Tatiana Soto from the Ministry of Justice in Costa Rica. We talked to the audience about how these violations have to be considered human rights violations, and how impunity remains intact as long as they are not considered as such.

FIRE's intense involvement in this movement continued. For the official Fourth Preparatory Conference for Vienna held in April in Geneva, UNIFEM organized an international Third-World Women's Caucus to lobby and network to strengthen recognition of the issue and recommendations by women. I was invited to form part of this caucus to report and accompany the other twelve women in this group. Together, we formed part of the broad Women's Caucus in Geneva with women from many countries and international organizations, specialized agencies, and governments.

Again, we were able to air the issues internationally through short-wave radio. Women from Africa, Asia, Latin America, and Europe and from specialized UN agencies such as the new chair of CEDAW and representatives from the Commission on the Status of Women and

UNIFEM came to speak on FIRE on behalf of all women. Women's specialized agencies and NGOs recognized that the conference would be a failure without a new vision of human rights that included women's perspectives.

At that conference, FIRE learned to lobby through radio. I remember the day Ivanka Corti, head of CEDAW, stormed out of the official plenary. She was in a rage because there was no room in the agenda for her to present the committee's analysis and recommendations on the floor of the meeting. I stopped her on the way out because things were becoming very difficult for NGOs also. The Women's Caucus was looking for ways in which to strengthen bonds with all specialized agencies who were promoting women's rights. "Ivanka," I called out to her with microphone on hand, "what is your expectation about the possibilities for women's issues? How do you feel and what should we do?" She stared at me, first fuming with anger, and then shifting to laughter when she read the sticker on my tape recorder that says: Feminists Are Everywhere.

Ivanka's reply to my question was, "It is a characteristic of feminists never to lose hope. Let's meet with the Women's Caucus!" Indeed, she was able to fit the recommendations into the Women's Caucus document, and women were able to get women's human rights issues into the official draft, free of reservations, for Vienna.

That year, under the title "Women's Rights Are Human Rights," FIRE produced a series that brought out on audio cassette much of what women were doing and thinking in preparation for the Vienna Conference on Human Rights. The sponsor was DANIDA, the Dutch International Cooperation Program. FIRE's brochure describes the series as follows:

The objective behind the series is to give women an audio instrument to share and expand the actions and debates around the issues so that before, during, and after Vienna, women can mobilize to make women's human rights effective in their lives.

- *Cassette 1. OUR TIME HAS COME: Reconceptualization of Human Rights. María, babe in arms, flees her home where her husband battered her near to death for years. She was imprisoned and tortured, yet this violence is not considered a human rights abuse. This program looks at "universal" human rights through women's eyes.*

- *Cassette 2. WOMEN'S RIGHTS ARE HUMAN RIGHTS: Campaigns and Activities. An international women's human rights movement is demanding that the United Nations address women's rights comprehensively. This program focuses on two campaigns to that end, plus a groundbreaking Convention on Violence Against Women by the OAS.*

- *Cassette 3. LATIN AMERICAN WOMEN SPEAK OUT: The final declaration of the Latin American Human Rights Preparatory Conference included an article affirming women's human rights. This is just one of the results of the dynamic women's rights movement in the region. This program picks up the strategies and actions by women to influence the conferences agenda.*

- *Cassette 4. BREAKING THE SILENCE, A FORM OF DEFENSE: Women's rights hearings provide women the opportunity to testify about the violations they suffer in the family, during war, of their socioeconomic rights, and of their bodily integrity. This program is a look at the global hearing process.*

- *Cassette 5. POPULAR EDUCATION: Recognizing Our Human Rights in Our Daily Lives. Answering the question, "When was the first time your human rights were violated?" is the basis of a women's human rights popular education strategy that originated in Central America. This program walks the listener through the process.*

- *Cassette 6. ART AGAINST GENDER VIOLENCE. Art against gender violence was present at an international arts festival held in Costa Rica. This program includes songs and theater from the Dominican Republic, Brazil, Costa Rica, Nicaragua, and the USA.*

Soon came the final gathering before the Vienna conference, and again FIRE's microphones were there. Calling for Change: International Strategies to End Violence Against Women was held in The Hague, Netherlands, in early June. The seminar was organized and sponsored by UNIFEM and the Netherlands Development Cooperation Special Program on Women and Development of the Ministry of Foreign Affairs. Technical assistance came from the North-South Institute of Canada. There, eighty feminists from forty countries—from grassroots to multilateral agencies—discussed and examined the issue of violence against women and articulated strategies to end it. Sharon Cappeling from UNIFEM was keynote speaker:

> *I imagine myself standing on this podium struggling to unroll a portrait of women's suffering. The canvas is so vast that it stretches beyond the confines of this hall, out the door and around the corner, beyond the field of political vision, beyond the power of imagination.*
>
> *Occasionally I long for a more containable cause. I think: if our ranks could be counted in the millions rather than the billions, how much easier it might be to focus world attention on violence against women, and to commit those brutal acts to public memory.*
>
> *Imagine a discrete group in any nation of the world, North or South, numbering, say, two or three million. Imagine the government of that nation allowing its citizens, with impunity, to beat members of this group in their own homes; to abuse them sexually at will; to mutilate them; to kick them to death and burn them. Imagine that government routinely denying this group land ownership rights or seats in schoolrooms and universities; imagine it demanding their labor with little or no compensation. Imagine the use of culture and religion to legitimize these acts. And imagine, finally, that these people are subject to all of this abuse simply on the basis of their membership in this group.*
>
> *We would have no trouble recognizing these acts as blatant and massive violations of human rights. We would have no trouble persuading human rights activists to champion their cause.*

Case studies presented at the seminar from Brazil, the Netherlands, Malaysia, and Zimbabwe showed that violence against women is systemic in all societies, making it universal. This was the message that the eighty women brought to Vienna a week after the seminar.

Vienna at Last!

FIRE went to the Human Rights Conference in Vienna and broadcast live for one hour daily for two weeks (thirty minutes each in English and Spanish). Jeanne Carstensen described the scene:

Besides grassroots, NGO, and international organizations and governments, delegations from every continent went live with us from our "studio"—a table strewn with cables and microphones smack in the middle of the hustle and bustle of the Rights Place for Women [the women's gathering place]. These broadcast conditions left us exposed to the ebb and flow of the women's rights lobbying, meetings, and gossip going on around us, which was, of course, just what we had in mind. When the NGOs held a press conference on short notice to criticize the [official] conference's decision to ice NGOs out of the drafting committee meetings, for example, it happened about thirty yards from our broadcast, which made finding a woman to comment on what happened a relatively simple matter.

But on our second to last day of broadcast the tide almost swept us away. Unbeknownst to our humble crew, a party had been planned for the Women's Rights Place coinciding exactly with the hour of our transmission..... Elizabeth Odio, Minister of Justice of Costa Rica, started giving María an address for dinner right in the middle of our broadcast. During another broadcast, wine corks popped all around us during the closing night celebration.

The Rights Place for Women was the organizational heart and soul of women's human rights activism at that event. Everything— from Women's Caucus strategy meetings, to gatherings of African or Asian regional delegates, to afternoon teas and late-night parties— took place in that not-very-large room on the NGO floor of the conference. Faxes, computers, and phones were in constant use and, of course, the walls were covered from floor to ceiling with women's rights posters and announcements. At 6:00 each evening, FIRE cleared the telephones and papers off one of the desks, set up four chairs and microphones and our simple telephone interface equipment, and broadcast women's voices live to over sixty countries around the world.

Broadcasting live was only one of the activities that FIRE organized in Vienna. We also held a Permanent Radio Tribunal on Women's Rights every day between 4:00 and 5:00 p.m. to receive the testimonies of any woman who wanted to tell her story of having her human rights violated. More than forty women sought out our microphones, and the experiences they shared were a lesson in the reconceptualization of human rights. Listening to the women from the Women Living Under Muslim Laws network talk about forced marriage, lack of access to education, and the spread of fundamentalism, and Asian women talking about the need to forge an identity around single women, for example, clarified the fact that human rights are indivisible. Civil, political, economic, social, and cultural rights cannot be separated as traditional human rights language would have us believe. The fifty-two testifiers on FIRE included the following:

• Kholoud Alfeeli, the first Kuwaiti female journalist and a member of the Kuwait Association to Defend War Victims. She was part of the Kuwaiti resistance at the time of the Iraqi invasion. Kholoud was an activist in defending the human rights of war victims. She testified about the importance of women's access to communication sources, and also spoke about her mother, who was the first Kuwaiti woman in radio.

• Naimat Farhat (testimony received by telephone call from California to Vienna). Naimat, a Lebanese citizen who lived in Kuwait for more than thirty years, along with her brother Osama, and their parents Ismail and Maimane Farhat, worked courageously with the Kuwaiti resistance at the time of the Iraqi invasion.

A few days after the Iraqi retreat, a Kuwaiti resistance fighter came to their house and accused them of collaboration with the Iraqis. He murdered Ismail and Osama Farhat, raped Naimat Farhat, and shot her in the head. Naimat survived, but with serious physical and psychological scars. On December 2, 1992, the Farhats filed a petition with the United Nations Commission on Human Rights, asking for an investigation of the pattern of human rights abuses in Kuwait. Naimat spoke to Jennifer Green of the Center for Constitutional Rights, one of the attorneys representing the Farhats.

• "Harib," a Palestinian woman who had suffered abuse by Israeli authorities. She testified about how she was incarcerated, tortured, beaten, and interrogated by the Israeli authorities. Harib also talked about discrimination against women who are political prisoners in Israel.

- Erica Fisheran, an Austrian feminist and journalist living in Germany, and Lepa Mladjenovic from Women in Black and the SOS Hotline in Belgrade, Serbia, spoke to FIRE about the war in Bosnia-Herzegovina and various feminist solidarity actions. Erica testified about the conditions in Bosnia, where Muslim refugees are living in towns that have been turned into concentration camps. She described two projects: Surviving Winter, a German refugee program where German families invite individual Bosnians into their homes, and Medica Zenica, a gynecological clinic for rape victims in Zenica, Bosnia.

    Lepa testified about her experience as a Serbian feminist at the World Conference on Human Rights trying to network with Croatian and Bosnian women, and the need for dialogue on divisive issues such as nationalism and the arms embargo, which have created huge rifts among feminists.

- There were also testimonies given by two Asian women who preferred to remain anonymous. They discussed the discrimination that lesbian women confront in their countries. They want to forge an identity around single women, whether they are divorced, widowed, or lesbian. They also spoke about the invisibility of Asian lesbians and how they are trying to create spaces where women can freely express their sexuality.

- "Kata," an Iranian-American lesbian who has been discriminated against for being a woman of color, Iranian, lesbian, and disabled. She works at a center that helps women who have been sexually assaulted. Kata is a feminist activist who wants lesbian women to gain voice and visibility.

- Myrna Mirelis, a Puerto Rican lesbian woman raised in the United States. In her testimony, Myrna strongly condemned homophobia in the United States and the way lesbian women are harassed and marginalized by their communities. Myrna also spoke about her personal experiences as a lesbian and all the discrimination she has had to confront.

- Nira Yural-Davis, an Israeli woman who lives in London. She is a feminist activist and member of the organizations Women in Black and Women Against Fundamentalism. Nira testified about how she has fought for the rights of Palestinians in Israel, against religious coercion, and for the equality and freedom for all people.

- Marieme Helie-Lucas from Algeria is a feminist activist and a member of the International Network of Women Living Under Muslim Laws. She testified about a dear friend of hers who has been a defender of women whose human rights have been violated by Muslim fundamentalist laws. She also spoke about how individual community laws are discriminatory against women, citing South Africa as an example.

Her daughter, Anissa Helie, talked about how she was born into a family of feminists, beginning with her great-grandmother. Anissa is also a member of Women Living Under Muslim Laws. She related the case of an Algerian girl who was secluded and abused by her parents for being pregnant.

Marieme Helie-Lucas and Nathalie Bruguera from Algeria, and Lynn Freedman, a North American professor of the School of Public Health at Columbia University in New York, told of how Women Living Under Muslim Laws has helped women whose children have been abducted, usually by their fathers. They related the specific case of a French woman whose child was abducted by her former husband (the child's father) and taken to the United States; the collaborative effort of women around the world who are members of WLUML was an important factor in the resolution of this case.

- Giving their testimonies in Spanish were Sonia Pierre, a Haitian-Dominican; Josefina Martinez Soriano from Mexico; Giovana Pagani from Italy; Fanny Samuniski from Uruguay; Montejo, a Mayan woman from Guatemala and refugee in Mexico; María Olea from Chile and immigrant to the USA; Berta Meneses from Cuba; Lilian Valverde from Chile and resident of Canada; Camila Choquetilla, a Quechua-Aymara Indian from Bolivia; Eva Bonafinni, of the Madres de Plaza de Mayo in Argentina; Senee Akhmed, a Shaharahi from South Africa; Petrona Sandoval from Nicaragua; and Alma Oseguera from Mexico.

The Permanent Radio Tribunal was picked up by other media producers, such as Erika Fisher from Germany and the Washington, DC-based Media Consortium, in their press releases.

The Global Tribunal on Violations
of Women's Human Rights

Another international women's tribunal took place outside of our "studio"—the Global Tribunal on Violations of Women's Human Rights, convened by a broad coalition of women's groups worlwide, and coordinated by the Center for Women's Global Leadership and the International Women's Tribune Center. The tribunal was the result of the efforts of thousands of women's organizations and networks around the world, which joined together to demand an end to the impunity surrounding women's human rights abuses.

The thirty-three testifiers related their personal horrifying accounts of violations in five general areas: Human Rights Abuses in the Family; War Crimes Against Women; Violations of Bodily Integrity; Socioeconomic Rights; and Political Persecution and Discrimination. The Global Tribunal, as one of the most important activities organized by the international women's human rights movement, played a crucial role in the overall strategy for achieving women's human rights gains at that important United Nations gathering. The stories would have shaken even the most callous listener. Women like Parveen Martha of Pakistan spoke about wife abuse:

> *I come from a poor, Punjabi-speaking family in Lahore. My parents arranged my marriage with Joseph, an electrician, whose family speaks Urdu. For some time the relationship with my in-laws was cordial, and during that time I had three children.*
>
> *But then my in-laws began to ridicule me when I spoke in my language. My husband started bringing strange women to the house. When I tried to stop him, he began to physically abuse me. I complained to his parents. Thereafter, they started threatening me with all kinds of violence like, "We will kill you or burn you to death." They stopped my family members from visiting me.*
>
> *On February 24, 1984, while I was cooking food for myself, my husband began screaming at me. He picked up a gallon of kerosene, threw it on me, and lit a match. I caught fire and ran here and there screaming so wildly that I could be heard outside the house. My body was so badly burned that I was taken to the hospital in Lahore. Nobody in the hospital asked me how I had gotten the burns; no police proceedings were initiated.*

I told no one what had actually occurred. I was afraid that my children would be taken away from me. My in-laws told me that if I kept quiet they would help me with medical treatment and take me home and look after me. "Even if you tell someone, you are not going to be believed. The police need witnesses; where will you bring them from?" they said.

After my wounds were healed, it became clear that my face was badly scarred for life. My husband refused to keep me in the house. He kept the children and told me to leave. He initiated divorce proceedings in the court, taking the plea that I had illicit relations with my brother-in-law. The case was decided against me.

Then I heard about Gina Jilani, but the period of limitation for appeal was over. My father had died with grief. At the moment I am fighting cases against Joseph for the custody of my children, and for maintenance. During the proceedings, what came up time after time is that I am an adulteress who has no rights to seek relief.

Others, like Gabrielle Wilders of the USA, described child sexual abuse:

In 1972 when I was ten years old, my mother was diagnosed with an inoperable brain tumor. After two years of chemotherapy, radiation, and other surgeries, she died. While she was still in a coma, my stepfather, a former priest, told me that the doctors at Sloane-Kettering Cancer Institute who were treating my mother were concerned about me because her tumor had been the result of an inherited immune disorder that affected only fair-skinned females who have a history of childhood illnesses. He explained that if this was not taken care of during adolescence, I would inevitably die at a young age, just like my mother. The cure was a new "therapy" involving sexual intercourse that would provide the necessary semen to strengthen my immune system.

"Therapy" took place every night for the next couple of years. He gave me pills, which I later discovered were tranquilizers. Although I knew this therapy was a sexual act, I believed this was medical treatment that my life depended on. I felt I had no choice.

When I was fourteen I became pregnant. I hitchhiked to an abortion clinic and, with money earned from a summer job, had the pregnancy aborted.

When I was sixteen my stepfather got a job transfer to California and said I had to go with him. I was frightened and decided to seek out the school psychologist. I told her that even though I desperately wanted to stay, I could not be separated from my stepfather or I would die. I was forced to explain. She was the first person I ever told. She immediately called the child protective services. I was not allowed to return home and was instructed to find another place to stay. Eventually I was placed in foster care. When the police confronted my stepfather he denied everything and accused me of lying and of insanity.

He was indicted and charged with first-, second-, and third-degree aggravated sexual assault of a minor. His bail was set for $100,000, but he only had to put up ten percent of that to walk free. Before the trial date, a psychological evaluation of my stepfather classified him as a "sadistic, manipulative, compulsive, and repetitive child molester." His lawyer counseled him to offer a plea bargain. Fearing I would have to endure a grueling and painful trial, my attorney advised me to accept the plea bargain.

Today, I know that if an environment had truly existed in which the rights of women to remain free of sexual violence were recognized, both my attorney and I would have felt empowered to reject the plea bargains. At the end he pleaded guilty and was sentenced to seven to nine years incarceration at a treatment facility for sexual offenders. But he was released after eighteen months after being judged to be responding to treatment.

I felt that all the anguish it had taken to get him convicted had been in vain, that my naive trust in the legal system had been betrayed.

Some women spoke about war crimes against them, such as Kim Bok-Dong from Korea:

One day in 1941 the official came with a Japanese man and said: "You have to go with the Chong Shin Dae." The Japanese man was wearing a yellow uniform with no sign of what rank he held. He demanded my mother's signature on a document. In those days women could not read, so my mother conceded, believing that I would be working in a factory and would come back after three years.

They took us first to Taiwan and then to Guangdong, where military doctors checked us for venereal disease. They ordered us to take our clothes off and expose previously unexposed parts of our bodies in front of unknown men. It made me extremely afraid. To prevent the examination, I kicked a lot. They forcibly removed my clothing and carried out the examination.

We were taken to the "comfort house," a fifteen-story building with soldiers on the first floor and the comfort house on the second floor. We were not free to go outside. They forced us into full-scale comfort work, servicing the soldiers. At the beginning, I resisted receiving men. For this, they did not give me food and they beat me up. Thinking that even if I refused I was being hurt, I decided to do as I was told. But I could not endure this sexual victimization, having had no experience with men. My internal sexual organs were torn and swollen. I cannot describe the suffering. Even speaking about this fact is humiliating.

My only thought was to escape or die, but I could not escape. The comfort house was located outside the army base. Ordinary soldiers would come from 8 a.m. to 5 p.m. At 7 p.m. the officers came. On weekends I usually received fifteen men. It is impossible to remember how many came in. We were in one place for two months and then transferred to another place for another two months. We kept following the war. The front line was only eight kilometers away from us, and we could hear the gunfire.

One year after the end of the war, I boarded a boat for home. I was twenty-three years old. It had been eight years since I had been kidnapped. Only my mother was left at home. She still thought I had gone to work at a factory. When I finally told her where I had been, I began to cry for the first time.

I met an older man whose marriage had failed, and we married. My husband did not know about my history. It's now five years since he died. I feel sorry for him because I was so damaged I couldn't bear children.

Emma Hilario from Perú was one of the speakers about enduring political persecution:

I am an indigenous woman from Perú. As a woman, I suffer the consequences of struggling with life, including defending the rights of my children, my husband, and my community.

In 1988 I was arrested because I started mobilizing against the high cost of food and unemployment and promoting means for farmers to improve their productivity. The police arrested 200 women, and I was one of them. I was so badly beaten that I underwent an intestinal operation. The country was under a declared internal war. The Shining Path was trying to control women's organizations. They were against popular organizations of women, and many women were killed as a way to instill fear and terror.

On October 19, 1991, three men came to my house and began to beat me—they dragged me to the bathroom by my hair. They put my head inside the toilet and continued beating me, calling me an enemy of the rightful leader, Guzman. The beatings took place before the eyes of my daughter who was only thirteen years old.

Then on December 20, five men came to my house pretending to sell bread. My mother-in-law was visiting me and opened the door. She was shot six times. My husband was shot; he still has a bullet in his back. I was paralyzed from the previous beating. Lying on my bed, I turned my head and I saw a man holding a Tommy gun and saying that I had not fulfilled their previous demands and that I was still looking for power. Then I put up my arm to protect my head, and it received the first shot, the second, the third, the fourth, the fifth, and the sixth. I pretended I was dead. My face was covered with blood from my arm, and thanks to that, I am still alive.

After a month of hiding, we left the country, leaving behind everything that we had built with our organization. We women build rather than destroy, we give birth and defend lives—we do not destroy them. Today, I live in exile, still persecuted and threatened. I do not have legal documents, but I live as a refugee. It is a hard life. It is difficult to find jobs and to be considered a useful citizen in society. I am here to say to the United Nations and to the world that we refugee women are here, and we also belong to this world. Millions of us from different countries and with different languages say: Human rights are also women's rights.

Violations of bodily integrity were often the subjects of testimonies, as was the one given by Dr. Nahid Toubia from Sudan about Dr. Asma El Dareer, the Sudanese physician who conducted the first national survey on female genital mutilation:

I stand here today to testify on behalf of many girls and women who had no choice when parts of their bodies were removed in the name of culture and social conformity. I testify for all the women in all cultures East and West who undergo the physical pain and psychological agony of bodily manipulations to conform to the prevailing social requirement of femininity.

Listen to the voices of African women:

I was circumcised in 1960, at the age of eleven. I remember every detail of the operation, and the worse part was when the wound became infected.... When I was eighteen, it was my younger sister's turn. I was totally against her circumcision. My father wanted the milder type [clitoridectomy], but my mother insisted on the more severe type [infibulation]. Eventually my sister had the intermediate type: virtually the same as infibulation. The suffering of my sister made me hate circumcision even more than my own earlier experience.

Nahid Toubia had this to say about female genital mutilation after reading the testimonies:

To justify this gross social injustice, we have been told that this is part of being a good woman and that it is a sacred requirement of religion. Neither Islam, Christianity, nor Judaism mentions female circumcision in their texts, although followers of the three religions, and others, practice it.

The concept of women's human rights differs from general human rights in that many of the violations against women—such as those described above—take place in what is considered the "private sphere" and not the "public sphere." Traditional "universal" human rights focus only on public, or state-perpetuated, violations. The United Nations and governments have failed to recognize these abuses of women's bodies because they are dismissed as private, family, cultural, or religious matters.

In July 1995 FIRE edited a six-part radio series about the Global Tribunal on Violations of Women's Human Rights. The series was funded by UNIFEM:

1. Cassette 1, part A: *VIOLATIONS OF HUMAN RIGHTS: ABUSES AGAINST WOMEN IN THE FAMILY.* The testimonies of human rights abuses against women in the family gave evidence of the universality of violence in women's lives, of the fact that the family is not a site of unconditional safety for women and girls, that there is a connection between women's economic vulnerability and the violations of their human rights, and of the dramatic factor that there are numerous obstacles to bringing the so-called private violations to public accountability. In the group of testimonies presented in part 1 of this six-cassette series, women from Austria, Brazil, Costa Rica, Pakistan, Uganda, and the United States testified in relation to abuses in family contexts.

2. Cassette 1, part B: *WAR CRIMES AGAINST WOMEN IN CONFLICT SITUATIONS.* The testimonies on war crimes against women in conflict situations provided evidence of the fact that women's bodies are figuratively and actually the site of combat in wartime; they also confirm that women's human rights are violated though the exploitation of familial relationships and that women suffer disproportionately from economic and social dislocations caused by conflict. Women from Japan, Palestine, Perú, Somalia, former Yugoslavia, and Russia gave their testimonies.

3. Cassette 2, part A: *VIOLATIONS OF THE BODILY INTEGRITY OF WOMEN.* The testimonies on violations of the bodily integrity of women exposed how patterns of coercion and violence against women permeate broader social, cultural, and economic institutions and practices aimed at controlling women's sexuality and reproduction. Testifiers in this part of the series were from Canada, the Netherlands, Nicaragua, Perú, and Sudan.

These testimonies had four major themes: (1) that international economic and structural upheavals are resulting in the proliferation of new or revised forms of exploitation of women sexually and economically; (2) that violations of women's bodily integrity and denial of their reproductive rights are often defended or excused in all parts of the world in the name of cultural and religious practice and expression; (3) that women's human rights abuses as the result of forced conformity to heterosexual norms are pervasive ; and (4) that women who are physically challenged or have disabilities face additional gender-specific socially constructed obstacles to the realization of their human rights.

4. Cassette 2, part B: *VIOLATIONS OF THE SOCIOECONOMIC RIGHTS OF WOMEN.* The testimonies on violations of socioeconomic rights rendered visible socioeconomic violations against migrant women, as well as the situation of indigenous women in the context of human rights violations against their group. They also exposed the human rights concerns affecting women who organize in trade unions and the women the trade unions represent. And finally, the testimonies exposed the human rights implications of structural adjustment policies for women's lives.

From Bangladesh, Barbados, South Africa, the Philippines, Chile, and the United States, the testifiers in this part of the six-part series addressed the impact of female economic marginalization, the increasing incidence of female-headed households denied societal support, and discrimination in a racist or colonial context. All of this fosters women's vulnerability to human rights abuses.

5. Cassette 3, part A: *POLITICAL PERSECUTION AND DISCRIMINATION OF WOMEN.* The five testifiers under the category of testimonies on gender-based discrimination and political persecution were from Puerto Rico, South Africa, Chile, and Algeria. Also included was a portion of the statement by the judges who commented individually after this group of testimonies.

The testifiers addressed three dimensions of the political and gender discrimination they suffer: (1) that women often face gender-based persecution in detention as well as state-mediated harassment in civil society; (2) that with the growing numbers of women migrants and refugees globally, a system of human rights protection based on one's membership in a nation-state is inadequate, especially where there is gender blindness to all kinds of violations of the human rights of refugee and migrant women; and (3) that women's political and civil rights are often sacrificed in the name of cultural and religious freedom of groups.

6. Cassette 3, part B: *RESULTS OF THE GLOBAL TRIBUNAL ON VIOLATIONS OF WOMEN'S HUMAN RIGHTS: ITS INFLUENCE ON THE UNITED NATIONS.* The sixth and last part of FIRE's series on the Global Tribunal of Violations of Women's Human Rights presented a report on the results of the tribunal and its influence in the official United Nations Conference on Human Rights in 1993 in Vienna.

When in the 1940s Eleanor Roosevelt and other women state delegates from the regions of Africa, Latin America, and the Caribbean struggled to get the word "sex" to be a type of discrimination mentioned in the 1948 Universal Declaration of Human Rights, little did they know that a whole movement of women would develop around the idea. Almost fifty years later, this movement broke though the reticence of international bodies and states to recognize the harmful laws and practices of discrimination on the basis of sex. They went beyond the need to acknowledge women's rights, but recognized that the violations of their rights is a human rights issue. The Global Tribunal played a role in that achievement.

FIRE's cassette series has been distributed throughout the world among women's human rights activists. It has also been requested by radio women from Latin America, the Caribbean, Asia, Africa, Eastern Europe, the USA, and Canada to play on their airwaves.

FIRE Goes to the Former Yugoslavia

Through the sponsorship of the Foundation for a Compassionate Society, FIRE was able to visit and gather testimonies of women who had been subjected to rape in the former Yugoslavia.

While in Vienna, I left the conference for a few days to join a small women's media and activist delegation on a trip to a Zagreb-based women's group, Tresnevjka. FIRE is responding to the ongoing need for solidarity and aid to the thousands of women who have been raped and tortured by Serbian forces by producing programs on the theme and organizing various public events in Costa Rica.

—Jeanne Carstensen, *Vista*

Aisa Hodo was a twenty-seven year old Muslim from Bosnia who was raped in her home some months earlier and living in a refugee camp in Zagreb when Jeanne interviewed her. Aisa's plea to her countrymen began:

> We are the same people, same nation, same blood. Muslims, Serbs, get up and destroy the guns so that this never happens again. Let us be together. Is it possible that I spent five months at a hospital, after the hell I went through? When I ran away and came to Zagreb to the hospital, I was pregnant from the rape and they would not do an abortion. I had to wait to give birth.

Aisa's baby died when she was giving birth. She continued:

> I learned from my parents not to make any difference among people. We want health, peace, and freedom, not war. My town in Bosnia might be in ruins, but I want to go and work the land, plant the fields, and see my ten year old daughter. It is hard to forget what has been done, but it has to be stopped.

At the time of the interview Aisa was still waiting to go back home.

Jeanne later broadcast a program about her trip to the Spansko Refugee Camp:

> NARRATOR: We were led by a group of about twenty women to a cluster of blankets spread out on the dusty ground.
>   Little children looked at us curiously from behind their mothers' shoulders and shy teenage girls monitored us at a safe distance from behind windows and trees.
>   We drank strong coffee together as the women began to talk, later joined by a few men. Approximately eighty percent of the refugees are women and children.
>
> Cut: First Bosnian woman
>
> TRANSLATOR: She just explained that she came from Gorazde on August 2, last year, in 1992. That she was also in the camp and she's

here now with her daughter and a son who was camp manager. He's now in London receiving medical treatment. And she explained who from her family has been killed—most of her family has been killed. She says she doesn't know anything about her husband or about her son. They both were led from their house, and from then, nothing. There's no information where they are.

Cut: Second Bosnian woman

TRANSLATOR: *She said, I too, have lost two sons, and my brother was killed. The son of my brother and two sisters were killed. I haven't heard anything from them for two years. All family has disappeared.*

Cut: Third Bosnian woman

TRANSLATOR: *My husband went to a concentration camp, and the Chetniks battered him very bad, and his back is destroyed. He is not living. He's here with me, but he's not living. He's dying, but he has had to try to survive. It is destiny. I have to realize it is destiny and continue to live with that. What else can I do? In other words, I could only go and kill myself.*

NARRATOR: *Mixed in with these accounts of terror, were some moments of humor. Many of the older women were dressed in the baggy Turkish-style pants and scarves traditionally worn by Muslim village women in Bosnia. They laughed as they showed us the huge billowing pants legs that let in plenty of air and joked about how they forgot to put on underwear when forced to wear a dress.*

Cut: Conversation

TRANSLATOR: *[laughter] She said when I have to go in town I have to wear a dress, and when I have dress, I forget the pants. [Laughter] She said when the Serbs came they didn't allow me to wear my traditional Muslim clothes, and I had to wear a dress. I never in my life wore a dress, always these pants. And another asked her, did you bring your [under] pants, and she said "No." [Laughter]*

NARRATOR: *Although many of the women we met in Spansko took great pride in their traditional dress, many of them told us that their identity as Muslims wasn't particularly strong before the war.*

In fact, they spoke with pride about the multi-ethnic composition of prewar Bosnia, which was approximately forty-five percent Muslim, thirty-three percent Serbian, and eighteen percent Croatian.

It was when genocide came to their villages and towns that their ethnic consciousness was really born.

Cut

TRANSLATOR: We never were believers. It was when we saw that they were killing us because we were Muslim, because of this different religion that we started—it is not really that we are believing, but we are starting to take care about who we are because we were without any consciousness about our nationality.

One woman said, "The first time I realized I'm a Muslim was when I heard my name at the concentration camp. That was the first time in my life I realized I'm Muslim."

The Campaign for Women's Human Rights Continues

The international work for women's human rights realized its great potential during the UN Conference in Vienna. Afterward, the struggle continued, and the FIRE kept on burning in the United States and in El Salvador.

In the United States

In October 1993, the Women's Studies Program at the State University of New York in New Paltz, New York invited FIRE to be the keynote speaker at their annual conference. Telling Our Stories: Women Breaking the Silence was the theme under which Jeanne shared the story and philosophy of FIRE and communication by and about women.

FIRE was also in charge of a workshop entitled Using International Shortwave to Tell Women's Stories, which included a live broadcast where many women shared the personal stories they had told in panels. They also helped Jeanne with the technical part of the live broadcast.

The first speaker was Pat Clark from the Women's Studies Department, who said, "We are glad to be able to tell our stories on shortwave." Student Carol Johnson talked about the Clothes Lines Project which displays the names and stories of women victims of domestic violence on T-shirts. Artist Lesley Bender talked about her work:

I have about ten paintings on display, and they also talk about violence against women. I myself have been subject to violence. It takes time to heal, but there is a light at the end of the tunnel.

Helen Viukasen, from Zimbabwe's Women's Bureau said that customary law in her country protects men's impunity, but is being changed by the women's movement. "We have been following the changes," she said. "There has been change in the social development of women, but it is slow."

Alex Green told how she is working to create a women's coffeehouse that will become a support center in the community of New Paltz. Also a singer, Alex ended her talk on FIRE with a song on the air.

Eckel Michelson, a member of the community, said that the workshop that moved her the most was the one about the holocaust, because women who had been there during the second world war gave testimony. "I am Jewish," she said, "and I totally connected."

Lee Bell supported Jeanne at the technical controls and came on the air to talk about a workshop on sexual harassment in schools:

Research done recently by the American Association of University Women in high schools in the United States shows that four out of every five students is sexually harassed in school. The title of the report is Secrets in Public, *showing that most of the incidents happen in front of others, who keep silent.*

Barbara, a member of the New York State Breast Cancer Coalition, came on the air to express the need to create awareness about the fact that there are 46,000 women dying every year in the U.S. alone from breast cancer. She herself was diagnosed with the disease and decided to work to help other women by "collecting signatures at this conference to send to President Clinton; money has to be allocated to the programs."

A member of the Bard University Coalition for Choice talked about the panels. Meanwhile, Barbara Scott, professor at the university and member of the RFPI Board, was finally able to participate in the broadcasts she had supported for years.

On that trip to New York, Jeanne also covered an expert group meeting on measures to eradicate violence against women, convened by the United Nations Division for the Advancement of Women, and organized by the Center For Women's Global Leadership. With topics such as violence against women in the family, violence against women in the community, and violence against women in armed conflict, the expert group considered the following:

> *The key element in the eradication of discrimination and, consequently, gender-based violence against women, is the principle of the universality of human rights, reaffirmed in the Draft Declaration on the Elimination of Violence Against Women and the Declaration and Plan of Action of the 1993 United Nations World Conference on Human Rights held in Vienna. These rights are non-derogable (cannot be eliminated) and no custom, tradition, or religious consideration may be invoked to limit their enjoyment. Moreover, all human rights are indivisible, interdependent and interrelated.*
>
> —Report on the Expert Group
> Meeting, point 13, 1993

In El Salvador

In the heat of controversy, the Sixth Latin American and Caribbean Feminist Encounter (Encuentro) took place in El Salvador from October 30 to November 5, 1993. Nearly 1,300 feminists met with the objective of sharing the achievements, obstacles and challenges of the movement in our region. FIRE was on the scene.

The main topics of the encuentro included the different expressions of the feminist movement in our region, feminist political proposals, and commonalties and diversities in the movement. The debates about these topics allowed the joy, sadness, commonalties and differences, encounters and lack of encounters to flourish, but we were particularly strengthened by the recognition of who we are and what we are struggling for.

There were also many workshops, but one of the most exciting activities of the encuentro was the Tribunal on Violations of Women's Human Rights organized by FIRE; Mujer, Justicia y Género of ILANUD of the United Nations; and the Feminist Media Group of Costa Rica. More than 350 feminists listened to the testimonies of nineteen Latin American and Caribbean women who denounced the violations of women's human rights suffered by them or by women who had come to them for assistance. Among them were testimonies about violence against women; violations of economic and social rights of women; the right to a safe and healthy environment; persecution and repression in contexts of war and internal conflict; persecution and discrimination on the basis of race and ethnicity, disability, political choice, or sexual preference; reproductive rights; and the forced disappearance of women from the arts and history. The tribunal reaffirmed the conviction of these women to break the silence by making their stories public and demanding justice.

The presence and testimonies of the women from Haiti, suffering from outrageous conditions of poverty, lack of self-determination and democracy, repression, and political persecution, strengthened our conviction that a strong solidarity movement in support of the women and peoples of Haiti is urgently needed.

Margarita Castro, a Quiche Indian from Guatemala, testified about the violence, exploitation, and discrimination suffered by indigenous women employed as domestic workers:

I make this denouncement so that women, and especially my indig-enous sisters, won't be afraid to denounce, so that they won't think that because they're indigenous they have to live in violence, suffering abuse.

Hemerenciana López from Mexico denounced the impunity sur-rounding the case of the rape and murder of two girls and a boy, de-spite requests for intervention by judicial and human rights bodies:

This process has gone on six years, and as compañeras of the affected mothers, since none of the lawyers wanted to help them, we've been struggling. There's no justice for the women who have lost their daugh-ters... isn't there justice for us, compañeras?

Elena Fonseca from Uruguay had this to say about the human rights of women:

Three women... were victims of domestic violence and didn't receive help from the state, despite having requested it. Two are dead and one is paralyzed in a wheelchair.... We consider that these cases have a systematic character and should therefore be conceived of as violations of women's human rights. We insist that domestic violence be understood as a global political problem, and not as isolated cases.... Penal law in Uruguay doesn't intimidate these domestic torturers who remain in impunity.... These cases we present before the tribunal show what we believe, that these women are confronted with a situation of "no-defense." They turned to everything society offers for their defense, and yet were not defended.

Patricia Juarez of Mexico referred to the case of a woman and her son who were brutally beaten by the woman's boyfriend. The aggressor was charged with attempted murder and grave injuries, but he appealed and was liberated. Patricia also called for victims of domestic violence to be granted refugee status.

From the voices of Simone Alexandre and Reinalde Valmir we learned of the brutal persecution and repression that had broken out against Haitian women:

Since the coup on September 30, 1991, a blind, massive, and selective repression has been established. More than 4,000 deaths, 300,000 internally displaced, 40,000 externally displaced, and more that 1,500 tortured and injured.... We call for all the women in the world to join together in solidarity against this continual violence and aggression against our rights.

Hernestina Hernández from El Salvador made a brief but poignant statement when she said, "I'm working for all women so that we can escape the massive *machista* violence we live in. They say the war has ended, but the deaths continue."

Christina Grela of Uruguay denounced the deaths of thousands of women in Latin America due to clandestine abortions and violations of their right to reproductive health:

I believe that each of us has experienced many violations of our reproductive rights, as have many well-known women, but it's the unknown Latin American women who have died in abortions in their homes, in hospital beds, or hidden somewhere, that should really be here. These cases... [plead for] maternity that is desired, conscious, and responsible, and not just destiny or an obligation.

Irma Campos, from Mexico, spoke about the intervention of the Catholic Church in women's reproductive rights, since it prohibits use of birth control, sterilization, and abortion and condemns divorce and relations outside of marriage: "Women have the right to decide the number and spacing of our children, and to do so we can use all methods that science and health institutions have made available to us."

Rosa Laverne of the Dominican Republic denounced racism against black women:

My name is Rosa Laverne, black Dominican woman, but I could be Marcela, Yolanda, or María, which is to say, Brazilian, Honduran, Puerto Rican, Nicaraguan, or Haitian. I am the voice of hundreds of black women who want to give our testimony on racism and the violation of our human rights through racism in our lives.

Rebeca Sevilla of Perú denounced the wide persecution of gays and lesbians, with total impunity, throughout the continent:

Everywhere, in all the cities, lesbians exist. Our existence, need for affection, identity, participation, and protection, our needs to able to communicate and to have relationships have been limited or denied.... While to some degree permits or licenses are granted for lesbian life... lesbian women are denied the status of being human. We want the right to live our lives with dignity, to organize ourselves freely as lesbians; we want to enjoy our capacity for loving, for organizing our families....

Maritza Melara of El Salvador referred to the discrimination against disabled women and testified about her personal experience as a woman in a wheelchair at the university:

I study at the University of El Salvador. I'm in my senior year, but it hasn't been easy because there are architectural barriers everywhere... to the extreme that I've been denied enrollment in a class because it was given on the fourth or fifth floor.

Yolanda Cortés from Nicaragua, also disabled, added, "I'm from Nicaragua. As a person I suffer two forms of discrimination: one, for being a women, and the other, because I'm blind."

Imelda Gaitán of Nicaragua spoke about the discrimination and exploitation suffered by blind women of different social spheres. She also denounced the fact that blind women are an "invisible group" with only small possibilities for development. Rosa Salgado from Nicaragua added:

Ninety-five percent of disabled Nicaraguan women have no access to education, health, work, or dignified housing. In addition to being disabled women, we're also victims of mistreatment by husbands, families, and/or the society. And due to our disabilities, we're doubly mistreated.

Political persecution of feminists was presented by Puerto Rican activist Esther Vicente:

In my country, the government carried out the practice of monitoring, labeling, persecuting, opening files, and compiling information on individuals and political and sociopolitical groups.... We have the right to be feminists, to practice feminism as part of our freedom, our right to freedom of expression, association, and gathering.
This persecution and these systematic human rights violation constitute violence against women. We claim the right to be feminists and to be subversive without being persecuted....

María Limón, a Chicana from the United States, testified about factory worker Rosa María Garcia's forty-four day hunger strike in protest of her unfair firing by the Mexican company Kemex (subsidiary of Union Carbide) after twenty years of labor:

Rosa María is only asking that she be paid what she's owed under the Mexican Labor Law. The quantity offered by the Kemex Company is only one-fourth of what is owed her. In addition, the amount is offered in coupons that are redeemable only at a Kemex store.

Xiomara Fortuna, a singer from the Dominican Republic gave the following testimony:

I was born with three marks: woman, black woman, and "poor thing" without a father. But at twelve I knew that I wanted to dedicate myself to singing and only singing and to take my song to forgotten corners where nothing ever comes, because I was born in a town where nothing ever came and I was always craving things. In this way I have had to confront many kinds of discrimination. Therefore I want to ask this tribunal to declare this depressing practice a mutilating crime, a violation of the right to expression, the exercise of creative arts, and the development of peoples' cultures, a violation against life and your right to a song that doesn't alienate.

After listening to the nineteen testifiers, a mother of Plaza de Mayo in Argentina got up, grabbed the microphone, and screamed: "This tribunal should demand an end to impunity!"

In June 1994, FIRE produced a radio series with the El Salvador tribunal's testimonies, as well as a book about the event. Funded by the International Cooperation of the Netherlands, these productions have helped multiply the effects of the tribunal. Through our links with AMARC, the tapes were distributed to 200 community radio stations, and FIRE distributed the book to the women's movement for dissemination in the hopes that women everywhere would be able to benefit from the experience.

We also helped the Colectivo Feminista de Video in Costa Rica produce a video about the tribunal. It was funded by UNIFEM and was first shown in the massive celebration in Costa Rica convened by the Central American Human Rights Commission the week that the OAS General Assembly approved the Convention to Prevent, Sanction and Eradicate Violence Against Women in 1974.

As the international movement grew to recognize women's rights as human rights, FIRE was there to record, listen, and broadcast women's voices to the world. The words of Mercedes Rodriguez of the Caribbean

147

Human Rights Network and Coordinadora Paz para la Mujer in Puerto Rico summarized FIRE's role in the process. She wrote about our involvement at the UN Regional Preparatory Meeting in January 1993 in San José, Costa Rica:

The presence of FIRE... nourished our dreams of freedom and gave us power. FIRE connects the voices of women around the world; the women who produce it constantly remind us of the value of friendship. They covered everything. They were serious, diligent, and always committed to the voices. They multiply the voices that have been silenced for centuries; they are committed to the urgency of our need to express ourselves in all our diversity, without censorship, without fear, and with the power behind words that speak of justice, peace and equality.

Local Tribunals on Violations of Women's Human Rights

At home in Costa Rica, together with other women's rights and human rights groups, FIRE organized three more tribunals. One in 1995, one in 1996, and one in 1998.

The 1998 tribunal, the Third Tribunal on Violations of Women's Human Rights, was organized by a coalition of organizations and institutions, including the Women's Political Agenda, the Collective 25 de Noviembre, CODEHUCA, the Costa Rica Human Rights Commission, FIRE, the Women's Studies Institute of the University of Heredia, the Women's Justice and Gender Program of the UN Institute for the Prevention of Delinquency, and the Women's Defensoria of the Ombudsperson's Office in Costa Rica.

This tribunal was held on November 23 in celebration of the fiftieth anniversary of the Universal Declaration of Human Rights and in commemoration of the International Day Against Violence Towards Women on November 25. The tribunal, held at the Supreme Court in San José, opened with the lighting of a candle that remained in full blaze throughout the event. The candle symbolized that women's words will light the way for those who, in having silenced women in the past, have lost the path to justice and peace.

In this, as in the past tribunals held in 1995 and 1996, women demonstrated the extensiveness of human rights abuses in all spheres of their daily lives. They also called attention to women's individual and collective strategies for survival and engagement.

The 1998 tribunal underscored some of the concrete results of the 1995 and 1996 tribunals. For example, the 1995 tribunal issued a resolution calling for gender sensitivity training for all personnel who work in the legal system. This resolution became the official program of the Supreme Court the following year. A testimony about domestic violence at the 1998 tribunal showcased results of the training. The 1996 tribunal received a Presidential Decree, signed on November 25 by the President of Costa Rica, declaring the 25th of November to be the Costa Rican National Day Against Violence Towards Women. However, many forms and incidents of violence against women continue to remain invisible even with official recognition of the need to address violence against women.

The 1998 tribunal also expanded on reviews of implementation of the Beijing Declaration and Platform for Action of the Fourth World Conference on Women (Beijing, 1995) and the Program for Action of the International Conference on Population and Development (Cairo, 1994). Testimonies emphasized that implementation of the documents from these conferences takes more than words. For example, testifiers reaffirmed women's free and voluntary choice of motherhood, and noted that this remains a challenge. Women's sexual and reproductive rights are not yet secure, and women's fertility is often controlled by others. From the perspective of the tribunal testifiers, external control of women's bodies is an abuse of power. As testifier Julia Pérez Cambronero, a thirty-five year old woman with six children who is eight months pregnant, said to FIRE:

At age twenty-seven I already had three children, and I had had two miscarriages. My husband was an alcoholic and drug addict, so it was very difficult for me to control my fertility with him. I went to the hospital at that time, and the doctors refused to sterilize me.... They told me I was too young, that I had too few children for a sterilization, and that there was nothing wrong with me that would justify the operation. I am very poor and can hardly look after my children.

A month after the tribunal, and due to the political pressure of the women's movement, she was finally granted the right to be sterilized. The need for a concerted effort among NGOs, government, and specialized agencies to translate the ICPD Program for Action into public policy was presented by Marisel Salas, from the Women's Political Agenda (WPA). The WPA is a coalition of women's organizations born in the context of the 1996 elections in Costa Rica. They are lobbying for further respect for women's rights within the framework of the principles outlined in the Beijing Platform for Action.

The WPA and other women's organizations are trying to get the government to adopt a regulation ensuring that hospitals recognize the right of women to decide about their own fertility. One recent victory was the adoption of a proposal by the Ministry of Health, which called for the creation of a Reproductive Health Committee whereby women's NGOs can be represented along with health workers, government officials, and the Ombudsman's Women's Office to guarantee that decisions about the issue will take into account the Cairo Program for Action.

Testifiers also addressed the denigration of domestic labor, which is often unpaid and unrecognized. The result is that domestic work is undervalued, and domestic workers are often exploited and abused by their employers. Currently this work is not fully protected by labor laws.

The following testimonies were also addressed: indigenous women's right to ownership of land; right of sex workers to a life free of violence as well as access to workers' rights; right of women prisoners not to be discriminated against; right to freedom of sexual orientation; women's right to political participation as decisionmakers in public office and political parties; women banana workers' right to health; right of women in Costa Rica to be free of racial discrimination; and protection of the rights of female maquiladora workers.

"Judges of conscience" for the tribunal issued recommendations and petitions, which will be taken to the United Nations, the Organization of American States, and the Central American Parliament (PARLACEN), as well as to the local public legal system, for consideration. Among the judges were the Ministers of Justice, Labor, and Women's Affairs, four female judges, and public officers within the national legal system, and the Vice Minister of Health. Several honorary judges also participated in the tribunal. They included the UN Special

Rapporteur on Violence Against Women and the head of UNIFEM's Regional Office for Latin America and the Caribbean.

In sum, the 1998 tribunal asserted that being a woman—immigrant, citizen, farmer, domestic worker, sex worker, lesbian, mother, indigenous, imprisoned, student, young—may be cause for oppression, harassment, discrimination, and abuse. And all too often, the perpetrators of abuse against women act with impunity. In order to eradicate gender violence, women must continue to speak out and demand action. Fifty years after the approval of the Universal Declaration of Human Rights, women have lit the way for humanity to have a chance of finding its way into a truly universal new millennium.

FIRE Writes a Chapter in UN History

In 1998, for the commemoration of the fiftieth anniversary of the Universal Declarations of Human Rights, a book was written "on behalf of and for the United Nations," *The Universal Declaration of Human Rights: Fifty Years and Beyond.* Editors Elsa Samatoupoulou, Clarence Díaz, and Yael Danieli asked various people from around the world to write chapters for the publication. Along with Shanti Darien from Malaysia, FIRE was asked to write the chapter in the book about the history of women's human rights since the 1948 declaration.

Because FIRE had collected so many women's testimonies about issues and facts that never made it to the history books, FIRE decided to use the opportunity to legitimize a large portion of the history that was in its audio archives. Some of the stories that appear in the book have seldom been heard. Official history attributes the fact that the Universal Declaration names "discrimination on the basis of sex" as a human rights issue to the efforts of Eleanor Roosevelt, a USA delegate at the time.

Yet Margaret Bruce, a ninety-year-old former employee in the first UN office in San Francisco, California, when the Declaration was being drafted, told FIRE in a 1992 interview that together with Eleanor were three Latin American women and three African women who were instrumental in placing that language in the UN Declaration. As a matter of fact, according to Margaret Bruce, the Latin American and African women were the ones who convinced Eleanor to include that language,

151

because originally Ms. Roosevelt wanted to use the words *equality among men and women* instead.

Margaret told FIRE that it was so hard for Eleanor to understand the argument favoring the word *discrimination* over *equality* that one of the African women became desperate. She finally told her "don't you understand that in the name of equality between man and woman, when a man dies in my country, the widow is buried with him?" Then Eleanor understood, and the word *discrimination* was included in the Declaration.

Another new piece of history unraveled through FIRE's audiotapes is that it was really the Latin American and Caribbean women's movement that placed gender-based violence as an issue on the international agenda during the U.N. Decade for Women 1975-1985.

FIRE's theory behind these revelations is that the true history of women is found in our oral stories, and therefore radio women have a privileged position to find historical data that is to be found nowhere else but in radio. Thus, radio women have to share their stories freely so their history can be printed in the books.

CHAPTER 5

Population and Development: Reproductive and Sexual Rights

Reproductive rights are not an isolated issue, but are intrinsically linked to macrodevelopment models. Women stress the importance of making women's needs central. It is therefore important not only to denounce abuses of population control, but also to show how population-control interventions are part of overall policies of the "new economic order," which do not put the fulfillment of people's needs in the forefront.

—Working group at the International
Women's Conference for Cairo '94:
Reproductive Health and Justice

In 1992, at the Earth Summit convened by the United Nations in Rio de Janeiro, Brazil, the Women's Action Agenda 21 was recognized by the United Nations. It expressed women's rights and perspectives on the issue of environment and development, and well as in relation to the planet.

In 1993, the global women's movement was present at the World Conference on Human Rights in Vienna to tell the world that women's rights are human rights and to make the United Nations recognize this fact.

The issue became part of the international agenda, and mechanisms such as the Special Rapporteur on Violence Against Women have since been created. Conventions such as the OAS Treaty to Prevent, Sanction and Eradicate Violence Against Women were included, as were declarations such as the United Nations Declaration on the Elimination of Violence Against Women.

Having had a strong influence on the global agenda concerning these issues, the international women's movement was ready to "engender" development further by making sure that policies related to population finally take into account women's needs and interests in the areas of health and reproductive rights and sexual rights. Our work was focused on the UN Population and Development Conference in September 1994 in Cairo, Egypt.

Of course, our FIRE burned throughout these efforts. It continued to burn strongly and clearly. And it spread.

Getting Ready for Cairo

In January of 1994, we were invited by DAWN to two activities in Rio de Janeiro. The first was their Interregional Meeting: "Four days of reason, magic, passion, and pleasure," as Peggy Antrobus put it. Thirty-two women from Asia, Africa, the Middle East, Latin America, and the Caribbean completed DAWN's document of analysis on reproductive rights. Our goal was to make sure that, through women's voices, our needs and interests were placed on the international agenda.

According to DAWN's preliminary report about the interregional meeting:

The context of the exchange among women from different regions should focus on how the debate on reproductive and sexual health and rights is related and connected to development models, with neoliberal policies and North-South relations. It should be a holistic approach, seen through the eyes of women from the South. We have to demonstrate that population policies have political motivations that are racist.... What we are looking for, in participating in this process around the Population and Development Conference, is to make sure that social policies consider and respond to people-centered development alternatives. The question is not so much one of "Should or can there be feminist population policies," but rather "What are feminists going to do to influence social policies?"

Directly following the interregional meeting, another event in Rio de Janeiro—the International Women's Conference for Cairo '94: Reproductive Health and Justice—gathered 215 women from over seventy-two countries. The International Conference, convened by an organizing committee of 15 regional and international women's groups from different parts of the world—such as DAWN, Isis Chile, the International Women's Health Coalition, Citizens-Studies-Information and Action (CEPIA), Women Living Under Muslim Laws, the National Black Women's Health Project, Women's Global Network for Reproductive Rights and Women in Nigeria—searched for new ways to reach agreement among women about the issue of reproductive health and rights in relation to social policies.

Women at that meeting drafted a 21-point statement. It dealt with women's perspectives on social and development policies aimed at promoting the right to sustainable livelihood for peoples, especially women, at times when neoliberal policies are aggravating the already unjust situation for the majority of the peoples of the world. The preamble to that statement follows:

Inequitable development models and strategies constitute the underlying basis of growing poverty and marginalization of women, environmental degradation, growing numbers of migrants and refugees, and the rise of fundamentalism everywhere. For women, these problems, and their presumed solutions through economic programs for structural adjustment, have particularly severe consequences: growing work burdens and responsibilities, spiraling process and worsened access to food, education, health services, and other basic rights; greater economic pressures to earn incomes; and growing victimization through violence, war, and fundamentalist attempts to control and subordinate women sexually and in a number of other ways.

The debates and positions about population policies showed that strong differences of opinion exist within the movement. The final report of the conference states:

A majority of participants agreed that women's health advocates should engage in making them [population policies] more democratic, women-centered, and integrated with health and development priorities. Some argued that population policies are inherently detrimental to women, and that women should instead promote social and development polices. Contraceptive technologies was another issue on which there are different views. These differences did not prevent the conference from reaching agreement on a range of important issues that formed part of the Rio Statement.

The more than 200 women present made a commitment to continue efforts and advocacy centered on building and strengthening the women's movement and bringing women's needs and interests into all agendas.

FIRE recorded panels, debates, interviews, and expectations, and also emphasized that we would follow the women's movement on the bumpy road to Cairo. The issues involved in the struggle to change the international agenda on population and development became a priority theme on FIRE.

As the UN Population and Development Conference approached, the third and final Preparatory Committee Meeting held in New York during the last three weeks of April became a stepping stone for women to bring their agenda to Cairo. I brought FIRE's microphones when I went to New York with the Latin American and Caribbean Women's Health Network, based in Chile.

Since the first UN conference on the issue in 1974 in Bucharest, and throughout the second such conference in Mexico in 1984, the Vatican had systematically opposed any language that had to do with the respect of women's right to free, informed choice or to adequate health care that takes into account women's needs and rights.

In 1994, an article entitled, "Linking United Nations Conferences in the '90s" published by ISIS Chile, I wrote about the invisible powers standing between women and the decisionmakers this time around:

The preparations for Cairo, held in the UN Building in New York, had no land in between as in the Earth Summit, no floors in between as in the Vienna conference. The NGO gathering and the official meeting were held in the same building, and on the same floor.

The women's movement and state delegates, together at last! Guess what stood between us and the states? The Vatican! Fundamentalist politics in the name of religion stood between us and the decisionmakers.

At that meeting in New York, the language regarding women's sexual, reproductive, and health rights as they relate to development was all placed in brackets [no consensus]. The challenge to get those issues out of brackets, so that the international community and the UN would recognize women's rights to reproductive and sexual health became the battle in Cairo. Policies without health and reproductive rights was unacceptable to women or to the majority of the 180 states at the Preparatory Committee meeting. Yet the Vatican, with its observer status at the UN and the unconditional support of eight state delegations, placed even *safe motherhood, sexual and reproductive health,* and *fertility regulation* in brackets.

FIRE undertook the challenge of putting women's voices on the air, contrary to the practice of most mainstream media. We affirmed that in Europe, the United States, Latin America, and the Caribbean, for example, most people only heard about the positions of the Vatican. Little was known about the overall agenda or women's voices on the issues, yet women were taking a strong stand about the need to get the issues out of brackets.

We are going to Cairo to close the gap between biological reproduction and social reproduction, by making sure that the Program of Action includes men's responsibilities in child caring, in sexuality, and in reproduction, at the same time demanding a shift from the attitude that focuses on women's fertility as the cause of environmental degradation and poverty. We want rights in those programs!
—Bene Maldunagu from Nigeria

FIRE was also preparing to do live broadcasts from Cairo. At the New York meeting, women told FIRE what they wanted to talk about on the air: religious intolerance against women's rights, development policies based on livelihood for peoples, respect for the international human rights framework in all policies, and testimonies about how women live their lives in regard to lack of those rights.

A new way of using FIRE emerged from that experience. The Women's Caucus asked me to interview Nicholas Biegman, the chair of the UN Main Committee that was holding the debates on sexual and reproductive rights. We wanted him to know that we were not going to let him be lax with the Vatican. One of the most interesting parts of the discussion was that he talked—off the air—about how he had learned that women's rights were important to the population issue during a trip to Egypt about twenty-five years before. In remembering, his sensitvity was brought back as a source of strength in his role as debate organizer.

Later, the Latin American and Caribbean Women's Caucus had designed a plan to interview, through FIRE, some of the most difficult delegations who were rejecting the inclusion of women's health rights, and also delegations who were supportive. Lobbying through radio interviews became part of their strategies.

One such interview was between one of the most outspoken anti-women's rights advocates at the Preparatory Committee meeting—a Honduran delegate from the anti-choice movement known to everyone as Lorena—and the coordinator of the Latin American and Caribbean Women's Health Network, Amparo Claro. The "interview" turned into a heated debate, in which the official delegate (who had a voice and vote in the UN) had to sit and listen to the women's rights advocate (who did not have a voice or vote at the conference). We learned of Lorena's (and the Vatican's) logic against reproductive rights—the notion that women are supposed to be the saviors of humanity, sacrificing everything, including their lives. She told FIRE that if the sacrifice of maternity were lost, all of humanity would be lost. Her words were very instructive to us and to our listeners for understanding the challenges ahead.

FIRE also empowered women at strategic moments by bringing them together through the radio to assess the situations collectively. For example, on the day that the Vatican bracketed the use and distribution of condoms in the draft document, FIRE immediately convened the NGOs to a "radio panel". Eighteen women voiced to a world audience their rage, analysis, and determination to work toward the lifting of the brackets in Cairo. Live on the air, they came up with strategies on how to articulate a response to the Vatican. It became very fluid after they listened to themselves and to each other. FIRE was right there when they needed to get their thoughts and feelings aired, and we captured the experience on tape for both present use and for posterity.

In addition, FIRE organized a meeting on radio where the Latin American and Caribbean women shared strategies on how to counteract the opposition of official delegates, and designed on-the-spot strategies to face it. FIRE also did a live broadcast that day, gathering the happenings of the day through the voices of five feminist NGO activists and two feminist women who formed part of the official delegations of their countries.

Toward the end of the meeting, women activists talked about the role FIRE had played. Claudia Garcia Moreno of the International Women's Health Coalition said, "FIRE has played an important role in propagating women's impact on health and reproductive rights issues around the world. You also always bring optimism and laughter, which is so important...."

After the preparatory meeting, FIRE produced a documentary about all the various voices we had broadcast from New York. It is entitled *Yemanya Spare Us of All Evil*—Yemanya is the goddess of both fertility and the oceans in the African and Brazilian mythology. The compilation was then used by the women's movement to lobby each country's delegates who were on their way to Cairo. Some of the positions advanced in New York were subsequently embarrassing for the governments back home, and the Women's Caucus worked to improve the official stances before they became written in the final document.

The Women's Caucus assigned FIRE the additional task of collecting testimonies gathered by women from around the world about discrimination against them by the actors who oppose the recognition of our needs and interests. Catholics for Free Choice, DAWN, WEDO, the Coalition of Reproductive Health of Women, CUNY's Law School Clinic, ISIS Chile, the Black Women's Health Project, and others gathered the testimonies and sent them to FIRE. They asked FIRE to take them to Cairo.

Debating the Issues in Egypt

Cairo, September fifth to the thirteenth—the International Conference on Population and Development-at last! A very tense situation in Cairo awaited us due to the threats of fundamentalist Islamic terrorists. Cairo is a city of fifteen million people, and the ten thousand attendees of the conference intensified the crowded conditions.

FIRE's presence in Cairo was possible because DAWN and ISIS Chile had invited me and Nancy Vargas to accompany their delegations. I summarized the goals of the international women's movement at the UN conference:

Known symbollically as the "mother of the world" for being the birthplace of civilization, the city of Cairo is now the crib for the International Conference on Population and Development. The "mother of the world" may now give birth to her second wanted daughter, an action plan and agenda that takes into account women's reproductive and sexual health rights, and a development plan with people's needs as central to development.

Again, we set up our equipment to broadcast live every day of the conference, to transmit "women's voices without brackets," telling their stories, giving their testimonies, and sharing their work toward having women's rights recognized as human rights, and reproductive rights recognized as a basic women's right—in spite of many obstacles to the broadcasts, such as the last-minute news that our RFPI studios in Costa Rica were unable to call Cairo! We ran downstairs to the administration of the hotel, worked with their technician in sign language (he spoke only Arabic), and got him to put a call through to RFPI for us. We got our connection, and with a fifty-foot telephone extension, FIRE went on the air in Egypt!

Charlotte Bunch of the Center for Women's Global Leadership spoke about a tribunal that was held at the NGO Forum entitled, "The Cairo Hearing—Reproductive Health Rights", which was broadcast on FIRE. Six testimonies of women from different regions of the world showed how lack of reproductive health rights in each of their distinctive cases violated their human rights. Five of those testimonies are presented on the following pages. The sixth, Wanda Nowicka speaking about reproductive rights issues in Poland, is reprinted in Chapter 10—

"Voices of Traditionally Underrepresented Women"—in the section entitled, "Women from Former Socialist Countries". The first testimony is that of Dr. Aida Self El Dawla, an Egyptian feminist and one of the founders of El Nadim, a center for the management and rehabilitation of victims of violence. She was a member of the New Woman Research and Study Centre, which coordinates reproductive rights research in Egypt, and she was also a lecturer in psychiatry at Ain Shams University.

I make this presentation as a member of a team of psychiatrists working at El Nadim Centre for the Management and Rehabilitation of Victims of Violence. The center has been founded to meet the needs of the hundreds of Egyptian women and men who are subjected to all forms of violence, be it torture, regular violence in police stations, or civil violence, and the hundreds of women who are exposed to domestic violence and rape or harassment in their homes, on the streets, or in prisons.

Salma is one of the fifty people who came to seek help at El Nadim for a trauma that clearly violated her psychological health and her motherhood for her living child. I am presenting this testimony in the name of Salma, who was too frightened to come herself. Salma is not the real name of the woman whose testimony I am presenting, although nobody would have identified Salma from her first name. Yet she is full of fear, to the extent that she would not run one chance in a billion [of being recognized].

Salma is a Muslim woman who comes from a lower middle-class family in Egypt living in a popular area of Cairo. Her mother is a housewife. Her father is a primary school teacher. Salma herself had finished secondary school and was training in secretarial skills. At the age of nineteen, Salma got to know a neighbor in the area who expressed his admiration for her beauty and expressed his wish to marry her. He was a young government employee who attracted Salma because he was so kind with her. He proposed to her father, who initially refused because the proposer's career was not promising. Salma insisted. This was the first time and, for very long, the last time that Salma really insisted on something that her father did not agree to.

Because she insisted, her father thought she was too dangerous and it was time to marry her off so that someone else could take charge of her. Salma had a wedding party. Family and friends were invited, and the party extended through late in the night until the bloodstained handkerchief, testifying to Salma's chastity and virginity on the night of her marriage, was shown to the guests who congratulated the parents, cheered the bride and bridegroom, and left.

Shortly after, Salma started to realize that something was not normal about her husband's behavior. He brutalized her and beat her severely for no apparent reason. He would not sleep with her, except after beating her up brutally. Salma was perplexed. She did not understand. She had no one to complain to. Her neighbors were new. She did not know them, and she could not complain to her family. Her mother would definitely tell her father, and her father would not support her because he was not happy about the marriage anyway. She had made a choice, and complaining would mean that her choice was wrong. She would be asked to pay for it.

After three months, Salma got pregnant. Her husband's aggression increased, and by the end of her pregnancy, when her belly had enlarged and she could not give in to her husband's desires, he would bring other women into the house. Every time Salma objected, she would be beaten to bruises.

Salma gave birth to her son. A month earlier, Salma's mother had given birth to a baby, too, and so she suggested that Salma come and stay with her for awhile after labor to help her through her puerperium and with the baby. It was then that Salma's mother saw the bruises and asked, and for the first time Salma spoke about what she had been enduring over the past months. She urged her mother not to tell the father, but the mother did. Furious that another man would do this to his daughter, the father went to the husband and negotiated divorce. The husband agreed at once, and both of them, father and husband, agreed that Salma was not to have her baby.

"I shall not bring up the child of this man," said the father. "If you think of bringing him into my house, I shall kill him." He took Salma's twenty-day-old baby away from her to the husband. Salma's tears did not help her. She was ready to go on living with her husband. She was ready to work for the maintenance of her son, but her father refused.

Egyptian law grants mothers the right to their children until the age of nine if a boy or eleven if a girl. But the law was irrelevant in this case. There was no one to enforce it. Salma was not allowed to ask about her son, nor to even see him. Her breasts swelled with milk. She would see her mother nursing and feel anguish and pain, both in her breasts and in her heart. She had to forget that she ever got married, and that she had ever had a child. Her milk dried by medication, and a few months later Salma was actually behaving as if she was never married, suppressing a part of her life that held the most precious thing she had.

The family moved into another neighborhood where Salma was introduced as an unmarried virgin. Soon, her family found her a job and she began to mix socially again. Everybody behaved as if Salma's past did not exist, and eventually she started to almost believe the same. Her marriage and baby became a faint memory with vague details. The clue to that past was a persistent anguish and frequent nightmares of a child with no features calling for someone who was not there.

A few months ago, Salma heard of our clinic and she came asking for help. She wanted to remember properly. She wanted to remember how her son looked and how she felt about him in those twenty days in which she had him. She said, "I wish I had continued to silently endure the pains of the beating. They are nothing to compare with the pains I feel now. My father and husband never agreed on anything, except to take my son away from me."

To this day, Salma's father refuses any attempts by our center to negotiate seeing her son. "She made a wrong choice. She will pay the price," said her father. In Salma's case, the price is her living child.

If you ask Salma, she would say her violators are her father and husband. But there is a long list of violators who contributed to Salma's misery. Salma was violated by a society that holds her guilty until she proves her innocence by the blood of her virginity exposed publicly on her wedding night. She was violated by a society that considers domestic violence a personal family matter that is not to be interfered with. She was violated by the fright of the image of a divorced woman and, like so many Egyptian women, paid an unnecessary price of endurance, bitter endurance. Salma, like so many other Egyptian women, was brought up to believe that motherhood is a virtue, the highest virtue for a woman, cherished and honored by customs, tradition, and religion in a religious society. She did not know that patriarchy is a stronger value than all others, that it is the most cherished value.

163

Finally, Salma's right to support was violated by the lack of support organizations, which could have intervened to save her the two years of endurance that did not even secure her motherhood. The violators here are a state and a government whose laws and legislations deprive Salma and thousands of Egyptian women of their right to organize against their violators and take control over their lives and reproductive health, both physical and mental.

Loretta Ross, National Program Director for the Center for Democratic Renewal in Atlanta, Georgia, USA, told her story. She had previously been Program Director for the National Black Women's Health Project and Director of Women of Color Programs for the National Organization for Women, work that she chose as a result of the injustices she suffered at the hands of the U.S. health care system.

I actually got introduced as a political activist, and I have about twenty years as a political activist. But the purpose of my talk today is to talk more about why I became a political activist. I represent many women of color in the United States whose stories are invisible. The abuses that women of color face in the United States are largely unknown. A lot of people don't know that they match the abuses that women face in developing countries.

My own story started when I was eleven years old. I was raped when I was eleven years old. I was a child to whom too many adult men had access. I was a victim of child sexual abuse. This abuse went on, so that by the time I was fourteen years old I was pregnant. I ended up having that baby at fifteen, and the abuse continued, so that by sixteen I was pregnant again. At sixteen, I decided that I didn't want to be a mother of two children, so I decided to have an abortion. I couldn't get permission from my parents, so I had to forge my mother's signature. It took so long for me to go through the process of both saving the money and making the decision to force the signature that I had a very late-term abortion. I was well over six months pregnant by the time I had the abortion.

After I had that abortion, I decided that I didn't want to even begin to possibly risk getting pregnant again, and so I sought a birth control method that would not fail me as other methods had. So, at age twenty-one, a few years later, I decided to accept the Dalkon Shield, an IUD that is no longer on the market. But if you all remember, the Dalkon Shield was a device that they made free and available to all poor women who asked for it, and I fit all the criteria. I was a woman receiving public assistance who had already had a child, who didn't want to have more children, so, of course, I was able to get a Dalkon Shield inserted into me totally for free.

Two years later, I started developing major problems. I began to suffer from all types of infections that I kept going to the doctors for. They kept telling me that I had some form of venereal disease, some kind of STD. They kept treating me for all of these diseases for well over six months, and it later turned out I didn't have them. What I had was a defective Dalkon Shield.

One night I almost passed out while I was at home. I ended up calling a taxi to go to the hospital. If you live in a poor neighborhood, you get to the hospital quicker if you call a taxi than if you call an ambulance. When I got to the hospital, I was barely conscious. I remember them putting me on a stretcher. Within a half-hour, they were wheeling me into surgery. On my way to surgery they put a piece of paper in my hand that I signed. When I woke up eight hours later I had been sterilized. My entire reproductive organs had been removed. I was twenty-five years old at the time.

What had happened medically was that my fallopian tubes had ruptured as a result of the Dalkon Shield, so my entire reproductive career lasted from age fourteen to age twenty-three. They didn't tell me why. They couldn't tell me why I had been sterilized. All they could tell me was that I was that unlucky woman they didn't catch in time. They never explained to me why, through six months of treatment, it never occurred to the head of the OB/GYN facility at a major hospital to remove my Dalkon Shield. Even when I was admitted to the hospital in a coma, I still had the Dalkon Shield in me. They never removed that until it was part of the surgery.

This is actually a story about victory, though, even though up until that time I had been a victim. Fortunately, I was so angry at what had happened to me that I immediately found a lawyer, and I became the first black woman to sue the maker of the Dalkon Shield, A.H. Robbins. It turned out that they knew more than five years before

165

mine was inserted that it was unsafe, yet they were still making it freely available to women like me, who got their health care through public family planning clinics. It also turned out that the hospital I was treated at knew that the Dalkon Shield was unsafe. But because it was a teaching hospital, they wanted their students to see what would happen to a Dalkon Shield patient who did not have it removed for six months. So I sued them, too.

I actually made a commitment in that moment that I would make sure that all the things that had happened to me would never, ever, ever happen to another black woman in America without somebody like me being there to fight for her. At the time these things were happening to me, my parents didn't understand, my community didn't understand, and the women's movement, such as it was at the time, didn't understand. They didn't understand that we who were black, who were poor, who were women of color, had a special kind of human rights abuse that America saved just for us, and that we had to be as vigilant in fighting to protect our lives as anything, because the rest of the world simply did not care. This doctor told me that what happened to me was a mistake, but as I pursue the fight to get rid of his medical license, I'm going to convince somebody that licensing that man was the real mistake.

The next speaker was Rubina Lal, a teacher of children with mental disabilities at the SPJ Sadhana School in Bombay, India. She presented the following testimony on behalf of a group of young women with mental disabilities who endured enforced uteri removal at a Government Certified Home for Mentally Retarded Girls at Shirur, India.

Friends, I am Rubina Lal. My daughter Shinjini is nineteen years old and multiply disabled. She has mental handicaps and autism. Years ago, when we were first told about her condition, we reacted in much the same way as all families do when they come to know that their child is handicapped. We were desolate and depressed, but mainly afraid, because we did not know what it entailed to have a child with disabilities.

Nineteen years later, I can say that the experience of bringing up Shinjini has enriched my life. Shinjini today enjoys and participates in many things that all of us do. She goes to work at the training center, helps in the house, watches TV, and loves going out.

My testimony is on behalf of Shinjini and other young women like her who also have many abilities, but are only called disabled. And because these women are disabled, they are subject to neglect, abuse, physical and emotional trauma, and a violation of their human rights. This is what happened at Shirur.

In the first week of February 1994, seventeen women inmates between the ages of 10 and 35 of a state-run residential home for the mentally handicapped were brought to a government hospital for the removal of their uteri. This Government Certified Home for Mentally Retarded Girls is situated at Shirur in the state of Maharashtra, India, and comes under the directorate of the Department of Women, Child and Handicapped Welfare, Government of Maharashtra.

An eminent and leading gynecologist from Bombay was called by the director of the department to perform the operations, which would be sponsored by the Rotary Club. Sufficient publicity was created for this "hysterectomy camp," which according to the good doctor, the caring director, and the generous funders, would provide human dignity and protection to mentally handicapped women.

But unfortunately, things did not work out exactly as planned. On February 5, 1994, the day of the operation, various women's groups and social activists staged a sit-in demonstration outside the hospital. Some employees of the hospital also participated in the demonstration. The Chief Minister of Maharashtra was asked to intervene and stop the surgeries, but protest notwithstanding, eleven women lost their uteri to hysterectomy.

Friends, since this testimony is on behalf of women with mental handicaps, I would like you to visualize the scene at this home at Shirur. Imagine that you are a woman with low intellectual functioning. Imagine that you live in an environment that provides very little by way of stimulation, attention, care, or training. You are mostly left by yourself with nothing to occupy your mind or body. Imagine also that you have a language and speech impairment and depend on others to understand your needs.

Now let us consider the Shirur hysterectomies and reasons given by the state and the medical community for performing the operations:

1) They say that hysterectomy was done because the women had no sense of menstrual hygiene: that during menstruation they played

with menstrual blood and smeared it on the wall, that they removed their sanitary napkins and soiled their clothes and bedding. If that were true, then these women would also be smearing fecal matter and urine. But if the home authorities could manage that, what was their objection to menstrual blood? It was obviously the stigma and dislike of the menstrual blood that led them to call it "messy" and resort to hysterectomy to "clean" the mess permanently. The operation has not taught the women to be hygienic. It has removed the source of something that was considered dirty and repugnant by their caregivers.

2) The second reason for the operation was that it prevented the women from pregnancy. I would like to know how a mentally handicapped woman who lives in a state-run home, managed by female staff, can ever become pregnant? Is it an indirect admission by the state to sexual abuse and custodial rape of its inmates? It is a commonly known, but officially denied, fact that sexual assault of women in institutional care happens regularly.

3) The medical community felt that hysterectomy was the best course of action, as it is the only solution science has for the management of menstruation of the mentally handicapped. Ironic, isn't it? This high-tech age has made us so dependent on science that we look for technological solutions to all problems caused by social attitudes and gender bias.

4) Sexuality and fertility of the women were cited as reasons for hysterectomy. The operation thus became a means to prevent mental handicap. The premise is that mental handicap breeds mental handicap, and as people with mental handicaps are considered economically nonproductive members of society, they should not be allowed to multiply. The followers of this eugenics movement used hysterectomy to reduce the population of disabled people. Research has shown that the majority of children with mental handicaps are born of parents who are of normal intelligence, but the authorities do not pay any attention to the researchers. It is easier to remove the womb of a helpless, handicapped woman living under their care and feel that they have done their best in prevention of disabilities, rather than to control environmental pollution, radioactivity, harmful drugs, malnutrition, and inadequate health services, which affect many women and often lead to the birth of handicapped children.

5) According to the authorities of the home, the women deserved hysterectomy because they were "untrainable." My experience with Shinjini and many other severely handicapped girls whom I have taught as a professional is to the contrary. A lot can be achieved by them if the caregiver has patience and understanding. The women at Shirur deserve better care and health services, not hysterectomy.

The mentally handicapped have a right to special facilities and proper support. It is the duty of the state to give them what is rightfully theirs. The Shirur incident proves that the state, with the connivance of the medical community, has abdicated its responsibilities, but we are not going to tolerate it quietly. The social activists and women's groups have held public meetings to condemn this incident, and they have filed a petition against the government.

Friends, I give this testimony at this international forum because I know that Shirur is a symbol of suppression and exploitation of the weak and the marginalized. Whenever a section of population is suppressed and exploited, the brunt of this fascism is borne by its women. In India, the women with mental handicaps had to suffer hysterectomy. In some developed countries they are treated like guinea pigs when drugs like Depo Provera and Norplant are tested on them. I leave you to decide which society is better for them. One thing that is clear is that exploitation of the weak and disabled does not have geopolitical boundaries. Viewed from this angle, Shirur is a global issue.

Amina Sambo, Executive Director of the Grassroots Health Coalition in Nigeria, had been addressing issues of women's health for more than two decades when she gave the following testimony. She also served on the National Task Force on Vesico Vaginal Fistula and was a regional consultant for the Center for Development and Population Activities.

My name is Amina Sambo, and I am the Executive Director of the Grassroots Health Organization of Nigeria. We are a nongovernmental organization with about 300 volunteers in village communities. The Grassroots Health Organization of Nigeria was founded in 1993 by concerned individuals who have the interests of women's health at heart, with special emphasis on VVF—vesico vaginal fistula—and other health-related issues.

What is VVF? It is a disease that affects women and girls only and is usually caused by early pregnancy. VVF is the internal rupturing of the bladder. A woman or girl who has VVF loses the ability to control her urine, which leaks continuously from the bladder through the vagina. Sometimes, in addition to this, the woman or girl may also rupture her rectum, so that feces also leak through the vagina. There are about 200,000 women and girls who suffer from vesico vaginal fistula in Nigeria. That means for every 1,000 women who give birth, two are likely to develop VVF. Ninety-nine percent of fistula victims have stillborn babies. After treatment for VVF, these girls can only have babies through Cesarean section.

One of the causes of VVF is prolonged, obstructed labor. About eight out of every ten cases of VVF seen in Nigeria are due to prolonged, obstructed labor during childbirth. The other cause is the Gishiri Cut, which is a traditional form of incision usually performed by local barbers (wanzamai) *and sometimes by traditional birth attendants. Indirect causes of VVF are early marriage, poverty, the loss status of women, and limited access to health and social services.*

On one of my regular visits to Murtala Mohammed Specialist Hospital, which is the national coordination center on VVF, I took time and talked with two VVF victims with whom I am quite familiar, who have been coming to the hospital and are still in rehabilitation from their operations. I will now present their testimonies.

Laraba comes from a village in the Dambata Local Government Area of Kano State in northern Nigeria. She is the fifth child of her father, who is a farmer. Laraba was fourteen years old when she was given out in marriage, without her consent, to a forty-five-year-old man. She never attended school. She became pregnant immediately after marriage. When it was time for her to give birth, she labored for two days. An untrained traditional birth attendant performed the Gishiri Cut on her. The Gishiri Cut is a traditional surgical procedure in the birth canal, usually done with an unsterilized instrument.

Laraba bled profusely. As a last resort, her mother took her to the hospital. The doctors found that Laraba had lost a lot of blood, sustained a severe laceration of the vaginal wall, and that her baby had died in the uterus. The doctors gave her a blood transfusion and removed the dead baby instrumentally through the vagina. After a few weeks, the family discovered that the young woman was wetting her bed. As a result, the husband refused to stay with her any longer. He divorced her, and she went back to her parents. After a few months, she became depressed because her own family treated her as an outcast. She could not socialize or eat together with her family as is customary tradition because she had VVF.

Habiba comes from a village in the Rano Local Government of Kano State. Her father is a farmer and has three wives and eighteen children. Habiba is his second child. Her father gave her in marriage, at the age of thirteen, to a man she had never known, who was forty years old. Habiba wishes she had been sent to school instead of getting married. Two months after her wedding, Habiba got pregnant. Apparently, she did not know about prenatal care, and the only medical facility she could recall was a dispensary about eighty kilometers from her village.

In the ninth month, Habiba went into labor for three days in her village. An untrained traditional birth attendant was called in, who administered some incantations and give her some herbs to drink, but all in vain. Her husband was informed about her condition, and it was agreed that she could be taken to the hospital. They took her on a donkey to the main road where they stopped a commercial vehicle and paid the driver to take Habiba and her mother to Murtala Mohammed Specialist Hospital in Kano. The doctors performed an episiotomy and delivered a stillborn baby.

Two weeks later, Habiba found that she could not control her urine. She wet her bed and clothes all the time. Habiba's clothes were full of stench. Her mother noticed it and asked her why she was smelling. Habiba told her about the urine leaking. They then told Habiba's husband and decided that she should stay with her parents until she was cured.

The family tried traditional cures for almost three years without any success. In the meantime, Habiba's husband sent a letter divorcing her because he did not want to wait nay longer.

Fortunately, both of these girls are now recovered. Both eventually went to the Murtala Mohammed Specialist Hospital in Kano, where they received corrective surgery. Laraba was operated on about three months after she developed VVF. Habiba suffered with VVF for three years before she learned of the Specialist Hospital.

There are about 200,000 women who have fistula problems similar to those of Laraba and Habiba as a result of giving birth at too young an age. Nigeria's Marriage Act, which is part of the statutory law, sets the legal age of marriage at twenty-one. However, women and girls can also marry under customary law in Nigeria. According to Islamic law, girls can be married at the age of puberty, or between ten and fifteen years old. The main reason given for this is to avoid promiscuity. Customary law in other parts of Nigeria also permits child marriage. Girls have no right to refuse such marriages, which are usually arranged by the parents. Boys are not forced into early marriage as are girls.

Nongovernmental organizations have on several occasions appealed to the Nigerian government to enact laws setting the minimum age of marriage at eighteen years. The problems of early marriage and early pregnancy are made worse by the lack of adequate access to health care, including maternal and child health care, particularly in rural areas. Women's rights to pregnancy-related health care are guaranteed by Article 12 of the Convention on the Elimination of All Forms of Discrimination Against Women.

Carmen Rincón Cruz challenged the Mexican justice system and medical establishment after the loss of her first daughter due to medical negligence. Her story, translated from Spanish, is one of personal struggle against a system that ignores the health rights and needs of pregnant women.

My name is Carmen. I am Mexican. I was twenty-eight years old, had a university career, a job in the health sector of my country, and was pregnant. My partner and I had decided to have a natural birth, so that he could be present during the whole process of labor, from the beginning to the end. We spoke with the doctor who would assist me, expressing our wishes and contracting the services of a private clinic. I was happy. I was going to have a child for the first time, never imagining the horror that this would bring me.

Upon arrival at the hospital the day of delivery, I was taken directly to the delivery room. They anaesthetized me immediately and without my consent. They didn't let my husband accompany me, despite what

172

had been agreed upon with the doctor. After inducing labor, having me push for hours and administering excessive doses of oxytocin, the doctor decided to perform an emergency Cesarean because the heartbeat of the baby girl could not be heard. Finally, they extracted the baby girl, completely purple and dead due to asphyxia or cardiac arrest. The doctors never verified the cause of death.

After gaining consciousness, I shouted that they were assassins and had killed my daughter. The doctors sedated me with heavy tranquilizers for hours. Later, when I awoke, I discovered that they had buried my daughter without even letting me touch her, without having the opportunity to hold her in my arms, without saying goodbye.

I then cry, scream, become desperate. At that moment, I think there is nothing I can do.

After two days, the doctor released me despite my continued physical illness. Nevertheless, the doctor said that this was normal due to my emotional depression, and that by walking enough I would recover.

The following week, I went to the clinic to get the stitches removed. After consecutively probing me, rectally and vaginally, the doctor said to me, with enormous coldness, that I was infected and that I need to be admitted to the hospital again. He also said that he couldn't continue to care for me because he was going on vacation.

The following week I went to another doctor, and after his diagnostic checkup he said that the uterine sutures were open, and that my ovaries and uterus must be removed. At the same time, the doctor told me that my hopes for surviving this infection were remote.

"She is going to die," he warned my parents. I suffered septic shock, and for weeks I struggled between life and death.

During the slow recovery, against so much abuse, the only thing I wanted was to die. Pus continued coming out of my vagina, my daughter was dead, and now I was sterile. My family, to console me, said that I was not the first nor the last woman to whom this had happened. They said that I would forget this nightmare and that I should resign myself.

And it is in the midst of my physical and moral pain, the anger and the powerlessness that I felt, that I asked myself, "Is the same thing that happened to me going to happen to girls who someday decide to become mothers? How long are we going to wait to denounce, talk, demand?"

I sued the doctor for medical negligence and professional irresponsibility. I then faced another horror as sinister as the one I had just lived through, which is the corrupt way justice is exercised in Mexico. The authorities refused to go to trial. After five years of economic, moral, and emotional drain, the doctor was sentenced to only a six-month license suspension.

What did I gain? They say that I just made a spectacle of myself, but I believe mine was an important victory, and symbolic for women. I gained the realization that in my country women do not denounce and do not demand justice. Instead, they die or are left handicapped and senselessly mutilated by the equivocations and medical errors of doctors. Within this society and in the legal field, the medical establishment is untouchable, united with a justice system that is corrupt and "buyable" according to social class.

I also learned that we women still carry taboos and stereotypes that do not allow us to talk and be heard. I learned that we are owners of our bodies, our lives, and that nobody, not even a doctor, has the right to decide over us. I also learned that in Mexico, postpartum infections continue to be one of the primary causes of maternal morbidity and mortality.

Now I have Estell, my daughter whom we adopted a year after the death of my first daughter. I also have José Luis, my partner, who continues to support and love me. To this day, I have not been able to have sexual relations with him, due to the horror that still causes me to remember the simultaneous vaginal and rectal probings by the doctors as they said, "You wanted it... screw you and put up with it!"

Charlotte Bunch also spoke to FIRE's listeners of the importance of making links between the Human Rights Conference (Vienna, Austria, June 1993), the Population and Development Conference (Cairo, Egypt, September 1994), and the Women's Conference to be held in Beijing, China, in 1995.

Three thousand journalists were present in Cairo. FIRE visited the commercial media outlets to inform them that we were there to provide them with contacts from the Women's Caucus to add women's voices to their coverage. Many of them accepted our offer.

For example, on the fourth day of the conference, I represented the international women's movement in a debate with the Vatican, which was broadcast on both FIRE and *The Christian Science Monitor's* world shortwave service. When I presented myself to the audience and to the Bishop, I began by saying:

The international women's caucus at the conference has selected me to be the feminist to go on the air with the delegate of the Vatican, not so much because I am a health activist, not so much because I am a feminist, but foremost because I am a former nun. I know from the inside that the Vatican is the most undemocratic state in the whole concert of nations that makes up the UN, and that there are no women in that state, so what do they want to tell all other member states what they should do about women?

From that moment on, the Bishop looked at the floor, unable to look me in the eyes throughout the whole debate.

During the debate, I also emphasized that the UN International Conference on Population and Development was not only about abortion—as the Vatican (and many others) would have the world believe—but it was also about the right to sustainable human development and health rights as a key component of that development.

We organized a press conference specifically to disseminate our message. Again, representatives of the anti-choice movement tried to block our efforts. As they were trying to interrupt the interviews between mainstream media and women's NGOs, FIRE drew them away to articulate their position on our microphones: "For Feminist International Radio Endeavour, I want to know what your position is about the right to development."

From that moment on, the anti-choice people argued on our microphone and tape recorder, frantically trying to defend their positions. After forty-five minutes they realized that they were fighting with us instead of disrupting the other interviews—one of them even tried to attack our camera as we photographed the scene. Debra Latham later wrote about FIRE's Cairo presence in *Vista*:

As the international media focus mainly on the issue of abortion as a point of conflict in the conference, FIRE, once again, is looking at all the issues involved in women's reproductive and sexual health rights and covering what is happening at all levels of the parallel conferences. FIRE and the women's movement have not forgotten the word "development" in the title of the conference.... We congratulate María Suárez of FIRE and the many women's rights networks gathered in Cairo for demonstrating once again that women will not be silent where our autonomy and human rights are concerned, and that no religion or state has sole moral authority over women's lives.

In response to the media coverage during and after Cairo, Rhonda Copelon and I wrote about the bias:

Once the Vatican and Islamic fundamentalists were stonewalled, considering that the Plan of Action approved reflects a new philosophy and set of actions that goes far beyond family planning as a demographic fix, and that it contemplates human rights, the participation of women, broad definitions of reproductive and sexual health, and the need for education, equality and the empowerment of women as official goals, mainstream media is distorting the Women's Caucus objectives in the conference.

After Cairo, most mainstream media are presenting women as advocates of population control with a prettier face. They ignore the transformative goals of women's participation in Cairo. They neglect the very serious difference between seeing women's empowerment as a means to an end, as opposed to an end in itself. They brush too swiftly over the dangers of continued coercion and disrespect that is inherent in continuing to objectify women even if empowerment is the new slogan. They neglect the other objective that the Women's Caucus brought to that conference: to shift the focus of alarm over poverty, development and fertility to the inhuman and world-threatening policies of the developed nations, the unconscionable debt burden and structural adjustment policies which have deepened poverty and depleted basic social services; militarism and globalization of the market economy with their accelerating exploitation of both human and natural resources; and inequitable and unsustainable patterns of consumption and development.

Our article pointed to some of the broader development issues that women around the world—and FIRE—had been speaking about for years. The work of the two world conferences that were to follow in 1995—the Conference on Social Development in Copenhagen, Denmark, and the Conference on Women in Beijing, China—was built upon the work we had done to defend our rights.

Rhonda Copelon, a U.S. feminist lawyer and women's human rights activist best expressed the role of women's media during the preparations for the International Conference on Population and Development (ICPD):

If having a voice in the preparations for Cairo and the ICPD document was a major struggle for the women activists, having a voice in media and holding our voices was an urgent need in such an adverse situation as was the Cairo conference. While most mainstream media reported ten-second soundbites from women activists, FIRE's live broadcasts allowed them to go deep into the issues and experiences. On the other hand, FIRE was a place where we could speak with journalists who were not putting us against the wall. We need that kind of space as a way of holding our own voice.

FIRE and the International Reproductive Rights Research Action Group

IRRRAG (International Reproductive Rights Research Action Group) was founded in 1992 and is coordinated by Professor Rosalind Pollack Petchesky at Hunter College, City University of New York, USA. IRRRAG gave a presentation in Huairou, China, at the NGO Forum that paralleled the UN Conference on Women in 1995. Two of their reports went out over the FIRE airwaves on International Health Day, April 9, 1996.

One was presented by Adriana Ortega from Mexico, and the other by Dr. Simone Grilo Diniz of the Colectivo Feminista de Sexualidade e Saude in Sao Paulo, which coordinated the research project in Brazil. They each presented the results of a three-year IRRRAG research study about reproductive rights issues in their respective countries.

The study examined how women perceive and define reproductive rights and explored women's values and decision-making. Research was conducted in seven countries: Brazil, Nigeria, Egypt, Malaysia, the Philippines, the United States, and Mexico.

Researchers interviewed more than 800 women living in urban and rural areas, including low-income women from diverse religious and ethnic backgrounds, women of different ages, and single and married women.

Membership in grassroots political and community organizations has helped women define and demand their reproductive rights. Membership in groups gives women, including very poor women, an opportunity to share their needs and concerns with others, to gain support, and generate ideas. Women develop a sense of identity as a group member that can positively affect their individual sense of self worth.

Joining a group has been very important for me because now people in my town see me in a different light. Before I was nobody. Not now. Nowadays everybody says, "Let's go see her, she knows." People in town come and share their problems with me, asking "What do you recommend about contraceptives?"
—Participant in IRRRAG study

The relationship between women's membership in groups and their sense of entitlement to reproductive rights is one of the preliminary findings of this international study on women's reproductive rights.

The IRRRAG research project focused on women's sense of entitlement to exert control over their bodies; their strategies for making decisions about sexual and reproductive issues, including childbearing; and strategies they use when they encounter opposition from family members, including husbands.

In Mexico, researchers interviewed women belonging to grassroots civic, community, and trade organizations concerned with problems in housing, food, child care, and health. Study participants lived in Oaxaca, Sonora, and Mexico City.

In addition to membership in groups, motherhood also helped give women a sense of self worth and the belief they are entitled to safety and control of their bodies. One of the women interviewed said:

I don't allow [my husband] to beat me anymore. If he hits me, I hit him back.... More than anything else, there is the courage my children give me... before I felt so alone without my parents' support, I would put up with almost anything.

During interviews, researchers learned that women feel strongly that decisions to use or not to use family planning should be made by women. Women used contraceptives in spite of fears that husbands would become angry, that husbands would beat them, or that the Catholic Church would punish their actions. One study participant told about taking a stand against her husband:

I think this decision should always be made by women. When I had the second child, I went to the Family Planning Department and asked for contraceptives. My husband got mad, but I told him I didn't care, and that I didn't want to get pregnant.

Sterilization is the most widely used family planning method in Mexico, and researchers learned that many women who have undergone sterilization avoid telling their husbands for fear of becoming victims of domestic violence. Women expressed outrage that some women might be sterilized without their consent but said they would not file a complaint because of distrust of authorities.

The second IRRRAG report presented on FIRE's broadcast that day dealt with the study in Brazil. Under the title "Brazilian Mothers Say Daughters Entitled to Control Their Bodies and Lives", Simone Grilo Diniz's presentation was synthesized in a press release by IRRRAG:

In Brazil, mothers say daughters are entitled to take control of their own bodies—and their own lives. Poor women who grew up in communities where traditional gender roles prevailed, where quality health care was scarce, and where ignorance about sexuality was common say they are determined their daughters will have a different life. They hope their daughters will acquire an education, develop job skills, marry later, have fewer children, and find fulfillment in paid jobs outside the home as well as through motherhood.

In Brazil, researchers interviewed rural laborers and sharecroppers in Pernambuco, domestic workers in Rio de Janeiro, and housewives in Sao Paulo. Researchers found that women's views of what it means to "take care of one's body" are changing. Women interviewed by IRRRAG researchers say taking care of one's body means freedom to enjoy sexuality as well as protection from unwanted pregnancy and sexually transmitted diseases. With AIDS as the principal cause of death among Sao Paulo women ages 20 to 44, mothers say their daughters are entitled to be safe from physical, emotional, and social risk and free from economic dependence on men. One mother in Sao Paulo said that a "good" girl is one who uses condoms during sex to prevent an unplanned pregnancy.

Brazilian women also are expanding the definition of "reproduction." Women defined reproduction not just as the biological event of giving birth but as a lifelong process that includes caretaking, work, and risks to women's health.

Brazilian women are rejecting the silence that traditionally has surrounded sexual and reproductive health issues. One woman interviewed told the story of how silence about reproductive health issues affected her: She continued to take birth control pills six years after she had a hysterectomy. When she stopped taking pills and her menstrual period did not begin she feared she was pregnant. Only after months of not having her period did she decide she must have entered menopause—never having been told that, without ovaries or a uterus, pregnancy was impossible.

Women also said that achieving a sense of purpose outside the home, through paid work, community work, or union activism, was critical in helping them develop a sense of self worth and entitlement:

Ten years ago, when I started participating, I was Mary Nothing who didn't have any awareness of anything. Here in the health movement, I gained the consciousness that we have to fight for our rights, for our space, and we have to think about tomorrow.

The findings, that generational differences influence one's perception of entitlement and that women define reproduction more broadly than childbirth, were common in all of the seven countries that participated in the IRRRAG study. In analyzing the cross-country data, IRRRAG researchers also found the following:

- While in all countries women affirm the importance of motherhood, they also say that motherhood carries burdens, pains and responsibilities. Consequently, women view motherhood as a role that entitles them to respect and decision-making authority, including decisions about family planning, abortion, health, and sex.

- Women's sense of entitlement to make their own decisions about marriage, childbearing, sex, and AIDS prevention may be enhanced by contacts and resources outside the family, such as work and membership in organizations. These activities also can generate anger, resentment, and violence from husbands.

- While women agreed that childbearing and motherhood gave them a sense of value, almost all said that decisions about the number of children and timing of pregnancies should be the woman's.

- Women's actions concerning reproductive health issues often defied their words. While many women considered abortion "wrong" or "sinful," they also described it as necessary and commonplace.

- Many women reported that their experiences with medical and health providers were often demeaning and did little to enhance their sense of entitlement. Experiences with traditional birth attendants and healers were more positive.

- Women's sense of ownership over their bodies was expressed in terms of desire to work outside the home, contribute to family income, and move freely in public settings.

- Women define reproductive health as a lifelong process. Definitions that limit the reproductive years to age 15 to 45 (the years when most women are biologically capable of becoming pregnant) are out of touch with most women's views. Women define "reproduction" as not just a biological event, but as a series of experiences, including caretaking, work, and risks to women's health throughout their lifetimes.

Following these coverages in 1995, FIRE became a member of the Latin American and Carribean Women's Health Network, thus expanding our commitment to the isues of women's health.

181

CHAPTER 6

Women and Development Around the World

> *Rio de Janeiro, Vienna, Cairo... Copenhagen, Beijing. This is the story of a long journey over new roads for which no previous route existed. Not even the sister with the most frequent-flyer miles could have drawn this route ahead of time. To participate in Beijing, we must integrate our experiences and agendas as a movement. No airline can do that for us. Either we do it together or we don't get there.*
>
> —FIRE, *Mujeres en Acción,* ISIS 1995

Indeed, by 1995, FIRE's path had crisscrossed the globe, broadcasting women's voices as they shared their own stories and demanded their human rights. FIRE was to play a role in the women's movement's activities at the UN's Fourth World Conference on Women (FWCW) in Beijing in September of 1995, but first it was to address issues of social and economic development in Copenhagen, Denmark.

182

Preparing for the UN Conference
on Social Development

In August 1994, FIRE was invited to accompany the women's movement to the New York Preparatory Committee (PREPCOM) meeting of one of the most significant but low-profile UN conferences: the Social Development Summit. Held in Copenhagen, Denmark, in March 1995, it was to address, according to the UN Information Note about the Conference:

> ...the major social development dilemmas facing societies the world over as they approach the 21st century... aim[ing] to achieve a conceptual and practical breakthrough by taking a comprehensive, integral approach to social issues.... Three core issues have been found to be of overriding concern to virtually every government: the eradication of poverty, the need for expansion of productive employment, and the enhancement of social integration.

FIRE analyzed the underlying obstacles surrounding the inclusion of women's and peoples' perspectives in the text about the summit. Our results were presented in August 1994, at a panel during the second PREPCOM for the Social Development Summit. The panel, convened by the Coordinating Committee of the Beijing NGO Forum, was held in the New York UN Headquarters Building. Following are my observations as reported on FIRE:

> Perhaps it is too early in the process to know for sure who of the invisible powers stands between women and the states in this conference. But I want to share with you a first image and gut feeling gathered during the first day of the PREPCOM.
> While Peggy Antrobus of Developing Alternatives with Women for a New Era was speaking at the plenary of the official meeting on our behalf, I looked over to the seats of the International Monetary Fund and the World Bank, which were beside each other.
> Lo and behold, the seats were occupied. Observer seats, voice, but no vote in a conference about social development. I thought they were listening to women's concerns as they sat there while Peggy spoke. But soon I discovered that this assumption was wrong. They had only been waiting

for their turn to speak. Only a few minutes after Peggy spoke, they had their turn. Immediately after they finished speaking, they left the meeting. Their seats at the meeting have been empty most of the time.

We have to consider that the states are no longer accountable to people, but to the international institutions that control economic and political power.

The meeting concluded just days before the Cairo International Conference on Population and Development. As economists and development specialists there were asking what type of human development is needed to bring about sustainable development, women turned the question around to ask what type of development is needed to bring about genuine human development?

Months later, at the last preparatory meeting for the Denmark summit, many women got their chance to speak live on FIRE. Anita Nayar from the Women Environment and Development Organization (WEDO) lined up women from different parts of the world: Chief Bisi from Nigeria, Olga Bianchi from the Women's League for Peace and Freedom (WILPF) in Costa Rica, Bella Abzug from WEDO, and Marta Benavides from El Salvador. They reported on the events of the preparatory meeting, where the Women's Caucus had brought an agenda calling for a restructuring of the development paradigm—a shift that would not come about unless people organized to demand what's theirs by right: the right to development.

FIRE was able to announce that women's voices without brackets would be aired live from Copenhagen, thanks to the invitations by many women's organizations for FIRE to cover the Social Summit.

International Women's
Day in Copenhagen

In March 1995, FIRE went to Denmark to cover the Social Development Summit and its relationship to the Fourth World Conference on Women, which was to be held in Beijing the following September. For FIRE's staff the two events were closely interrelated.

About 130 heads of states gathered in Copenhagen to begin discussion of the Social Development Summit's agenda: poverty, unemployment, and social integration. Debt cancellation, accountability of the World Bank and the International Monetary Fund, and sustainable development were among the hot issues for which there had been no previous consensus. Another particularly controversial concern was the allocation of new resources for social development, for which the "20/20" proposal asks developing countries to devote at least 20 percent of their national budgets and donor nations 20 percent of their aid budgets to basic human needs.

Economic and social equity between men and women merited particular attention. According to UN Under-Secretary General for Policy Coordination and Sustainable Development, Nitin Desai, "We cannot address environmental or social concerns without addressing the problem of gender inequality."

Bella Abzug, co-chair of the Women Environment and Development Organization (WEDO) pointed out, "Women perform two-thirds of the world's work but earn only five percent of the world's income and own less than one percent of the assets."

Many unique women's activities took place in Denmark, one of the most difficult UN conferences for women and other underrepresented people. It was up to us to challenge the political will of governments and financial institutions, to get them to commit to a review of macroeconomic policies and the way they make economic profit their top priority, thus sacrificing social development. Women knew that those commitments would not come easily, so we especially organized to have a voice at that summit.

One of the most outstanding activities of the summit was the celebration of International Women's Day on March 8. That day, women from around the world launched the 180-Day Global Campaign to support positive change in women's lives. The campaign would end on September 6, during the Beijing conference. The celebration began when hundreds of activists attending the UN World Summit for Social Development rallied with colorful banners, live music, and speeches by an array of women leaders. Later, participants joined thousands of Danish women in a torchlight procession through downtown Copenhagen. FIRE covered this activity.

Another memorable action was a women's hunger strike, staged in the center hall of the Bella Center, where the official summit was taking place. From the 8th of March up to the 11th, some 15 women fasted, accompanied by others at different times. At the end of the strike they issued a press statement about the objectives and development of the activity:

One billion women, men, youth and children go hungry every day as a matter of necessity. On International Women's Day, March 8, 1995, a group of women began a fast to highlight the plight of the poor who are mainly women and children, to express solidarity with them, and to express the need for urgency in addressing their needs at this World Summit for Social Development.

Our fast is meant to point out that the basis of the problem of the poor and the hungry is the organization of international finance and the distortion of political power, which has burdened many of our countries with debt that can never be paid. In too many countries, this debt is used to justify decreasing expenditures in health, education, and other social services. This debt and its consequent adjustment programs force the payment of unlivable wages, and increase the amount of unwaged and unvalued labor, especially of women.

We invited delegates here at the Bella Center to join the fast, to sit in our circle here as an open act of solidarity, and to fight hard for our basic demands, which were contained in the draft document they were finalizing here at Copenhagen.

Delegates joined our fast, some for hours, others for twenty-four hours. Many more came to be with us, including the President of Guyana, Dr. Cheddi Jagan, Chairman of the Conference; Ambassador Juan Somovia, UNICEF Special Ambassador; Sir Peter Ustinov, Danish Minister of Social Welfare; Karen Jaspersen, many other UN officials.... NGOs, journalists, and scores of women participated in this spiritual action intended to push for meaningful political outcomes.... This is the first time the United Nations language has taken a holistic approach to the eradication of poverty. Nevertheless, recognition is not enough....

To eradicate poverty, member states must begin with the drastic reduction of military spending beginning in fiscal year 1996. To eradicate poverty, bilateral and multilateral debt MUST BE CANCELLED NOW. We welcome the initiative of the Danish government to cancel $118 million debt with immediate effect from March 1995 and urge *governments to follow this lead and extend it. To alleviate poverty, we call for a transformation of the Bretton Woods Institutions into People-Centered Development Institutions.*

The recognition of women's equality and gender equity and the right of people's participation in the document are new and welcome; however, this is not enough. Now we call on ALL governments to ratify without reservations the Convention on the Elimination of All Forms of Discrimination Against Women [CEDAW], BEFORE the opening of the Fourth World Conference on Women in Beijing, China, in September 1995.

Acceptance of 20/20. This must be seen as a moral minimum. The opportunity was missed to see poverty as existing in the North, as the G-77 called for. We will monitor this commitment and call for more and more social spending, as needs dictate.

These recognitions and commitments enshrined in the Draft Declaration and Program of Action must be seen as a minimum. Women will insist on the implementation of this minimum. We stand ready to play our role in civil society as promoters of transparent accountable systems of governance; we stand ready to work with governments to continuously search for and implement a new paradigm of people-centered development that understands [that] the market system does not address the majority of humanity's needs, especially those of poor people.

We commit to making the contents of the declaration finally negotiated here in Copenhagen accessible to women worldwide and call on governments to honor their commitments.

Finally, we salute all those, especially Ambassador Juan Somovia, who have advanced our collective human needs at this conference.

FIRE covered the hunger strike and its culminating activity described in the following announcement:

Women welcome recognitions and commitments,
but these are not enough!
Cancel debt!
Improve civil society's access!
MAKE WOMEN'S RIGHTS UNIVERSAL IN LAW (CEDAW)!
END MILITARISM!   *March 11, 1995*

Among the 15 direct participants in the four-day hunger strike were Dessima Williams from Grenada; Iman Ashara from Nigeria; Wangari Mathai from Kenya; Paninga Fulani, member of a refugee organization in the Netherlands; and Jocelyn Doe from the Caribbean. Other women were from Africa, Canada, Japan, the Caribbean, the United States, and Europe.

Many people laid handwritten posters on the floor around the strikers with some of the following messages: Fast for poverty eradication. Join! / The USA does have poverty! / Bosnia is dying, if not now, when? If not Summit, who? / The rich need to live in poverty for a week! / The planet earth and its resources should be our common heritage / For the people who produce the food for the world! / There is hunger in Canada, yes there is / Structural adjustment has no positive impact on the poor / Lift the economic sanctions: USA remove the brackets off women's lives in Cuba / The economic framework places the highest value on war and destruction, pollution, and greed. The basics of life are nothing to economic markets / Stop the capital gain that causes human pain / Build communities, not markets alone / When we dream together, reality begins!

At the end of the strike, Fatima Allo of the Tanzania Women's Media Collective interviewed women for FIRE. One of them was Wangari Mathai, leader of the Green Belt Movement in Kenya. Asked about her assessment of the Summit, Wangari answered:

The document is not bad, nor good. What is important is what we can do at the national level now with this document. The poor have been brought to the center of the agenda, but further marginalization of people is what will happen if we do not mobilize at the national level.

Fatima then asked Wangari if she thought Africa was poor.

It is not poor! It is so rich that other countries have used it to enrich themselves. What we lack is leadership. Governments have to stop being corrupt; they should involve civil society and exercise good governance and free flow of information. Civil society has to demand accountability.

Fatima then spoke with Eva Quistop who presented herself as a "freelance" politician. A former member of the European Parliament representing the Greens, she represented herself and the antinuclear movement at the summit:

In the last 20 years we have struggled a lot but have achieved very little. We in Germany have been working on getting Germany to give one percent of its national budget to economic cooperation, and still we have to come here to repeat the same demand.... Denmark is an example. It has no nuclear energy, fantastic alternatives for social projects, and is giving one percent of its budget for social development.

I had the opportunity to interview Fatima about the relationship of this summit with the Fourth World Conference on Women. Fatima reminded us, "As media women we have our own challenge. When we go to Beijing we need a good media strategy there."

FIRE's Firuseh Shokoo interviewed Dessima Williams, of the Island of Grenada in the Caribbean, who said:

We are taking the energy expressed here to Beijing. Our presence has been important here at many levels. We have seen some new commitments on the question of gender equity, an integrated approach to ending poverty, a new energy, and respect for civil society, but we have not seen enough. [Issues such as] demilitarization, macroeconomic frameworks, and so on [still exist].

Asked by Firuseh to summarize the demands of the strikers, Dessima talked about support of people's rights, more spending on social development, more demands for cancellation of the debt, demilitarization, open space for civil society, indigenous peoples' land rights and participation, women, youth, and ratification of the CEDAW Convention:

We believe that through women's democratic inclusive action, we could open more democratic space for all of humanity, and this is what we have been doing here!

Fire Goes on Satellite

FIRE held its own unique activity during the Copenhagen summit. On the eighth of March, while the 180-Day Campaign was being launched, our first live broadcast via satellite and digital phone line took place. Broadcast on National Public Radio in the United States through the satellite connection, women present at the Social Summit talked and answered the questions of journalists in the United States who were covering the summit for their local media.

At the Denmark end, I organized women from different parts of the world. Participants were Fatoumata Sire Dakite from the Association of Malian Women's Rights and member of the Coordinating Committee of the 180-Day Global Campaign; Ishrak Shamin from Pakistan and member of the Association of Development Agencies in her country; Rachel Kite from the USA and member of the International Women's Health Coalition; Eugenia Piza from Costa Rica and presently working in the Gender and Development Team of OXFAM in England; and Magaly Pineda from the Dominican Republic and advisor to the Latin American and Caribbean NGO Focal Point for the NGO Forum and the Fourth World's Conference on Women in Beijing.

Coordinating with us in the U.S., Frieda Werden of WINGS organized journalists for the radio show. Reporters were María Martin, executive producer of Latino USA, and Susan Richardson, a member of the editorial board of the *Austin-American Statesman*.

It was quite a complex operation. Frieda described her setup:

...[it] took place in the studios of KUT-FM [in Austin, Texas]. The transatlantic link was an ISDN line rented from the Dade International Radio Corporation and picked up at National Public Radio in Washington, where it was transmitted to Austin by a satellite. It was mixed and uplifted by another satellite channel for reception by other public radio stations.

At the other end it looked rather simple, although it probably was not! As FIRE walked into the magnificent studios installed at the conference site by the Danish Telephone Company, a woman technician was sitting at another ISDN telephone line and immediately welcomed me.

The line was not working, and I panicked. We were used to dealing with simple technology, and doing the controls ourselves. The Danish technician was as nervous as Katerina, Nancy, Jeanne, and I had been in previous live transmissions when something had gone wrong. To make matters worse, she could not talk to me because of language barriers. However, the problem was solved when, by some accidental magic touch, I hit something that opened the line, and the show went on.

Eugenia Piza talked about the campaign she was involved in:

We are here to demand a radical rethinking of the actual draft of the Platform for Action of the Fourth World Conference on Women. We are concerned that the present draft does not reflect the demands of the women's movement, North and South, East and West. We are trying to place macroeconomic issues as a gender agenda of this summit.

Asked by journalist Susan Richardson about the way in which women's concerns relate to poverty, Eugenia responded:

...people do not make connections between economic policy and women's well-being. It is usually assumed that women will make significant changes if they are granted their rights. However, the granting of rights requires an enabling environment, which makes the enjoyment of those rights a reality for women. What is the right to vote without informed choice?

Frieda Werden asked her how women in the NGO Forum received the news about the U.S. administration's announcement that it will grant, through the U.S. Agency for International Development (USAID), $11.7 million to keep girls in school in Africa, Asia, and Latin America. Eugenia answered, "It is a pitiful amount, not only given the needs, but the real potential that the USA has to provide aid. We cannot take it very seriously." When María Martin asked her about the media coverage, she said:

I believe that there is some coverage in the international papers, but the media image of the Social Summit is rather low. They look for the issues that [are] unusual, and the issues of social development and women are not of interest to them.

Fatoumata from Mali came on the air next. One of the co-sponsors of the 180-Days, 180-Ways Campaign, she talked about the event:

The whole day today was a day of women, in the plenary of the official conference, the halls, the NGO Forum. But the rally that is taking place now is the opening of the women's campaign. It seeks to place women's concerns and needs at the center of the agenda.

Asked by Susan Richardson about Malian women's main concerns, Fatoumata referred to "...poverty, effective social integration, and knowing their rights. The right to a job, shelter, participation in political and social life." She said that women from different regions can come up with a common agenda:

Discrimination against women exists in Mali and in the United States. It takes different forms, but it exists. In Mali working women have the right to maternity leave, and in the USA some working women do not benefit from this right. We need to share our expertise and experience.

Ishrak Shamin from Pakistan told the audience that she had come to the summit because she is a member of the steering committee of the Bangladesh NGO PREPCOM for the NGO Forum and FWCW. "We identified feminization of poverty as the number one issue for the South Asian region," she said. "That is why I am here, so that the governments take it into account." Frieda asked Ishrak about the problems in her country with programs for alleviation of poverty by which men feel that women should not receive special treatment. She replied:

In the field, it is a different situation. There, it is the women who are more successful in building the credit facilities and they are more serious. Women are getting more credit facilities, men are sending their wives, sisters, and mothers to organize and get the credit facilities, but men use the money for their own needs. Women have no control.

Frieda then asked about the acceptance of the ideas of the International Conference on Population and Development (Cairo, 1994) by some women in Bangladesh. Ishrak answered, "My view is that women should not be the targets of population policies, because women do not make the decisions, so males should be targeted!"

Rachel Kite from the USA was just returning from the negotiating table of government delegates when she came to the microphone:

I have just left the negotiations about basic needs, and one of the essential elements of individual basic needs is the right to health care, and for someone in particular it's also reproductive rights. This was agreed to in Cairo, but what we see here in Copenhagen are two things. One, a general lack of clarity among some delegates as to what it was that they agreed to in Cairo; and secondly, the desire by some forces— especially by those who were not happy with the Cairo agreements— to use the opportunity to roll back some of those agreements. I can happily announce that it has not prevailed. The document of this summit will reinforce what came out of Cairo.

Susan asked about financial commitments to population policies. Rachel responded that the Cairo financial package

...attacked the way in which population funds are spent. It basically says that they need to be reoriented to take a women's health and rights approach and deliver comprehensive services of which family planning is one. The discussion here [in Copenhagen] is wider, and therefore more complex, because it addresses the whole enabling economic environment. Women's health groups are here looking at the amount of money that is allocated to the provisions of basic services that are needed to deliver reproductive health services: primary health care systems worldwide, education systems, and the basic economy of countries. The two issues that are going to go down to the wire here in Copenhagen are the alleviation and eradication of debt and the release of new and additional resources for development.

Last on the show was Magaly Pineda from the Dominican Republic. She spoke in Spanish, while I did a live consecutive translation:

I'm very happy to be able to talk to you in Spanish. One of the special things that marks this summit is that women have the determination

to intervene decisively in macroeconomic policies and to prevent our governments from indebting us further, and that with the new links among women that have been established here, we will move into a better world.

FIRE ended the program by announcing to the audience that it was 7:00 p.m. in Denmark, and women were about to begin a candle-light march and vigil:

We will honor the women who 85 years ago, declared the 8th of March International Women's Day. [We will] honor the women who have died of violations of women's human rights throughout those 85 years, and [we will] bring in all the women who are not here, by remembering them in our candlelights!

Involving Youth in Radio

Another special feature on FIRE at the summit was made possible by an initiative of UNICEF and the Association for Progressive Communications (APC). Students from around the world were able to write about their concerns through e-mail to the heads of state at the Social Development Summit. Young people from 69 countries sent in thousands of messages this first time ever that the UN requested input from youth over the Internet.

While in Copenhagen during the meeting, Firuseh Shokoo and I collected many of the letters and read them on the live broadcasts. It was our first link of radio with the Internet, a connection that FIRE later expanded.

CHAPTER 7

FIREPLACE in China

Women in media in all the regions of the planet are undertaking efforts to make sure that the [UN Fourth World] Conference's agenda takes into account the need for support and funding of women's media such as women's publications, radio programs or stations, and women's television. The issue of equal participation in production, management, and decision-making in mainstream media has also been highlighted by women in media, in their advocacy and lobbying work to influence the Platform for Action that will come out of the conference.

—UNESCO, February 1995

More than 30,000 women and a few men gathered at the Fourth World Conference on Women (FWCW) and the NGO Forum, Women '95, in China in late August and early September of 1995. The event was not only of major importance because of its theme, but it was extra special to FIRE because one source of inspiration for the creation of FIRE came from the previous such meeting: the Third World Conference on Women in Nairobi, Kenya, in 1985.

Getting to Beijing was a long process, full of struggles, tears, laughter, and some (what seemed to be) miracles. As the conference drew nearer, we started strategizing with our women colleagues all over the world about how we could best participate. What follows is how our vision became a reality.

On Our Way to Beijing

Our journey to Beijing entailed eight preparatory planning stages before we were actually airborne for China. In those stops along the way to Beijing, we met with women's groups who were developing plans to be sure the important issues were included as an integral part of the conference.

First Stop: Mar del Plata, Argentina

The Latin American and Caribbean Regional Preparatory Meeting for Beijing was held in Mar del Plata, Argentina, in September of 1994, as was the accompanying NGO Forum. FIRE was there, along with hundreds of other women:

Welcome once again to FIRE broadcasting live. This time we have jumped from Cairo last week, to Mar del Plata, Argentina today. Come and share your voices without brackets.

Women from China, Thailand, Haiti, Cuba, Argentina, Costa Rica, Guatemala, Honduras, Chile, Barbados, Trinidad, Tobago, and Jamaica heeded the call. They shared their uncensored voices on the issues at stake at the conference.

Voices without brackets were the voices of the "democratizing rebellion of women" that Gina Vargas, convener of the NGO Forum, talked about in the introductory speech. They are the voices on FIRE's airwaves of rebellious Haitian women denouncing the injustice that is taking place in their country, the very same day the marines had come into their country without expelling the military.

Voices without brackets include the voice of Rebeca Cutie from Cuba denouncing the U.S. blockade against Cuba's aim to fulfill people's social, economic, civil, and political needs in the midst of a world crisis. They include the voice of the Panamanian worker who said that it was her first time at a conference, and she could not sleep that night from the excitement of finding out that women from so many other parts of the continent have the same concerns that she did. They are the voices of young women telling us on the air that they don't want the future for later, but they want it now. Voices without brackets were also represented in the voice of Supatra Mazdit, convener of the NGO Forum in Beijing, as she said, "What I have seen of the Latin American and Caribbean women in this, my first visit to the region, is that they not only want their claims to be met, but they want to change the world."

They were the voices of Chinese women belonging to nongovernmental organizations in their country, saying that the level of flexibility in organizing is something that they value in the women's movement of Latin America and the Caribbean.

Some special experiences happened to FIRE in Mar del Plata, as well. One was the radio work with the women from the Caribbean subregion at the meeting. A month beforehand, FIRE had called CAFRA (Caribbean Feminist Research Association) to let them know that the English program during the NGO meeting and the official conference was going to be dedicated exclusively to them, since it would probably be the only activity in their language.

As soon as women started gathering in Mar del Plata, FIRE looked for the Caribbean women to coordinate the live broadcasts in English. They had their own plan, having decided to take over the programs by planning them daily and collectively in their subregional caucus, and having their own host. Every day Ivette Dwlef, a radio woman in Barbados, interviewed the preselected guests.

Another very special experience was having Ana Virginia Duarte from CODEHUCA at the conference as a replacement for Katerina Anfossi, who was in her seventh month of pregnancy and was not able to travel. In less than one hour of on-the-spot training on using the tape recorder and coming live on the air as a host in the Spanish program, Ana Virginia brought to the airwaves her strength, energy, and capacity to communicate with women on FIRE.

See Chapter 2 for the full story of FIRE's experience at the Mar del Plata conference.

Second Stop: Toronto, Canada

According to the UN Education, Science and Culture Organization (UNESCO):

Media issues are for the first time prominently on the agenda of a conference on women. Therefore, the international community recognizes not only the place of the media in our societies and its growing role in shaping opinions and attitudes toward women and gender issues, but also its potential to make a far greater contribution to the advancement of women worldwide.

In 1994, UNESCO held seven regional workshops—in West Samoa, Cuba, Malaysia, Ecuador, Bulgaria, Tunisia, and Zimbabwe. In February of 1995 in Toronto, Canada, 130 media women came together at an international symposium entitled "Women and Media: Access to Expression and Decision-Making". A preconference to the United Nations Fourth World Conference on Women, the symposium was convened "to work out ways of improving women's representation in media."

There they drafted the Toronto Platform for Action, which specifies strategies for media enterprises, professional associations, educational and media training institutions, and governments to encourage and improve women's representation and leadership in the media.

Among the recommendations were: promotion of equal opportunity programs to ensure equal access by women and men to expression and decision-making; training in new technologies; preparation of guidelines for nondiscriminatory reporting; and monitoring and denunciation of attacks on media professionals who expose or speak out against extremists.

UNESCO's meeting not only drafted the declaration about the issue, but it acknowledged women's alternative media productions and their influence on mainstream media. At a forum entitled, "Demystifying Media for Social Change," which focused on ways of communicating information on women's issues, 180 radio, video, and written productions were displayed and screened. Selected productions were presented by UNESCO at the Fourth World Conference on Women. FIRE was given two of the four awards for radio production. (See the section on FIRE's Awards at the end of Chapter 11 for more information about these UNESCO awards and other awards FIRE has received.)

The World Association of Community Radio (AMARC) reported about the Toronto meeting as follows:

Panelists from developing countries compared the obstacles that women in the media face trying to be heard with the imbalance of reporting between North and South countries. Urvashi Butalia, editor of Kali for Women in India, said her publishing house was founded because "the concerns of the women's movement are not articulated in mainstream publishing." She continued, "Because of the Third-World perspective, both nationally and internationally, we felt on the receiving end of knowledge and wanted to do as UNESCO and reverse the flow of information."

Patricia Made, managing editor of the Zimbabwe-based Southern African Economist, *stressed the difficulties of writing stories that fall outside of the standard definition of news. She said, "One set of values becomes the norm.... We don't know how to test the waters of in-depth reporting, how to move outside of self-imposed censorship," a practice which takes place all over Africa.*

Butalia added, "The news is shaped by events, not process, and is made mostly by men." India is democratic, she said, "but censorship is imposed by the government," particularly on pornographic and politically sensitive material.

Moderato Barbara Barde, vice president of programming for the Women's Television Network (WTN) of Canada, said women in the media must examine, "How do we self censor so we don't even pitch a story anymore because [the editors] don't want to hear it?"

Self censorship can stem from other concerns, said Butalia. Her publishing house turned down a controversial Mauritania book, The Rape of Sita, *because "we were afraid of what would happen if we published it—it would have been suicide. We didn't want another Rushdie-like situation on our hands."*

Katia Gil, regional officer of the International Federation of Journalists (IFJ) in Venezuela, concurred: "In Latin America, self-censorship means that you are afraid." This fear can be for one's life or simply because as a journalist it is necessary to toe the line if you want to eat. In many Latin American countries, particularly Guatemala and El Salvador, censorship results because "there is little tolerance for criticism of the government," said Gil.

"Censorship is a very troubled issue, and freedom of expression is even more troubled. It has to be located in the political context," concluded Butalia.

Third Stop: Austin, Texas, USA

Also in February 1955, Nancy Vargas represented FIRE at the conference, Reframing Frontiers, held at Stonehaven Ranch near Austin, Texas. The conference brought together women working in radio, video and electronic communications from North and South America. The participants were IPAL, APC, Cine Mujer, Mujer a Mujer, CENECA, CALANDRIA, CEMINA, Puntos de Encuentro, FIRE, CICAM, SIPAM, LANETA, and Telemanitas.

The conference drew from, and aimed at building upon, previous plans for alternative media spaces as a basis for more work and discussion with other women's media groups. Convened by Telemanitas (a video network based in Mexico) and the Foundation for a Compassionate Society, one of the many objectives was to coordinate efforts for the Fourth World Conference on Women and the NGO Forum to be held in China.

What women in media at the Texas meeting wanted was expressed in one of the reports by Telemanitas:

Women's media groups are calling for a space dedicated to information and communications at the NGO Forum in Beijing. This space is critical to our ability to communicate and share information with each other as well as to effectively get our messages out to our constituencies and the world. More than a press room, we see this space as a place that will provide a space dedicated to women's alternative media; will allow communication/information groups to pool information and resources; will give us access to technical facilities; will include print, radio, electronic, video, popular, and other media; and will provide support services to women's alternative media.

The types of activities that could take place in the Alternative Media Space were already being planned by women's media groups present at the meeting:

- *FIRE*: Planning radio broadcasts by sending telephone transmissions to Radio for Peace International. It would broadcast women's stories and voices during the NGO Forum and official conference.

- *WINGS*: Planning a live women's radio call-in show between Beijing and the U.S., as well as cover the meetings.

- *IWTC*: Organizing a women's bookstore to sell books and videos, and possibly a women's alternative media center.

- *AMARC/FIRE/SIPAM*: Planning to collect six-minute cassettes of women's voices and concerns for Beijing. To be broadcast locally and at Beijing.

- *Chinese-American women's group*: Developing a portable dictionary of useful terms.

Other issues discussed at the meeting related to possible coordination of video work in Latin America, the Caribbean, and the USA. Throughout the conference, FIRE did daily live broadcasts from the kitchen table at Stonehaven.

Fourth Stop: Manitoba, Canada

In March 1995, I represented FIRE at the Twelfth Annual Conference of the Manitoba Committee for the UN End of the Decade for Women in Canada.

Titled Onward to Beijing: Hearing Women's Voices, the conference drew 300 women to Canada to make sure women's voices would be heard by governments before the Fourth World Conference on Women, to be sure that their issues would be on the agenda of the conference.

Women of color, migrant women, native women, women in government, and women who had gone to Nairobi 10 years earlier listened to each other. They also heard FIRE talk about radio, and they heard the Association for Progressive Communications talk about the advantages of electronic communications.

The event emphasized the need to develop media strategies so that all women's voices could be heard.

Canada's National Women's Television Network (WTN) discussed their recently begun TV station. FIRE was on their show that week, and we observed that, much like FIRE, the all-woman staff does the technical work, the broadcasting, the script writing, and everything else. I commented, "I felt like I was back home at FIRE... women running everything for themselves!"

Fifth Stop: Back in Costa Rica

In April 1995, FIRE drafted the final proposal about what had come to be known as the FIREPLACE, a place where FIRE would be broadcast live from China. There was confusion and controversy over where the NGO Forum would convene in China, but no matter where it would be, FIRE would be there. Shortly thereafter, the final decision was made to move the forum to Huairou, a town several miles from the site of the official UN conference in Beijing.

We issued a call to women around the world to start the process of organizing for live broadcasts. Many women's groups responded to the simple call (shown on the following two pages) to organize the broadcasts from the NGO Forum: Asia Pacific Media Task Force (South Pacific Islands), Tanzania Women's Media Collective (TAMWA), International Women's Tribune Center (IWTC), Women's Feature Service (India), the World Association of Community Radio (AMARC's Latin American and Caribbean Women's Desk), Women and Development KULU (Denmark), SIPAM (Mexico), RED ADA (Bolivia), Radio Tierra (Chile), Pacifica Radio (USA), Women's International News Gathering Service—WINGS (USA), Women Living Under Muslim Laws, the Youth Caucus, the Latin American and Caribbean Women's Health Network, the People's Decade of Human Rights Education (DHRE), the Foundation for a Compassionate Society, the

CALL TO WOMEN IN RADIO AROUND THE WORLD:
WHAT?

A FIRE-PLACE is being organized to do an eight-hour daily SHORTWAVE LIVE BROADCAST on Feminist International Radio Endeavour (FIRE) at Radio For Peace International.

Feminist International Radio Endeavour (FIRE) is a shortwave radio program produced and broadcast in Spanish and in English daily by Radio For Peace International, a shortwave non-commercial radio station located on the campus of the University for Peace in Costa Rica. It reaches over 100 countries worldwide.

WHERE?

At the NGO FORUM as part of a Women's Alternative Media Action and Service Center at the 4th United Nations World Conference on Women to be held in Beijing, China in September, 1995.

The aim of the Center is to celebrate and demonstrate the work of women's alternative media networks, provide services for women's alternative media networks attending the NGO FORUM, and facilitate strategizing around media policy for the Platform for Action being considered at the official Conference.

The FIRE-PLACE will consist of two glass rooms located in the middle of the CENTER: one for the shortwave broadcasts, and one for production, telephone reports to local radio stations and reception of letters from the E-Mail Conference. Each will have an international telephone line, telephone interface for quality sound through phone, and editing equipment.

WHO?

The Women's Alternative Media Action and Service Center will be the product of a broad coordinated effort. The emerging core group for the activity are: ISIS Manila, ISIS Santiago, FIRE, TAMWA, APDC Malaysia and the International Women's Tribune Center.

In keeping with the aims of the Action and Service Center, Radio FIRE broadcasts will: celebrate the work of women's alternative media; ensure wide coverage of the event beyond that provided by other media; allow women to participate without leaving home; and provide a case study to support the efforts of alternative women's media networks, and efforts to establish a women's satellite into the next century.

The emerging core group for the Radio FIRE-PLACE initiative within the Center are: AMARC—World Association of Community Radios, RCNA—Radio Caribbean News Agency, TAMWA—Tanzania Women's Media Collective, WINGS—Women's International News Gathering Service, and FIRE.

WHAT'S IN IT FOR YOU?

FIRE is currently networking with women around the world who do local radio programs so that they can organize their own segments on FIRE's broadcasts in Beijing from the 30th of August to the 8th of September from 8:00 a.m. to 4:00 p.m. in China.

Segments will include the following: news, E-mail messages from women, reports for the caucuses, radio speak outs, interviews, live coverage from the entire Forum, music, poetry, etc.

If you are interested in taking part in the programming, you are most welcome to do so in any of the following RADIO ACTIVITIES:

1. You can take responsibility for organizing a half hour segment of the eight hours every day in any of the following languages: Spanish, English, French or Portuguese. (Other languages can be used for special programs, so long as you organize on-site translation into any of the four languages)

2. You can organize and host one of the segments of the newscast program every day.

3. You can bring relevant audio tape productions that you have produced to be broadcast on THE FIRE-PLACE.

4. You can produce programs right there.

5. You can record interviews, panels, press conferences and women's meetings to report about them on THE FIRE-PLACE.

6. You can help us organize an E-mail Conference, process the letters to read on the air while at the NGO FORUM, and answer the letters.

7. Contact and line up women's networks and caucuses to come on the air to speak about special issues.

204

Central American Human Rights Commission (CODEHUCA), and individual journalists Nadezhda Azhgikhina from Russia and Varaporn Chamsanit from Thailand.

When she learned about our plans, Florence Butewa of WILDAF in Africa said, "What a great name for the place that FIRE will organize in China! Did you know that in Africa, the fireplace is where people gather to talk and share?"

The month of April was central to the organizing of FIREPLACE activities. FIRE had to figure out a way to create a two-way communications venue in Beijing—between the women who would be in China and the international audience who would not be there but would communicate through media.

A format of call-in shows for the FIREPLACE would have been expensive, as FIRE would have had to pay for two open phone lines from China while the broadcasts were on, and we would have had to provide for collect calls from all over the world. This alternative was out of the question. FIRE's best bet was electronic mail, but training in the use of cybercommunication was necessary, as FIRE had a kind of "cyberallergy" that had prevented us from getting online.

Ana Sisnet (Technomama) from the Foundation for a Compassionate Society came to Costa Rica to train FIRE staff (and to help us overcome our cyberallergy) so we could include the information superhighway in our strategy for the FIREPLACE.

FIRE learned to use e-mail, and the next day we were connected to the rest of the world, this time not only through shortwave, but also through computer communications. When the first e-mail came in, it was like magic to us.

Date: Sat, 22 April 1995 16:01:12—0700
From: Institute for Global Communications
Subject: Re: Greetings from Austin, Texas
Dear Friends of the Family Learning Centers: What a wonderful surprise for FIREmamas to have opened the mail ALONE FOR THE FIRST TIME, and find such a beautiful message from such a beautiful family. We know something about it from conversations with Ana Sisnet, our trainer!
Regards: Katerina and María from FIREMAMA.

Sixth Stop: Bridgetown, Barbados

Young women's voices were also given priority on FIRE prior to the Fourth World Conference on Women. Perhaps this is because of Mary Powers of the Ms. Foundation, who organized a Girls' Speakout during the last PREPCOM for Beijing, which we played on FIRE very often. Mary's words stayed with us: "Girls are our forward-looking strategies." Or perhaps it was because, when given the chance, girls are perfect radio women for FIRE.

This is what happened in Barbados on May 12 during the Strategies Meeting convened by DAWN and the Latin American and Caribbean Focal Point for Beijing. Susie Sen, daughter of Gita Sen from India, was trained by FIRE on the spot. She thus became the youngest forward-looking replacement for FIRE's staff in the future... but also in the present. Susie did interviews and took responsibility for the technical controls. Vivian Wee of DAWN was her selected guest on FIRE for the following script:

SUSIE: Good morning, my name is Susie Sen and today I will be interviewing Vivian Wee, with María from FIRE. Vivian, what did you say this morning at the discussion?

VIVIAN: What I said this morning is that there has been a conflict of realities. We women think that this is going to be a women's conference. But it is becoming clearer that this is a conference of governments, by governments, about women. Women are becoming the objects of discussion. This has placed us in a worse position than we were in previous conferences. We were the discussers at the conference on environment, for example. Even the site of the forum has been placed far away so that we have less of an input.

MARÍA: What role do you see women's media having in this context?

VIVIAN: We need a balance between being pro-active and reactive. We need to respond to the challenges, but if we only react, we will be thrown in all directions. We need to know our long-term strategies: what will constitute a women's agenda for development for the twenty-first century... the change of venue cannot distract us.

SUSIE: Thank you. In Barbados, this is Susie Sen and María Suárez of FIRE, with Vivian Wee from Singapore.

Seventh Stop: Kalmar, Sweden

The Institute for Further Education of Journalists (FOJO), based in Kalmar, Sweden, convened a 10-day institute in June 1995 for 20 Third-World women. These women were mainstream and alternative media communicators who would take part in the coverage of the FWCW. It was one of FOJO's International Women and Media Seminars, which they have held every year since 1991.

Women from Bangladesh, China, Costa Rica, India, Jordan, Kenya, Malaysia, Sri Lanka, Algeria, Morocco, Pakistan, Brazil, Malawi, Perú, Nepal, Ghana, Mongolia, Papua New Guinea, South Africa, Haiti, and Zimbabwe were all there. They met to share what they would do in China, to learn more about the conference in Beijing, to share an assessment about women in media in their respective countries, to learn about women in Sweden, and to develop a strategy toward a collaboration on the coverage of the UN world conference.

The highlight of the meeting was the drafting, by the 20 women, of what was later known in Beijing as The Kalmar Declaration. It is a five-page document in which the signatories assess the current situation of feminism, freedom of the press, the image of women in the media, and the status of women the world over. The document, which is reprinted in part on the following pages, also contains a series of recommendations and strategies to pursue in preparation for the FWCW and in each woman's own country and region.

In the press statement drafted by the group of women about the Kalmar Declaration, they state:

> *The struggle for gender justice goes beyond the fight for women's equal opportunities and equal rights... women's human rights are inextricably linked with the very concept of justice for all... feminism in its true perspective also recognizes the basic injustices that exist among nations, within nations, and within societies due to race, class, ethnicity, age, abilities, sexual orientation and religion.*

Participants also organized a workshop convened by FOJO to be held in China in which women media practitioners would read, discuss, and sign their names to the Kalmar Declaration.

KALMAR DECLARATION

Adopted by the participants at the International Women and the Media Seminar convened by FOJO in Kalmar, Sweden from 19-28 June 1995.

Preamble

We, women in the media, meeting in Kalmar from 19-28 June 1995 , to discuss the role of women in the media, in preparation for the Fourth UN World Conference on Women and the NGO Forum '95 to be held in Beijing, state the following:

- That we are media women from 20 countries comprising five regions: Africa, Latin America, Asia, the Middle East and Eastern Europe.

- That throughout the 10 days of discussions and exchange, and throughout our participation in the preparatory processes toward the Beijing Conference, we have been guided by and herein acknowledge the efforts of women to have the issues of women in media included for consideration in the final Declaration and Platform of Action for the World's Women.

- Among these documents are: the Bangkok Declaration of the "Women Empowering Communication Conference" in February 1994; the Regional NGO documents and Platforms of Action of the Ministerial Conferences of Asia and the Pacific, Latin America and the Caribbean, Africa, the Middle East, and Europe and North America; the Toronto Platform for Action adopted in the UNESCO International Symposium on "Women and the Media: Access to Expression and Decision-Making" in March 1995; and the official and NGO documents from the Final Preparatory Meeting in March 1995.

- That while these documents call for commitments and action from media organizations, governments, and international bodies, there is need for us women in the media to state our assessment of our situation and the issues involved and to declare our commitment to specific and concrete actions that we ourselves can undertake.

I. ON FEMINISM

Feminism is perceived by many, especially in the media, as a rather threatening phenomenon, regarded as a fanatic movement of unhappy women who have been unsuccessful in their private, and perhaps professional, lives. This attitude may stem mainly from the dynamism with which the feminist movement has grown and developed throughout the world, so that there is fear that women will soon take over men's dominant place in society.

This may explain why we now find ourselves struggling against an anti-feminist backlash, symbolized as a whiplash which comes back with the same force with which one cracks the whip. The backlash is especially reflected in media portrayals, government policies, and an increasingly strident campaign among conservative groups in religion and other sectors of society.

We believe it is fitting therefore to expound on what feminism truly means to us as women, particularly as women working in the media.

Feminism to us means the ability to create a just society where both men and women can affirm their diversity with choices and full participation in the development process.

Feminism is about gender justice whereby our bodies, the home, the streets, the workplaces and the planet are all places of security for women. It is then that gender violence, discrimination and subordination of women would no longer be issues.

Feminism includes but goes beyond women's rights as it deals with gender justice which is integral to the concept of justice for all.

Women's rights to us mean equal opportunities, equal rights and universal human rights. Feminism, however, recognises basic injustices that also exist among nations and within societies based on race, class, ethnicity, age, abilities, sexual orientation and religion. There is also imbalance in the way we relate to the environment. Feminism therefore seeks to contribute to the eradication of these injustices.

Along with taking part in the meeting, FIRE interviewed the women about the significance of the declaration. Rouquia Alami from Palestine said that for Palestinian women and for Beijing itself, "The document is very good for lobbying for the Platform for Action, and also [a statement of] what to be aware of in terms of media for the next 10 years."

Malaysia's Pang Yin Fong believes that the Kalmar Declaration is an important step toward "making right the portrayal of women in media, because it shows the personal convictions about what is not right in media now."

Orie Rogo-Manduli from Kenya affirmed that the declaration is an instrument to work with in her country. "This will go a long way, because it has the feeling of women worldwide," she said.

Jordanian Leila Debb agreed that it will be valuable as an instrument for women and media in her country where there is little work about women and media as such, although women constitute 50 percent of the journalists in the country.

Rina Jimenez David from the Philippines pointed out the significance of the document as a statement of women in mainstream and in alternative media:

This is the first document I have encountered in which women in mainstream and alternative media have come out and declared themselves as feminists, openly, have produced their own analysis of feminism in the world, and have linked feminism to our work in the media.

Sometimes women in the media have locked themselves outside of the mainstream of the women's movement. We have felt like resources for their needs, and we have distanced ourselves as observers and reporters. Now, with this declaration, we are proclaiming that we are taking our place within the mainstream of the international women's movement, that women in media have our own thoughts, work, and analyses to contribute to the women's movement, that we are not conduits or instruments only, but that we contribute to the growth of the movement.

I will use the document to begin a dialogue between women in mainstream media and women in alternative media for some sort of work that we might do together. In Beijing, the issue of women in the media will be highlighted with this declaration as yet another lobbying document.

Nerun Yakub from Bangladesh affirmed that she was glad that the Kalmar Declaration defines our position as feminists:

As feminists we are deep humanists because we look at the human state of affairs in terms of development, a just world.... today, everything has become a commodity, and feminists fight that. There is a distorted idea about feminism, so I am glad we are taking the declaration to China.

Chinese journalist Chen Ya said:

The most important thing about the Kalmar Declaration for Chinese women is the concept of feminism. There, people usually think that feminism is something very funny. With this declaration, we can see that feminism is the ability to create a just society where both men and women can affirm their diversity with choices and full participation in the development process. It is very important for women in China to know these ideas.

The Eastern European women stated that many of the concepts had been new to them, but now they have an instrument to take back to help them work with women journalists in their countries.

FIRE also organized a live broadcast from Kalmar, in which some of the participants talked about their experiences at the seminar.

With Chen Ya from China, FIRE created a radio Mandarin Chinese–English dictionary: FIRE asked Chen Ya a world in English, and Chen Ya repeated it in Chinese. A fun dictionary that was, for FIRE had asked the 19 journalists to write down the words they would want to know before going to China. Some of the requests for phrases in Chinese were very pragmatic:

I'm lost, show me the way to Huairou!

How do I get from Huairou to Beijing?

Where is the bathroom?

What is the price of this?

But it is too expensive!

211

Other phrases expressed the main concerns that women were bringing to China: *violence against women, women's rights, equality, human rights, journalist, communications,* and *reproductive rights.* Some words requested for the dictionary were evidence of the attitude with which women from other parts of the world were going to meet women from China:

What is your name?

What do you think about this issue?

Welcome to this workshop!

The experience of recording the dictionary was a great indicator of the language barriers that women would face, but also of the ways women find to overcome them. FIRE also created a Spanish version of the dictionary and distributed it in Latin America and the Caribbean. A similar dictionary was made in Swahili and taken by Orie from Kenya and by Fatima Alloo from Tanzania back to their countries.

Eighth Stop: Lima, Perú

A Strategic Adjustment Meeting of women from Latin America and the Caribbean aimed at designing the plan of activities of the regional women's NGOs in Beijing took place in Perú between August 20 and 22, 1995. Katerina Anfossi was FIRE's representative at that meeting.

The representatives of the subregional focal points of Brazil, the Southern Cone, the Andean Region, the Caribbean, Mexico, and Central America were convened by Gina Vargas and her Focal Point Team for the region to develop a plan that aimed at:

> *...influencing the Platform for Action that will be approved at the Fourth World Conference on Women, and rendering visibility to the political proposals of women from our own region in the NGO Forum.*
> —Letter of Invitation to participants

Communication was identified as an area for special attention for giving visibility to the region within the forum and the conference, and to report to the regional constituency in China about the development of both the official conference and the NGO Forum. It was considered critical to coordinate information about women's activities and to create a team of journalists and communicators to disseminate information to the media.

"Beijing: More than Mere Words" was the theme under which Latin American and Caribbean women left the last regional meeting before the conference. With this plan and many concerns about what to expect in China, women went back to their countries to prepare for Beijing.

The Last Stage: Flight to China

Just before the Beijing conference, a set of unmet promises had to be faced by women globally. Many women in all regions were being denied their visas, although the Chinese Organizing Committee (COC) had made a commitment to give visas to all registered participants. FIRE's staff members were among the first to be denied visas in the Chinese Embassy in Mexico, although we had presented all of our documents. We finally received our visas, thanks to an international campaign launched by the International Women's Tribune Center.

In addition to our trademark bags of radio equipment, we carried along the expectation of being able to produce the daily four-hour live broadcasts with women in community radio and women in alternative media from around the world. We had a detailed schedule of participants who had prepared to produce shows from China: fuel for the FIREPLACE.

We left Costa Rica alone, but women boarded the plane at every stop, and by the time we arrived in China, women had filled the plane.

Our work began while we were still airborne. A woman from the United States recognized us on the plane and came with her tape recorder so that Katerina could train her to become a radio woman for the FIREPLACE during the NGO Forum.

Others came to tell us that they had heard about our problems with visas and had written to the United Nations asking to put pressure on the embassy in Mexico. Indeed, we got our visas because many women's groups throughout the world mobilized, along with a former Undersecretary General of the UN and a Latin American Ambassador to the UN. More people than we had thought had worked to secure our visas for us. They were convinced that the FIREPLACE had to happen!

A special greeting that had been requested by FIRE through a flight attendant came over the loudspeaker of the airplane: "United Airlines wants to congratulate all the women on the plane who are traveling to take part in the conference. In five minutes we will be landing in China." Applause followed. We all had made it!

Beijing: The End of the Long Journey and a New Beginning

Upon our arrival at the airport, hundreds of young Chinese men and women helped us at the different stages of disembarkation. We had learned that Chinese people who volunteered to work at the conference had to learn a list of 500 English words. The government would have done women a great favor if they would have given us the list! Sometimes it took us a long time to use the right word. Here is a typical exchange:

> *I have to wait for my suitcase.*
> *Excuse me, please, I do not understand.*
> *Bags? Luggage? Briefcase? Backpack?*
> *Wait a moment, please!*

Moving into our hotels in Huairou was an adventure. When the security guard—a nice young girl—opened our radio equipment bag, she almost died. "What is it?" she asked. (There were more than 500 words just inside that bag!)

Radio equipment? electronics? radio gear? instruments for broadcasts?... I put together a no-language show. I took out one of the microphones, and began a make-believe broadcast. The guard understood but then began to look even more perplexed. "Wait a moment, please!" And she ran out to get the head of security.

He came and looked at the equipment, but could not say anything or ask anything. Perhaps the heads of security did not have to learn the 500 words. He did, however, let us register at the hotel.

The next day—two days before the NGO Forum was to begin—we went to the venue of the FIREPLACE: the Women's Alternative Media

214

Action and Service Center (WAMASC). Nothing was ready! Everything else around it was set up. The mainstream media center had carpeting, chairs, tables, computers, telephones, and faxes. It also had a big bright sign in front: The Business Center. It was time to bring our contingency plans into play. (See Chapter 11 for a discussion of the technical planning that preceded our trip to China.)

The blueprint for the FIREPLACE had long been sent to the Chinese Organizing Committee. Joan Ross Frankson of the International Women's Tribune Center had left a week before us, money in hand, to make sure the place was built within the Women's Alternative Media Action and Service Center.

The difficulties that women's media face all over the world were exemplified that day in China. It was happening again—the unpredictable!

We had to take matters into our own hands. We started clearing the place, asking the workers to put tiles on the dirt and cleaning up the mess. Hardly anything media-related happened there that day or the next.

At that point—the day before the inauguration of the forum—we had given up the idea of the glass, soundproof FIREPLACE that had been our best-case scenario, but the phone line was not there either!

That evening Catherine, a young woman member of the team who had been working to get the Chinese Organizing Committee to agree to finish the WAMASC on time, went as pale as can be:

I was just told by the COC that there will be no booth for the FIRE-PLACE, and no phone line for the broadcasts. I am so sorry. I worked hard on it. Now I do not know what has happened... there is nothing I or you can do.

I do not remember that moment very well now, but I do know that I burst out crying. I felt like the world was crumbling down on me. I had such a feeling of powerlessness that I was paralyzed!

After a while a couple of journalists and communicators passing by came across the scene. Both were women who had worked with FIRE at previous meetings: a journalist from Thailand and a radio woman from the Fiji Islands who had registered to do programs at the FIRE-PLACE. They were shocked and dismayed. "No, it can't be," they said.

"The FIREPLACE has to take place. It is ours by right.... Wait here, we'll take care of that."

At a table only 18 yards away sat the women who make up the NGO Facilitating Committee and the Chinese Organizing Committee, discussing the final arrangements about the coverage of the Inaugural Act the next day. The journalists from Fiji and Thailand approached their regional representatives, got them out of the meeting, and talked to them about our missing FIREPLACE.

Neither one needed an explanation. Both representatives—Supatra Mazdit of Thailand and Salamo Fulivai of the South Pacific—knew about the FIREPLACE in detail from newspaper reports or personal connections. In less than 10 minutes they addressed Madame Huang Quizao, vice chairperson of the COC. She agreed to allow the FIRE-PLACE to happen, signed the letter authorizing the international direct telephone line, and set the process going. However, it would take a couple of days because the line had not been assigned in the previous planning process. The COC had been concerned about direct live broadcasting from the NGO Forum and were resisting letting it happen.

The women returned to me, only to find me crying even harder. "Now I am crying of joy because of what I just saw happen," I told them. "FIRE has always believed that it has developed because of the existence of a strong women's movement. But today I felt it stronger than ever!"

Indeed, the next day, August 30, FIRE went on the air. Its phone line at the NGO Forum was delayed until September 1, but the Asia and Pacific Women in Media had given us their hotel room, which had a direct international line.

On September 1st we finally went on the air from the FIREPLACE at the WAMASC of the NGO Forum. It was magic: there was no glass booth, we were out in the open surrounded by many women communicators who had created a beautiful and colorful media center.

The following is the script of the first live broadcast from the FIRE-PLACE:

NARRATOR: Today, a huge cloud of transparent, clean smoke is coming out of the FIREPLACE. It has been possible because of the warmth of the alternative media women's movement, those who are here and

216

those who have stayed behind in their countries also spreading the word that women are here to demand our rightful place in society and in this forum.

Control: Music by Sinnead O'Connor, "FIRE on Babylon"

NARRATOR: The Hopi Indians of the Sierras in South America have an ancient story that talks about how, if one were able to fly beyond the earth, as you looked back down, you would see, instead of people's bodies, the fire in them. Millions of fires: big ones, small ones, dwindling fires, and strong fires... little sparks in some, and shinning flame on others. The fire that you would see in this FIREPLACE today is hot and strong.

Control: Music

NARRATOR: Welcome to Feminist International Radio Endeavour—FIRE—broadcasting live, at last, from the FIREPLACE at The Women's Alternative Media Action and Service Center in Huairou, China, venue of the Women's Nongovernmental Organizations Forum that has brought together the sparks of women from all regions of the globe. Those who are here have also brought the light of the hot-hearted protest for those who could not make it.

Control: Music

NARRATOR: Women in alternative media have created a space here, in the midst of the forum, where women communicators can celebrate and demonstrate the work of our networks. This center also provides services for women to communicate, while at the same time it facilitates strategizing around media policy for the Platform for Action to be considered at the Fourth World Conference on Women to be held in Beijing next week.

The FIREPLACE for shortwave radio broadcasting is proudly a part if it, and when I said that women in alternative media created this space, I meant it literally. Here, women have had to light this FIRE from the ashes.

Control: Music

NARRATOR: Thus, what we are really celebrating here today with our first broadcast from the FIREPLACE is nothing else but women's tenacity to put this place together. Welcome to the FIREPLACE. It will definitely be burning until the last day!

From the 30th of August to the 8th of September, FIRE went on the air systematically, bringing women's voices to an international audience that could not attend the event:

Welcome to FIRE, broadcasting live from Huairou, venue of the NGO Forum, Women '95. As we begin the first FIREPLACE live broadcast, the more than 17,000 women already gathered here are making final arrangements to begin the more than 5,000 panels and workshops that have been registered for the next 10 days. As we open this broadcast, women from all regions and all walks in life are traveling from Huairou to Beijing to take part in the Inaugural Act that will begin at 5:00 p.m. at the Workers Stadium. With us today are Katerina Anfossi, María Suárez, and Nancy Vargas from FIRE, with the support of Firuseh Shokoo and Sara Benitez....

In Huairou, the FIREPLACE was a simple corner with friendly radio technology fit to broadcast through an international telephone line. Equipped with a telephone interface, a mixer, and five microphones, women celebrated the work of women's own media. We provided a case study to support women's efforts to establish women's satellites and a broader voice in the world of shortwave radio in the next century. We ensured wide coverage of the events beyond that provided by other media, and we allowed women and men to participate without leaving their homes.

Reports about the FIREPLACE were featured in two of the main newspapers published during the NGO Forum and official conference. Chinese journalist Ma Dan of the *World Women*, a *China Daily* publication during the activities, wrote an article (September 7, 1995) entitled, "Shortwave Radio Is on FIRE", in which she said:

In one corner of the building next to the Business Press Center of the forum site, which few participants pay attention to, the Women's

218

Alternative Media Action and Service Center has a base... FIRE is doing live broadcasts!

Another article was published in *The Earth Times*, in its section entitled Beijing Watch. Women's Feature Service journalist Linda Newman reported (September 9,1995) about us under the title: "Setting the Airwaves on Fire," in which she said:

> *It was supposed to have been broadcast out of a soundproof glass booth at the NGO Forum. But the FIREPLACE—Feminist International Radio Endeavour—has been burning up the airwaves since day one, despite the unsuccessful attempt to secure a noise-free environment from the forum organizers. The setback was no detriment for the FIREPLACE.... Program producers, hosts, and engineers from 17 countries are participating in the FIREPLACE daily programs at the forum, with others lined up hoping for a spot on the air. For most, FIRE is their best bet to get their voices and concerns heard internationally.*

Many other media featured FIRE prior to the Beijing conference and during the broadcasts. In July 1995, we were written about in the *Latin American and Caribbean Newsletter Towards Beijing '95*, the *NGO FORUM Newsletter*, *People and the Planet*, and in *Vista* of RFPI in Costa Rica. In Thailand's newspaper, *The Nation*, an article by Veraporn Chamsanit described the plans for the FIREPLACE.

August reviews appeared in *The Tribune* of the IWTC in New York, on the worldwide web in Womensnet of APC, on WBAI's Talk in the Morning with Patrika Dallas, in *The San Francisco Chronicle*, on the Voice of America, and on TV Channels 16 and 15 in Costa Rica.

The publicity continued in September with reviews on WETV (September 3), CNN (September 4), and the Latin American and Caribbean Communications Team (September 6). Articles appeared in Costa Rica's *The Tico Times*, *World Women* of the *China Daily*, and in *The News*, reported by Casandra Balchin of Lahore, India.

Anchors of the daily Spanish program were FIRE's staff Katerina Anfossi and Nancy Vargas with the support of Olga Rey from Spain. I was host of the English programs, with the support of Firuseh Shokoo from Puerto Rico and Christine Butewa from Uganda.

Productions at the Swedish conference were the result of a coordinated effort of many women's groups that had previously registered to take part in broadcasts from Beijing:

- Asia Pacific Media Task Force (South Pacific Islands)
- Tanzania Women's Media Collective (TAMWA)
- International Women's Tribune Center (IWTC)
- Women's Feature Service (India)
- The World Association of Community Radio (AMARC's Latin American and Caribbean Women's Desk)
- Women and Development KULU (Denmark)
- SIPAM (Mexico)
- RED ADA (Bolivia)
- Radio Tierra (Chile)
- The People's Decade of Human Rights Education (DHRE)
- The Latin American Women's Health Network, Pacifica Radio (USA)
- Women's International News Gathering Service—WINGS (USA)
- Women Living Under Muslim Laws
- The Youth Caucus
- Individual journalists Nadezhda Azhgikhina from Russia and Varaporn Chamsanit from Thailand

We also made our international telephone line available for radio women to receive phone calls from local radio stations in their own countries in order to send in their reports. Women on the Line from Australia, and Beijing Watch Women's Center in the Philippines did their broadcasts from the FIREPLACE. Rina Jimenez David, a Philippine journalist, reported about this in her local radio program:

August 31, 1995. Manila. FIRE plays host to the first Tele-Press Conference of Beijing Watch Women's Center, an information center on the Women's Conference. Speaker was Remmy Rikken of the

Philippines who spoke to members of Philippine media. Maraming Salamat to FIRE!

Others, such as Women's Feature Service from India, Viqui Lofquist from the U.S., World Association of Community Radios (AMARC), and the Pacific Media Task Force brought radio productions and music to play on the programs.

Another feature of the FIREPLACE was the use of electronic media combined with shortwave radio to expand the voices on FIRE even further. A group of women at the Central American Human Rights Commission (CODEHUCA) were trained by FIRE to listen to the programs and report about them in other media. Throughout the 17 days of broadcasting they monitored the programs in Costa Rica and produced a daily press release for written media, women's groups, and electronic mail networks.

The Association for Progressive Communications (APC) created a FIRE web page from Beijing and provided us with an e-mail account through which we received many reception reports from all over the world. Some were in English:

From: Joan Boyle
Organization: Dowling College
To: fireplace@wcw.apc.org
Subject: Keep it burning!!!!
Just received your FIREPLACE in N Y. Congratulations and keep the Fire going. We're counting on you!
All the clippings from the NY Times will be in the mail soon to C R. We're standing with you!!!!!!
With love, Joan, Jim.

Others were in Spanish, like this one received from England, thanking FIRE for providing information in both languages, and for providing "a Latin American perspective about all of it."

Estimadas colegas:
Me parecen muy buenos los informes que estan enviando sobre el foro de ONGs y el esfuerzo de ponerlos en dos idiomas. Lo que les

recomiendo es que envien los informes en ingles a las conferencias en ese idioma. Sería bueno que usaran tambien la <africa.wcw.news> y la <apngowid.meet>.... ¡Adelante con el trabajo! Nos viene bien tener una visión latinoamericana sobre todo esto.

Saludos:Dafne Plou
Equipo de Informacion de Londres
Date: Tue, 5 Sep 1995

More than 200 women's voices came on the air to talk about their experiences and their perspectives on the issues at stake. The 17 groups that produced programs brought a broad group of guests on the air. Not one single region of the world was excluded.

Delta Pasingan from Papua New Guinea was one of the producers at the FIREPLACE. A member of the Asia Pacific Women's Media Task Force, she later shared with FIRE what the experience had meant to her and her group:

I never thought I would see something like the FIREPLACE in Huairou. It certainly put a lot of fire among the women in media from the Pacific Islands. After the broadcasts, we had two discussions. One was with the Melanesian Spearhead Group which includes women from Vanuatu, Fiji, Solomon Islands, and Papua New Guinea. The other discussion was among the Pacific Media Task force. We talked about how wonderful it would be to have something like FIRE in the region. You know, a mobile radio station would help women from small islands work together!

Another thing that came out of the FIREPLACE that has created a lot of interest is that somehow your broadcast was picked up by women in radio in Melbourne, Australia. The Pacific Bit Program recorded the broadcast and used it in their own program on Radio Australia.... after Beijing, the producer in Australia sent me a copy of the tape, and now it is being broadcast locally in my region.

A rainbow of diverse women had their voices heard internationally from the FIREPLACE: black women, white women, and mulattas; women with disabilities and able-bodied women; indigenous women and mestizas; girls, young women, middle aged and older women;

lesbians, bisexual, and heterosexual women; women from the North, South, East, and West; married women and single women; women who were official delegates at the UN meeting, women belonging to NGOs and grassroots organizations, and women in specialized agencies.

Those "voices without brackets" spoke about the themes of the agenda of the NGO Forum: Politics and Economy; Environment; Humankind Peace and Security; Human Rights; Political Governance; Education, Health, Arts and Culture; Religion; Science and Technology; and Media and Communications. Many spoke about the situation of women in their countries of origin. They also related the themes of the forum to the issues covered at the official UN conference: Development, Peace, and Equality.

CODEHUCA's reports of FIRE's broadcasts provide a sample of these women's words. Petrona Sandoval, of the Association of Nicaraguan Women with Disabilities, reported that the issue of women with disabilities is frequently silenced. Veronica Chavarria offered her opinion on this situation. She is a Nicaraguan woman who has a visual disability and is a member of the Autonomous Commission of Blind Women of Nicaragua. Veronica asserted:

> Despite difficulties, it has been our challenge to come here and give testimony on our accomplishments as well as our difficulties. Similarly, we expect to receive the solidarity of the women participating in the NGO Forum and the official conference to bring increased visibility to the issue.

In an interview for FIRE, Alicia Fournier, head of the official delegation of Costa Rica, gave her opinion on the issue of resources, saying:

> It is certain that economic means are indispensable to gain progress in these countries; however, we, from our governmental level, must consider and revise our own budgets and channel resources to programs for women.

With respect to Costa Rica, she added:

> We cannot forget that we are half of the population. Nor that we are in a process of state reform, a moment of transition in which we will

revise, reform, and look ahead, and look where we are allocating our
budget. In addition, we should be thinking of how to promote the par-
ticipation of civil society in looking for solutions.

Sonia Casino from El Salvador, a delegate of the Inter-American
Institute for Human Rights, explained how the Salvadoran Women's
Platform was built after a process supported by 40 Salvadoran
women's associations who consulted with 600 women from different sectors. Some of the topics mentioned in the survey that are
now incorporated in the national agenda are violence, work, health,
and sexuality. She said, "This will serve as a guide for the work in El
Salvador after Beijing."

Beverly Ditsie of Soweto, South Africa, was interviewed by FIRE
the day before she was to represent the lesbian caucus at the plenary of
the official conference about the need to recognize sexual orientation.
"Feminism to me is about women having choices, it's about women
knowing that women have choices."

Sonia Correa, delegate of the Women's Health Network of Latin
America and the Caribbean, who was an observer of the official meeting, reported that the most significant event that could change the
course of discussion was the meeting of the G-77. Prior to the conference, the members of the group had decided to take an individual position on the issue of women's health:

At the current moment, however, they have indicated a new intent.
At their meeting they are seeking a consensus position to lift the
brackets. The women's NGOs stress the need for action to be taken
in each country.

Gina Vargas, NGO Forum coordinator for Latin American and the
Caribbean, talked about the role of religious groups as decisionmakers:

Religious postures should not be imposed on the states. We cannot
allow the Vatican to reverse the advances made in other global meet-
ings, like in Cairo. What women don't achieve through the official
platform will be achieved in our countries and regions through the
action of civil society.

Ligia Martin, coordinator of the Women's Rights Program of the Ombudsperson's office of Costa Rica, came on the air to say that "structural changes are needed."

When the NGO FORUM was over, FIRE broadcast the voices of women's groups accredited to attend the United Nations' official conference. The studios of Radio China International at the conference were the location for the FIREPLACE on that occasion.

The Chinese staff there shared their space with FIRE during the late-night hours so the broadcasts could continue until the last day of the event. At last, the FIREPLACE had a glass booth studio! Although we did not have a common language when we began broadcasting with the support of their technicians, soon we developed sign language to direct the operations.

A thumb up meant "open microphone now," and a thumb down meant the opposite. A thumb to the left meant "fade in tape deck now," and to the right, it meant "fade out tape deck now." Soon after the first such broadcast in Spanish, all the staff of Radio China gathered around the FIREPLACE to watch the show.

Many of the more than 200 women who came on the air left us written messages about what being able to have a voice on FIRE meant to them. Zsuzsa Kadar, representative of the Autonomous Confederation of Hungarian Women Workers, said that she struggles about issues of migration and ethnic conflicts. "I organized international women's conferences in East-Central Europe about women at work," she told us. "We women haven't only one nationality. The world is our place."

Michaeline Mashigo from South Africa, representing the Young Women's Network, said, "I greatly appreciate the opportunity to represent young women from my country, especially because we have been left out of the process for a long time. My hope is that the resolutions taken at this conference will be implemented."

Mahfoudla, from Tanzania, read a poem on the air and said, "It was an enjoyable experience to be a participant on a live program of Radio FIRE. My only hope is that my interview and the poem have inspired many to fight for the cause of ending violations of women's rights."

President of the Feminist Dalit Organization in Nepal in India, Durga Sob told us, "I am so happy to have had a chance to be interviewed on FIRE! I would like to wish you success, because I will never forget this moment in my life."

Robin Morgan from the U.S. added, "FIRE is that: warmth and light, and dancing energy and power. It is the politics of the airwaves—invisible, everywhere, able to go beyond the walls of tyranny—like feminism...."

A total of 54 hours of coverage were aired on shortwave from the FIREPLACE. Reports, interviews, live concerts, testimonies, news, and poetry were heard internationally. It was the only systematic live coverage that came out of Huairou, and FIRE was one of the media outlets that did the most hours of broadcasting from the events.

CODEHUCA's report of September 12, 1995, summed up our feelings about and participation in the conference:

According to FIRE, broadcasting from Beijing at the site of the official UN conference, "The climate of the conference is one of confidence that the results might be favorable to women and to the achievement of peace, equality, and development in the world. However, concerns continue as the hard-core debates began this week." We would like to mention that on September 3, Feminist International Radio Endeavour was recognized in Beijing with the UNESCO Award in Communications. FIRE has demonstrated its dynamism and creativity in covering the NGO Forum and the conference with only a few microphones.

We received a total of 70 reception reports from North America, Europe, South America, and Central America directly or indirectly through CODEHUCA. Added to the list of listeners were the hundreds of women who gathered around the FIREPLACE on a daily basis, simply to hear, write reports, record, videotape, or photograph the activities of the live broadcasts. Also the thousands who never write to a radio station.

FIRE's Sparks Fly Outside the FIREPLACE

In addition to the live broadcasts, FIRE staff took part in various panels and workshops at the NGO Forum in Huairou.

Katerina Anfossi was a panelist on "The Document and Its Passage", an activity organized by the International Women's Tribune Center. The panel looked at the different uses of documents, and Katerina emphasized that documents should validate women's voices and oral language skills.

Nancy Vargas was a panelist at a Women and Communications panel at the Women's Environmental and Development Organization (WEDO) tent. She described FIRE's radio communications experience, saying, "Radio is a means of communication where women can speak for themselves without mediation."

I was a panelist at the plenary session—"Media, Culture, and Communications: Global Forces"—organized by the NGO Forum Facilitating Committee. I took the audience through each one of the previous UN conferences in the decade, showing that there are global forces in the world that do not have a seat at the United Nations, yet dictate global politics on all levels: Big business, fundamentalists, the military, the International Monetary Fund, the World Bank, media, and the drug Mafia.

I also organized a training workshop about media work for 33 participants of the International Reproductive Rights Women's Network. At the workshop they planned their media strategies for the conference. This consisted of writing and distributing a press release in which they invited media to come and cover the panel where the network would present the results of research undertaken by countries in Africa, Asia, Latin America, and North America.

Another activity that I organized was a workshop entitled "The Popularization of Women's Human Rights." It was part of the Institute of Human Rights Education organized by the People's Decade of Human Rights Education.

Other projects I was involved in included the coordination and moderation of an activity organized by the Latin American Women's Health Network at the regional tent, where five women from the region gave testimonies about violations of their reproductive rights. I also participated in a discussion about FIRE's experience at the ISIS Chile workshop on Women and Media. At the workshop organized by the Swedish Institute for Journalists, I presented an analysis of the role of mainstream media in placing more attention on geopolitics than on the issues addressed at the NGO Forum and conference.

FIRE also trained women in live broadcasting: Olga Rey trained women organized in the Youth Caucus, and Katerina and Nancy trained Christine Butewa to operate the technical controls during the

CN11 - 0250   Issue No 10   Thursday, September 7,1995

published by China Daily

Shortwave radio is on Fire

by Ma Dan

"Hello, this is Maria broadcasting from Huairou. As we go into our sixth day of broadcasting, I want to share with you that things are very active here in the Non-governmental Organizations' Forum."

In one corner of a building next to the Business Centre of the forum site, which few participants pay attention to, the Women's Alternative Media Action and Service Centre has a base. Maria Suarez-Toro, from Costa Rica with Feminist International Radio Endeavour, is doing a live broadcast.

Inspired by the Women's Peace Tent in Nairobi in 1985, where the need for consolidating women's communications networks to confront the information new world order was reaffirmed, Fire was founded as a shortwave radio programme.

Produced and broadcast daily in Spanish and in English. It is the only feminist shortwave radio project in the world.

"What characterizes Fire as an alternative media is that it is media in women's hands," Suarez-Toro said.

Technically, they are quite simple, using friendly radio technology fit to broadcast through an international telephone line. Their facilities consist of a telephone interface, a mixer and five microphones.

With this lightweight equipment, Suarez-Toro and two other permanent staff some helpers are able to broadcast four-hour "on the spot" productions.

They have also made live broadcasts from the UN World Conference on Human Rights, the UN World Conference on Population and Development and the UN World Summit on Social and Development.

"We estimate that about 30,000 people across some 100 hundred countries can hear us," Maria said proudly.

"And some listeners around the world continue to write to us through electronic mail, offering their comments on our programme in Huairou."

The contributions and strength of Fire, she said, come from its practice of making news, reporting and providing testimonies from "our own voices and our own format."

"That sort of experimentation without pressures from commercial media or mainstream media and without strict professionalism allows us to re-create with our own creativity what women's communication is all about," she said.

As an activist for women's right and a literature teacher the past two decades, Suarez-Toro realized that people at the grassroots level, especially women, don't have a say in media, yet have many strategies, solutions, suggestions and perspectives about everything that happens in the world.

"When I was asked to begin the feminist radio programme," she said, "I said that's gonna to be a venue for those voices and perspectives and strategies that people never got to hear, yet they are so full of wisdom and the experience of life."

Fire has grown increasingly popular worldwide since it went on the air five years ago. To listeners, it's "warmth and light and energy and power," Suarez-Toro said.

FIREPLACE in China—The Beijing newspaper *China Daily* reports on FIRE's live broadcasts from Huairou, China.

228

FIREPLACE broadcasts. In October, we received a letter from Christine in which she wrote, "Thank you for giving me the opportunity to work with the FIREPLACE. What I liked most was doing the technical work!" Many panels, workshops, tribunals, tent activities, interviews, and marches were registered on audiotape for broadcast after the forum and conference. Among the tribunals recorded were the "Global Tribunal on Accountability of Violations of Women's Human Rights" (organized by a coalition of groups coordinated by the Center for Women's Global Leadership); the "Tribunal on Violations of Women's Human Rights in Conflict Situations" (organized by a coalition coordinated by the Asian Women's Human Rights Council); and the "Girls' Speakout" organized by the Youth Caucus. Panel recordings included IRRRAG's report about the findings of their research on reproductive rights in seven countries, ABANTU's African Panel "Women and Political Participation", WEDO's panel on "Women in Media", and many others.

Bringing It All Back Home

During our flight back to Costa Rica after the events in China had come to a close, Radio for Peace International celebrated its eighth anniversary with the traditional Fiesta on the Air live call-in show, during which listeners called from 10 locationsas close as Brasil de Mora, just a few miles from the station, to as far away as British Columbia, Canada, and all points in between. Among the callers were men and women who talked to RFPI about FIRE. Grace Moulton from Florida in the U.S. was among them:

I think you have lots of great programs, but my favorite is FIRE, and I think they've been doing an especially good job with the coverage on the women's conference in Beijing. That must have been quite an undertaking.

Moises Juan Corilloclla, from Perú, wrote to RFPI, sending "...special congratulations to FIRE for covering [the conference] in Beijing." Jerry Mukatos from North Carolina in the U.S. called to say that he was relieved to know that the FIRE staff had been able to go to China:

...and were able to do the reports from there.... there is quite a contrast between your coverage of the conference, and the other sources I heard.

The Costa Rica newspaper *La Nación* reports on FIRE's struggles and successes in China.

REVISTA DIARIA DE LA NACION

SECCION B   25 DE SETIEMBRE DE 1995

Peripecias en Pekín

HAROLD LEANDRO CAMACHO
Redactor de La Nación

María Suárez, primer plano, Nancy Vargas (izquierda) y Katerina Anfossi celebran el regreso a nuestro país en la cabina de Radio Paz Internacional, en Ciudad Colón.

Tres periodistas cuentan su experiencia en la Cumbre de la Mujer, donde transmitieron en vivo para Radio Paz Internacional

Hubo montones de problemas. Pero ganaron el entusiasmo y el deseo de cumplir un objetivo: hacer llegar a todo el mundo los detalles de la Cumbre de la Mujer.

Tres periodistas, dos costarricenses y una chilena radicada aquí, se impusieron esa meta. El canal para lograrlo fue Radio Paz Internacional, que funciona en la Universidad para la Paz.

Cargadas con su equipo, las ticas María Suárez Toro, de 47 años, y Nancy Vargas Sanabria, de 31, así como la chilena Katerina Anfossi Gómez, de 32, emprendieron su periplo por Asia.

"Fueron muchas las carreras y presiones, pero nuestro máximo orgullo es que fuimos la única emisora que transmitió en vivo durante la reunión más importante de mujeres", afirmó Suárez.

UNA CABINA, POR FAVOR

El principal escollo que tuvieron las periodistas en China fue que durante el Foro de Organizaciones no Gubernamentales, que se desarrolló en Huarou, previo a la reunión cimera, no dispusieron de una cabina para transmitir.

"Cerca del edificio donde se efectuaba el encuentro había un galerón viejo. Allí hicimos un conato de cabina", dijo Anfossi.

Cuentan que utilizaron un tubo de metal en lugar de martillo; recogieron clavos viejos, usaron made-

ra casi inservible, mas al fin tuvieron un espacio donde entrevistar a sus invitados.

Desde allí, las funcionarias de Radio Paz Internacional transmitian cuatro horas, dos en español y el resto en inglés.

Ya en Pekín, para la cobertura de la Cumbre de la Mujer, toparon con mayor suerte: Radio China Internacional les cedió parte del equipo para salir al aire.

"Ahora el problema era el idio-

Una anécdota

En una de las reuniones durante la Cumbre, María Suárez observó el rostro de cine que le era conocido. En inglés, le escribió una nota: "Usted es Sally Field, me encantó su actuación en la película Ríos salvajes, no tardó por cómo manifieste los reímos, sino a los hombres fue el mensaje". El rostro del cine le respondió: "Gracias por sus halagos, pero no soy Sally Field. Soy Meryl Streep".

ma, puesto que los técnicos chinos no hablan español ni inglés. Ante ello, utilizamos el lenguaje de los gestos", indicó Vargas.

De esta forma, un pulgar hacia arriba, significaba "abrir el micrófono"; hacia abajo, "cerrarlo"; hacia la derecha "abrir linea con Costa Rica".

VOCES DE ALIENTO

Según cuentan, fue muy gratifi-

cante la cantidad y calidad de las invitadas que tuvieron en cada una de sus emisiones.

"Fueron mujeres de todo el mundo, con realidades y puntos de vista muy diferentes. En eso, cumplimos con creces la misión de darle la palabra a la mujer desde su perspectiva", comentó Suárez.

"Por nuestra frecuencia pasaron mujeres de India, China, Nepal, Tanzania, Europa, Puerto Rico. Pero lo más importante fue saber que mucha gente nos escuchaba y nos enviaron sus voces de aliento", aseveró Anfossi.

Y así fue. "Vía Internet pronto comenzaron a llegar cartas de apoyo de todas partes del mundo. Nos querían seguir oyendo la voz de la mujer directamente desde Pekin", añadió Vargas.

Dado el trabajo que ha desempeñó Radio Paz Internacional, el Fondo de las Naciones Unidas para la Infancia (Unicef) les concedió el premio Producciones hacia Pekín. "Pero lo más emotivo fue que nos lo entregaron en plena transmisión. Nosotras sabíamos del galardón, pero nunca imaginábamos que nos iban a sorprender en medio de nuestro trabajo", afirmó Anfossi.

¿Quiénes son?

- María Suárez Toro llegó hace 25 años, es maestra y activista de los derechos humanos de la mujer. Vive en Curridabat.
- Nancy Vargas Sanabria tiene 31 años, es periodista y tiene dos hijos. Vive en Vargas-Araya, en San Pedro de Montes de Oca.
- Katerina Anfossi Gómez tiene 32 años y un bebé; es abogada y egresada de periodismo. Vive en Ciudad Colón.

I never heard anything about structural adjustment on the other [mainstream] sources.

FIRE's followup to Beijing continued for the next several months. Our flames continued to burn through the post-Beijing media coverage: *Viva* of *La Nación* in Costa Rica (September, 1995); *Yes—we can do it!* a newsletter for Women in Journalism; an article in *FOJO* by Margareta Furberg (October 1995); *BRECHA* of CODEHUCA (October 1995); WBAI on Talk in the Morning by Patrika Dallas (October 1995); *Interadio Newsletter* of AMARC (October 1995), *DAWN Informs—Developing Alternatives with Women for a New Era* (October 1995); *Swedish International Development Agency Newsletter* by Marianne Englund (October 1995); *Dialogue* of the University for Peace in Costa Rica (November 1995); *Vista* newsletter of Radio for Peace International (October 1995); and SWAN—School of Women Artists Network—in *Post Patriarchal Newsletter* no. 9 (November 1995).

Virtual Sisterhood's Barbara Anne O'Leary and Steve Wise of *The Earth Negotiations Bulletin* helped us organize a sound panel for cybercommunications on the worldwide web <www.iisd.ca/linkages/4wcw/fire.html>. In it, women from the Philippines, Africa, and Latin America and from WEDO interpreted the results of the United Nations' Fourth World Conference on Women.

In late September, Laura Flanders' Counterspin radio program featured the FIREPLACE, and new listeners responded to it. Following are some of the e-mail messages FIRE received about that broadcast.

Date: Sun, 24 Sep 1995 11:53:07—0400 (EDT)

I was pleased to hear the coverage of FIRE and the Women's Conference on Counterspin last night. Very good!

Charlie W.

Subject: More info please

Greetings Ms. Suárez,

Having just heard your interview with Laura Flanders of FAIR at the Beijing Women's Conference, I was much impressed (not in any particular order) with your commitment, eloquence, command of English, and the effort you are putting forward on behalf of both women's role in the world and alternative means of communications. Greater grassroots, decentralized media such as yours is more necessary than ever, particularly in the U.S., the most manipulated, unaware, and brainwashed constituency probably in the world today.... Keep up the good work, and keep in touch. Muchas gracias, señora, y buena suerte.

Ron Landskroner

From: Alice

Some time ago after the conference I heard about FIRE over the radio when an interview with María was broadcast. She told about FIRE's experience at the NGO Women's Conference trying to set up the FIRE-PLACE in Beijing. At the same time the regular broadcast frequency was given as 7.385 on the 41 band. Could you please let me know the time you broadcast and if this frequency is correct. I live in California. I was so impressed with the work you are doing and hope to be able to locate you at last on the shortwave. Looking forward to hearing from you.

FIRE also prepared a comprehensive report about the FIREPLACE, including the voices broadcast from the FIREPLACE, to give back to participants. Some of the broadcasts were transcribed by Amber Sharick, a language student from the U.S. who came to volunteer at FIRE as part of her field work. Following is the inspiring letter we received from Amber after her return to the U.S.

Subject: FIRE

I want to thank you again for a wonderful experience working at FIRE. You truly influenced my life and now I hope to continue working as a woman in radio and in other forms of communications. I hope things are wonderful down in Costa Rica. I hope to obtain a shortwave radio from a pawn shop soon so I can listen to the lovely ladies of FIRE. Tell Kata and Nancy hello.

I am editing a piece on radiation victims and am including Rosalie Bertrell from Beijing. It reminds me of all those tapes I listened to at FIRE.

Amber

Oh P.S. If you want to do a collaboration or have an idea for a show or could use some tapes, I will be here until the end of July. I know you are busy, but if you get a chance, drop a line and say hello.

Other messages of encouragement kept coming in:

Date: Thu, 30 May 1996 08:48:46 +0000
From: Waldemar Mellquist
Hello. Thank you for interesting information in Kalmar. I will try to tune in to your programs.
Friendly regards.

Dozens of women from Latin America and the Caribbean met in Perú to evaluate their participation and achievements in Beijing and Huairou, and to develop plans for their post-China activities. The group agreed that the FWCW had been positive, but that it had not been all of what women needed and expected.

FIRE was assessed as a very successful project, originating from within Latin America but being a global effort. As feminists from the region, our airwaves would definitely be in the plans for the future.

That future of implementation of the Platform for Action in Costa Rica began on November 25—International Day Against Violence Towards Women—when FIRE recorded its first post-Beijing action. It was marked by Costa Rican feminists in a new way. Among other activities such as the traditional march, they held the first Tribunal on Violations of Women's Human Rights in Costa Rica.

Signs of possible backtracking by the government of Costa Rica became very clear at the public meeting to report about the results of the conference in China. There, Alicia Fournier, head of the governmental delegation to Beijing, who also had spoken from the FIREPLACE, said, "...in Costa Rica, the results will be implemented in accordance with our traditions and culture."

It was against this background that feminists, women's human rights activists, and traditional human rights NGOs in Costa Rica decided to organize the first-ever Tribunal on Violations of Women's Human Rights in the country. The public event was held in the Lawyers' Bar Association of Costa Rica and had as an objective the promotion of wider knowledge and understanding of the gross violations of women's human rights, which adversely affect the lives of many Costa Rican women.

The 22 testimonies presented at the tribunal gave evidence of the fact that Costa Rica's traditions and culture have excluded women from the enjoyment of full human rights. However, Costa Rica holds international and regional prestige for its record of respect for traditional human rights, peace, and formal democracy—it is known as the Central American Switzerland. The voices of women about the exclusion of their rights have been silenced in this global image.

María Eugenia Dengo, an elder in Costa Rican politics since the 1950s, testified about the history of Costa Rican women's political participation, affirming the ongoing struggle with ample gestures:

Women have been at the forefront of every major struggle in Costa Rica's history, for example to overcome dictatorships during the last century and to include social and economic rights for people during the liberal revolution in 1948. Yet when it came down to who was going to govern, women were put aside, or at most, were placed in secondary, nondecisive political positions.

Livia Cordero Gene testified to having been a prisoner of conscience from 1991 to 1994 without due trial. She was living proof of political persecution due to being a peace activist and human rights defendant.

Seven women testified about the horrors of domestic violence, and the lack of administration of justice in their cases. More than 2,000 cases of domestic violence had been presented by other women between the date of the tribunal and the 8th of March, 1996.

A case presented by the San José Women's Police Station Coordinator, Zayra Salazar, was that of "María," a pseudonym for a woman now dead, whose husband stabbed her 19 times. When she denounced him formally, the court judged the act as a minor offense. He later killed her.

Another was the case of Olga, a street girl subject to abuse by her stepfather when she was six, thrown to the streets by her stepmother after the girl took the case to court, abused by men in the streets when she was nine, and sexually harassed by police officers who picked her up on the streets of San José. The testimony affirmed the conclusions of recent research done in Nicaragua and Brazil that show that street children are not only the product of lack of economic and social rights, but that many take to the streets to run away from domestic violence and abuse.

Other testimonies at the tribunal gave evidence of racism in Costa Rica. Loraine Powell, an Afro-Costa Rican women, told her story of harassment in the workplace at a local university and of the use of racist language against her to discredit her formal complaint. Ethnocentrism in the multiple forms of denial of indigenous women's rights was presented by native Costa Rican Marina López. A case of discrimination on the basis of sexual preference was also presented at the tribunal, as well as two testimonies of how women in the arts are rendered invisible.

Carmen Bustos Bustos presented her case about denial of reproductive and holistic health of women by the multinational corporations who sell and use toxic fertilizers that have been banned in the U.S. She discussed her seven miscarriages while working at a banana plantation between 1967 and 1976, and the pain she still suffers from exposure to the toxins that were used. "I had four kids after I left the plantations," she said, "and they each have the same symptoms I have had since then: permanent headaches, pain in my bones, and skin problems."

Organized by the Costa Rican Commission of Human Rights; the Institute of Women's Studies at the National University; the Women, Justice, and Gender of the UN Institute for the Prevention of Delinquency; the Earth Council; the collective, 25th of November; the Central American Human Rights Committee; and FIRE, the tribunal documented violations of women's human rights committed by private actors, private institutions, and the state.

FIRE has been there for women all over the world as they speak out for their rights, and we continue to burn warmly and brightly beyond Beijing.

What you have seen, Katerina, Nancy, and María from FIRE doing throughout the past few days at this NGO Forum—the live broadcasts, the recording of panels, interviewing women—is also being done at the local level by many women who form the global movement of

women doing radio everywhere. Why? Because radio in the hands of women is a medium where women can be themselves, where women have a voice of their own to share with others, and it is a medium that is accessible to most women!
—María Victoria Polanco, vice president of AMARC

In a *Vista* article, Nancy Vargas wrote about her impressions of the conference and challenged the women of the world to protect the ground they gained there:

For the international women's movement, nongovernmental organizations, and civil society, post-Beijing means more than a written document. It is a reminder that UN member states, the United Nations, and other international organizations have made a commitment to implement, for the sake of the improvement of the daily lives of women, the commitments they agreed to in the Platform for Action of the Fourth World Conference on Women held in China from the 4th to the 15th of September, 1995.

There is an old saying that "from words to action stands a long trail." Although the NGO Forum, Women '95, and the Fourth World Conference ended only two months ago in China, and despite the fact that it showed, without doubt, the strength and the process of empowerment of the international women's movement, and the fact that the 183 member states of the UN adopted the platform by consensus (except for a few reservations by some states to critical areas such as reproductive and sexual health and rights), the responsibility remains to remind them, and demand of them, that this written document is to be transformed into concrete actions for the effective development of women in the world; a development accompanied by peace and equality. It is the NGOs, the international women's movement, and civil society who are called to remind them and hold them accountable.

Here is an example of a reminder that occurred during the conference itself. Throughout the official UN meeting, women heard the voices of delegates of member states talking and talking, one after the other, about the improvements that they had undertaken at the national level since the last UN conference on women in Nairobi 10 years ago. When the turn came for the "unofficial" delegate of

236

the Latin American and Caribbean women's organizations—Virginia Vargas—to speak, at the plenary session, she said, "Almost everything has been said, almost everything, with the exception of justice, resources, and funding commitments for the implementation of the Platform...."

It is important to emphasize that the issue of women and media became part of the Platform for Action for the first time. Part J of the document places emphasis, among other things, on the importance of access by women communicators to decision-making in media. The Platform also calls for the equal participation of women in the media and even in monitoring bodies. It calls for the establishment of codes of conduct for the portrayal of nonstereotyped images of women in media, and access to new technologies. According to a study by UNESCO, in Latin America, Asia, and Africa women in broadcasting and print media comprise an average of only 25 percent. In Europe it reaches 30 percent for the press and 36 percent for broadcasting.

Meantime, throughout the world, women are coordinating activities to promote national reforms and actions to implement the Platform.

I'd like to end by telling our Vista readers that it is not by chance that the Fourth World Conference on Women became the biggest ever UN conference in its history. It gathered 31,000 women and some 1,400 men. It is also not by chance that there were substantial advances in the recognition of women's human rights, just as it is not by mere chance that the common call by women was: "Not one step back."

Thus, although there is the old saying that "from the word to the action stands a long trail," women are saying that there is no going back!

CHAPTER 8

Beyond Beijing and into the Future

May 1, 1996, International Worker's Day, is also FIRE's fifth anniversary on the air. We will celebrate this occasion with joy and enthusiasm, because of all the good and memorable moments we have lived.

But on this occasion we will not share our travels, marches, or live broadcasts. Today we want to talk about some simpler things: the weaving and embroidery.

You might ask yourself what needles, thread, and scissors have to do with a feminist program and its fifth anniversary. I can tell you that it has a lot to do with it!

Ever since I was little, my grandmother Paquita would sit us down in front of the sewing machine or the rocking chair that she used for weaving and embroidering. She taught me that a good piece would result only from the completion of each row or stitch as if it were one whole piece in itself, and that at the end, all rows would form the total picture; that at the end it should be so well

*put together, that the right side and the back side would be of the
same quality.*

*Today, when I remember the multiple weavers who have built
FIRE, and the many colored threads that have given it light and
joy, and the cross stitch or rice stitch, I believe that this dimension
of weaving and of embroidering has taken place on FIRE.*

*Today I also remember those who have given us the warm wool
for the cold in December, as well as the warmth that emanates from
FIRE, for that warmth has also shielded me on rainy and humid days
and in the eternal nights when I have been in faraway countries.*

*There are so many things I learned form Tata Paquita. My
grandmother also taught me to undo and begin again, to refuse
some wool, and to combine textures. And when I see her today, at
the age of 86 still weaving and embroidering for her grandchildren,
I can't help but affirm that embroidery and weaving have a lot to
do with life.*

—Katerina Anfossi in *Vista*, April 1996

The first four months of 1996 were illuminated by the fact that
we were approaching our fifth anniversary on the air! By this time, in
the months following the FWCW, we had become a strong FIRE whose
flames had reached all around the globe. Our sparks were flying!

Gathering Our Strength
for the Future

As our anniversary approached, we assessed our current situation
as the only ongoing global feminist radio program produced in the
South, and we looked toward the future.

With the rush of international conferences behind us, we decided
to strengthen our coverage of local, regional, and international women's
activities. FIRE would be on the scene as women struggled to implement their own feminist agenda, as well as to monitor the commitments by states and the United Nations in the world conferences of the
first part of the decade.

Throughout FIRE's first five years, we had been networking with women around the world who produce local radio programs to help them organize their own permanent programs on FIRE. We had received tapes from many parts of the world, and the experience of the FIREPLACE collective production had increased this influx.

During the first few months of 1996 alone, tapes had come in from United Nations Women's Radio, the Population Reference Bureau, PANOS Institute, Tanzania, Canadian Women Farm Radio Collective, Diane Post from KAFR in Arizona, Women on the Line in Australia, WINGS, AMARC, CEMINA in Brazil, SIPAM in Mexico, RED ADA Bolivia, Radio Tierra Chile, and more.

We further facilitated these interconnections by continuing to develop simultaneous programs with local radio programs by women around the world. Such broadcasts had been featured on FIRE in previous years by Interkonexiones in Germany in 1995, by the Women's Caucus of The World Association of Community Radios from Senegal in 1995, by the Black Women's Network from the Dominican Republic on FIRE's Anniversary in 1994, by six women journalists from Third-World countries broadcasting from Sweden in 1995, by WEDO in New York during the Second PREPCOM prior to Beijing in 1994, and by the Latin American Women's Health Network in 1994. And, of course, we had our jointly produced broadcasts from the FIREPLACE in China. We were committed to continuing to expand this work.

FIRE and Women's Health in 1996

In January 1996, we received a special request from Carol Vlassoff at the United Nations World Health Organization (WHO) in Geneva:

We are planning to implement a radio cum pictorial material project which we are calling the Healthy Women Counseling Guide. I have talked with Sophie Ly of AMARC and Sharon Fonn of the Women's Health Project in South Africa and they both felt I could learn a lot from you, and figuring out ways of collaborating. We are especially interested in reaching illiterate women in rural Africa at this point. I will provide more information, but we want you to come to Geneva next May for a workshop with African women in radio.

We are always ready to share our knowledge with women around the world, and right away we started making plans to help out.

Carol went live on the air on FIRE, when she visited on January 22, 1996. She talked about the work of the WHO, and the African women's health project:

> *I am from Canada but have worked in Geneva at the World Health Organization for the past eight years. Our research places emphasis on the perspectives of people themselves, understanding the disease, and the way people understand it and deal with it. Malaria is the one we work with most. Particularly the interest now is to look at how women understand disease. They are usually left out of the picture in the dialogue about health. They want to find out about it, and there is hardly any information available. We want to figure out how to reach women with more information.*

Carol recounted an earlier WHO experience to explain how she knew of the importance of women's participation in the definitions and strategies about health:

> *The meeting began in the typical WHO fashion: everyone sitting around a table, everybody with name tags, and a formal presentation by one of the assistant directors. We told the participants what our objectives were for the meeting, and then we asked each one to introduce themselves... Halfway through the presentations, a very well-known feminist who works with UNIFEM stopped the round of presentations and told us that we were doing this the wrong way. She explained that she could present herself, but this was not why they came; they had their own objectives and wanted WHO to listen to them.*
>
> *This was the first time in WHO that anyone had dared to voice their own opinion and declare their objectives in coming to a meeting. Over the week we had many people from the organization filtering in, because they had heard that this was a very unusual meeting. From that process we learned not just about women's health and issues, but how to actually conduct a meeting that is meaningful. At the end of the meeting the women did not tell us what we should do— they recommended that we go and ask women themselves and ask them the questions that we were asking the group of experts!*

WHO went on to do research projects in three African countries to learn from the women in those countries. Carol continued her story:

Although there were differences in the countries, overall, the messages that came from the women were very similar! One thing that we realized is that women have a real wealth of information, themselves. They know a great deal, because health is their work throughout the world. We found out that what we needed to do was to find a way for our information to mesh with theirs, and to realize all the constraints they have—constraints that do not have to do with lack of knowledge. Because of their constraints, these combine all different kinds of strategies!

In the research we also asked people whom they listened to. They talked about meeting in groups and face to face, but they all said that they listen to and like radio. However, the one thing they did not like about the radio is that they could not ask questions....

Carol talked about what she had learned about women in radio in Africa:

The South African experience is very interesting because they combine television, radio, and written material to work on health issues. They accompany the programs with booklets... and place them in the clinics and elsewhere. Then people take the written materials home.... Another advantage is that women can copy the tapes and take them to their communities to listen to them.

Carol then requested that the audience write to her at the World Health Organization with suggestions for materials, articles, and experiences about the combination of radio and written material to provide information about women's health.

Response to the program came through e-mail from ADEFRA—a black women's network in Germany.

Subject: Geneva

I read in your messages that FIRE is going to Geneva on May 29th. Why don't you came to Munich afterwards? We would be happy to have you and whoever is with you here in Munich. I already told them a lot about you, so they are very curious to meet you finally. If you can't come, than maybe I could try to come. The article about the WHO and this woman Carol Vlassof was very interesting. I will get in touch with her also. So my dear, so much for now. Greetings to all the FIRE women.

Love and Peace, Jasmin

Women's health was also explored by another team of researchers. On February 26, more than 70 women from rural and urban areas met in Costa Rica to talk about their findings throughout two years of popular research on the topic. Alianza de Mujeres Costarricenses convened the national event, with the objective of sharing the results of their consultative popular research about the issue.

Katerina Anfossi and I were there to cover the activity for FIRE. Ana Hernandez, president of Alianza de Mujeres Costarricenses, framed the event in her inaugural speech:

Our biggest challenge today is to debate, analyze, and design affirmative proposals. A year after the population conference and a few months after the Fourth World Conference on Women, we know that there is a need for this consultation so more grassroots women take part in the process.

She reported that the meeting was preceded by 32 local and regional *encuentros* (meetings) among women. The major finding was the need for three basic processes to occur—strengthening of women's organizations at the local level, strengthening of interregional coordination and communications, and use of legal rights by women, themselves, to protect their sexual, reproductive, and labor rights.

Gabriela Prado, coordinator of the grassroots research on women's health, presented the global situation that formed the backdrop for their research:

Today in Costa Rica we are in a state of crisis. Twenty-eight percent of families live at poverty level. The resources assigned to social development have been reduced substantially.... This affects the quality of life, and women are affected most.... What we will do today is share the results, but we will also identify strategic actions to propose at all levels, in order to find solutions. Because our need for health is holistic, we have dealt with the issues of housing, work, violence, sexuality, and other topics.

Ana Hernandez reiterated the need to look for ways to dialogue with the government to look for solutions.

Nancy Vargas Moves On

In February 1996, Nancy Vargas left the FIRE staff to undertake professional work with rural groups in Costa Rica on a national level. Having been with FIRE since 1992, Nancy became a feminist at FIRE, she re-created her professional experience by producing feminist communications, and she grew to develop an international consciousness. She also brought to the program and team of women her sense of simplicity, her knack for combining feelings with consciousness, and also the benefits of her journalism studies.

Nancy's presence had been stamped on FIRE, and we hoped the benefit would be reciprocal: that her feminist commitment would be stamped in the groups with which she was to work, and that her international consciousness might help other Costa Ricans understand that no man, no woman, and no country are islands unto themselves.

Nancy became coordinator of a rural women's radio network with a local radio collective, Voces Nuestras, in Costa Rica. However, in 1998 she returned to collaborate with FIRE "because," she said, "the international links are so important!"

Concerts on FIRE

Throughout our years on the air, FIRE has periodically shared with our listeners when feminist musicians in Costa Rica held performances—sometimes in our studios. Two such concerts took place in February. 1996.

The first was a concert by "Marta and Juan" (as they wanted to be known), two young Costa Rican flamenco guitar players we had met while covering a youth festival in San José. Marta shared her story of

244

how stereotypes about women and flamenco always make people think that she will be the dancer who will dance to the man's guitar sounds. When she appears with her guitar, people are surprised.

Guadalupe Urbina, Costa Rican folk singer, came to sing live on FIRE, as she had done several times before. She was thrilled about having received letters from our listeners who had heard her on the short-wave programs in Cuba and in Ecuador.

The following song by Guadalupe, translated from the Spanish, is one of our audience's favorites:

Together, but Not as One

You see how hard it is to love after the fire and the lust;
after the passion, we have to talk about what is left.
I have returned, my love, from a thousand olden pains.
I am not willing to relive them.
Rather, my love, let us be together, but not as one.
I love you, my beloved, but I will not stand new pains
because I already have hundreds of them.
My beloved: it's better together, but not as one.
So much happiness built by us,
so many dreams painted.
And if you touch me, you can still see that my
skin blossoms in your hands.
But tiredness reaches me,
and I get tired of having to struggle to live with you
trying to make a joy out of each day.
That is why I prefer, my love....
I saw your sacred hands build walls and floors
where my feet stand.
Those hands filled with cement, perfumed at night
always caressing me.
Losing you will not be easy,
since we have so many other dreams to live through.
There are so many dreams ahead, that I'd rather be....
Together, but not as one.

Remote Live Broadcasts from the U.S. and Mexico

Expo '96 in the U.S.

From February 2nd through the 4th, Expo '96, a gathering of feminists in the United States, was broadcast live on FIRE in both English and Spanish. Convened by the Feminist Majority in the U.S., the event presented the perspectives, strategies, and actions of feminists in that country to influence the political agenda of their national political leadership.

The three days were filled with exhibitions, symposia, roundtables, personal exchanges, networking, training seminars, and development of strategies for the 1996 U.S. elections. Participants also demanded accountability from the U.S. administration for implementation of the Platform for Action of the UN Fourth World Conference on Women.

Producer of the Women's International News Gathering Service (WINGS), Frieda Werden, broadcast live for one hour daily over the telephone from Washington, DC, to FIRE in Costa Rica. Following is an excerpt from her opening report:

Expo '96 opened its doors to 2,700 women for the opening session at 9:00 this morning. Outside, they had faced a cold snowstorm that closed down the schools today, as well as the coldness of nearby Congress in its eternal debates about the budget, behind closed doors, closed to women's claims.

Inside, the lavender-colored carpet at the Sheraton Hotel in DC awoke today to find its rooms filled with warm exposition booths displaying all kinds of dreams, hopes, works, campaigns, and actions that women have undertaken to change their stake in U.S. society in anticipation of the year 2000.

Organizer Dean Martin explained the purpose of the conference:

[We are] showcasing women's issues and how women envision their issues in the future. What we are asking all participants to do is to envision a feminist future.... By doing so, we are moving into the next century.

Diana Pierce spoke to Eliza Graney of WINGS about the organization Wider Opportunities for Women (WOW)—a project that works on poverty issues with low-income women. Welfare, welfare reform, unemployment, homelessness, low-wage employment, and poverty trends are among their emphases, as Diana explained:

We do research, organizing, fact sheets, Congressional testimonies, and more.... We have about 500 women's employment training organizations across the country, and many of the women from those organizations are here. We all need to have a safety net, because we are all economically vulnerable. Thus, we need the backup. This year we have worked very hard to keep welfare programs from being decimated and cut.... [welfare is] a guaranteed safety net for women when they fall into poverty... losing their jobs or other means of support.

Diana was quick to say that what is at stake in the debate and proposals in government is the future of welfare itself:

They [in Congress] started out trying not to make welfare reform, but instead they are making welfare cuts so they can cut the federal budget; they are sending the responsibility down to the states. The reason there is a federal welfare program in the first place is because the states were doing such a lousy job of it during the depression.

A survey demonstrated that half of the counties in the USA did not even have programs for women and children. Welfare was federalized so that it would be available to everybody, so do we really want to send it back to the states? The answer is no.... If you live in a state that does not have very much money, or in a state that has run out of money, or if you go at the wrong time, you will not get the money you need. No woman should be in a position of depending on "just luck."

She went on to describe another of WOW's campaigns:

[We are also] working to get women into nontraditional jobs, because those are the kinds of jobs that pay higher wages and enable a woman to support a child or two. Only seven percent of women are in nontraditional jobs. There is higher unemployment among women than among men. While it is true that men's wages are going down, women's wages are going down as well, particularly for women who

are at the lower levels of education. Wages are declining for everyone in this country, not only for men.... We develop teams: unions, employees, and so on, so that we have a confluence of all the important people who have a stake in this. It's not only the co-worker, but supervisors, managers....

Burlette Allan is the coordinator of the Washington, DC chapter of the YWCA—Young Women's Christian Association. She coordinates a pre-vocational program to introduce women to the trades in nontraditional work:

We work very closely [with WOW], trying to model how service providers, women working in the trades, and women training other women can make a difference in terms of women's wages and benefits.

Cindy Morano of WOW added:

At Expo '96 we are working on building a structure on which we can place the planks for women's economic security, and most of the people who have been building that structure are young women.

Kathy Rogers, executive director of the NOW Legal Defense and Education Fund in New York, came on the air to talk about the fund's litigations in defense of women's legal rights:

Just recently we had a case [in Massachusetts] that went up all the way to the Supreme Court. The case had to do with pornography in the work place. A woman was running for a union election. Her opponent took a picture of her face, pasted copies of it on pornographic photographs, and put them up all over the workplace. We actually succeeded in that case; the other union employees were disciplined, and she won damages. The Supreme Court said that was fine, and would [therefore] not hear the case.

Interviewer Martha Burk of the Feminist Fax Net based in Washington, DC, asked Kathy about the educational equity cases at the Virginia Military Institute and at the Citadel:

Both of those cases are [dealing with] very prestigious military institutions, each of them over a hundred years old and producing some of the greatest leaders in the states of South Carolina and Virginia—not just in the military, but in business and in politics. In both cases, these institutions have been publicly funded, but the state says "no women need apply," and this also means "no women will be admitted" to these institutions.

NOW has challenged both institutions:

Our position is that women should have exactly the same opportunities as men, and they have the capabilities of succeeding in these institutions.... It's public money used to provide a tremendous opportunity to men and denying it completely to women.

Dixie Horneig, executive director of the Grey Panthers in Washington, DC talked to Martha about their new project called Age and Youth in Action. Dixie shared the news of a summit of young and elderly people to be held in Washington, DC the following May 30 and 31:

We will bring young grassroots people and elder people to talk about issues.... What we hear in [mainstream] media is that young people are blaming old people for their lack of economic progress. In fact, that is not the case. They are not blaming older Americans, yet it is portrayed this way. It is the "divide and conquer" syndrome. It's been very effective, and it's not [allowing] us to talk realistically to each other.... We the people have problems, but we the people are not the problem. Let the corporate world as well as the economic players [take] full responsibility.

Dixie also talked about other programs for women:

In Boston, we run a program called Jobs for All. We understand that women are at the lowest levels of the economic scale, particularly older women.... What we want to do is show that we are in support of women's issues as being all people's issues.

WINGS' Frieda Werden introduced María Jonas of the Austrian Social Democratic Women who would then run for a seat in the European Parliament. In 1993, the Feminist Majority selected her for the Feminist of the Year award for having fought for quotas for women in the political parties and all other social spheres. Frieda asked about the results of that struggle, and María shared her success story:

Until a year ago, I was the general secretary of Socialist International Women, a world association of social democratic and labor women's organizations. When I started out in that position, back in 1985, about six parties had quotas introduced. When I left the position last year, it was 30 parties, not only in Europe, but also in Latin America, Africa, and Asia. This success means that more women get into politics, parliament, town councils, and [other] government [positions].

Her ideal formula is 40 percent men and 40 percent women. She explained that Norway was the first to take up this formula, and in the long run women will have 60 percent:

What began as an affirmative action program for women, turned out to be a protection system for a species that is endangered in politics, and that is men!

Loud laughter come in through the microphone. Our anchor on the other end faded out her own reaction. Nothing like technology in women's own hands!

Experiences of other countries mentioned by María Jonas took place in Sweden and Austria. Frieda asked her about quotas being seen as putting women at the bottom of the lists, to which María wittily responded:

This is not like being at the bottom of the list in the Olympics, [because] the important thing is to have been there. That is not what we [women] want. We want to be in the parliament, and not only on the lists!

Ann Zill from WEDO in New York framed the setting as she sees it:

We have, in the United States, a country that is in deep despair: there is no trust in our government, there is no trust in other people, there is a feeling that we do not have a world that is working correctly. We are not making as much money as we used to, there is no safety net for us, many of us do not have any health care, we do not have a sense of community, we do not have [as women] basic rights that we have been struggling for, many of us most of our lives, and suddenly they [the rights] are not there anymore.

So what is the answer to this? I think it's time for women to take leadership, to assert their basic stance on what should be done in this world.... Let's talk about values. Good values have to do with trying to understand that we should not be killing each other.... And when you have a country at the end of the 20th century, and I am talking about the United States, that is not in a big war or even a cold war, spending a mind-boggling figure of nearly 300 billion dollars a year on weapons of individual and mass destruction, and is spending that money in a way that has made it the economy of the country, and that is selling those weapons all over the world, then it is time for women—who have a sense about life as opposed to death—to take charge....

Laurie Mann, webmaster of the Women Leaders on Web Site, and staff of the Feminist Phone Line Super Booth, stepped up the mike. Expo '96 was her first big feminist conference since 1977. "I've been to a lot of marches," she said, " but [in them] you do not get the opportunity to sit back and see what women are actually doing, so I'm thrilled."

Elayne Clift, also of WINGS, joined hosts Frieda Werden and Eliza Graney. They interviewed Laura X, who works at the National Clearinghouse on Marital and Date Rape. The clearinghouse works to change the laws, as well as to educate young women about sex and power. A formerly battered woman and abused as a child, Laura X became involved in these issues because "all of the work of the women's movement on these issues has resonated in me."

She talked about her visit to Costa Rica in 1993, where she learned that Costa Rica was the first country in the world to make marital rape a crime back in the twenties, because there was a specific legal statement for prosecuting a rapist who had attacked his own wife. She commented,

"This is not so in our country [the U.S.], where we have exceptions for husbands in rape prosecution in 40 states...." She also talked about her experience in Beijing during the United Nations Fourth World Conference on Women:

> *It was an astonishing event. The 185 UN member states decided to repeal the most popular male privilege: sex-on-demand in marriage. The power of the women in those countries [was felt]. They have become an economic force, a social force, and also [a force] in the religious communities there. We do not even have that [law] here!*

Alaskan ecofeminist singer Libby Rhoderick was one of the entertainers who went live on FIRE. "Every issue [in the world] is a local issue," she said. She sang a song she wrote entitled "Is That What You Really Want," which speaks to the dreams and visions we need to keep in life. "It is a question we have to constantly ask ourselves, certainly in a new year!" she explained. "Especially for women, because we are not asked what we want." Eliza commented that asking what a person really wants gives her value.

Comedians Judith Goodman and Becky Pretis, members of an all-female comedy group at Cornell University also talked to WINGS about their impressions of Expo '96. They commented that they were surprised to find so many feminist comedians: "We saw a great bumper sticker here that says, She Who Laughs, Lasts."

Laurie Barnam, director of the Susan B. Anthony House in New York, was also a guest in the broadcast. The house is a national resort landmark because it is where the suffragist leader lived and where she was arrested for voting for the President of the United States. Laurie described the house as "an inspiration for girls and women, and a great source of education for men and boys."

Also beaming out of the broadcast booth at Expo '96 was Bella Abzug, director of WEDO and author of a proposal entitled "My Contract with the American Women." She spoke about the proposal, which summarized the commitments that the U.S. (along with 188 other countries) had signed at the United Nations Fourth World Conference on Women. The 12 points in the document are about the burden of poverty on women, equal access to education and training, health care and related services, violence against women, the effects of armed conflict on women, inequality in economic structures and policies, power sharing and decision-making, mechanisms to promote women's advancement, human rights of women, the role of media, the environment, and the rights of the girl-child. She reminded the shortwave audience:

> We came from Beijing with a very important document [by consensus], which I have called a contract with the world's women. [The contract] is politically impossible, so we are the ones to [enforce it]— the women of the world. It is our document; we own it. We insist that the contract be carried out. Here in the United States, in order to counteract this terrible contract ON women that our friend Gingrich has put on us, we have developed, with other groups, an adaptation of the Platform for Action from Beijing, relevant to the particular areas that we are in, in every locality.

The challenge was clearly stated:

> Together, we are going to make 1996 a year that counts! And that means that it has to be won by women, to see that those who would take away our rights are TAKEN AWAY. We take them out of the Congress, we take them out of the legislature, and we make sure that we keep the White House where it is.... Take it over, because we are moving into the next century, and it is ours.

Asked by the audience at the booth about her international experience, Bella answered:

> I am a product of the American women's movement... but I have to say that working internationally has given me a new sense of inspiration. Women who are so deprived, women who have such an enormous struggle, they have given me a sense of knowing that women can do anything, because they have, in their struggle for survival. So I am in love with my work internationally, but I'm determined to be influential in my work nationally as well. That is why we are working on the Contract with the American Women.

253

She continued:

When we come from different cultures, then we have to learn from each other.... If you can accept and have an understanding and willingness to work to accomplish a goal with those with whom you may differ, or those who are different from you, whether it is by reason of race, religion, geographical background, or sexual orientation, you become a stronger person. You understand the meaning of humanity. It gives us strength to be diverse, and to be able to respond to change and difference.

Expo 2000, a followup initiative of the Feminist Majority Foundation, was planned to be held four years later, with women from all over the world meeting to present, share, and discuss their actions. This idea was also shared by Vivian Wee of DAWN on FIRE's live broadcasts from China during the Fourth World Conference on Women when she put forth the following proposal:

After the UN and the states have gathered here [in Beijing] to organize a World Conference on Women, it is about time that women around the world organize ourselves to convene a Women's Conference about the World.

After the live broadcasts, FIRE shared the Expo '96 tapes with women who were U.S. citizens living in Costa Rica, members of the Democrats Club, the Quaker community, and the Women's International League for Peace and Freedom (WILPF). We all listened to them at a special forum at the Quaker Peace Center in San José.

Dorothy Hagely stated that for her, listening to the broadcasts was the closest thing to being in Washington, DC in person. "Thank you FIRE," she said. "You have taught me today how to evade the cold weather in the United States, without missing the boat there." Gretchen Nielsen added:

I'm so glad I came to listen to this! I have lived here for many years and went back to the United States for a visit last year. I found it a different country: the anger, the hatred, the bad politics, and the despair is what I mostly saw and heard. However, now I come to listen to Expo '96, and it has given me hope and joy. I did not hear what women are doing and promoting when I was there.

Francis Chavarria, coordinator of the Global Women's Net based in Costa Rica, suggested the organization of monthly listening sessions to share information about the U.S. elections. Thus, Expo '96 has not only provoked strategies and new venues of coordination of women in the U.S., but has definitely influenced what expatriates in Costa Rica will do to be involved in politics back home.

Feminist Congress for Social Change in Mexico

FIRE was committed to following up on the results of Expo '96, and to building on our experience there in conducting remote broadcasts produced and hosted by other radio women.

On March 24, 1996, FIRE had an opportunity to do just that. Margarita Argot from SIPAM in Mexico and a producer at the FIRE-PLACE in China, called FIRE to organize a live broadcast. Her opening words were "From Mexico, we greet all of you. We are over 200 women who have gathered in the Feminist Congress for Social Change."

Topics of the activity were: (1) reform of the state, political participation, and democracy and women's citizenship; (2) development and equity, and globalization with equity and social policies; (3) political alliances, feminist coordination, and women's programs.; and (4) the right to information, media, and culture.

The Plan for Action of the Fourth World Conference on Women in China was also analyzed. Josefina Chávez, a Mexican feminist and member of one of the groups that organized the conference, talked about the gathering:

This conference is very important. It came out of the groups that took part in drafting the national NGO document for Beijing. Other women who did not go to Beijing are also here. We seek to discuss how to take further qualitative steps to have more political influence in relation to feminist demands. We want to design our

255

own feminist agenda, the agenda that we need in today's Mexico to enter into the process of transition to democracy, where women can participate in a coordinated, independent way in order to have an impact.

Lucero Gonzalez, member of the Information on Reproduction Group (GIRE), talked about the need for a feminist agenda:

We have assessed that the international agenda approved in Beijing is a useful instrument, but we want our own agenda, a feminist agenda that goes beyond [the Beijing agenda], that has a forward-looking strategy. We want to arrive at the next millennium with grounded and clear proposals. This is why one of the main topics discussed here is the ways we link with each other, our alliances, and how to influence the National Women's Program where four feminists from our group have been accepted.

Gloria Cariaga, also coordinator of the event, and member of the group Sor Juana's Closet, spoke about the political essence of the feminist movement—transformation of society:

In these past ten years we have specialized, both in terms of issues and also in sectors in which we work, and that has been important. But it sometimes seems as if modernization and specialization separate us from the political perspective that we have in regard to transformation of society. In this sense, the debates here about the reform of the state, alliances, the links between what each of us is doing, and social development in our country is very important for the recovery of our political essence.

Gloria also talked about another critical issue for the feminist movement—leadership and power:

In some discussion groups [in the event] we were able to sit down to discuss the issues about feminist leadership: the recognition of the leadership of women and the ways in which we are going to exercise representation and criteria about political representation.

She also talked about her thoughts on the challenges ahead:

We have to break away from the power issues through leadership and allow it to help us identify with each other and recognize what each is doing. We have to support leadership and create mechanisms of trust and support for those women who have developed substantively in different fields. These are two of the major achievements here: the recovery of our political essence and the acknowledgment of our feminist leadership.

Laura Frade, member of the group Alternatives in Training and Community Development, urged women's organizations in all countries to:

...follow up the implementation of the Plan for Action in each country and at the international level, because we run the risk of [having governments] backtrack.... It is important that we continue to share information about the commitments that governments signed on to, and implementation of those commitments.

Margarita Argot reported about the deliberations in the Mexican Feminist Conference in regards to communications, media, and culture, saying, "One of the substantive issues was the discussion about the need to work closely with media and the need of the movement to design and implement its own information, communication, and cultural strategies."

FIRE Covers Two More Protests in 1996

On March 1, 1996, the march in protest against the kidnapping of two women in Costa Rica took place at 12 noon in San José. Thousands of students, public workers, women, peace and human rights activists, families of the women kidnapped, and tourists marched silently, dressed in white. Convened by a coalition coordinated by the University for Peace, the day marked the second month of the kidnapping of

Nicola Fleuchaus (German) and Susana Sigfried (Costa Rican of Swiss descent). The women had been kidnapped by Comando Viviana Gallardo, who had undertaken at least two known previous terrorist actions in Costa Rica during the decade.

Nicola Fleuchaus and Susana Sigfried had been kidnapped from the Laguna de Lagarto Lodge in Santa Rita de Boca Tapada, San Carlos.

FIRE broadcast the march live by using the public phone in the Plaza de la Democracia as all the marchers came into the plaza. With the support of three policewomen who understood my explanation about the international broadcasting of the activity, many tourists, Costa Rican teachers, and passersby spoke live on FIRE. One of the speakers was Carlos:

I am Carlos, a teacher. As Costa Rican teachers we will not accept terrorism of any kind in this country. That is why I came to march today: for peace and justice for these innocent tourists.

The two kidnapped women were released by their abductors on March 12. Apparently, none of the governments of Costa Rica, Switzerland, or Germany became involved. Rather, it was the families of the women who negotiated their liberation.

Apparently the captors settled for a ransom of $200,000 private money. Not everything had been said about the issue, the captors, or the circumstances. The women were alive and free on March 22, but the threat of further kidnappings weighed on all who came to Costa Rica while silence and impunity remained.

Silence and impunity were also denounced on the 5th of March, when FIRE received a call from Perú. Women from that country had just ended a meeting where they decided to make a public international urgent action regarding the assassination, the day before, of Pascuala Rosado.

Having recently returned to her country after years of exile in Chile because of the persecutions of the Shining Path guerilla group, Pascuala was killed by them while traveling to the marketplace. Caller Victoria Villanueva said that Pascuala had suffered previous persecution by the terrorist organization, and "She will be in our hearts and in our work forever!"

Celebrating March 8, 1996

We celebrated March 8, International Women's Day, of 1996 in several ways. Locally, we covered a mobilization of women to the Supreme Court of Costa Rica. A meeting was held at 7:00 a.m., where 12 feminist delegates of women's human rights groups and human rights NGOs met with the president of the court. He was to respond to the findings and recommendations of the First Tribunal on Violations of Women's Human Rights in Costa Rica, which had been held on November 24, 1995.

The president of the Court, Dr. Edgar Cervantes, stated that he had decided to send the document to the Plenary Court composed of 19 magistrates. This gave the document the highest legal profile it could have. Women hoped this would also mean the highest commitment!

During the meeting, Dr. Cervantes expressed his admiration for the feminist movement and recognized that there were flaws in the administration of justice as it related to women. He promised the delegates, "I will do everything possible on behalf of women."

As we know, everything possible for women was full implementation of the Platform for Action of the UN Fourth World Conference on Women and respect for all human rights standards in the country—no more, no less.

As the women came out of the meeting, other women were waiting outside the court building to hear the president's response. Katerina Anfossi interviewed some of them for FIRE's broadcast two hours later.

One of the women interviewed was Cora Ferro, feminist theologian and former director of women's studies at the National University of Heredia in Costa Rica:

It is important to point out that this 8th of March is very significant for all Latin American women because everything that is done in any country affects all. What we have done here at the court was to defend women's rights!

Esperanza Castro, a grassroots organizer of San José, said, "Because this day honors women workers of many years ago, today we have to think and support women in the maquilas [U.S. industries in northern Mexico] who are so exploited."

María Eugenia Barquero, an urban community activist, added, "Women in marginalized communities and campesino women should also be honored today. Neoliberal policies are denying us our rights."

Marcela Jagger, one of the testifiers at the Tribunal of Violations of Women's Human Rights in Costa Rica, said that she was very excited about the morning's activity "because women's rights are being claimed."

Human Rights activist Luisa López talked about the importance of the activity: "By bringing the resolutions of the tribunal to the court, we are demanding a change in legislation, and an end to androcentric legislation that contributes to the violations of women's human rights."

Ana Elena Obando, lawyer and organizer of the tribunal declared that by bringing the resolutions to the court, "We are bridging the gap between nonformal activities like the tribunal and formal institutions like the Supreme Court."

Ana Virginia Duarte, coordinator of the Women's Human Rights Project at the Central American Human Rights Commission, read a statement drafted by women's organizations. The statement addressed the murder of Pascuala Rosado, which had been denounced on FIRE two days before. It called for justice and an end to violence and expressed solidarity with the family of Pascuala in Perú. The pronouncement also affirmed solidarity with Nicola and Susana, the two women who had been kidnapped by terrorists in Costa Rica on March 1, and demanded their release by their abductors.

That day FIRE's English broadcast was dedicated to the women from Algeria who were simultaneously organizing their first-ever local Tribunal on Violations of Women's Human Rights by fundamentalists. Caught between the religious fanatics and a government that has not protected women, women's rights seemed to be the bargaining chip in the "peace" negotiations. According to Radio Algiers' own broadcast that same day, "In the past year alone, 342 Algerian women were killed by fundamentalist terrorists, and another 353 women were wounded."

FIRE received a call from an Algerian activist who did not want to be identified. She said that there had been a call for a dialogue toward peaceful resolution to the conflict in that country and that women's rights were being sacrificed at the negotiating table. "The government, in the process, might give up the rights of women," she added. She described the women's action:

On this day in Algeria, women have gathered together as one to denounce the crimes of the fundamentalists against women in the whole of Algeria, the violence against them, the rise of fundamentalism. Women from political parties and organizations have come together today. This alone is news because women have not been able to unite as such.

On that day, women from the Algerian Group of Democratic Women and the Association for the Promotion of Women had organized a tribunal on violations of their rights. The testifiers, their families and the press had come to the tribunal to give or hear the testimonies. Our guest continued:

Religious fanaticism in Algeria has led to various crimes, killings of intellectuals, democrats, but especially women because they are women. Women are killed if they do not wear a veil, and also if they wear one. They are killed in the home and in schools, villages, and cities. It is really a massive massacre of women, just because they are women, and according to fundamentalists, the place of women is at home.... [A woman is killed] not for what she does, but for what she is.

When asked what she recommended for other women to do, she said:

As women we should side together and show solidarity; women should approach the representatives of Algeria in their own countries, write to the President of the Republic in Algeria and denounce the fact that the fundamentalist program is sexual apartheid—the complete separation between the world of men and the world of women, and this separation of women would be decided by men, and not by women themselves. [Women should denounce that] any compromise with the fundamentalists would be cutting severely women's human rights in Algeria. For instance the family code that is now enforced deprives women in Algeria of all their rights within the family, as well as some rights as citizens.

She issued a further call to the international audience:

Women in Algeria have called on women to come to their country despite the situation because women in Algeria were cut off from women in other parts of the world for many years. There is hope that because of solidarity, things can change.... So right now in Algeria the government is prepared to end the war, not a civil war, but a war against civilians, because it is only civilians, the ones who are being massacred by both sides: by the army and by the fundamentalists. So in this context it is important to let the world know that the Algerian government is prepared to compromise with the fundamentalists to end the killings, but at the cost of women's rights. If we can prevent this by making public and shaming the Algerian government for this attempt, then it would be a big achievement.

Asked by FIRE about what else it could do, the caller said:

FIRE should put Algerian women on the air on a regular basis at this time, so that the world starts knowing about what is happening there, and how horrendous the crimes against women are during wars and conflicts.... FIRE can be a link between women who have suffered in war and conflict situations and bring them together so they take action together, not as individual victims, but as women victims coming together, and women judges coming together. These crimes have to be judged!

FIRE was featured on the March 8 broadcast of WBAI in New York. We talked about how the Arias Foundation for Human Development had organized the signing of the Contract with the Costa Rican Women. Similar to WEDO's Contract with the American Women to enforce the promises gained in the Fourth World's Conference on Women, the Arias document included the commitments made by members of the United Nations at the FWCW. Media, an issue forgotten in WEDO's contract, is included in the Costa Rican contract. It was promoted by former First Lady Margarita Penon and signed by local legislators, women in government, women in specialized UN agencies, and women in funding agencies.

Parallel to the March 8 activities throughout the world, the UN Commission on the Status of Women (CSW) was preparing to meet in New York from March 11-22. Media was one of the issues to be discussed at the Beijing followup meeting. The CSW stressed women's access to new technologies among other issues in the platform.

FIRE Online

In March 1996, FIRE consolidated the e-mail/shortwave radio experience we had started developing during and after Beijing. A new permanent segment was created on FIRE: an e-mail radio system where the audience is asked to write messages online, to be read on the air. The response was great from the start. Following are some of the messages we received.

Date: Sun, 18 Feb 1996 20:38:50—0800 (PST)
From: Dorothy Kidd, Canada

I'd love to hear about your FIREPLACE stories as I'd like to do something with them on Vancouver Cooperative Radio. As well, I am forwarding your name on to Marjorie Beaucage, a Canadian filmmaker who is completing a video about Beijing and is looking for more sound material. So talk to you soon.

Date: Friday, February 23, 1996
From: Jean Parker, Colorado Coordinator, Cross Disabilities Coalition

I just wanted to tell you that I received the tapes you sent about the tribunals. I have listened to them all and found them very informative. I want to pass them to others I know who would benefit from the information presented in this way. Thank you for sending them.

Subject: Asking for information from Spain!!!
Date: Thu, 15 Feb 96 15:36:00

My friends,

This a new Spanish shortwave listener who would like to get some information about your programs, frequencies and everything you consider suitable for someone like me. Moreover, I can tell you that I am a Journalism postgraduate student at the University of Navarra, in Pamplona, Spain. I would love to write my doctoral thesis about the future of shortwave radio stations, in particular, and the future of international broadcasting, in general. It would be great if any of you could send me some information (more Internet addresses, brochures that you publish, where to find articles about this issue, discussion groups, etc). I would truly appreciate it very much. On the other hand, I offer myself to keep in contact with you and give you all the information you ask for (if any) about this kind of activity in Spain, which is not much, by the way.

Date: Friday, February 9, 1996 7:13am

Dear María,

I'm sorry you were not able to make it to the Expo, but I understand you had a class to teach. I did have the opportunity to wander over to the FIRE/WINGS booth and hear some of the live broadcast. There was a group of Dominican women from New York City whom I had a chance to hear—they had interesting things to say on their impressions of the Expo. The Expo was a rousing success, despite the fact that we had a snowstorm. Over 3,200 people actually showed up—we could have gotten more if the weather had been better. In a way it reminded me of the NGO Forum—except that it was more orderly and was taking place in a nonhostile context (if you forget about the U.S. Congress and the right wing attacks on women).

I still dream of coming to Costa Rica There is a young woman in my office here—Justine Andronici, who is very interested in coming and doing the FIRE internship in Costa Rica. I will give her your e-mail and phone so that she can contact you directly.

Christine O., Feminist Majority
Washington, DC, U.S.

From: Arnel Martinez Reyes, Cuba

Greetings to Katerina, María and the rest of this enthusiastic FIRE collective. I want to tell you that a few days ago, while I was browsing my shortwave radio I found your program and listened to it attentively. I find it very interesting, and I wish you the best, and that you keep working just like you have so far. I am a 29-year-old young guy, single, and a fervent collaborator in radio. I am the president of a listeners' club of Radio BANES; at the archeological city of Cuba. I love to read, collect stamps, postcards, picture magazines, and like to get letters from friends in other countries. I would like to get the magazine Gentes from you, so that I can document my information about AIDS. I would also like to get your QSL card, pictures, calendars, frequencies, and please put me on your friends list.

Besides these types of messages and reception reports, FIRE began receiving news that women wanted posted on shortwave alongside the posting of the information on e-mail conferences. Following is an excerpt from the first set of announcements we received after we announced the new segment:

SEXUAL HARASSMENT IN BRAZILIAN UNIVERSITY BECOMES POLITICAL WAR— YOU CAN HELP

- -

This message is about a serious case of sexual harassment in Brazil. We are asking for the HELP of concerned people and organizations. Please forward this message to whomever you think appropriate.

- -

This account is about power and about its abuse. It is about the unwritten prohibition of stating sexual harassment, spurious allegiances and other power games freely played by some university professors, protected from truth by their violent corporate practices.

Vera Helena Monezi is an administrative worker at the University of Sao Paulo (USP) since 1981. She used to work at the Biology Department, at the Institute of Biosciences and she also had regular political activity in her local Union. In October 19, 1993, she was forced to report sexual harassment to the police department: the head of her department had been insistently harassing her and, in the face of her open refusals, he made her life in her workplace unbearable. Finally, he threatened to fire her.

Vera had a witness to one of her boss's strikes: a colleague of hers. What followed her report was an incredible series of attacks. First, they threatened her witness until he denied having seen or heard anything that could impute guilt on their boss. Then they refused to transfer her if she didn't agree to withdraw her denouncement. The agreement where they stated their conditions is properly documented. With no witness and—documents attest to it—the interference of influential people in the high courts of the country, the charge was filed in March 1994.

Vera was transferred this same month to the Center of Marine Biology of the USP, in a little town about three hours from Sao Paulo. The director revealed herself a server of the Institute's policy toward Vera's reports: despite the acknowledged competence of this worker (and the director wrote letters stating her position), she was put "in disposability" in June 1994. Well, the electoral period in Brazil started in May 1994 and the law is clear about the impossibility of transferring public workers for seven months around the election....

Palestinian women also began sending their reports:

The Women's Affairs Technical Committee (WATC), has started its Palestinian women's network project within which contacts are established with various women's organizations all around the world. We are very interested in establishing contacts with prominent women's organizations in your country. We would appreciate it a lot if you could circulate this message to all people concerned with women's issues. Hope this will be the first step toward establishing the wide supportive network we admire. With all my respect and hope to hear from you soon.
Yours sincerely, Shuaa Marrar,
Coordinator of Palestinian women's network

December 5, 1995
This is just a little note to keep you informed about the most recent challenge in the Palestinian women's arena. The Women's Affairs Technical Committee has been very busy recently with the mobilization against various measures imposed by some of our Palestinian Ministries who are violating some of the basic human rights of Palestinian women....
WATC, which includes representatives of women from three main political groups, a number of women's study centers, and independent women activists, held a meeting on December 4, 1995, with the Palestinian Deputy Minister for Internal Affairs, Mr. Ahmad Tamimi at the WATC offices in Ramallah.
We informed Mr. Tamimi that we are astonished to learn that our Ministry for Internal Affairs is requiring women to bring along a

266

written consent from their husband, father, or brother before a Palestinian traveling document is issued. Another permission from the father or the husband is also required before a woman is permitted to leave the country.

The Deputy Ministry praised the role of the Palestinian woman stressing that traditions, Palestinian culture, and religions should be taken into consideration when issuing our Palestinian laws. We stressed that this is the time for abolishing all traditions that do injustice to women. We are already networking with more women's organizations and activists for a strong stand against these discriminating laws that violate the Universal Declaration of Human Rights, the Convention on the Elimination of All Forms of Discrimination Against Women and most important of all, the Palestinian Declaration of Independence.

We are, at this point trying to use the information tool to its utmost, appealing to all human rights institutions and to all countries who have stood by the Universal Declaration of Human Rights to stand by Palestinian women in their rightful demands for equal rights.

We hope you can join us in our just struggle. We thank you again for your support.

Sincerely,
Suheir Azzouni Mahshi, Director

To All Women All Around the World
"United We Are Strong"
We, the Women's Affairs Technical Committee (WATC), would like to establish a wide supportive network with different organizations all around the world. We want to exchange our successful and failed experiences with you and benefit from each experience in solidarity....

Another e-mail message came from women in the United States:

PARTICIPANT INFORMED CONSENT FORM
March 7, 1996
Hello! We are members of a graduate seminar in Communication Studies at the University of Northern Iowa, U.S. For our group project

we wanted to help in some small way to carry the work of the United Nations Conference on Women in Beijing forward. Thus, we are asking anyone who reads this to answer the few questions below. Our objective is to help assess the usefulness of the section of the Platform for Action on Women pertaining to violence against women (section D, which we have included at the end of this survey for your easy reference).

We are not attempting to obtain a statistically generalizable sampling of responses. Rather, we seek information from as many sources as possible. Thus, we ask that you forward this survey to others on e-mail or post it on your Worldwide Web Home Page....

A Witness for Peace who had visited Guatemala sent us the following report:

Feb 11-26 I participated in a Witness For Peace human rights observer mission to Guatemala. Forty volunteers from around the U.S. gathered in Guatemala City for briefings and then split into two groups. One group traveled to Xaman, the site of an Oct '95 military massacre of returned refugees who had purchased land and had been guaranteed freedom from military intrusion. The other group visited Rio Negro, after studying the World Bank-funded Chixoy dam project....

The group I followed went to Pacux, the government-built model village, next to a military base, where the displaced survivors of the Rio Negro massacres have been relocated. There is a monument to those massacred, which is located near Pacux, within sight of the military base. Along with commemoration of other massacres, it names 71 women and 107 children killed on March 13, 1982, as well as those who killed them—the civil patrol from the nearby town of Xococ, in the presence of Guatemalan military officers.

We also heard several accounts from witnesses, some of whom were children taken as slaves to serve those who had killed their families. This was done under the policies of "low intensity conflict," with training by the U.S. military through the School of the Americas and other programs. The goal was to destroy movements calling for social justice and economic space for the survival of the indigenous majority.

268

My role on this trip was to document the experience with photographs and sound recordings. I asked each speaker for permission to record. After telling them about the work of RFPI, I asked if concern for their personal safety should restrain broadcast of their accounts in Central America. They all agreed to broadcast.

In a few days I should have a log of material, most of which was spoken in Spanish and English (Spanish speaker would pause and translator would deliver the English). Some talks were entirely in English. The dignity and strength of the women who deliver most of this discussion is clear and impressive. As a longtime listener to FIRE, I'm grateful for the prospect that some of this material, if broadcast, can live beyond our memory and our notes, and reach far beyond the four walls and the small group of us who heard it.

From Jerry Markatos

FIRE's Activism Continues in 1997

The dynamics of 1997 were crucial in grounding FIRE in the region, while maintaining and developing its international scope. The year 1997 was also crucial in helping FIRE's staff understand the issue of institutional identity.

Jennifer Harbury's Search for Justice

At the very beginning of 1997, Harvard graduate attorney and human rights activist Jennifer Harbury began producing 15-minute phone programs for FIRE about her husband's disappearance and murder in Guatemala, and about the cases she has submitted to the court of the Organization of American States (OAS) about it.

Bámaca Velásquez, known as *Everardo* in the indigenous resistance movement in his country, disappeared in the hands of the Guatemalan army in 1992. His widow was searching for the truth about the crime and for an end to impunity of human rights violations in that Central American country:

My husband was a Mayan citizen of Guatemala, who was captured by the Guatemalan army in 1992. I tried for three years to find out what had become of him, and the army would only state that he had been killed in combat, and that they knew nothing more about him. In fact, he had been seen alive and being tortured to death by a Coronel Julio Roberto Alpérez.

During the next three years, I went to the government of the United States, to the State Department, to the National Security Council, again, and again, and again asking for help and information about obtaining a fair and balanced trial for him, and treatment in conformance with the Geneva Convention: no torture, no secret prison, no murder without a trial, basic medical care.... The torture that I had heard about him receiving was truly terrifying. I got no help whatsoever from the U.S. government. After three seriously dangerous hunger strikes, one of which lasted 32 days. I eventually learned that he had been killed by Coronel Julio Roberto Alpérez, the same person the eyewitness had seen torturing him earlier.

And not only that, but I also learned that Coronel Alpérez is someone who is paid by the CIA to send information over to them. In fact, the same month that Alpérez was seen torturing my husband, he received $44,000 from the CIA. In short, what we have learned is that the CIA pays for information that they know is being extracted from prisoners who are being secretly detained, tortured, and eventually assassinated. This information is not being given to family members, who never really do learn what becomes of their loved ones.

This is a practice that I would like to bring to an end. What we need is to have that bright, bright line drawn so that there is a clear signal sent to all military dictatorships in the future that [what they have done] is against the law, [that they are] not above the law.... That's what I hope to get out of the Inter-American case against the Guatemalan army.

FIRE broadcast Jennifer Harbury's programs whenever she was able to send them to us, as she traveled back and forth between the USA and Guatemala to prepare the cases.

Throughout 1998, the Inter-American Court of the OAS held three public hearings about the Bámaca Velásquez case presented by Jennifer

Harbury. Claims include the possible responsibility of the Guatemalan state in the disappearance, torture, and extrajudicial execution of Bámaca. The Inter-American Commission has requested the OAS Court to declare that Guatemala has violated human rights, and that it should investigate the facts and punish those responsible for the case. The OAS Commission has also stated that Guatemala should inform the family about the whereabouts of Bámaca's body and give them his remains. The proposed resolution also calls for reforms in the methods of training the army, and suggests that the state should compensate the relatives of the victim.

On June 18, 1998, as Jennifer came out from the second court hearing in Costa Rica, FIRE approached her again about the case.

It is an important day for me for two reasons. One, today is the birthday of Everardo, my husband. He would have been 41 today if he had lived. He was tortured by the Guatemalan army several years ago, as most of you know.

The second reason it is an important day is that we have just finished the first phase of our trial, an international trial against the Guatemalan army here in the Inter-American Court of the OAS here in San José, Costa Rica. The Guatemalan army was finally forced to stand trial [in a place] where they cannot shoot the judges, or intimidate them, or buy them. They are not in Guatemala where no intellectual author of a war atrocity has ever stood a trial for any of the 200,000 assassinations and tortures, or for any of the 440 massacres of the Mayan villages in that country.

So it is a very special day [because] we were able to force them [the army] to try to defend themselves in an international tribunal where they were not in command of the situation and could not prevent justice. It was really good for me to be heard just once in front of a panel of judges that the Guatemalan army didn't own or control with guns to their heads.

Throughout Jennifer Harbury's search for justice, FIRE coordinated with the Central American Human Rights Commission (CODEHUCA) for a transcription of her programs in Spanish and English and publication of them in their newsletter to the region. As a result of FIRE's programs on the air, where we called for people to send Jennifer cases that would support her cases in the courts, Jennifer received three more cases.

One of them was about a woman survivor who disappeared in Honduras in 1982. While she was imprisoned, she heard people with U.S. accents talking to the Honduran military who were performing the tortures. Her testimony appears in the introduction to Harbury's cases in the U.S. courts.

I have two different lawsuits against the United States government. One is against the CIA and several other agencies under the Freedom of Information Act to force them to give me the rest of my files—what they haven't given me so far.

The most important one to me, though, is a civil rights case that I have brought against close to 30 defendants. All are U.S. officials, either in the CIA, or in the White House National Security Council, or in the Department of State, including the former U.S. Ambassador [in Guatemala] Marilyn Macafee.

There are two halves of this case really, under different parts of United States law, and in particular, the Constitution. The most important half of the case is that United States officials have in fact collaborated, and cooperated, and contributed to torture and assassinations and clandestine prisons not only in Guatemala, but everywhere—number one, by paying for information they know has been extracted through torture and assassination; also by failing to properly supervise and screen people who are on their payroll as informants, by not revealing information that they should in order to save human lives.

So they have actually covered them up, not only promoted torture and assassination and secret detention, but covered for it, and shielded it, and protected it through official impunity so that it would continue.

And the fact that it is continuing this day in Guatemala is reflected in the recent brutal assassination of Bishop Gerardi in Guatemala. The 75 year-old bishop had been run out of Quiche during the massacre era, returned from exile, and had written an exhaustive study of the war crimes in Guatemala, assigning 85 percent of the atrocities to the Guatemalan army and paramilitary, and 10 percent to the guerrillas. Forty-eight hours later he was bludgeoned to death in his garage. They tortured him to death. It took him 15 to 30 minutes to die, drowning in his own blood. We've [the USA] been helping this situation by paying these people and shielding them from justice for all of these years.

The second half is related to the shielding of justice, which is lying to family members, withholding information that would have saved lives.

If we know where a torture center is, such as the one where Sister Diana Ortiz was held, we cannot shield that from the outside world, we have to report it immediately so that those lives can be saved.

So we are not only covering up for people, we are actually in torture chambers. Maybe our [USA] officials are not using their hands to carry out the torture, but they were paying for information extracted through torture, they were present at the torture centers, they knew where the tortures were, [they knew] who was being tortured, who was about to die, and where the torture centers were. And they have lied all these years about it to the United States government and to the United States people. And I think that it is time that practice comes to an end.

As of the beginning of 1999 the OAS Court had not yet issued a verdict regarding the Bámaca Velázquez case.

Women's Health, 1997

From March 17-20, 1997, FIRE did daily live coverage of the Seventh International Women's Health Conference in Rio de Janeiro, Brazil, giving priority to the voices of women of color present at the conference, and also to Brazilian domestic workers and elder political activists.

On March 18, African American April Taylor from the International Black Women's Health Network interviewed another African American woman live on FIRE. Loretta Ross, a member of the Georgia-based National Center for Human Rights Education in the USA, shared her impression of the conference:

My impression of this conference is that it is like a global feminist meeting about women's health issues. It has been going on for two decades. We've come together a lot in these global gatherings outside

273

the auspices of the United Nations where male-controlled organizations set the agenda. This is the time we set our own agenda, and we talk about our own issues, and it is the time when we draw our own ideological lines on a lot of issues. So this is the place to be, and I encourage women listening to go to the next one, which will happen in three years in Canada.

April Taylor also interviewed Evelyn White, author of a black women's health book published in the United States, who said:

There is a stereotype about black women being strong, and that affects the way we look at our health problems, and they way others do, too. The issues of sexuality are also full of stereotypes, so we have to talk about our personal lives at these meetings. I got involved in this issue through the links with the Brazilian black women in a project by the Global Exchange in San Francisco. I am writing about this conference, because this conference has given me a better understanding that black women in other countries need solidarity, and we need to learn from them!

Jasmin Edding, a black German from ADEFRA, also became a producer on FIRE's live broadcasts. She interviewed Evelyn White also, because the day before she had heard in FIRE's broadcast that Evelyn had written a book about black women's health, and she wanted to know more about it.

JASMIN: Tell us about the book, because you mentioned it yesterday, but you did not explain.

EVELYN: Yes, I edited the book, and it is called Speaking for Ourselves. *The first edition of the book was published by Zeal Press in Seattle, Washington, in 1990, and then an expanded edition [was published] in 1994. The basic impetus of the book was to bring together a collection of African American women writing on a variety of issues, especially to demystify that black women are strong and invincible in the USA, that we can handle any problem. When you look at statistics, we have high rates of diseases such as breast cancer, diabetes, stress.... On the other hand, it is hard for us to talk about these issues because*

274

it is expected that we concentrate on oppression, racism, and such,
and not deal with our own selves. I addressed that. Alice Walker writes,
Angela Davis writes in it. And so does Audre Lord.

Throughout the broadcasts, FIRE celebrated the tenth anniversary of the Catholics for Free Choice on March 18.

FIRE also broadcast the day the groundbreaking news that Algerian women's groups had issued an international case against one of the fundamentalist terrorists in their country. The case concerned a growing threat to women's human rights and to women's lives by non-state actors, such as fundamentalist groups in much of Algeria as well as in many other places in the world. Therefore, special attention needed be given to the fact that, in the name of human rights, freedom of speech, and freedom of expression—all values that are cherished—many of the worst perpetrators of abuses against women are seen exclusively as victims and thus granted privileges that are denied to women.

Many countries had given asylum to Algerian fundamentalists on the grounds that they would be persecuted by the state if they were living in Algeria, totally ignoring the fact that asylum cannot be granted to perpetrators of crimes. Meanwhile Algerian democrats and especially targeted women, running for their lives and fleeing from persecution by fundamentalists, have been denied asylum, on the grounds that they were not persecuted by the state but by non-state actors.

This de facto ruling gives impunity to fundamentalist perpetrators and their being granted asylum. Moreover, their being labeled victims rather than perpetrators also gives them a wide audience in human rights circles. A leader of the network Women Living Under Muslim Laws said on one of FIRE's broadcasts:

We need to stand against their enjoying such impunity. This case is
very symbolic of the general problem, but because it involves a promi-
nent leader, it is the occasion for us, as women who suffer from funda-
mentalists' anti-women policies and practices, to make our voice heard.

The case was brought to the courts in the USA by the Center for Constitutional Rights and CUNY Law School in New York. Both organizations represent Algerian people, among whom are many women, victims of fundamentalists and calling for for democracy in Algeria. They have initiated a lawsuit against Anwar Haddam of the Islamic Salvation Front in the U.S., where he happily lived for several years. He is facing charges of crimes against humanity. As of February 1999, the case had not been decided in the U.S. courts.

FIRE in Spain

The Intercontinental Gathering for Humanity and Against Neoliberalism took place in Spain in the last week of July and the first week of August in 1997. FIRE's Katerina Anfossi covered the activity, which was attended by some 3,000 people from 50 countries. Among them were men and women from Italy, Spain, Mexico, Switzerland, France, Germany, Denmark, Canada, the USA, Finland, Ireland, Britain, Belgium, Sweden, the Czech Republic, Greece, Austria, Portugal, South Africa, Chad, Cameroon, Rwanda, Senegal, Togo, Morocco, Turkey, Israel, India, Bangladesh, Australia, and Indonesia, as well as nearly every country from South America.

It was the Second Encounter—based on the preceding First Intercontinental Encounter for Humanity and Against Neoliberalism, convened by the Zapatistas and carried out in Zapatista communities in Chiapas exactly one year before. It was at that first meeting where participants agreed to convene the second gathering.

As part of the official inauguration ceremony on the evening of July 26, the two Zapatista representatives—Dalia and Felipe, both Tojolabales from the exiled community of Guadalupe Tepeyac—addressed the thousands of delegates with a message from the indigenous Zapatista communities of Chiapas. In her inaugural speech, Dalia presented her view about power:

We did not come here to fight among ourselves, to see whose word is best, or to find out who has the truth or who is the strongest. Freedom is not achieved by defeating one's brother. We can only become better with others, and not on top of others.

Major working groups into which the delegates at the encuentro were divided included the following:

- The neoliberal economy against humanity: Our lives beyond the economy
- Work, and the means of production: Creating the conditions for a worthwhile life
- North-South and East-West relations
- People and identities: Old and new problems
- Human mobility and forced destinies
- Struggles for culture, education, and information
- Women and their struggles: The struggle against patriarchy
- Struggles for land and the earth: Ecology
- Against all forms of marginalization

The Zapatista representatives presented the following paper on the struggles of women:

Friends: women and men. I am going to tell you a little about the women who provide support for the Zapatista Army of National Liberation. First, I would like to say that the women of the rebel village of Guadalupe Tepeyac are by nature very strong. We do not give in, and we struggle with great dignity. As Zapatista women, we believe that there should be not only men in control, because we women have our way of thinking and our ideas, too. We, the women of the Zapatista villages, see our children with nothing to eat, without a proper house or proper clothing. We also see that the family does not have land to grow crops on. But apart from this, we indigenous women have no education.

Very few of us can read and write, and we also have problems with our health. Many of us die when giving birth or from malnutrition. That is why we struggle, and that is why we support the Zapatista Army of National Liberation. When the insurgents came down to our villages from the mountains, they started to explain to us that we women had rights and we had to fight to make sure those rights were respected. Women's rights have to be respected first of all by the community since that is where everything starts. We realized then that the men who drank beat their wives. That is why we agree completely that there should be no alcohol in the communities. The insurgents taught us about the struggle and later the different communities discussed laws for women in the Zapatista villages.

In these laws the women of the villages said that they deserved respect, that women have a right to work, to receive money, to decide how many children they want to have, to marry the person they want to—because it was not like this before. There are still many villages where women are forced to marry against their will. That is why in the Zapatista villages there is the law that says nobody can be forced into marriage. The women's laws also say that women can join the EZLN if they want to and that they can hold positions of leadership just like any man—in other words, they can be part of the military command. This is what we can tell you about our struggle. We see the struggle of women as a long one that varies from place to place. We, the women of the Zapatistas, see women struggling in other countries, but sometimes we see them struggling for things that we do not understand. I want to tell you that the Zapatista women respect all of your different ways of thinking.

We want to learn about your struggles and talk about how we struggle and how we organize. We want you to listen to us, but above all we want to listen to you. Perhaps some people think that our struggle is very minor and that we should fight harder. We say to them that our struggle, like that of many women, is only just beginning. That is all, companions in struggle.

—Compañera Dalia and Felipe, EZLN support

Although in the midst of the event, Katerina was not able to find the working group about women, she did a live broadcast on FIRE where she raised some of the issues regarding women's political participation, stating that there was little representation in the organization of the event. She also thanked the Foundation for a Compassionate Society for having contributed to the presence of more women at the Encounter.

Community Radio in El Salvador

In July 1997, we were also in El Salvador at AMARC's First Central American Regional Community Radio Conference. The main issue dealt with at the conference was the legal status of community radio in the region. In El Salvador, for example, only the eight community radio stations already in existence were able to get licenses and frequencies. The rest of the licenses were assigned to those who could pay. FIRE's Katerina Anfossi, who attended the meeting, observed:

Commercial interests are overriding the fact that the radio spectrum should be of service to the communities, thus communities should have access to some of the frequencies. It seems that privatization is also affecting communications! That is a violation of the right to communicate!

Katerina also shared the fact that the Latin American and Caribbean Women's Health Network met to issue actions to strengthen their organization with AMARC. One of the main actions agreed to by the women radio producers was to work together in gender training.

Economic Violence
Against Women

On November 25, 1997, FIRE broadcast live from Vancouver, Canada, at the alternative women's activist meeting that was held parallel to the Asian Free Trade Agreement Summit of businessmen and heads of states.

On the live broadcast organized by Vancouver Community Radio producer Dorothy Kidd, the women from the Vancouver Commission on the Status of Women came on the air to talk about their protest against the Asia Pacific Economic Forum (APEC). Dorothy said the forum was considering "a new kind of free trade agreement that will be made by the Asia Pacific countries and also Australia, New Zealand, the USA, Canada, Mexico, and Chile." She also explained that at the meeting the governments were on the sidelines, and the real negotiators were the businessmen.

A lot of activities were planned to counter this neoliberal agenda, among them the two-day Women's Forum, the Second International Conference of Women Against APEC, which took place a week before the gathering of the corporations and the governments. It was attended by women from all the countries involved in the agreement.

Participants in the program were Ema Alicia Cortéz, originally from Mexico, and Carmen Miranda. Carmen, a Guatemalan woman living in Canada, is a member of a women's radio group in her country called Nuestra Voz. Ema talked about the potential impact on women if APEC is approved:

It will be very dangerous in Asia, because the corporations will have the power to devastate the economy of any one country in the region. When a country turns into economic crisis, women have to do most of the work and also suffer most of the pain because of the oppression. And once there is a crisis, all human rights are erased. So if APEC continues, the consequences are going to be devastating, and not only for Asia, but for the world!

Carmen Miranda talked about the impact of structural adjustment in her country.

Because neoliberalism is about privatization, in my country now the national hospitals are charging money for people's health to be taken care of. They ask for a "donation," but the fact is that if people do not pay, they will not get the service.

Economic violence against women was the main topic of the women's meeting. Called feminization of poverty in Latin America, it means that women have always been the poorest of the poor, with lower wages and less ownership of land, so declines in real wages and jobs have a particularly strong impact on these groups.

Feminization of poverty also means that increased privatization has led to higher costs for health care, such that an increasing number of families cannot afford proper medical care nor to send their children to school. In that situation, it is the women who take on the extra tasks as substitute nurses or caretakers, often in addition to working at paid jobs. As with other domestic unpaid work of women, serving as caretaker has no economic value in a market economy.

Cuts in daycare services and support also create additional burdens for women. A third characteristic of feminization of poverty is that structural adjustment policies have fueled growing economic polarization with a wider gap between rich and poor, along with higher unemployment and lower wages, which have taken a greater toll on women. Although in some cases the number of jobs have actually increased, particularly for women, these tend to be private-sector positions with low pay, few benefits, and no job security.

Finally, women are more likely to put themselves last, focusing more on their families when it comes to limited availability of food, education, and health care, and so are far more likely to be malnourished, illiterate, and have chronic health problems left untreated. Declines in economic prosperity have contributed to a deterioration of social conditions, with widespread increases in crime and violence—particularly against women.

The actions of women's NGOs during the official APEC summit included the organizing of a "ribbon of hope" containing demands, which women presented to the dinner place of the official delegates while they were eating. Ema described their entrance:

It was called to my attention that there was an Indonesian guard taking our picture as we walked in. Women from Burma, women from East Timor, and others were there, but they were not able to go in because they were stopped, and others were photographed.

The participants in the live broadcast also denounced the fact that the Canadian police disrupted the peaceful marches, saying that those kinds of activities could not happen "because this is a democracy!"

Reflection and Reformulation

Also in 1997, FIRE received funds from the WHO, and we began our reception report study. Norma Valle spent a month with us here in Costa Rica, and we looked at all the letters we had received during the past six years and distributed almost 300 questionnaires to listeners who wrote in 1996 and 1997. We received more than a fifty percent response to our questionnaires, and the Reception Report Study was completed on March 8, 1999 (see Chapter 13).

Most of the end of the year 1997, FIRE staff spent time reflecting about building a stable present for its growth and development to be ready for the future.

Staff reflections about the way to tackle our entry into the millennium included issues such as legal status, funding, autonomy, and others. As a starting point for reformulation, FIRE drafted the following statement:

The time has come to make some major changes. Change is part of growth, and growth is what needs to happen for FIRE.... We have chosen to face the challenge, the growing pains, and the risks. And we feel we have designed ways to do it successfully.

That is our choice in the context of today. Looking at other women's media, it seems that many women-owned media organizations are faced with that same challenge of profound change, one way or another.

This year ISIS International, based in Manila, Philippines, published a book about women-owned media in the world. The publication was originally thought to be one that would depict outstanding alternative women's media outlets that today could be considered "success stories." But in the process of selecting from the many women-owned media venues—community, local, national, regional, and international in the world, they realized that instead of calling them "success stories," they would make an introduction calling them "survivors" at this point. FIRE is among the significant survivors.

FIRE has survived the backlash against women, the homogenization and forced abortion of women-owned media through globalization, and the cutbacks in funding for women's projects.

FIRE is a survivor because of the broad support and its grounding in the local, regional, and international feminist movement. A very important factor has been the unconditional financial support of Genevieve Vaughan of the Foundation for a Compassionate Society. Yet another factor has been the permanent staff of producers' own convictions and work as part of the women's movement. The support of the audience has been crucial and very affirming. Another factor that has contributed to FIRE's continuing existence through the past seven years is that the Global Fund for Women and many other foundations and funds have supported FIRE's special projects. None in isolation has been the source of our strength for survival.

The other interesting thing about the survivor stories in the ISIS book is that out of the total of survivor stories, FIRE knows that at least 12 of them are currently undergoing very major transformations from what they have been and done in the past 10 years. These include, among others, Fempress, ISIS itself, Women's Feature Service, and the International Women's Tribune Center.

It seems that it has been characteristic of feminist media organizations today to make the big changes that the times demand of us. The following are the transformations FIRE will undertake:

1. *Giving FIRE a legal entity in Costa Rica as part of Latin America and the Caribbean, while at the same time strengthening the buildup of FIRE's international character through our links with the international women's movement. FIRE has been a nonprofit nongovernmental organization based in Costa Rica "de facto" for the past seven years. What FIRE will do is legalize that fact.*

2. *FIRE will look for diversified funding to alleviate the burden that the Foundation for a Compassionate Society has had in providing all of the core funding for FIRE. Until it has its own legal status in the region, this is hardly possible. In the globalized world of neoliberalism today, to the funding world, any organization (FIRE included) belongs to the place (read country) though which it gets its funds. Throughout the seven years of FIRE, it has received its core funds though the legal status that Radio for Peace International has in the USA though Earth Communications. Therefore FIRE would not qualify as a Southern-based organization when it really is precisely that!*

3. *The feminist movement has been a major force in struggling locally, regionally, and globally so that the issue of composition in decision-making is taken into account and is a key factor in defining what social or political organizations are all about. FIRE needs to have its own board of directors, because, although the staff has been an autonomous team of women within the radio station that hosts FIRE, it can be subject to the relations that RFPI has, unless it stands on its own.*

At the end of the year, FIRE informed the Foundation for a Compassionate Society about the proposed changes, which were very much welcomed by Genevieve Vaughan, who had been suggesting to

FIRE that we adopt our own legal status. FIRE then began to negotiate with RFPI about the terms in which this change would take place.

We stated that FIRE would formalize its status as a nonprofit organization in Costa Rica. We also said that FIRE would continue to develop a relationship with RFPI, separate from the one with the Foundation for a Compassionate Society, based on the concept of interactive autonomy—making explicit, as separate entities, where we need each other, and negotiate explicitly the terms in which we will support each other in those needs. We further stated that FIRE would set up its own office and would come to the radio station to do the FIRE broadcast. We said that FIRE would continue to pay the sum of $60 per hour of air time on RFPI for FIRE's broadcast and that RFPI and FIRE should agree to and sign a contract based on the proposed changes.

CHAPTER 9

FIRE Spreads from Latin America to Cyberspace

FIRE is needed now more than ever. Women's voices need to be heard.... FIRE allows women to tell other women truths and to remind them of their struggle.... Its success is the evidence that its truthful approach is the best approach.... Radio is a magic tool that gives people power.

—Jessica Green, USA Spanish student in Costa Rica

In the beginning of 1998, FIRE started creating the conditions to give itself a legal status in Costa Rica. The statement of objectives of FIRE's new status was to explicitly include in the legal organization all that FIRE had become and done throughout its seven years, beyond producing its shortwave radio program—the promotion of the presence of women in media; the affirmation of and respect for diversity;

the promotion of the human rights of women and all human rights; and the affirmation of women's right to communicate. FIRE had also contributed to the strengthening of women's media efforts by promoting and participating in networks, and in local, regional, and global initiatives undertaken by women. FIRE had become a forum where women from around the world sent their local radio programs to be broadcast internationally.

Under an integrated theme, "By all means: connecting voices, technologies, and actions," FIRE affirmed and made explicit its combination of local radio, international broadcast, Internet presence, and written press around the world.

A Time of Transition

RFPI's International Board Meeting was scheduled for the beginning of 1998. In a negotiated agreement with RFPI, FIRE presented its proposal of separation to their international board. After the presentation of FIRE's proposed plan, everyone at the meeting, including the International Board of Advisors of RFPI, who were all present for the announcement, celebrated the change. They wished FIRE well!

The only question asked by one of the board members was whether FIRE would continue paying RFPI for the air time of FIRE's broadcasts, to which FIRE responded affirmatively.

As of that moment, the process was on its way. During the next few months, RFPI and FIRE were engaged in a bilateral negotiation process to design a contract between the two organizations that would make explicit the new terms of their relations. Finished in March of 1998, the contract needed only the approval of the dean of the University for Peace, who had asked RFPI for an opportunity to review it before the signing, and who had stated that he wanted to include a clause about the fact that the contract between RFPI and FIRE should be renewed on an annual basis.

In the interim, Genevieve Vaughan, head of the Foundation for a Compassionate Society, had announced that she would close down the Foundation as of April 31, 1998, but would continue to fund some of its projects. Among them was FIRE with its core funding budget, but with a reduction of air time contribution to RFPI. FIRE would continue its broadcasts two hours per week, instead of six. Upon the reduction of hours, RFPI decided to donate to FIRE an extra hour of repeats on Sundays. Thus, as of March 1998, FIRE was on the air three times a week.

Fire's Legality Becomes a Reality

The Asociación de Comunicaciones Feminist Interactive Radio Endeavour (AC FIRE) was born on March 8, 1998, as a nongovernmental, nonprofit organization based in Costa Rica. It is composed of 11 Latin American and Caribbean feminists, and an honorary member—Genevieve Vaughan from the United States, who founded FIRE in 1991 and placed it in the hands of Latin American and Caribbean feminist producers.

From that time on, AC FIRE has continued FIRE's international work in communications from a Latin American and Caribbean feminist perspective. AC FIRE's activities have included the continued production of the FIRE radio program and its shortwave broadcast on RFPI. AC FIRE developed the following objectives:

- Promotion of the presence of women in media.
- Affirmation of and respect for diversity.
- Promotion of the human rights of women and all human rights
- Advocacy for the right to communicate.
- Strengthening women's media efforts by promoting and participating in networks and in local, regional, and global initiatives undertaken by women.

AC FIRE also defined itself by the following characteristics:

- It is a feminist communications alternative that contributes to the creation of new and alternative communications venues.
- It is a channel of expression, analysis, and research in communications from women's perspectives.
- It is a communications endeavor through which the voices of the voiceless among the voiceless (women, and especially Third-World

women) are broadcast to a local, regional, and international audience. Thus, it contributes to the alteration of the information flow in the international world order of communications where women's voices, and especially those of Third-World women, are hardly heard in any systematic way.

• It is a feminist communications endeavor that promotes, creates, and defends the right of women to express themselves and to be heard; that promotes, creates and defends the right of those who do not have access to the voices and proposals of women to be able to hear and know them; that promotes, creates and defends the right of the women's movement to influence local, regional, and global politics with its voice.

The work undertaken by FIRE throughout its seven years in communications had confirmed that the feminist analysis and proposals have supportive ears in a broad diversity of peoples and places. The Reception Report Study of the letters received from male and female listeners gives ample evidence of this fact. FIRE's experience suggests that this way of communication not only transmits ideas and knowledge, but it is also capable of generating individual and collective commitment.

In its *Vista* newsletter of April 1998, Radio for Peace International published an article by FIRE about its changes: A New FIRE-Place for FIRE. In another article, RFPI announced the changes in FIRE's structure and celebrated its transformations. After a brief introduction about FIRE's beginning at RFPI, the article continues:

It is therefore with joy and sadness that RFPI embraces the closing of this chapter in the history of FIRE. As [the producers of] FIRE form their own new legal entity in Costa Rica, we wish them well. As they set up their new offices and face new challenges, may they achieve their greatest aspirations. It is a time, not of endings, rather of new beginnings....

In the same issue of *Vista*, the Program Corner on the front cover listed the new FIRE schedule of three days a week and stated that the reduction in hours was unrelated to the changes in FIRE's organizational changes.

Troubled Waters

Not long after we had adopted our legal status, and despite the fact that all negotiations between RFPI and FIRE had gone smoothly and the new schedule and relationship were already in place, FIRE received a letter from the Dean of the University for Peace. The letter stated that, together with RFPI, whose studios were located on the campus of the University for Peace, the dean had decided that the FIRE program broadcast by RFPI would be suspended as of the July 12, 1998. The following is a translation of his letter.

UPAZ-SE-152
June 12, 1998

Feminist Interactive Radio Endeavour Communications Association
Dear Sirs:

After having analyzed with Mrs. Debra Latham, Director of Radio for Peace International, the need to introduce changes, amendments, and adaptations to the broadcasting program of Radio for Peace International, I have come to the conclusion that the F.I.R.E. Program (International Feminist Program), which in the past has been produced together with your organization and which has currently drastically changed its legal name and its field of duties, due to these same reasons, should not be included in the broadcasting program. A period of 30 days is granted for broadcasting the last programs according to the terms that had been negotiated with the Director of Radio for Peace International.

Cordially,
[SIGNATURE]
Francisco Barahona, Dean

cc: Debra Latham, Director of Radio for Peace International
   María Suárez Toro and Katerina Anfossi Gómez

After that surprise, FIRE wrote to Debra Latham on June 26 to request reconsideration:

We are addressing this letter to you for the following reasons:

1. We consider that the unilateral decisions made by you and Mr. Barahona, which mainly affect our organizations, are inadequate

289

since they override your authority as Director of Radio for Peace International and our condition as independent producers.

2. You are the general director of the broadcasting station with whom we have developed our labor and contractual relationships.

3. Direct communication with you has been the mechanism used throughout the seven and one-half years in which we have produced the program.

4. Direct communication with you has been the mechanism used even after March 8, 1998, the date on which we legally and physically separated from Radio for Peace International, after establishing our own legal status and moving to our own office in Ciudad Colón.

5. All other independent producers of paid and non-paid programs that are broadcast on Radio for Peace International communicate directly with you as Director of Radio for Peace International...

We want to request the following actions from you, in conjunction with the Dean of the University for Peace, Mr. Francisco Barahona (if the procedures deem the actions of both of you to be appropriate):

1. To create an internal or external assessment committee that will be responsible for analyzing the Feminist International Radio Endeavour (FIRE) program from March 8, 1998, the date on which it established its own legal status and field of duties, until the present time; and to analyze the changes, amendments, and transformations of Radio for Peace International in order to establish whether or not said changes in Radio for Peace International and the FIRE program are indeed contradictory, so as to merit termination of the broadcast of FIRE on RFPI. As of this day, we have no knowledge of the changes, amendments and adaptations introduced in the broadcasting program of Radio for Peace International, as mentioned in the letter by the Dean of the University of Peace.

2. To assess the definition and descriptions of RIF/FIRE, from 1991 until today, and the present definition of AC RIF—producer of the radio program—in order to determine whether or not our legal status is indeed contradictory to the principles of Radio for Peace International.

3. *To analyze the work report prepared by our organization and delivered to Radio for Peace International on May 11, 1998, and later updated and presented to the second AC FIRE Associates Assembly on May 31, 1998. We will be glad to provide the assessment committee with said report in order to verify whether or not our actions are contradictory to the guidelines of Radio for Peace International and/or the University for Peace as claimed by Mr. Barahona in his letter.*

4. *To review the RFPI International Advisory Board report of January 1998, regarding the presentation made by FIRE in which it explained the reasons why it was separating legally and administratively from Radio for Peace International and why it was reformulating the relationship with RFPI in order to continue broadcasting the program, both in English and in Spanish. According to this report, there was no opposition nor controversy from the RFPI staff, its International Board of Advisors (all of whom were present), or the members of the RFPI International Advisory Board.*

5. *To analyze the contents of the letters from the audience received by RFPI and RIF/FIRE from March of 1998, when the relationship between the two organizations was modified, until today, in terms of what listeners have said about the program.*

6. *To analyze the final contract draft negotiated by RFPI and RIF/FIRE in April of 1998, which was to be signed when the dean of the University of Peace included the time periods covered by the agreement.*

7. *To analyze whether or not the changes, amendments, and adaptations introduced by Radio for Peace International and mentioned by Mr. Barahona in his letter to the producers of FIRE were communicated to the other independent producers in order to determine whether the procedure followed by the University for Peace and RFPI is consistent, or if it was applied exclusively to our organization.*

After the assessment committee has analyzed thoroughly all pertinent information, it should prepare a report of the findings, indicating whether or not the program we produce is contradictory to the broadcasting guidelines of Radio for Peace International, taking into account that from the first FIRE broadcast on May 1, 1991, until June 12, 1998, there has never been any controversy over broadcasting the program.

We also want to identify several other factors that we feel are important considerations in this matter:

> *1. The producers of RIF/FIRE, who are also co-directors of the Feminist Interactive Radio Communications Association (AC FIRE), have not been notified of the changes, amendments, and adaptations referred to by Mr. Barahona in his letter. In spite of the fact that we have produced FIRE and also have generated the necessary financial support for more than seven years, these changes have been applied without us having been granted our right to know about them. The assessment procedure proposed above would grant us the democratic right to informed participation in deciding whether or not we would adapt the program to the new RFPI broadcasting guidelines and would also grant us the right to explain the reasons why our program does in fact comply with the guidelines of RFPI and University for Peace.*

> *2. Even if we have no information regarding the changes, amendments, and adaptations mentioned by the Dean of the University for Peace in his letter, we want to point out that the goals and activities of AC FIRE are completely in accordance with Costa Rican law....*

We want to point out that the goals and activities of AC FIRE are not only in complete accordance with the Costa Rican legislation, but also comply with the following:

> • *The guidelines of the Action Platform of the UN's Fourth World Conference on Women (1995), Chapter J on Media, in which it stresses the importance of women's access to media decision-making processes. It also calls for the creation of implementation policies and programs for the promotion of a positive image of women in the media, and it promotes women's access to new technologies, among others.*

292

- *The articles on nondiscrimination against women included in the UN's Convention for the Elimination of All Forms of Discrimination Against Women.*

- *UNESCO's current efforts to promote nonsexist communication and women's access to media. According to a recent UNESCO study (1995) conducted in 10 countries, women media workers are a minority equivalent to an average of 25% of all media workers in Africa, Asia, and Latin America. The same study indicates that only 1.4% of all TV programs refer to women's issues and three-fourths of these are presented by men. Although the study did not include shortwave radio programs, according to the editor of Passport to World Band Radio, both the proportion of women media workers and of women's news is estimated to be even lower on shortwave.*

Therefore, the formation of women's independent media, directed by women who approach the issues for a broad audience from a women's perspective, is one of FIRE's contributions to the shortwave and communications world that should not be superficially underestimated. The question is, what logic and arguments will Radio for Peace International use to explain to the local and international community the cancellation of FIRE's paid shortwave broadcasting space and its search for financial funds "to try out some new things" (Vista, April 1998), given the fact that FIRE pays RFPI for its hours on the air, and also that the audience loves the program, and the program has been granted several awards and is an already existing program?

Likewise, what logic and arguments will Radio for Peace International use to explain how the right to the freedom of press, the right to nondiscrimination, and the contribution of mass media to world peace do not apply to our FIRE program and organization? We request your support for our proposal in order to resolve this situation in the most satisfactory way for all those involved. Meanwhile, and until the final report of the assessment committee is issued, we request that the FIRE program continue broadcasting on RFPI.

The letter was signed by Katerina Anfossi Gómez and myself, as co-producers of Feminist International Radio Endeavour (FIRE).

RFPI director Debra Latham replied that "RFPI is a program of the University for Peace." She also stated that the decision to discontinue FIRE's broadcasts would not be changed.

The reasons given for the suspension of FIRE had to do with its new legal status, which positions it as an autonomous women's organization.

Friends of FIRE Speak Up

When FIRE was suspended from RFPI broadcasts, FIRE became part of what producer Katerina Anfossi described as:

...the never-ending migration of women-produced radio programs that face the prejudice, in many radio stations where they broadcast, of being considered the "least listened to," the "worst produced," and "the least profitable," and therefore, the easiest to substitute.

FIRE had demonstrated throughout its seven-year presence in the world of shortwave that it is one of the favorites at Radio for Peace International where it was broadcast. According to the number-one shortwave monitoring book, *Passport to World Band Radio*, in their yearly monitoring reports in 1994, 1995, 1996, 1997, and even in 1998, FIRE is one of the stars of RFPI programming. On page 175 of their 1998 report, the editors wrote:

FIRE (Feminist International Radio Endeavour) is one of the better offerings from the melange of programs that make up RFPI's eight-hour cyclical blocks of predominantly counterculture programming.

FIRE had been the most profitable program for RFPI, since FIRE air time payment to the station amounted to $60 an hour for two hours a day, seven days a week.

Also, from 1994 through 1997, FIRE received more international awards than any other program broadcast on RFPI.

Furthermore, according to the Reception Report Study, the letters of protest about the suspension, and the letters of support to FIRE for its continuation beyond the shortwave radio broadcasts, provided concrete and ample evidence that FIRE was one of the favorites among RFPI's listeners.

Some of the letters received by FIRE between February and May 1998, when the negotiations between RFPI and FIRE were taking place, are evidence of our popularity. Following are some of the messages of support we received:

- February 1998: Jorge S. wrote from Cuba to say that he thinks FIRE in very necessary "considering the marginalization of women in the world, especially in the countries in development where the differences are more blunt, and this is why the program is even more important...."

- February 1998: Marian del Carmen Daza wrote from Mexico to say that she stopped listening for a while when she had to move to another zone in Mexico where she could not get a shortwave radio. "Now I am back to my place and listening again. Please give special regards to Nancy Vargas, whom I hope is still with you."

- March 1, 1998: Ary Nigard from Finland wrote about productions in Perú in February 1998. He said he heard the news about FIRE when the Swedish Ambassador in Perú was talking about women's rights.

- March 11, 1998: Arthur Boston from Liverpool, UK, wrote to say that he heard the interviews produced in Perú in February 1998. He said he had heard a woman from Bolivia, and he found the program "really interesting with women's points of view." He wanted to know how often FIRE broadcast, and when he could tune in to it again.

- March 1998: Amanda L. also wrote from Cuba to send FIRE an article for the program. The article is about the work women in Cuba do to support children whose health has been affected by the Chernobyl nuclear power plant accident.

- March 1998: Anarda G.M., also from Cuba, said that for "the millions of women who live in oppression and discrimination, this FIRE program is very necessary." She also offered to help FIRE by sending poetry and literature from her country for the program, as she is a university graduate in literature.

- April 1998: Lisa Benni from the USA, presently a Peace Corps activist in Honduras who listens to FIRE there, wrote to thank us for the information about our program schedule, and asked for the new one with FIRE's new hours of broadcast at RFPI. "Good luck in your excellent work," she said.

- April 1998: A.S. (female, name not revealed) from Virginia, USA, wrote to say she was sorry FIRE was not on the air every day any more, but she will look us up in the new schedule and wishes us well in our new endeavors.

- April 1998: Gladys A. wrote from Cuba wishing us well on Mother's Day on the second Sunday of May. She thanked FIRE for the Christmas card sent to her, and attached articles for FIRE to read on the air.

- April 1998: Maribel wrote from Cuba to share her concern's about the difficult situation Cuba is facing, which makes it very difficult to get medicine and food for her five grandchildren, whom she takes care of. She asked FIRE to read the letter on the air.

- May 1998: Craig MacKinnon from Halifax, Canada, said that he hardly ever writes to a station, but has made the exception this time around because he heard a program on FIRE that was very useful to him: a woman talking about the swap of debt for nature.

- May 1998: Dariga Atajanovna D. from Kazajstan and presently living in Cuba wrote to tell FIRE her tragic story about having lost all contact with her family in her country of origin after she came to Cuba. She was operated on for a brain tumor, lost her sight, and her husband divorced her. She asked FIRE to read her story on the air.

- May 1998: Elena A.L. wrote from Cuba to say that although she did not get FIRE's response, she knows FIRE read her letter on the air because she received a letter from a listener who has become her pen pal.

Facing up to the Challenge

Continuing her analysis of FIRE's sudden suspension despite its success, Katerina said:

The frequent success of these programs has often prompted the desire of many media owners to try to take them over by substituting others for the women creators of these programs, while keeping the successful names of the programs for themselves. This factor is one of the many issues that make evident the fragile status of programs produced by women in relation to the owners of media.

This is one of the reasons why the continuity of women-produced radio programs does not stem only from their profitability, their ideological content, or the audience. Their continuity is linked directly to the sexist prejudices of the owners of media, as well as to the unequal balance of power between men and women.

When we analyze the spectrum of communications, we find that the power of the media has allowed their owners to define what and who are socially and politically relevant, rendering invisible large sectors of the population, especially women.

The right to democratic communications faces many obstacles: The concentration of media ownership in ever fewer national and international monopolies; the unidirectional flow of information from north to south; the pre-established ideological content of media that are sexist, violent, and that alienate many; and the globalization of the economy. Thus, the right of the voiceless to communicate will continue to be a challenge in the years ahead.

The rapid development of communications and new technologies, as well as access to cyberspace, challenges us to ask ourselves whether these developments will duplicate the fate of traditional broadcast and print media, again depriving many of a voice—or whether these new technologies will instead benefit those who have been excluded in the past.

Decisions that favor putting the appropriation of media venues in the hands of producers, as well as the connection of different technologies, voices, and ideas, will make more viable the possibilities for true democratic communications in the local, regional, and international context.

With the sudden suspension of its broadcasts, FIRE's efforts to diversify had to be intensified. One of our first steps was a campaign to strengthen our links to the women's movement and radio producers by explaining to them about FIRE's suspension from shortwave broadcasts and requesting letters suggesting how we could continue to work together.

The response was broad and immediate. Women in radio opened their local radio venues in different parts of the world to FIRE's productions!

In 1998 alone, FIRE's reports or programs were picked up by other shortwave radio stations or programs such as Radio Netherlands, BBC, and WINGS on RFPI. We were also featured on numerous local radio stations and programs around the world, including Radio LoRa, Switzerland; Radio Universidad de Costa Rica; Voices in India; 2 XX 10008 AM Community Radio in Canberra, Australia; the radio program of the Canadian Women's Federation in Canada; Radio Ghana ACCRA in Ghana, Africa; and Radio Pirate Woman, Ireland.

We were also carried by KUMD (103.3 FM), Duluth Public Radio, the university radio of the University of Minnesota in Duluth; the radio station of the University of Wisconsin in Superior, Wisconsin; KUVO (89.3 FM) community radio in Denver, Colorado; and Vancouver Co-op Radio in Canada.

Encouragement Continues to Pour In

Messages of support from our listeners continued to arrive. The following is an e-mail message that was prompted by a FIRE broadcast:

Date: Monday 28 de December de 1998 8:50 AM
Subject: FIRE
María Suárez Toro:
My name is Teri. I heard you speak on a local public radio station on Xmas eve and I became intrigued. I came home and called up your website on my computer. I am now very interested in finding out more about your organization and if there is anything I can do to help. As soon as I found out about you, I wrote to my friend in Mexico. She says she knows you. Though I am an American, born and raised, I have always had a strong pull and affection toward the people of Central and South America. I visited Costa Rica last year and am now in love with your country. I live in New York, not the city but the eastern end of Long Island. I am a registered nurse/acupuncturist. Please tell me how and if I can become involved with your organization. Even if only to spread

the word and educate people about you. Looking forward to hearing from you and perhaps even meeting you some day.

Regards, Teri

In Spanish, FIRE's programs were featured on the AMARC community radio network, composed of almost 200 radio stations or programs in Latin America. José Ignacio López Vigil, head of the AMARC Latin American office wrote to us about the broadcasts:

I want to thank you for the valuable contribution from Milan. About the broadcasts in Radio Planet Earth, a few people have told me that they received the programs, and they liked them. I am sorry we did not have time to talk more about the future plans for AMARC and for the women's network especially. We will find time....

Accolades in Print

Print media also featured articles about FIRE's new directions:

- *Action*, the newsletter of the World Association for Christian Communication (WACC) published an article entitled "Feminist Radio Fortified in Costa Rica."

- In June 1998, *Mujer/Fempress* had an article entitled "Genevieve's Dream." Written by Costa Rican correspondent Yadira Calvo, the feature points out that the change to AC FIRE affirms FIRE's Latin-American roots, and that in it, Genevieve Vaughan's dream since the Third World Conference on Women in Nairobi, had become a reality.

- Also in June 1998, issue No. 2 of *Women/Health Journal*, the Latin American and Caribbean Women's Health Network magazine, published an article entitled "AC FIRE, Feminist, Interactive and Latin American." It describes the history and perspectives on the change in legal status.

- In the August 1998 issue of *Tertulia*, a magazine in Guatamala. Laura Asturias wrote with alarm about the suspension of FIRE from RFPI's broadcasts. It quotes FIRE's letter about the suspension, asking how RFPI will justify looking for funds for a women's radio program of their own, when they suspended FIRE.

- Services Especial de la Mujer, the Latin American and Caribbean Women's Feature Service, is produced in Costa Rica by Thais Aguilar. In August 1998, it denounced the suspension of FIRE from RFPI's airwaves. It also quoted FIRE's letter to RFPI.

- In September 1998, *Diálogo* of the University of Puerto Rico featured an article about the Reception Report Study under the title, "Fire Opens Venues in Latin America."

- *Interadio*, AMARC's newsletter, featured an article in December 1998 based on a interview with me about the chapter entitled, "Of Sexual Politics and Women's Human Rights," in the book written for the United Nations in commemoration of the 50th anniversary of the Universal Declaration of Human Rights.

Support from Former Members of the FIRE Collective

Individual women who had formed part of the FIRE collective in past years wrote to express their solidarity.

Dear Kata and María:
I received the statement about what has happened with RFPI and UPAZ. I really could not believe it. My solidarity and strength to you....
—Jeanne Carstensen, California, USA

We have received through the mail the explanation about the closing down of your radio program.... I think it is terrible that they would cut the wings of such an important initiative for so many women... and one that has taken so much effort to build. I am sending the notice to women's organizations; if there is anything else we can do, do not hesitate to let us know. Keep it up!
—Olga Rey, Spain

I want to let you know that I am with you, even though I am far away. FIRE is a unique and necessary media venue. You, and all the voices of women that you have broadcast have created an indispensable space for women all over the world. For me in particular, it has been an unforgettable experience to have had the opportunity to work with you. The experience in FIRE strengthened me as a woman and as a journalist. Please continue forward, and count on me for whatever. As the saying goes, "Whatever does not kill you, strengthens you." So despite the obstacles, FIRE will be stronger than ever!

A solidarious embrace, Firu.

—Firuseh Shokoo, Puerto Rico

Nancy Vargas did not write; because she was in Costa Rica, she immediately came to our office to offer to work on a volunteer basis with FIRE if needed.

Support from Our Shortwave Listening Audience

Sixty-six of FIRE's listening audience wrote directly to FIRE, some to find out where they could locate FIRE. Shortwave operators from Cuba and the United States suggested that we build our own radio station and offered to help us do so. Others gave FIRE ideas on how to get broadcasting on other stations, and many supported our endeavors. Many others, especially from the USA, Cuba, and the rest of Latin America, expressed their dismay at the suspension of a venue where they had learned so much.

August 1998

Dear FIRE,

I have been following you for some time and have 'ried in the past to contact you to no avail. I am trying again because I cannot find you on the current RFPI broadcasting schedule. Where and how might I listen to you? All the best in your endeavors.

Signed, Mary L.H.

301

November 1998
From Cuba, Gladys A.A
Dear friend Katerina,

I was surprised as I turned and turned the shortwave radio dial looking for your broadcast and could not find you. I thought something was happening, but I never thought you were suspended! In your programs, through the women you interviewed, you denounced many of the situations that Latin American women face. Maybe someone did not like the fact that you are so progressive, and the argument about the legal status is just an excuse to take you off the air. I am glad about your optimism, and that you will continue working on behalf of women. Let me know how I can help. Although I do not have Internet here to be able to listen, I like just knowing you are there. Send me the written information.
Love, Gladys

December 1998
Dear FIRE,

First thank you for producing such important and informative programs. As a Peace Corps worker in the Dominican Republic, I listened to FIRE broadcasts. Now here in the United States I want to continue listening to them on shortwave but I haven't been able to pick them up. Do you have any information that might help or suggestions for tuning in? Your programming is excellent and I don't want to miss it. Thank you for your help. I know you are very busy.
Sincerely,
Lisa Benni

December 11 1998
Jaguey Grande, Cuba
Dear friends of FIRE:

Greetings to the joyful FIRE collective! From Cuba, I want to send you my support and my strength in this moment when RFPI has shut down your marvelous and exquisite program. I am very sorry that they tried to destroy such a professional and eloquent team of women like all of you. I was new to your shortwave broadcasts, but I can tell you that I loved your programs, because without much money, but with a very practical, joyful, and humanistic approach, you did your program.

Signed, Yasbel (female)

Hi, María, I hope you are all well. I only want to say that what you people do is something that is just wonderful for the feminist movement because of the way you give an opportunity to so many Latin American, African, and Asian women to express their opinions and [tell about] the realities that they live.

—Susana, Duluth, Minnesota, USA

December 18, 1998
Cuba

Dear FIRE:

I hope your spirit remains, and that you find a radio station with a better quality. For my part, you will always be the FIRE that once made me stick to a whole morning of work, and to you, the women in charge of making that complex system work, I wish you congratulations. Be assured that I will never forget you.

A friend always,
Yosbel (male)

November 27, 1998
Mexico

Dear Katerina,

I just received your letter and here I am, still fuming in anger, looking for a way to vent my anger. Such a vacuum! What should I be feeling? Nothing. I just feel what I feel because of what you are going though. My solidarity to you! With a friendly embrace, I wish you a good future. I trust in you, because I know that on top of every mountain you climb, there will be a voice. Go forward always!

Marco R.

November 1998
Attention Katerina Anfossi Gómez:
From Mexico, I am Rafael G.G

The news you mention as to why your broadcasts were suspended is too bad, and it has been very surprising to me because your program focused on the realities of women on the whole planet, and thus were very interesting to me. They showed me other aspects about the participation of women. This is why I wish you well in this next phase of work. Good bye.

My dears, warm greetings. I am very sorry about the decision of the directors of the University for Peace to take away your program, which you produced with such professionalism and enthusiasm on behalf of Costa Rica, the Americas, and the world. Good luck in your future!
          —Arnulfo A., Panama, October 1998

About the fact that you were cut off from Radio for Peace International, do not worry. That is just a small obstacle to your big objective of owning your own radio station. Move forward! Congratulations for having your own legal status. That is of much more value these days, than having a little program on someone else's radio station!
Attentively,
YSCB in Sononate, El Salvador

I hope that by the time you get this letter you are all fine and have the will to continue in the work that you do. This work is so necessary for all women, because, although I am a man, I defend all women of the world!

I am deeply affected by the fact that I cannot listen to you any more since you are off the air. The only way we can communicate is by mail or through a newsletter you could publish if your economic conditions allowed you to do that. As the world is being globalized, that means more unemployment and poverty, and it is women who suffer most from it. I hope you realize your dream of having your own radio station.
          —Michael R.M., Cuba

It hurt me deeply when the FIRE women went off the shortwave broadcasts... their voice became a part of me....

However, I can see from your letter that you women have grown into a formidable organization! Prophesy has it that women will rule the world....

Love, Bernard

—Bernard Di Santo, Clyde, New York, USA

Thank you for your recent letter.... I had been wondering what ever happened to FIRE on RFPI! Now I know. Hopefully this is a forward move for you.... I know that sometimes AM transmitters in the range of 200-500 watts can be obtained for free. With modifications, most can be converted to shortwave.... I have no knowledge of Costa Rica, but I urge you to explore the possibility of getting your own radio station—a voice of your own on the air!!!!

Take care, O.C.

—Oscar C., New Orleans, Louisiana, USA

You have been undertaking a very important task in radio, and thus, I hope you will accept me as a collaborator.... I know that building a radio station is about money, and I do not know what the situation is in Costa Rica, but I have already built three radio stations here, and if possible, I will voluntarily build one for you.

Shortwave is a bridge between countries, and the work that you do is very important, so it has to go around the world! It is necessary for women to hear your message of liberation and the knowledge about their role in society. What happens? We are all equal, and women have shown themselves to be as capable as men, but society does not want to see it. In this world ruled by men, the success of women is not recognized, or it is minimized by men. Please accept me as your collaborator.

—Octavio M., Cuba

I am very sorry that RFPI has taken you off the air! For so many women, your broadcasts were the only hope for peace and freedom! You can count on my help and my best wishes that in the future you can have your own international radio station. That is the dream of your listeners, and we hope it comes true, because I bet most of your Latin American audience does not have Internet access. I would like to receive a photocopy of your web page since I do not have access. Good luck to your enthusiastic team, and success in your professional endeavors.

—Jesser A. (male), Cuba

Women's Organizations Write In

Women's organizations also protested our dismissal from RFPI's airwaves. Viqui Quevedo from Chile, founder of Radio Tierra—the only all-women's radio station in her country, and first in Latin America—wrote the following:

Please tell me where I have to write to protest energetically in light of such an absurd, discriminatory, and neoliberal measure that those people [RFPI and UPAZ] have taken by closing down your radio program. I think it is too much! I have many arguments to defend FIRE, and a treasure of feeling to humanize my analysis. It hurts, but it also potentiates my fury.

I am always with you,
V.Q. from Chile, and from FIRE, damn it!

Puntos de Encuentro, a Nicaraguan NGO wrote:

...feminists from the continent have had historical relations with FIRE, and now we see you are on the verge of disappearing from the radio dial. Our immediate solidarity to you, and please let us know what we can do to help.

From Puerto Rico, María Teresa from the Center for Research in Social Studies at the University of Puerto Rico wrote the following:

I work in the Center, and just recently I became the coordinator for the Caribbean Region of the Latin American and Caribbean Network

Against Domestic and Sexual Violence Towards Women. It is part of the Coordinating Commission, Peace for Women. I have received the information about the situation you are facing. I am interested in knowing [more] about your situation. Here [in Puerto Rico] we are beginning to obtain a radio space for gender issues. Thus, the contact with you is an opportunity for our development. We could also establish collaborative links.

Subject: support for FIRE.
From: Women in Black Against War, Belgrade.
Dear activists of FIRE:

The Women in Black from Belgrade, Serbia, want to support you in continuing the very important political work with FIRE's radio program. FIRE is one of the radio programs around the world that cares about injustices. Women in Black have had the opportunity to work with FIRE during the UN Conference on Human Rights in Vienna in 1993. It was a pleasure to work with women who are so committed and who are supportive of the small nonviolent acts that tend to promote human rights and peace. As peace activists and feminist activists, ourselves, we strongly support FIRE.

The Latin American and Caribbean Women's Health Network (RSMLAC), based in Chile, sent us the following protest:

We send you all our support and solidarity in light of the situation that is affecting your radio broadcasts. Your program is known regionally and worldwide for its deep commitment to the cause of human rights—especially to the cause of the rights of women—and its commitment to global peace and to the environment has for a long time been a very clear and valuable example of committed feminist journalism..... Our network has worked with FIRE in many international campaigns, and we demand that RFPI revoke the decision to ban the normal broadcast of FIRE....

From Radio Milenia, the recently created women-owned radio station in Perú:

Dear María and FIRE,

Our Director, Gaby Ayznoa from Milenia told us she saw you in Milan, Italy, at the AMARC conference, and that you were able to talk extensively.... Gaby told us you are interested in our news and reports.... We opened your web page, and we heard your program and liked it! We hope our information is useful for your reports.

M.J.

New Paths to Our Listeners

FIRE's founder and sponsor, Genevieve Vaughan, had expressed her commitment to continue funding FIRE on an ongoing basis. Other agencies, such as the Global Fund for Women, funded a project for institutional support of FIRE; HIVOS of the Netherlands funded FIRE for the creation of a local radio program in Costa Rica; and the Dougherty Foundation funded support for FIRE's Internet website. After the adoption of our legal staus, FIRE also received financial support from UNFPA, UNIFEM, Shaler Adams Foundation, Mama Cash, and private donations by Martha Drury, Anne Thompson, and Ralph Fine from the USA.

Traditional Broadcasts in 1998

Before FIRE lost its airspace with RFPI, we had begun 1998 with a continuation of our live broadcasts from home and around the globe, including the following:

- Perú (February): Interviews with women from Latin America who were participants in the event Women in Management, organized by the University of Lulea in Sweden.
- Costa Rica (February): Interviews with students from the USA studying at the Institute for Central American Development Studies in Costa Rica.
- South Africa (February): Interviews with women in media, development, and nonviolence movements from different countries in Africa, organized by the Institute for Further Education of Journalists.

- Nicaragua (March): A workshop organized to train grassroots activists in influencing politics in the Central American region— Capacitación Para Capacitadoras en Incidencia Política—with Valeria Miller of Global Women in Politics, and coordinated with CENZONTLE, a Nicaraguan NGO. FIRE was also invited to be on the selection committee.

- Kalmar, Sweden (June): Fifty African, Asian, and Latin American mainstream journalists speaking about democracy in media at the Institute for Further Education of Journalists.

- El Rodeo, Costa Rica (June): Interviews at the Institute for Community Development and Communications by Women.

Local Broadcasting with "Está Legal: (It is Fair)

With all of the support we had received from our listening audience and from our networks and sponsors, we were able to develop new venues for traditional broadcasting at the local level, enhancing our recognition as Costa Rica radio producers.

In early 1999, we began our local broadcast of Está Legal (It Is Fair). Funded by HIVOS of the Netherlands, the program is broadcast in Spanish with various formats, including interviews, live broadcasts, discussions, and call-in shows on a variety of current issues and events from women's perspectives. Katerina Anfossi, director and host for the program, spoke about the advantage of FIRE's new venue:

We are launching this local program in response to requests by local women, including many in the women's movement. Many have participated in FIRE programs through the years but were unable to hear them in the past when we broadcast mainly on [international] shortwave.

We are continually developing new programs, such as the program we began on International Women's Day, March, 8, 1999. Although it is primarily a local program, it is also regional and global in scope under

309

the slogan, "Fem Interactive: Global women's voices from within the part of the continent that is Latin!"

FIRE in Cyberspace

While seeking ways to continue FIRE's traditional broadcasts, we also found ourselves once more forging innovations in women's international communications by connecting voices, technologies, and actions in a new way.

It began in August 1998 at the Seventh Annual Meeting of the World Association of Community Radio (AMARC) in Milán, Italy, when the AMARC Women's Network asked FIRE to produce its two-hour daily live program on Internet, satellite, and AMARC's Pulsar radio press agency. Thus, FIRE coordinated and hosted two hours daily of international live broadcasting on the AMARC Women's Network of Radio Planeta Tierra. From that space, women from all over the world talked through the Internet in Spanish, English, Portuguese, French, Swahili, and many other African languages. They talked about the democratization of media, about women's human rights, about the right to communicate, and about the impact of structural adjustment programs on their countries.

Radio Planeta Tierra broadcast 24 hours a day from August 25-30 during the AMARC conference. The broadcasts went out via satellite to all continents, and via the Internet to all computerized corners of the globe.

On that occasion, FIRE also broadcast live from Milan to Costa Rica. At 10:00 p.m. Costa Rica time on August 25, 1998, these introductory words launched one of the live broadcasts from the AMARC conference:

Welcome to this live broadcast from Milan, Italy, venue of the Seventh International Conference of the World Association of Community Radios. This is María Suárez from FIRE, for the program Noche Tras Noche at Radio Universidad de Costa Rica.

With FIRE correspondent Luisa Cruz from Perú, we also organized and hosted the daily half-hour show of the Latin American and

Caribbean men and women present at the conference. From Radio Planeta Tierra, this was an international Internet and satellite broadcast.

Another first for FIRE was a live broadcast posted in sound on our website by Katarina Anfossi in Costa Rica. The program featured a report about the role and history of the AMARC Women's Network, and the voices of the recently elected president of AMARC, María Victoria Polanco from Colombia, and of Bianca Miglioretto from Switzerland, the new head of the Women's Network. Other women came on the air to celebrate the consolidation of the Women's Network within AMARC.

FIRE wrote daily press releases for AMARC's PULSAR Press Agency, and these announcements were picked up by other radio stations in the region. In this way, FIRE continued to amplify women's voices at the 1998 Seventh AMARC Conference and to multiply our own impact though the diversification of media outlets.

About FIRE in the Internet

Dr. Margaret Thompson, director of the M.A. in International and Intercultural Communication at the University of Denver in the USA, had this to say about FIRE's new outlets:

Launching women's voices into cyberspace placed the feminist radio program broadcast from Costa Rica at the cutting edge of a new age of media technology. From that day on, FIRE—Feminist International Radio Endeavour—could be heard in both Spanish and English over the Internet, in addition to its ongoing venues of radio and written press focusing on women's perspectives on a variety of local, regional, and international issues.

With this new media format, FIRE joined a new age of creative broadcasting, which is radically different from traditional radio because it is broadcast through a desktop computer hooked to the Internet.

One of the results is that it decentralizes the power to communicate because it doesn't require a fully-equipped radio station to broadcast, nor a license to use the airwaves. Furthermore, it can be accessed from anywhere in the world.

The Internet format represented FIRE's first step toward developing a women's Internet radio station. The station will eventually do live broadcasting (real time audio) over the Internet, including live coverage of local, regional, and international events and issues from women's perspectives.

Such a station will be one of hundreds of new Internet radio stations, which are attracting millions of listeners worldwide who have downloaded listening software onto their computers. What would set FIRE's Internet radio station apart is that it would be owned, designed, and run by women of the South; that rather than a simultaneous repeat or rebroadcast of the programming of a traditional radio station, it would produce radio for the Internet (which would than be rebroadcast by radio stations); and also that it would be regional, and at the same time local and international.

Tackling the Virtual Invisibility of Women of the South on the Internet

When FIRE launched its new media venue of broad/netcasting through the Internet and the worldwide web, one of its objectives was to give ever broader visibility to the voiceless among the voiceless in media—that is, women, and especially women in the South. However, FIRE very soon discovered that the politics of identity on the Net keep many in virtual invisibility—especially women from the South—by defining them as the *other*.

A few days after we decided to go into broad/netcasting, we began to surf the Net for computer software. At the same time, we were searching for statistics about the people who use the Internet, as they would become the potential new audience for FIRE in cyberspace broadcasting, which we knew would be different from shortwave. We also needed to register the FIRE website on search engines in order to gain visibility, thus drawing visitors to FIRE's website.

Our first encounter with being defined as *the other* came when we looked at statistics about Net users in the USA. The Simons Market Research Bureau did a survey that is reported in Yahoo's special anniversary edition of September 1998. Classification of users according to race were the following: *white, African American, Asian,* and *other.*

312

We soon learned that in registering ourselves as FIRE producers, being Latin American and Caribbean women, we would fall into the category of the *other*.

But we did not give up. Katerina Anfossi and I continued surfing the Net, this time for the software we needed. After a few hours we came up with a program that we felt could be useful for our purpose of placing our radio programs online. It was also a program that seemed to be available to us, as it was free.

So we began to fill out the online form. First, it asked about our organization, meaning the type of institution that FIRE is. The choices were these: *private, governmental, cultural, educational,* and of course, *other*.

As a nongovernmental organization, we clicked *other*. Unlike written forms, where usually when you write *other*, you are asked to specify *what other*, this Net form skipped to the next question. It left us hanging in no one's land in cyberspace. So once again, we were the *other*, period, click, and skip.

We continued to the next category of questions, eager to get through the ordeal in order to get access to the software we needed to give visibility to the *other* voices.

The next question was about us as individuals. The categories were *student, professor, government official, public worker,* and again, *other*. Once again, we clicked *other*, as we are feminist activists in communications. That category was not there, and of course, the program did not care to know who we were. It automatically took us to the next question, whether we wanted to go there or not. By the way, I believe this is what they call *interactive*.

And so we passively continued until the questionnaire came to the end. Then we waited for the computer to process the data and give us the long-awaited access to the software. Finally, the cyberscreen flashed the answer: "Sorry, access denied. You do not qualify."

We sat there, looking at the screen in dismay. The free Internet democracy does not include *Latin, NGO,* or *feminist activist* as subjects! And if these categories of users exist in real life, they have to pay in order to have access to cyberspace.

After we recovered from the shock, we realized that this Internet ordeal was not so different from FIRE's recent experience with other international media:

- When we received the letter from the University for Peace telling us that FIRE broadcasts were being dropped from RFPI's programming, the reasons were very similar to our recent experience with the Internet—legal status does not fit. Click. An NGO is a nonqualifiable *other*.

- In its letter to FIRE following the one from UPAZ, RFPI stated, "[Our] intention remains to open a new program dedicated to analyzing gender issues within different parameters than the ones you hold." Click. Latin American women producers are the nonqualifiable *other*.

- RFPI went to the World Association of Community Radio Broadcasters Conference in August 1998 to request women's radio programs *other* than FIRE's, and those programs would not even have to pay for air time! Click. Feminist is the nonqualifiable *other*.

Any similarities between the politics of the Internet and of shortwave must not be by chance. The politics of identity used by owners of media to decide who has a voice and who does not seem to cut across international media, be it modern cyberspace or traditional shortwave.

What is it about the way media decisionmakers have shaped that world? Dr. Laurien Alexander, dean of Antioch College in the U.S., and researcher in the field of shortwave said at an RFPI board meeting in 1994:

> If I were to call global communications flow—information, satellite, computer technology, telecommunications, direct broadcast satellite—a "family," I guess I would call it a dysfunctional patriarchal family: the father owns and controls the modes and means of communications, the children are afraid of talking, and the mother is silenced.

In reference to FIRE in international communications she added, "but I have been told that the women are no longer afraid to speak."

Creation of a Women's
Internet Radio Station

As of our experience with AMARC broad/netcasting on August 25, 1998, AC FIRE began to create an experimental women's Internet radio station based in Costa Rica: <www.fire.or.cr>.

The concentration of media in the hands of ever fewer (and male) hands denies women and other excluded sectors of society the right to communicate. Ensuring that the ownership of some regional media venues are in the hands of women helps to guarantee that alternative political proposals and views will not be silenced arbitrarily because of sexism and the unequal power relationship between men and women.

FIRE's Internet radio allows women communicators to explore the diverse possibilities of democratic communications that can connect voices, technologies, and actions by linking traditional radio, Internet, and written press in an innovative way. It makes available to the women's movement—and especially its radio producers—a communications venue that helps balance the presence of women's perspectives in radio and in the new communications technologies, thus enhancing the capacity of the movement to influence agendas. FIRE's Internet station also validates women's due right to democratic communications through their voices, experiences, and expressions.

The strategic aims of FIRE on the Net are twofold:

1. To guarantee the property of a women's international, regional, and local media venue in the hands of women who will strengthen gender democracy toward equality and social change.

2. To guarantee that this media venue will become a strong center of experimentation and innovation where the richness of the cultural diversity that characterizes our region can have an expression that will contribute to the democratization of communication.

As with any other radio program FIRE has produced, it is *by* and *about* women, but *for* all! Many different constituencies benefit from FIRE's Internet radio:

- The *audience* has a communications venue where they can access information, voices, and perspectives that they can seldom tune in to in other media venues, thus having access to alternative analyses, criteria, and experiences. They can participate interactively, with the opportunity to respond, ask questions, and expand on what they listen to on the Internet station, and also to request programs of interest and information.

- *Women's groups, women in communications, and networks of women in media* now have a media venue that facilitates the continuous dissemination of information, of styles, and perspectives at the local, regional, and international level. They also have the options to participate in workshops, to design and produce regional programs, to learn new technologies, and to articulate their ideas with traditional radio technology.

- *Feminists and the women's movement* have a channel of expression and experimentation that is directed by women. It guarantees them the right to communicate and to influence agendas.

- *Other radio stations* have a continuous flow of programming produced by women to download and rebroadcast on their own radio stations.

Since August 1998, the following programs of global interest have been broadcast on FIRE's Internet radio, in English and in Spanish:

- Milan, Italy (August 30): From the AMARC Seventh World Conference, women's voices about the results of the AMARC elections where women from Eastern Europe, Western Europe, Latin America, Asia, Africa, Canada, and the U.S. were elected to AMARC's board.

- Kalmar, Sweden (September): Twenty journalists from Africa, Asia, and Latin America—specialists in ecology—speaking about media coverage of environmental issues in their regions.

- El Salvador (September): Coverage of the resolutions of the eight working groups at the forum, "Communications and Citizenship."

- Kalmar, Sweden (October): Twenty women journalists from Africa, Asia, and Latin America speaking about women in media in their respective countries.

- Denver, Colorado (October): Coverage of the event at which the Peace and Justice Committee presented Carol Richardson with an award for her strength and courage in the struggle to close down the School of the Americas.

- Fort Benning, Georgia (November 21-22): With Margaret Thompson for an update about the results of the SOA Watch protest outside the School of the Americas.

- Palo Alto, California (November): With Sara Valls from the Global Fund for Women to announce, first hand, the news about the allotment by the organization of a special fund of $150,000 for women in Nicaragua and Honduras affected by the devastation wrought by Hurricane Mitch.

- Nicaragua (November): An interview with Ana María Pizarro of Nicaragua's CIMUJER about the effects of the Hurricane Mitch on women.

- Cocoyoc, Mexico (November); A special report featuring various health activists in preparation for Cairo+5, including Frances Kissling of Catholics for Free Choice and Marianne Hasselgrave, coordinator of the NGO Forum.

- The Hague, Netherlands (February 1999): The NGO Forum at The Hague in the Netherlands with Ana Elena Badilla of the Arias Foundation, Marisel Salas of the Costa Rica's Women's Political Agenda, and Anna Arroba of the Costa Rican Women's Health Association.

FIRE Answers the Need
for Experimental Radio

There has long been a need in Latin America and the Caribbean for an Internet radio laboratory to experiment with the development of global and regional productions through the convergence of local programs and experiences.

There has also been a need to experiment with regional productions in terms of the audience who very seldom get the opportunity to receive an integrated regional women's vision in radio productions, even though FIRE's research indicates a very strong interest. FIRE produced regional programs for years on shortwave, and both the regional listeners and radio producers participated and celebrated the initiative as a way of integrating experiences and visions, and as a way of sharing diversity in light of commonalties.

With FIRE's Internet radio, others besides the producers of FIRE can come to Costa Rica to experiment with designing, producing, and broadcasting Internet radio programs. Both Internet users and the local audience provide feedback from the listeners' perspectives. At the same time, producers in the region can use the Internet productions in their own countries and provide their local listeners with a women's integrated regional vision.

There has been a need expressed by women in radio in Latin America and worldwide regarding a gender perspective in the radio stations where they broadcast their programs. The women producers have emphasized the necessity of having regional training and production workshops that will facilitate the difficult process of integrating a gender perspective into their programs.

Many of the regional training workshops currently offered do not include collaborative production where the trainees can experiment with new concepts without pressure from the owners, but FIRE's Internet radio station provides that space. We started developing a track record for providing a safe place where women producers can experiment when we opened the FIREPLACE microphones to other producers to speak and produce live broadcast programs in China.

Internet FIRE has also given women producers the opportunity, the training, and the means to access new communications technologies. This need was identified in the UN resolutions of the Fourth World Conference on Women in Beijing, 1995. It was also included in the resolutions of the 1998 Seventh AMARC conference, as well as in the resolutions of the forum, Communications and Citizenship, held in El Salvador in 1998.

Another concern in the Latin American and Caribbean region has been the devaluation of programs produced by women. This devaluation stems from the prejudice that most media owners have about women's programs, thus making them the most fragile to sustain on the air. Many women radio producers in the region are greatly concerned because they recognize how frequently they are forced to move their programing to other radio stations, always subject to the arbitrary whims of their owners. These women's testimonies confirm the constant threat of the exile and segregation of women's radio programs.

Such vulnerability supports the need to consolidate media in the hands of women—not only media produced by women, but the promotion of media owned by women—as the legitimate right of women to communicate as a means of guaranteeing the continuity of their voices. FIRE's Internet radio ensures a continuity in the broadcasting of women's radio programs, even in the interval where they are searching for a new venue because they have been dismissed from a previous one. Through FIRE, women's programs can be broadcast internationally on the Internet, and it also provides female producers with a far stronger negotiating capacity in their search for new venues because they are never totally off the air.

FIRE continues its collaborative broadcasts with women radio producers who send their programs to FIRE for international broadcast via the Internet. The strong interest in continuing joint ventures is evident in the request for such collaboration from the Latin American and Caribbean AMARC Women's Network regional office, a request for FIRE to work with the regional coordinator in training for production with a gender perspective, and also for training in new technologies starting in 1999.

There are several features that make Internet FIRE a unique experience:

- FIRE Internet radio positions—in a continuous way—the voices of Latin American and Caribbean feminists, and of all women, in local, regional, and international media, both traditional and modern. This positioning helps reverse the traditional unidirectional north-to-south flow of information.

- FIRE Internet radio combines traditional media and new technologies in the hands of women. Traditionally, women have been the carriers of oral histories and traditions, and now they can bring their capacity for oral expression to a medium that up until now has consisted mostly of images and writing.

319

- FIRE has created a cyberspace regional venue that is at the same time local and international.
- FIRE's Internet radio makes it possible for other local, regional, and international communications venues to get programs by simply downloading them from the Internet. This simplifies the exchange, lowers the cost, and quickens the access of other radio stations to women's programs.
- Also the flexible format with text and photos that stand alone for those unable to get audio.

FIRE Finds a New Audience

The creation of a new audience for FIRE has been evolving gradually as people find out about our Internet broadcasts. Among them was Rita Lucey, who had been a prisoner of conscience in the U.S. for having trespassed onto Fort Benning, Georgia in 1997. In protest against the School of the America's located there. The SOA is where Latin American soldiers are trained by the US government in military tactics. Countless SOA graduates have been implicated in gross violations of human rights throughout Latin America in recent decades. Rita served a six-month prison term during the first half of 1998. Here is her e-mail message to FIRE:

Date: Wednesday, 6 January 1999 8:50 AM
Subject: Applause

Great web page. I have copied it, especially since much is in Spanish, to send to sister inmates at the Federal U.S. camp—this is a hope-filled message—a women's Spanish network—international in scope, that will address many of their issues.

Rita Lucey

From: Mavic Cabrera-Balleza
Isis International-Manila

Dear María and all friends at FIRE,

Warm New Year greetings from all of us here at Isis International–Manila! We're delighted to know that you're now broadcasting on the net. I'll be accessing it as soon as I've sent this message. It's really inspiring to learn that the interface between radio and the new information technologies is now materializing.

A second e-mail came from ISIS after they tuned into FIRE's web radio:

Mabuhay! (Welcome, hello, long life in Filipino)
I recently visited your Internet radio website. It's very focused and informative. I showed it to the other ISIS women and they're all impressed. We are conducting a training for women radio broadcasters in Fiji from 22-26 Feb. 1999. We will open and present your site as an example in the workshop on using Internet for radio. I have a question and suggestion to make: Are you planning to make this in real audio?... This would be all for now. Thank you for inspiring us to continue providing alternative spaces for women to communicate.
Affectionately, Mavic

Subject: Web
From: Adriana Gómez, Red Salud
To: FIRE

First of all, congratulations for the FIRE web page, it is so much fun to surf it! I hope you can train us in the use of electronic technology the way you use it. We need that. I need an interview with Ana Elena Badilla about The Hague for our newsletter. Can you provide us with that?
Adriana Gómez
Editor, Women's Health Journal

From: Margaret Thompson
To: FIRE

Wow—the web page is GREAT!!! You folks have really been putting a lot of time into it... great info about Cairo+5. I also like the combination of text and audio. Felicidades!!! Plus it's fun to hear familiar voices.

From: Cotidiano Mujer, Uruguay
Subject: Programa Cairo+5

Congratulations for the Internet radio idea, and for the materials it has! I need to learn how to download the sound! As you know, we have a daily local radio program and would like to both send you some programming to put in your WEB-radio, and we would also download your programs and play them on ours! Great!

Elena Fonseca

From CIMAC (Mexican Women's News Agency):

Dear Colleagues: We have learned that you have posted the resolutions of the event, "Citizenship, Democracy and Media" held in El Salvador last September in your website. Please guide us as to how to download them!

Lourdes Barbosa, Coordinadora de Radio
Servicio Informativa de CIMAC
Comunicación e Información de la Mujer, A.C.

Two radio women from rural Grecia in Costa Rica wrote:

Hi Colleagues! We are Rosemary and Emma, who are undertaking a course in Internet and came across your address. We would like to know which frequencies we can tune in to in order to hear you. We work in a local radio station, Radio 16 in Grecia, Alajuela, Costa Rica. We hope to hear from you, and to help you.

Another woman from the rural town of Ciudad Colón, where FIRE is located, wrote to FIRE after she had listened to it on the web:

From: Marjorie Mora Chavarría, Ciudad Colón's Pharmacy
Subject: Reception Report
Dear friends of FIRE:
Congratulations for this new form of being consistent, independent, and of great courage in defending the sacred rights of women and peoples in general. Good luck to you and best wishes that you move into the XXI century recovering your morale and continuing to defend human rights that are so violated by many enemies who do not want peace on this earth.
A friend in the struggle,
Dr. Marjorie Mora, Ciudad Colón, Costa Rica

Also from Costa Rica, Grazia Lomonte wrote to say:

...I went to visit your Web page, and it is wonderful. I hope that you open many opportunities in this new cyberspace, and that you continue joining forces and voices with those who live for creating the possibility of a better world for all. I am truly proud of the work you do. An embrace of FIRE...

From Puerto Rico, Marie Berrocal wrote:

It is fabulous to hear you so clearly on the Internet speaking from Milan, Italy. The advancements that have been made in Internet technology are amazing, and especially knowing that it is free and accessible... democratization? Congratulations for a clear, concise, and informative program. I see you are getting into modern communications—lightly and with audacity.... How wonderful!

Subject: Live broadcasting (and live-on-tape)
Date: Tue, 11 Aug 1998 13:36:37—0700 (PDT)
From: Frieda Werden
Dear María,

Maybe WINGS and FIRE (and maybe even some other women producers around the world) could set up a consortium to do live broadcasting on a regular basis. I'd love to do more live international programs myself—such as roundtables from conferences, or international women's conference calls on different subjects.
In sisterhood,
Frieda

Frederik Norona from India wrote:

Hello from India! I am a journalist here, and learned about your website from the bulletin of the World Association of Christian Communication. Incidentally, I hope to meet you in Sweden in September, as I am part of the class you will be teaching at FOJO-Kalmar about your radio experience.

From The Hague in the Netherlands, Sara Sharat wrote to say she was told about FIRE's webcasting, heard it, and likes it!

Global Activism in Communications

FIRE was the first systematic feminist program in the world of shortwave radio. For more than seven years, the ideas and actions of the feminist movement were disseminated for six hours daily (a two-hour daily broadcast that was rebroadcast twice). This fact was of immense value because it allowed for the necessary continuity that the women's movement required, and so enabled the audience to hear a continuous voice on behalf of women. Most radio programs or stations broadcast feminist voices only rarely, and then only on specific topics, on days of commemoration, or about events related to women.

For the past seven years FIRE had done live broadcasts from a variety of events at the local, regional, and global level. Through this communications strategy, FIRE had facilitated the process and impact of actions taken at these events. This strategy also allowed FIRE to be present at a multitude of events where women developed both internal and external strategies on behalf of the women's movement.

Disseminating the spoken words of women—broadcasting the individual and collective testimonies of women globally—has been an important achievement in FIRE's international communications strategy because it has fostered the recognition that women's words constitute a political analysis of reality. With this emphasis on women's oral language, FIRE has given to women's words the value they deserve. When brought together, the personal testimonies of women can be seen as links in the chain of oppression. We are continuing to bring these testimonies to our audiences through our work in traditional radio, and we are bringing them to the Internet as well.

In addition to establishing a new base for FIRE in Costa Rica, the year of 1998 was also a year of continuing global action through training in radio techniques and technology, participation in women's networks, and development and dissemination of communications theory and practice

Training in Radio
and Other Media

FIRE's constant efforts to expand its audience beyond the shortwave radio listenership has enabled us to create channels for distribution of programs to other radio venues, to become a source of news and information for other media, to use other media to further disseminate the voices broadcast on FIRE, and since 1995, to combine the use of radio with new communication technologies such as the Internet. Thus FIRE has been able to maintain its personality as an international communications venue and has articulated its mission of "connecting voices, technologies, and actions, giving voice to the voiceless."

In addition, one of our key strategies has been to ensure that women operate and control the communication technologies used in our broadcasts, and to seek ways of simplifying this technology in terms of cost and operating techniques, thus expanding access to a wider range of participants in FIRE productions. This strategy ensures that broadcasts can continue even under extreme conditions of scarce economic resources or adverse political conditions.

Throughout 1998 FIRE continued training women around the world in the use of radio and other media:

- In February, FIRE trained 17 Latin American women in Perú who were engaged in management of different types of projects in 15 Latin American countries to interview each other for radio. Fifteen productions were broadcast on FIRE.

- In April, we went to Minnesota in the USA to train Victoria Lucia Ibanez of the American Indian Community Housing Organization in the use of a tape recorder to do interviews for FIRE. Three radio productions were broadcast on FIRE.

- Also in April we made arrangements with Joyce Kramer at the University of Minnesota, Duluth, whom we had previously trained, to record and interview women at the Conference for Solidarity Among Women held in Cuba from April 13-16. MADRE agreed to send FIRE the recordings and post the frequencies and dates of the broadcasts of the proceedings in their bulletin.

- In April, FIRE also organized a training workshop for women members of the Asociación de Salud de Mujeres en Costa Rica, in which we trained 12 health activists in the use of the tape recorder and in interviewing techniques.

- In May, we made arrangements with Margaret Thompson of Denver University in the U.S., who had been previously trained by FIRE, to do interviews for FIRE with women who visit her university. She did two programs that were broadcast on FIRE. One was with Robin Morgan (journalist and former editor of *Ms* magazine in the USA); the other was with Polly MacLean (black journalist from the Caribbean, working as a mass communications professor in the US and also in Africa.

- In May, we also trained two women of the local and regional Brahma Kumaris movement to record and interview women for FIRE broadcasts about their initiative to promote the values stated in the Universal Declaration of Human Rights in this year of its 50th anniversary.

- In the months of May, September, and October, FIRE trained 38 female and 22 male journalists from Africa, Asia, and Latin America in live broadcasting.

For the near future, FIRE together with the AMARC Women's Network, plans to organize a training workshop in electronic editing and broadcasting in Costa Rica for Latin American and Caribbean women.

Strengthening Women's Networks

FIRE's participation in women's networks at the local, regional, and international level, together with the constant exchange of ideas and experiences provided through these networks, has resulted in a constant evolution of innovative communications alternatives within the feminist movement.

As an international communications venue since 1991, FIRE broadcasts have provided a forum for locally produced radio programs sent to us by women from all parts of the world, thus amplifying women's voices and strengthening the impact of their media productions.

Since its inception, FIRE's organizational strategy has emphasized its role in participating and strengthening existing women's networks rather than creating a separate network. This served to affirm FIRE's successful strategy of *interactive autonomy*, by which a communications venue that is part of the women's movement can at the same time maintain its independence.

FIRE continued strengthening women's networks, and being strengthened by them, through the following actions in 1998:

- In February, FIRE met with 25 other women from regional media networks in the Latin American Women's Media Forum convened by the World Association of Christian Communication (WACC) in Perú.

- FIRE accepted an invitation by AMARC to take part as keynote speaker in its seventh conference in Milan, Italy, in August.

- FIRE nominated Marieta Quezada, director of the Blind Women's Bakery in Costa Rica, as a 1998 candidate for the Women's Rural Creativity Award in Rural Life—offered by the Women's Summit Foundation in Geneva, Switzerland. The following is the reason FIRE submitted her name:

  Under her direction, the bakery provides the service of wonderful bread to the city's community, while also standing as an example of the capacity of a group of women who have shown to all of us that a disability such as blindness is not necessarily an obstacle to development, given the tenacity of the women and community support.

The nomination was rejected because the award is for rural projects, and the bakery is in the city.

- FIRE joined the Sponsoring Committee of the Milenio, an initiative organized to celebrate the change of the millennium by convening people to come to Costa Rica at the turn of the year 2000 to demand and celebrate peace.

- FIRE was a participant and associate convenor of the International Forum: Communication and Citizenship (San Salvador, September

9-11). The forum was a meeting point to seek consensus on proposals and actions in favor of the Right to Communicate.

- FIRE was invited by the Global Fund for Women to be on its Advisory Board and was invited to participate at their November meeting in California.

- FIRE developed a campaign through women's organizations calling for economic support to Nicaraguan and Honduran women single heads of households. FIRE collected U.S. $600 and 2,000 Costa Rican colones.

- FIRE took part in the international women's meeting, "Confounding the Critics: Five Years After Cairo," held in Coyoac, Mexico on November 1998. At this meeting, 135 women and several agencies met to design strategies for Cairo+5 in February 1999, where world governments and the UN would assess the implementation of the Platform for Action of the 1994 World Conference on Population and Development.

- FIRE was elected by the Coordinating Committee of the Cairo+5 NGO Forum to be the focal point for Costa Rica. The appointment was ratified by local groups in Costa Rica. Throughout 1998 and the beginning of 1999, FIRE organized activities with women's health groups in Costa Rica to have an influence on the Cairo+5 process at The Hague and at the UN.

- FIRE supported the SOA Watch Campaign to close down the School of the Americas at Fort Benning, Georgia, and undertook two additional activities in support of closing the SOA. FIRE (1) organized a meeting with Democrats Abroad in Costa Rica about the campaign, and (2) went to Denver for the presentation of an award to the co-director of SOA Watch.

- FIRE was present at the re-opening of Tree Radio Berkeley— microradio broadcast from a tree in a park in Berkeley—on November 22.

- On November 23, FIRE also held an exchange of experiences with the Latino producers of Radio Watson in Watson, California, another microradio experience.

- FIRE presented the story of their experiences in an exchange meeting of women in radio in San Francisco. It was agreed that we would all look at ways to go into shortwave radio together, looking for an open station.

- FIRE was co-sponsor of the Third Tribunal on Violations of Women's Human Rights in Costa Rica held on November 23.

- FIRE was co-sponsor of the Women's Cultural Festival in Costa Rica, in commemoration of the 50th anniversary of the Human Rights Declaration, held from November 30 to December 10.

Feminist Communications Theory

FIRE has presented courses, workshops, panel presentations, and talks about feminist communications theory and practice, both at the local, regional, and international level, as well as in educational activities in communities, conferences, schools, institutes, and universities. Through these activities, we have been able to systematize the communications theory and practice that has emerged through our experience, while also disseminating these ideas beyond the radio program itself.

FIRE's feminist communications strategy has included the organization—together with other women's groups and coalitions—of tribunals on violations of women's human rights. With these activities, FIRE has been able to prove that the only place where the reality of women's human rights can be found is in the oral history of women, precisely because those rights have not been recognized, and therefore do not form part of written history or historical documentation. FIRE continues organizing these activities and providing its proceedings to audiences around the world.

FIRE efforts to develop and disseminate information about feminist communications theory and practice during 1998 include the following:

- In February, I was invited to represent FIRE as guest professor for the event, Women in Management, organized by the University of Lulea, Sweden, where I presented our theory and practice of feminist communications. The event took place in Perú, where 17 Latin American and Caribbean women in management met to share their projects for engendering management in the region.

- In April, I represented FIRE as keynote speaker for Latin American Awareness Month and Women's History Quarter at three U.S. universities: College of St. Scholastica (Keynote: "Women's Rights as Human Rights"); University of Wisconsin, Superior (Keynote: "Women and Peace Movements in Central America"); and University of Minnesota, Duluth (Keynote: "Mundialización, Women's Voices from Central America").

- At the three universities visited in April, I also taught five university classes about FIRE's theory and practice in women's international and regional media in the areas of Political Science, Developmental Psychology, Women and Literature, Ethnicity and Media, Democratization of Third-World Countries, United Nations and International Politics, Women in Different Cultures, and related topics.

- Together with the International Rights Action Watch (IRAW) in Malaysia, FIRE was selected by the United Nations in March to write the chapter about the history of women's struggle to get the UN to recognize women's rights as human rights for the United Nations historical book in celebration of the 50th anniversary of the Universal Declaration on Human Rights.

- In May, September, and October, I taught three courses at the Institute for Further Education of Journalists (FOJO) in Sweden. All three courses were attended by journalists from Asia, Africa, Latin America, and the Caribbean. The first course was on Women and Media, with 20 women journalists. The second was Media and Democracy, attended by 40 male and female journalists, including journalists from Sweden as well as from Asia, Africa, Latin America, and the Caribbean. The third course I taught was Media and the Environment with 20 journalists attending.

- In April, Zhong Xin, a journalist with the Institute of Renmin University in China, did an extensive interview with FIRE for a feature that was published in China's *Educational Magazine for Journalists.*

- On April 8, FIRE's theory and practice was featured on the front page of *The Daily Telegram* newspaper in Superior, Wisconsin, in the U.S.

- UNICEF has featured the testimony about the violations of the human rights of girls in Costa Rica from the First Tribunal on Violations of Women's Human Rights in their online UNICEF materials for the Girl Child at <www.unicef.org/voy/meeting/gir/girhome.html>. FIRE's material about the tribunal can be found at <www.unicef.org/voy/meeting/gir/gir3tx1.html>. According to UNICEF, "The materials for the Girl Child are being translated into Spanish and French and will be online in those languages by about the end of May, 1998." The translation was a contribution by FIRE and the Organizing Committee of the Tribunal in January 1998.

- FIRE staff were on the panel at the conference, Promoting the Organized Participation of Women in the Cancer Epidemic, held May 12, 1998, in San José, Costa Rica. FIRE presented the regional and global perspectives about the issue, and also proposals about how the Costa Rican women's movement can connect globally and regionally to other initiatives about the issue.

The letters we received throughout FIRE's eight years on the air confirm that our international feminist communications strategies have opened the ears of men and women from a broad diversity of cultures, races, languages, ages, and sexes who listen to the feminist perspectives broadcast on FIRE, identifying with various issues and perspectives that they rarely have access to in other media venues and programs. Therefore, it seems that feminist media not only disseminate the voices and perspectives of women but actually serve to create new and different perspectives.

In addition, the vast number of messages we have received from men from around the world have helped us understand that perhaps the intimacy of radio (which so far has been studied only from the perspective of women listeners) enables nonfeminist listeners, and men in particular, to listen to feminist perspectives on radio without feeling threatened, and thus helps to bridge the gender gap in communications.

Into the New Millennium

By the end of 1998, FIRE had expanded its team to include Brenda Azúa, daughter of Chilean exiles in Costa Rica. Brenda came to work on FIRE's website and in documentation for the local FIRE radio

Feminist International Radio Endeavour
Radio Feminista Internacional

El Programa Radio Internacional Feminista RAIF
Feminist International Radio Endeavour FIRE

A Genevieve Vaughan,
con profundo respeto, admiración y cariño
por haberlo creado, fundado, apoyado y patrocinado
desde sus orígenes en 1991 hasta el presente,
por haberlo puesto en 1998 en manos de mujeres
feministas latinoamericanas y caribeñas para
compartirlo con el movimiento mundial de mujeres.

En gratitud por acompañarnos hacia el nuevo milenio,
al haberse convertido en miembra honoraria de la
Asociación de Comunicaciones Radio Interactiva
Feminista productora de FIRE
desde su fundación en 1998 en adelante.

¡ Muchas Gracias !

Dado el 10 de Diciembre de 1998 en San José, Costa Rica.

Katerina Anfossi Gómez
María Suárez Toro
Co-Productoras - FIRE

program, Está Legal. She worked at FIRE throughout 1999. Ana Elena Obando Mendoza joined the FIRE team to co-produce Está Legal during three months in 1999.

FIRE also hired Ana Ugalde, a Costa Rican administrator and accountant, to handle our administrative functions. Nancy Vargas Sanabria became a FIRE consultant to undertake research about local radio stations in Costa Rica that could broadcast FIRE programs in 1999 and into the future.

FIRE continues to seek out innovative ways to serve our listening audience. To comply with requests from listeners who do not have access to the Internet, FIRE plans to publish a semiannual newsletter with the Internet radio information. The newsletter will be distributed to those of our audience who have "lost us" temporarily. We also plan to look for other shortwave venues, and we are investigating the possibility of getting our own radio station in Costa Rica.

On December 11, FIRE closed out the year of 1998 by celebrating a change that had became a strategic jump into the next millennium. AC FIRE gathered the members of its association in a celebration to honor FIRE's founder and sponsor, Genevieve Vaughan.

The celebration was special and very energizing. FIRE gave Genevieve a scroll, reproduced below, expressing appreciation for her support.

When I presented the scroll to her on behalf of AC FIRE, I said:

> *...this homage to Gen is done in little Costa Rica, but we assume we do it on behalf of the thousands of women around the world whom we have met in FIRE's travels, who have also benefited from Genevieve's generosity and vision. We still have little idea about the number of projects like FIRE that have been able to emerge and grow because of her support.*

Katerina added:

> *I want to thank Gen because she has allowed us to be where we are now. When we were first taken off shortwave the feeling of solitude was so big, and it was when we found each other that we found the way. Not everyone would do what Gen did. She put this program in*

our hands even before she knew us. She trusted women from the South, herself being from the North!

Genevieve, on her part, stated that she learned to be an international feminist in the Italian feminist movement, saying "They taught me I could trust women from other countries! And it has proven successful with FIRE." She told the story of how FIRE was begun, and she wished us well. She also stated that at the beginning she wanted to create a women's radio station, but, she said, "Maybe we had to wait for the technology to develop. Now is the time!"

After the presentation of her scroll, FIRE formally admitted Genevieve Vaughan as the first honorary member of the association AC FIRE.

This celebration also presented the first occasion for AC FIRE's board members to share with the founder of FIRE what the Feminist International Radio Endeavour has meant to them. Ana Elena Obando, a Costa Rican women's human rights lawyer said:

> *...the process by which FIRE erupts into cyberspace is very important to us women in a world where justice is globalized now with Pinochet's case in England, the economy is globalized through neoliberalism, where feelings are also globalized though our international links, and now, so are the voices of women through cyberradio! It has infinite possibilities because of the way FIRE is using it. We felt an immense blow when FIRE was taken off the air on shortwave, but the staff has turned the blow into a very positive energy to move forward!*

Roxana Arroyo, women's human rights activist and lawyer said:

> *Last year, I said that FIRE was important because it gave a voice to the silenced stories of women. But now, listening to the report of this year's activities—what happened to FIRE and how it faced the challenges—I also have discovered that the spirit of FIRE is in the movement, and not in the particular media venue where it broadcasts! They can remove us from one media venue, but FIRE's value is not whether it is cyberspace, shortwave, or whatever, but its essence is a very urgent message—that of women.*

FIRE has gone from place to place, media to media... but always women's voices! The particular venue is a mirage of power, the real power FIRE carried with it, which is the commitment to give voice to women. As a Costa Rican, I have to say that listening to FIRE's programs has put me in contact with the voices of women from all over the world that I will never meet. Yet I identified with their issues, and those voices made me grow as a woman.

Anna Arroba from the UK and resident of Costa Rica, who is currently building a women's health organization, told board members:

FIRE opens venues; it gives us examples. Only when we open our own autonomous spaces can we really grow. For a time we rent space and borrow space, but eventually we have to build our own that no one can take away from us.

Brenda Azúa updates FIRE's website.

Informática y Tecnología Electrónica Digital

6 EDITORIAL

2 mujeres al aire por Internet

Por: Guillermo Mata Palmieri *gmata@guate.net*

Katia prepara una transmisión para sacarla al aire

En días recientes tuve la oportunidad en Costa Rica de entrevistar a un par de mujeres muy emprendedoras ajenas totalmente, hasta hace unos meses, al área de informática o tecnología. Sin ellas quererlo así, se convirtieron en pioneras en Latinoamerica en muchas cosas, demostrando al mundo que con muy pocos recursos económicos, pero una gran voluntad de hacer las cosas y el amor a una causa se pueden hacer milagros. Maria Sánchez y Katia Anfosi, trabajan ambas para una ONG denominada FIRE. Esta es una organización de apoyo al movimiento feminista que salió del aire cuando transmitían programas de interés para las seguidoras por onda corta. Debieron clausurar actividades debido a algunos problemas con frecuencias en Costa Rica. Al no querer quedarse fuera del aire y dejar a sus seguidoras sin la información de vital importancia, se dieron a la tarea de montar un sitio de Internet con toda esta información. Sin embargo, este no es un sitio cualquiera. Ambas se dedicaban a transmitir por radio y no sabían absolutamente nada de Internet, pero necesitaban colocar en la red sus voces, pues el sitio no podía ser un lugar textual. Una de las creencias más fuertes de esta organización es que la voz femenina es imprescindible escucharla, pues de acuerdo a Katia, está compuesta de una sensibilidad que denota el estado de ánimo de las mujeres. Además, no podía ser un audio malo, sino que tenía que ser de alta fidelidad. La experiencia en radio les enseñó como grabar sus voces sin interferencia y ruido. Lo más importante es que muchas oyentes son analfabetas y con la voz el mensaje llega sin ningún problema.

Montar el sitio para quienes no sabían absolutamente nada, pero nada de Internet fue realmente un reto completo. El esposo de una de ellas les enseñó a utilizar un programa tipo Publisher y allí empezaron a hacer sus primeros experimentos Maria y Katia. Esta era la parte más sencilla, aunque se tomaron su buen tiempo para dejarla como ellas la habían concebido. Investigaron con un buen número de profesionales en informática cómo introducir el audio a su sitio y que este fuera de calidad y accesible a todo el mundo en un tiempo bastante razonable, ya que el material que está en el sitio son por ejemplo, conferencias de hasta 4 horas de duración. Nadie les pudo dar una solución concreta e investigaron mil programas diferentes para audio. Al final, empezaron a grabar y pasar su información con el tradicional Real Audio y éste fue el éxito más grande, pues lo más sencillo les resultó lo más efectivo. Todo salía perfectamente bien y el audio es de gran calidad. Lo más importante es que se puede cargar tan fácilmente y sin interrupciones, que es posible escuchar toda una disertación de media hora como si se estuviera en el mismo lugar donde se está dictando (Obviamente depende en gran parte de su conexión a internet). El sitio de ellas es uno de los más visitados en Latino América para consultas acerca de la causa que ellas representan y a él llegan radioemisoras para "bajar" la información en audio y retransmitir la misma a través de sus frecuencias. A este sitio llegan diariamente hombres y mujeres de toda latinoamérica en busca de información "audible" con respecto a temas feministas. El No. de hits es altísimo para un sitio tan especializado y ahora esperan convertirse en la radio en vivo de mayor audiencia dentro de sus seguiroas. Este proyecto es aún más ambicioso, pero de seguro lo van a lograr. El sitio es www.fire.or.cr. y vale la pena verlo para relamente ver el trabajo de estas 2 pioneras.

Estoy seguro que como FIRE, existen otras organizaciones a nivel mundial, que han visto en Internet un potencial para comunicarse con el mundo. No es necesario estar en los países más desarrollados para poder generar algo grande, no es necesario tener una infraestructura millonaria para montar un gran negocio en Internet, solamente hace falta una idea y una gran fe en ella para ponerla en el aire. Estas 2 mujeres nos demostraron que lo más importante es la idea, la implementación del sitio es algo tan trivial como utilizar un procesador de palabras. Y lo más importante de acuerdo a Maria y Katia es la simplicidad, ingrediente fundamental en el sitio de ellas. Un notable periodista hace muy poco le hizo una pregunta a un alto ejecutivo de una de las empresas de informática más poderosas del mundo y fue ¿Y cuándo llegarán todas las oportunidades y ventajas de Internet a Latinoamérica? La respuesta del ejecutivo, para ser exacto un Vice Presidente, fue Nosotros creemos que en uno o dos años estarán disponibles en la región. La pregunta del periodista fue un tanto vaga, pero la respuesta de un VP de una de las compañías líderes en informática fue la peor respuesta que jamás haya escuchado yo. Internet y todas sus ventajas están ya disponibles para todo el mundo. En realidad Internet es la oportunidad más grande que se le puede presentar a Centro América para darse a conocer en el mundo y dar a conocer y vender sus productos

María y Katia diseñando su sitio.

a un mercado que no conoce diferencias geográficas y que son miembros de una sola comunidad, la comunidad del Internet. Imagínese y puede manejar YA su negocio, desde el garage de su casa (o la cocina, como FIRE), sólo falta un poco de creatividad y dedicación, elementos que nos dieron a todos los seres humanos por igual sin importar nacionalidad, raza o sexo. Asi es que, ¡no hay excusa! Ω

The February 1999 Central American edition of *Compudata* reports on FIRE's innovative Internet broadcasting.

THE TICO TIMES

CENTRAL AMERICA'S LEADING ENGLISH-LANGUAGE NEWSPAPER
Member of the Inter-American Press Association

VOL. XLIII N° 1518 — 36 pages

San José, Costa Rica, Friday, April 16, 1999

₡250

Lifeguards at Cocles "Weekend"

Internet FIRE Spreads Flames into Cyberspace

By Margaret Thompson
Special to The Tico Times

LAUNCHING women's voices into cyberspace has put a feminist radio program broadcast from Costa Rica at the cutting edge of a new age of media technology.

FIRE (Feminist International Radio Endeavor) can now be "heard" in both Spanish and English over the Internet, in addition to its ongoing venues of radio and written press, focusing on women's perspectives on local, regional and international issues.

With this new media format, FIRE joins a new age of creative broadcasting, radically different from traditional radio because it's broadcast through a desktop computer. It doesn't require a fully equipped radio station to broadcast, nor a license to use the airwaves. And it can be heard anywhere in the world.

Co-produced by María Suárez and Katerina Anfossi since it began in 1991 as an international radio program on shortwave, last year FIRE began to broadcast internationally from Ciudad Colón — west of San José — over the Internet. The initiative is funded by the Foundation For a Compassionate Society, the Global Fund for Women, and the Dougherty Foundation.

CURRENT audio clips available on FIRE's Web page range from a report in their own voices on the impact of Hurricane Mitch on women in Nicaragua to interviews about women's involvement in the movement to close the U.S. Army School of the Americas at Fort Benning, Georgia, which trains Latin American military.

FIRE's Internet Radio also features a special report entitled "A Crack at Impunity," about the detention of former Chilean strongman Gen. Augusto Pinochet in the U.K., seen from the perspective of female political prisoners of the military dictatorship in Chile in the '70s and '80s and Chilean women political leaders.

The Internet format represents FIRE's first step toward developing a women's Internet radio station, according to Suárez. The station will soon do live broadcasting over the Internet, including live coverage of local, regional and international events and issues from women's perspectives.

Such a station will be one of hundreds of new Internet radio station now operating, which are attracting millions of listeners worldwide who have downloaded listening software on their computers.

FIRE'S Internet Radio Station is owned, designed, and run by women, and rather than a simultaneous repeat or rebroadcast of traditional radio programming, it produces programs designed specifically for the Internet that are also being picked up for rebroadcast over other radio stations.

"The Internet will allow us to give a 'voice to the voiceless' in media — that is, women — and particularly women of the Global South, by reaching an even broader audience worldwide," Suárez said.

Over the past eight years, FIRE staff has traveled around the world to collect women's ideas and voices for the programs, covering major summit meetings and UN conferences on the environment, population, human rights, social development, media, and women.

FIRE is just one activity of a new non-governmental organization called AC Fire *Asociación de Comunicaciones*, formed March 8, 1998 (International Women's Day) in Costa Rica.

AC FIRE is dedicated to promote the presence of women in media, the affirmation and respect for diversity; the human rights of women and all human rights, and the right to communicate. It also strengthens women's media efforts by promoting and participating in networks, and in local, regional and global initiatives undertaken by women.

AC FIRE is a full member of the World Association of Community Radios (AMARC). It has also launched a local radio program entitled *"Está Legal"* (It's Fair). Funded by HIVOS of the Netherlands, the program, broadcast in Spanish on Radio América on a weekly basis, features interviews, live broadcasts, discussions, and call-in shows on a variety of current issues and events from women's perspectives.

"WE are launching this local program in response to requests by local women, including many in the women's movement," producer Katerina Anfossi noted. Many have participated in FIRE programs through the years, but were unable to hear them in the past when we broadcast mainly on shortwave."

The program will feature programming produced by women from Perú, Ecuador, El Salvador, and Brazil, as well as from Latinas in the U.S., Canada, Europe, and elsewhere.

FIRE can be heard over the Internet via its Web page at: **<http://www.fire.or.cr.>** It can also be heard locally Wednesdays at 10 a.m. at 780 on AM radio.

(Margaret Thompson is the director of the master's programs in international communications and intercultural communications of the University of Denver).

FIRE broadcasters include Tatiana Mora, Brenda Azua and Katerina Anfossi.

Tico Times/Will Wilson

Meet the Women of FIRE

AT their Ciudad Colón headquarters, a kitchen is as good as any other room of the house to install equipment and broadcast to the world, for the four women who run the Feminist International Radio Endeavor (FIRE), the first feminist radio station over the Internet in Latin America.

"We'd like to have more technology to do live broadcasts, but we have learned to work with whatever resources are available, and, by doing that, we have become pioneers of this new type of media," Katerina Anfossi, a Chilean who has been involved with FIRE since its 1991 birth, told The Tico Times.

For Anfossi, the advantage of radio over print journalism or written material on an Internet site is that, through the voice, women from all corners of Latin America — many of whom don't know how to read or write — can express their opinions and tell their stories, which will be heard just the way they spoke them, without intermediaries.

"WE are trying to make a point that women's poverty is not the same as men's poverty," she said. "Women face more health, education, and human-rights problems, and we want to take a stand against it."

Anfossi is honest about FIRE's ideology. "If you're looking for objectivity," she said, "don't listen to us." She explained that the radio station works exclusively for the cause of women and is not afraid to tell things just the way they are.

"We are also trying to change the traditional view of women working in the electronic media," Anfossi said, referring to TV's obsession with image and modern views of 'beauty.' "We don't look like that, we don't want to look like that."

IN addition to Anfossi, the women of FIRE are Puerto Rican María Suárez and Ticas Brenda Azúa and Tatiana Mora.

—Mauricio Espinoza

The Tico Times of San José, Costa Rica, devotes a page to FIRE's activities and plans for the future.

Margaret Thompson, a USA journalist visiting FIRE for the occasion added:

As a woman from the USA, and as a journalist trained in traditional journalism, I really learned the patriarchal way of doing media. A magic wand gave me "editorial judgment" upon graduation. And editorial judgment usually means framing information into familiar stereotypes to keep groups under control! I have seen in FIRE's media work how they have a methodology that has turned things around. By letting women speak for themselves, FIRE lets women frame their own way of presenting themselves and the issues!

Grazia Lomonte, an Italian psychologist and resident of Costa Rica said:

I feel I am celebrating a birth of new cosmic forces. FIRE's new millennium has already begun here. Katerina and María have sustained it emotionally, even though politically it has been the whole movement. But the emotional losses and the gains, you have held onto with your passion, and you have grown and made this project grow. It is only when we have something that is really ours that we feel the loss and the fear of loss. FIRE was non-negotiable because it always belonged to the movement!

Indeed, a year ahead of real time, the new millennium was born for FIRE by the end of 1998. Reincarnated seven years after its shortwave debut, FIRE had moved forward with the voice, the choice, and the strength of women.

CHAPTER **10**

Voices of Traditionally Underrepresented Women

I'd say they [radio women] are a powerful tool, getting women together somehow. So I encourage them not to limit themselves; go all the way with this, because this is quite a great thing; they should really go for it!

> —Tumy, a young South African who had just learned
> to do radio, in her message to radio women in other
> parts of the world. Johannesburg, South Africa, 1994

Ever since our first days on the air, FIRE has been strongly committed to listening to the voices of the most voiceless women: Women of color, women with disabilities, senior citizens, women imprisoned for political reasons, refugee women, lesbian women, girls, and women from underrepresented countries. FIRE has worked to amplify all women's

339

voices from around the world. We continue to bring our warm glow to places where women find themselves and their ideas in the shadows.

Women from Cuba

In March 1993, the FIRE team covered an important activity in Cuba: a conference entitled, "Cuban Women about the Economic Boycott," coordinated by the Federation of Cuban Women (FEDIM). The Reverend Eunice Santana, from Puerto Rico and president of the World Council of Churches, spoke at the conference:

> It is a privilege to be in Cuba, and an honor to take part in the conference that will promote solidarity with women of Cuba.... We have a commitment to justice and unity.... We believe that there can be no suffering, scarcity, repression, or blockade, or pain that can be foreign to us. Cuban sisters, this blockade is not only against you, it is against all alternatives of life and liberation, against dignity, sovereignty and hope, against all peoples and against each of us. We are here to express a solidarity in the way that only women have experienced it in life.

Katerina Anfossi, who covered the conference for FIRE, said:

> When I went to Cuba to that conference, I established a beautiful relationship with the organizers and the participants. We were among the few media that covered it all. But when I posed the idea about doing live programs through the phone line and getting their voices on tape systematically, the relationship changed. I believe that when we establish a relationship, not just as a journalist covering [an event] and gathering information, but offering a space for women to speak for themselves, it makes difference.

One and a half years later, on September 7, 1994, we concentrated on these issues again at ICPD in Cairo. In a panel organized by DAWN—Women Without Voices—women from Cuba, Haiti, and Puerto Rico shared their realities.

A Cuban woman expressed how, in spite of 35 years of an unjust economic embargo, women still have hope for a better future:

I have great faith that the world will change because things cannot continue the way they are. This unjust economic order can't continue, the economic blockades can't continue.... I have the faith and the conviction that the accumulated wisdom of the peoples of the Economic South are going to overcome. Above all, the women, with their talent and intelligence, will be capable of overcoming this injustice that we have against us... the illegal blockade of the U.S. against Cuba that seeks to make my people surrender through hunger, but they aren't going to succeed.

Another statement by a Cuban woman was the testimony of Rita María Pereira, a Cuba-born lawyer for the Federation of Cuban Women. Her testimony was presented at the NGO Forum of the Social Development Summit in Denmark in 1995, a tribunal that was organized by a coalition of NGOs. María spoke in Spanish but was translated by interpreters. FIRE broadcast her testimony in both languages.

My name is Rita María Pereira. I work at the Federation of Cuban Women. From the moment that I was invited to be part of this tribunal, a gesture that honors me and for which I am thankful, I have thought a lot about this moment and the great responsibility I feel before my people, our women, and all of you who are here today. I think about the difficult but necessary art of communication. I reflect on this because this is a matter of focusing on an issue very controversial of simply unknown, like the economic, financial, and trade blockade imposed by the United States on Cuba for more than 35 years. There lies the challenge: being able to communicate some facts and experiences that will contribute to understanding the reality of my people, our women.

I live in a country that carries out great efforts to survive and develop, to maintain the advances made in the fields of health, education, and social security while maintaining its right to sovereignty and national independence. It is a country that does not pretend to be a paradigm. It is a country that simply wants to be dignified and respected in the construction of its social project. Because of this, it is punished through an economic blockade, which has had adverse consequences on the enjoyment of the human rights of its people.

I am a witness to this reality of the economic and social consequences of the "Cuban Syndrome" plaguing U.S. administrations from 1960 to the present, its most recent and irrational expression called the Torricelli Amendment. Its objective is to force the Cuban people to change their political system—hence its euphemistic name, *The Cuban Democracy Act*—as an addendum to the U.S. military expenditure budget.

What does this mean for our country, for our lives, and for our normal development as human beings? It means the aggravation of the country's economic crisis due to the loss of its markets when its main trade partners, mostly located in the ex-socialist countries, disappeared. It is not only a matter of not being able to trade with a nation that represents a great market only 90 miles away from our coast, but it also implies, among other restrictions, that the products manufactured by third countries using Cuban raw materials cannot be exported to the United States. It means that we are obligated to trade and transport merchandise from distant places like Asia and Europe, which makes prices higher due to transportation costs. Also, the costs of imports increase because the ships that touch Cuban ports cannot touch U.S. ports until six months later. This is why the ship owners of naval enterprises charge us much more for merchandise transportation. It means that we do not have access to external financing due to the pressure that the U.S. exerts upon financial institutions. These are only some of the implicit measures in the economic sanctions that have a very negative impact on the standard of living of the population and which, unquestionably, affect one of the most vulnerable sectors—health.

While organizing my ideas to address you today, I recalled the epidemic of Dengue hemorrhagic fever that developed in the country a few years ago; 355,230 people became ill, and 158 died. Of those, 101 were children. I could not stop thinking about the pain of those families, of those mothers. I could also not stop thinking and remembering the refusal of the U.S. Department of State to sell and send to Cuba the insecticide needed to tackle the epidemic. It had to be purchased in other countries. We bought it in Asia at a higher price and, of course, its arrival was delayed, creating difficulties in the effective treatment of the disease.

That is why I decided to present the testimony of a Cuban woman physician who could not be here today due to her work, but whose personal experience reflects the reality of many health professionals *who day-by-day suffer the pain of not having at hand the best medicine to alleviate the ailments of their patients.*

Dr. Abela Lazo, a specialist in anesthesiology and reanimation at a hospital of internal medicine, testifies:

> *In my hospital, we carry out a great number of surgical interventions of high risk, which do not take place in any other part of Cuba. This surgery requires an extraordinary amount of resources in order to carry it out with success and offer quality medical assistance. On many occasions, these resources are limited, the medicines are scarce, and generally the anesthetic medicines are very expensive on the international market. They are not sold to us directly, so we have to buy them through third countries. This doubles the cost of the medicine and makes the sales transactions difficult.*

> *I have the daily obligation to distribute with absolute equity all the available resources to enable the work to be done. I want to clarify that the fundamental principle of our endeavor is to carry out the operations with absolute security and quality. We prefer to postpone a surgery if we cannot count on all the necessary resources for its success.*

> *In many places in Cuba, alternatives are practiced to solve problems of basic scarcity within public health, mainly in our system of primary care, a truly strong sector, because here the family doctors, jointly with the community, have developed many valuable solutions to substitute imports like the use of green medicine and acupuncture.*

> *We also confront serious difficulties with materials or spare parts to repair equipment when it breaks down. On occasion, these unexpected breakdowns of necessary pieces of equipment affect or even suspend the development of a surgical program. We do all that is possible to fulfill these surgical programs as planned, but sometimes the work that we may be able to accomplish in six hours extends to eight, to ten, or to twelve hours. This also results in extension of the work shift.*

> *Often, we arrive home late and then must face responsibilities that are as demanding, or more demanding, than our jobs. There*

is the question—What do I cook?—because there is a scarcity of food. We have to care for the children and their school needs. We have to have a good relationship with our partners in order to have a harmonious family life.

Sometimes, we don't have time or are exhausted. The challenge of acquiring certain products for the home also falls upon us. Products for personal hygiene and the home are very scarce. We feel great pain and sorrow for not having adequate clothing and shoes for all members of the family, particularly for the children. They outgrow their clothing and shoes every year.

She stated that on occasion she has to send her children to school with a pair of broken shoes, but one thing is clear: All children in Cuba go to school, even if their shoes are broken. This is something very hard. For what mother is this not painful, moreso in a country that has had so many achievements? We sometimes create a sort of slipper to alleviate this situation. Many times we pass on to the little ones the school uniforms of the older ones. We search for ways to solve the basic needs.

Finally, Dr. Abela Lazo referred to an aspect of special importance to me, and this is why now I not only speak on her behalf, but on behalf of millions of Cuban women. It has to do with the diverse expressions of solidarity that we receive from people and friends from all parts of the world, which are relevant not only because of their material value, but for their great moral value. We want you all to know that we struggle with the objective of overcoming each day, facing each problem. Our women face their daily lives aware of what the revolution means, and we have decided to resist and defend it. In spite of the blockade, we shall overcome.

Women from Puerto Rico

Because of the colonial status of Puerto Rico, where the island has no self-representation in official international forums, and the ambivalence of many organizations and specialized agencies that insist on placing Puerto Rico as part of the USA in delegations, Puerto Rican women hardly have their own voice internationally.

In FIRE, Boricuas have had a place to be themselves and represent themselves in their own right. One such case is the 1993 coverage (originally in Spanish) of the testimonies of Norma Valle and Ana Rivera-Lassen at the Global Tribunal on Violations of Women's Human Rights at the NGO Forum parallel to the UN World Conference on Human Rights in Vienna.

Norma Valle, a feminist writer, teacher, and journalist, presented the following testimony:

My name is Norma Valle. I give my testimony as an individual and also as a voice for the many other women who, like me, have been persecuted, harassed, and monitored by the state for more than a decade. The reason for this monitoring and harassment is that we are feminists who believe that the women's movement is an instrument for our struggles. The state has persecuted us by infiltrating our women's rights organizations, by interfering with our human right to organize toward a just cause, and by persecuting us in our professional and personal lives.

I believe that feminism should be an integral part of all aspects of my public and private life. I have been a feminist activist since 1969. I was president of the Sociedad de Mujeres Periodistas and la Federación de Mujeres Puertorriqueñas, and I was a member of the Directive Junte of the journalists' union.

I have done all that while continually being harassed and pressured by the government. I started to feel the discrimination just after I had been elected president of the Federación de Mujeres Puertorriqueñas. I was also persecuted and discriminated against during the years of work at the newspaper El Mundo. *I was transferred between five different departments of the editorial office in a period of five months. First, I was a political reporter; then I was transferred into the sports section; later I was a community reporter; and finally, they changed my working hours—all to try to make it too difficult for me to work. I constantly felt targeted. I remember one day, my work partner called me in and reprimanded me for a mere eight-minute delay in a report. I looked at her and said, "Maggie, why are you doing this to me?" Both of us cried. In 1976, tired of struggling against co-workers whom I hand once considered friends, I left my job.*

For many months I could not find another job. I worked as a sales clerk in clothing stores. I wrote freelance articles for public relations agencies. I did many odd jobs to survive. A friend got me a part-time job at a private Catholic university teaching two journalism classes. At the beginning of each semester, the director would question my presence there. Why should they keep this "feminist communist"?

Just after I had my baby, I was offered a job to write "human interest" articles. It was at first a part-time job that turned into full time, but after I had been at this job for three months and I was about to be made a permanent employee, my boss fired me. The president told me that "every time my name was mentioned, the structure of the newspaper would shake." I was unemployed for many months. I was a single mother.

During this period, I continued to feel persecuted. When I was driving my car, I felt people following me. Sometimes I would park my car in one place, and later I would find it someplace else. I really believed I was being watched by the government. Once, I was in New York doing research for a book, and two men followed me around the whole city. I was scared, and I was angry at those who had been my friends. I almost felt that I was losing my ability to reason, that I was going crazy.

In 1980, I was employed by the Puerto Rican State University. First, I was a part-time worker, and later became full time, thanks to the director of the School of Communications and to some friends who mentioned my name for the job. But in 1982 I was fired, before the documents for my permanent job were completed. I then started a new period of economic instability that lasted for two years.

Many of my friends were also subjected to such persecution and harassment, and they gave up, but I have not because I have had the support of my family and friends who recognized my struggle.

The "feminist" or "too feminist" label has caused me to be persecuted until today.

When, in 1989, the Supreme Tribunal of Puerto Rico ordered that 130,00 files of those considered subversives be turned over, I received the file kept on me, with information that had been collected for over a decade by the State Police and the Justice Department. For being a feminist, I was considered a subversive. I found out that the discrimination and persecution I had suffered in my personal life, the discrimination at work, and my frequent unemployment, were a result of numerous visits by intelligence agents to my neighbors, my parents, and my bosses at my various jobs, and the investigation of everything I had ever said or done. They had the license plate numbers of all the cars I had ever had; they investigated all my private and confidential documents; they documented people who had dated me. The harassment had been real, concrete—I had the evidence in my own hands.

According to the Puerto Rican government, which is controlled by the FBI, it is a crime to talk about women's rights. To talk about the right of Puerto Rican women to struggle for self-determination and the independence of its people, to say that women have always been excluded throughout history, is the crime that I perpetrated.

I declare myself guilty of pointing out women's exclusion, and I have come here to share with men and women who want to hear me and work in defense of an egalitarian humanity. I am also guilty of teaching my university students and my daughter that feminism is a legitimate doctrine that must be valued by the United Nations and other international organizations. I believe that women's organizations have been threatened and subjected to persecution and harassment by governments. This danger is what we are fighting against here today.

When I received my police file, I had to laugh at the stupidity, but I was also filled with a horrible anger against the intelligence agency, and I cried. I cried for my daughter, for my sisters, and for my friends from Puerto Rico and all over who have been exposed to harassment and the denial of their human rights.

The following testimony was given by Anna Rivera-Lassen, a feminist lawyer from Puerto Rico.

> *November 25th, 1985*
>
> *Memorandum to: Captain Carmelo Malendez,*
> *   Director of the Intelligence Office*
>
> *From: Agent Israel Santos*
>
> *Issue: Demonstration sponsored by the*
> *   coordinator of the feminist movement*

Reason for the Activity: To celebrate the International Day
Against Violence Against Women

The following feminist organizations are listed on this document: Encuentro de Mujeres, Feministas en Marcha, and la Organización Puertorriqueña de la Mujer Trabajadora. Collaborators in the activity mentioned above are: Collective Taller Salud, Circulo de Concientización Gay, Mujeres Artistas de Puerto Rico, and Circulo de Estudios Feministas de Trujillo Alto.

This is an example of the memoranda that appear in dossier #6288 of the Puerto Rican Police Intelligence Office. This dossier was compiled on the woman who speaks to you now.

The Puerto Rican police have been watching me and keeping information on me under the category of "subversive and terrorist." This is due to my participation in the feminist movement and in activities to promote women's rights.

Feminists organized in Puerto Rico during the 1970s, in accordance with the rights that we had under the laws of the island. Under the constitution of Puerto Rico, all people are guaranteed the right to meet and to free association. It is also guaranteed that we cannot be discriminated against for reasons of race, color, origin, sex, and political or religious ideas. During the decade of the 1970s, especially in 1972 when we founded the Mujer Integrate Ahora, I was very young, only sixteen years old, and I believed in justice. I did not then know its consequences.

The practice of keeping files on people or persecuting people due to political ideas has a long history. But in Puerto Rico, the fact that this practice was discovered to be related to a far more serious practice—a series of murders of "terrorists" by the police—had a strong impact on public opinion. The police, the Justice Department, and the state were watching people and keeping information about them, even when they had not been involved in any crime. It was done just because these people had opinions and ideas different from the state. This practice was questioned by a national tribunal, which demanded that the Puerto Rican police and the Justice Department stop and give the files to the respective subjects. When we received these files on our activities, we realized that, for the Puerto Rican government, working for better opportunities for women in the society was considered to be subversive.

The file on the feminist organization Mujer Integrate Ahora, for example, had data from as far back as 1976. The file on this organization was full of wrong data about its founding, its ideology, and objectives. It contained pictures and information about activities, and documentation related to women's rights. It also combined newspaper clippings about activities of the organization.

In the case of individual feminists' files, the watching and recording had started early, at least since 1974. The watching of the individual members of the organization, Mujer Integrate Ahora, as well as of members of the Alianza Feminista por la Liberación Humana, and of the Federación de Mujeres Puertorriqueñas, started in the 1970s.

During the 1980s, it was extended to members of other organizations. For all the members of these organizations, the persecution had personal consequences that directly affected these women's lives. Some of them lost their jobs because officials would come to the workplace to talk about them. Others had problems with their neighbors due to the police coming to interrogate them. Many times, it caused problems with family and close friends.

I, for example, suffered for many years because I did not know that they had invented a false case about me at the Puerto Rican University. It almost prevented me from continuing my law studies. And all we get for all the pain caused are these files.

The feminist activities that were documented by the police included forums, rallies, public demonstrations, conferences—anything related to the promotion of women's rights. Any public defense of women's reproductive rights, expressions against the violations against women or in favor of abortion or someone's sexuality were considered subversive activities. We denounce this practice of keeping files on people because of our ideology and feminist activities. We denounce it as a repressive and illegal action of the state.

Throughout this city, we have been talking about the eradication of oppression and the recognition of women's rights as human rights. The domestic violence, the violation of women inside and outside war situations, the violations of our physical integrity, the traffic king of women, the denial of our rights as indigenous peoples, and the prejudice *against lesbians are all based on a patriarchal system. This system will change only through our organizing against patriarchy. It is ironic that our human rights are guaranteed, but our basic right to organize to meet is not.*

A denunciation by this tribunal would serve as a clear and impressive message that women have the right to organize in order to participate in the social and political life of their countries, and that interference with this right is a violation of our human rights.

Women from Nicaragua

One of the conferences that FIRE first covered was the Nicaraguan Women's Conference (Encuentro), held in January of 1992, which explored the reality of Nicaraguan women and new alternatives for building a more just internal order. The theme of the conference was United in Diversity. Women of color from Nicaragua's Atlantic Coast, disabled women who had been victims of war in that country, and indigenous refugee women from the Central American region were given priority on FIRE's microphones at that meeting.

Liliam Amador Martinez, a Nicaraguan woman with a disability that had relegated her to a wheelchair, talked to FIRE about the issues she faces and shares with other women like herself:

I am working with a center for rehabilitation and integral development for people with disabilities, because we can make a contribution to society from our wheelchairs. We need the social support, not only from our families, but from everyone. When I had my accident, my life changed totally. My accident happened in the earthquake of 1971. I thought my life had ended.

After a year I began to pull myself together. I am mother to five children, four of whom I had before I was disabled. I have put them all through school by learning to sew. This feminist encuentro has given me, for the first time, an insight about women's particular subordination and discrimination. My disability was an accident, but the situation that I face as a woman is hereditary. Yes, we inherited it from our great grandfathers, grandfathers, and fathers. Life has to

change for women, we have to conquer through our dignity. I learned
so much at the workshop about violence and rape... I found out it's
not a class issue, but a gender issue.
In their final declaration, the 800 Nicaraguan women present stated:

This encuentro has meant the beginning of a new political culture.
We want to find our definition of power and ways of exercising it so as
to move beyond masculine ways that we have internalized and repro-
duced. We reaffirm the self-convened encuentro, autonomous and plu-
ralistic, as a will of all of us in the democratic way of building effective
solidarity among women.

Refugee Women from Guatemala

In Guatemala, 1992, Katerina Anfossi covered a Refugee Women's
Conference, sharing experiences with Central American refugees and
recently repatriated Mayan Guatemalan women, gaining a more profound understanding of the lives of these diverse women and how their
situation as refugees affects them so deeply. FIRE learned that the greatest hope for our refugee friends lies in knowing that many international and nonprofit organizations left the conference committed to
implementing new programs that employ a gender perspective. This
perspective will better reflect the reality of refugees in general, the majority of whom are women and children.

Katerina, Nancy Vargas, and Jeanne Carstensen traveled to Nicara-
gua in March 1992 for the first Central American Feminist Conference.
Five hundred women from Belize, Guatemala, Honduras, El Salvador,
Nicaragua, Costa Rica, and Panama, as well as Central American refu-
gees living in Mexico, gathered at Nicaragua's Pacific coast resort of
Montelimar for five days of workshops on the central theme of power,
"The power we have and don't have, and the power we want to build."

Throughout the week the emphasis was on the sharing of
experiences. Together for the first time, the women experienced an
ongoing process of discovering their commonalties in the face of
tremendous diversity. The first two days focused on How Women Live
in Central America, with 34 workshops on topics such as sexuality,
pleasure, feelings, law, black women, indigenous women, and the current

351

structural adjustment policies that are impoverishing women. The effect of this interchange was, as Salvadoran Morena Herrera told FIRE, "To confirm that we share a common history that, until recently, has been unknown."

Throughout the conference, FIRE reiterated its commitment to bringing women's voices from around the world to every corner of the globe. As a result of our recordings and interviews during the event, FIRE produced a series of cassettes about the conference. It was distributed throughout Latin America, not only for use on radio, but also for popular education. The cassette series, "The History of Gender in Central America," was made possible by the Foundation for a Compassionate Society and the Global Fund for Women, who gave FIRE the funding to go to the event and to produce and distribute the series.

The FIRE broadcast on March 5, 1996, was dedicated to women in Central America. We played the series, "History of Gender in Central America," where women from each country speak about their feminist perspectives. Women in a region that was immersed in civil wars throughout recent decades have organized autonomously, because they have learned that no one will make their revolution unless they organize and struggle for it themselves. The half-hour program describes Central American women's expectations in organizing the 1992 Central American feminist conference. It highlights the need for autonomous women's organizations and a common agenda for change in the region.

Women Forgotten in
Costa Rican History

Tatiana Lobo, a Chilean–Costa Rican writer and winner of the 1995 Sor Juana Ines de a Cruz literature award for her book *Asalto al Paraiso* came to FIRE in 1996 to do a special program about her most recent book: *Entre Dios y el Diablo (Between God and the Devil)*. The book is based on research about women in Costa Rica's colonial period, but she believes "the history of Costa Rican women is still to be written."

Because there is so little information about women in that period, Tatiana went to the few sources available: The registry of marriages, deaths, protocols, testaments, and letters of freedom granted to slave women. The book is a compilation of what she was able to gather about

12 women of the period, some white Spaniard, others black slave African women, others indigenous, and others mulattas and mestizas.

Tatiana believes that Latin American women's identity was shaped during that period of the eighteenth century. The stories of these women give evidence to the fact that "women's resistance to the patriarchal domain during the colonial period took different forms."

For white Spaniard women, the norms about sexuality and child-bearing were very strict, but for the black and indigenous women there was a "permissibility" because their children added to the wealth of the state and of the Church.

The book shatters the myth that women of those times were ladies dressed in black, with their eyes always looking down, always standing in the kitchen, always praying to saints by lighting a hundred candles to them, and frigid in their sexuality. Tatiana discovered in the legal books the many illegitimate children that are registered, the divorces, and the rebellions, the sufferings, punishments, and abuses against these women. Tatiana also believes that the situation for women has not changed much since then.

Katerina Anfossi asked her if she believes that women themselves have changed since then, to which she answered with a very emphatic yes:

We are stronger, we have a sense of empowerment, but structures and the way society treats women have not changed much. We have to own a sense of history to understand the challenges.

While still on the air, Tatiana received a phone call from Alma Molina, a Salvadoran living in Costa Rica, who wanted to tell her how much she appreciated and enjoyed the book when she read it. For the author, it was the first time she had received direct feedback about her work.

Black Women from the Americas and Germany

FIRE's links with black women from all of Latin America and the Caribbean began to strengthen when in July of 1992 Nancy Vargas attended the First Encuentro of Black Women of the Latin American and Caribbean region, held in the Dominican Republic.

The women at that meeting analyzed their black identity, the racism, sexism, discrimination, and gender violence they suffer. They decided to create a network of Afro–Latin American Women and Afro–Caribbean women, aiming to connect and unite black women of the area.

Nancy Vargas made a live phone call from the meeting, where Sergia Galvan, coordinator of the organizing committee, talked about the need to reconceptualize language and culture to end discrimination, saying that phrases such as "the black market, the obscure side of history... [are part of] a language that discriminates against us."

It was at that meeting that FIRE announced for the first time—since it had just happened that day at the conference—the nomination of July 25 as International Day of Black, African Latin American, and Afro-Caribbean Women.

In Costa Rica, preserving Afro-Limón culture was the main objective of the Workshop on the "Situation of Black Women from Limón on the Atlantic Coast" from January 21-22, 1993. Coordinated by the Limón Afro-Cultural Foundation, this activity was based on an interchange between black women from Limón and emphasized the need to reconnect with their own identity. The women created an intercountry network for rescuing the Afro cultural values in the province, emphasizing the need to create opportunities for the involvement of black women in economic activities based on society-wide re-education in African culture.

In April of 1995, Jasmin Edding from the Black Women's Network ADEFRA in Germany came to the FIRE studios to learn how to produce radio programs. She was there at the same time as Ana Sisnet, who is a black Panamanian woman from the Foundation for a Compassionate Society. Jasmin talked on FIRE about her organization and her work:

Ours is a very young organization. We began 10 years ago in Germany, and in recent years have done outreach in Africa, Latin America, England, and the USA. It always surprises us that even black peoples in those countries do not know about the existence of blacks in Germany. Black people have been in Germany for hundreds of years, and not only after the second World War, which is what many think.

Asked by Nancy about the meaning of the outreach, Jasmin said:

It has allowed us to know our history and heritage because it is not only our history in Germany, but the other side of our history. It is a history that we never learned in school, but in networking around the world. For me, getting to know black women in other countries is like finding pieces of my family, an extended family. There are differences among us, but also many commonalties. [For example], most of us in Germany come from mixed couples, and are raised German, and we live in white communities. I have been interested in getting to know the experiences of women who live in black neighborhoods, because they have more role models. What we have in common is that we have all experienced racism, and our common goal is to fight it.

She talked about the actions undertaken by her network to render visible their identity:

ADEFRA is a forum for black women where they can study about their history. We have also organized an archive, and we hold workshops for white women, which is very important. We have had a newspaper called African Look *that is not produced right now because of [lack of] funding. We also organize tours to other countries. That is very important; that kind of activity has been my school. We have done research on black women and health, so that people know what our issues are. We have to counteract the stereotypes. We not only work, but take time to have a good time!*

Jasmin thanked FIRE for the opportunity to come to Costa Rica to learn about radio, and about black women in Costa Rica. As she was leaving the studio after the program, she received a phone call from a Costa Rican listener who thanked her for the program because, as she said, "I am one who had no idea there were blacks in Germany. Thank you for the very informative program." Jasmin and the listener exchanged addresses to keep in touch.

With the help of Nancy Vargas, Ana Sisnet and Jasmin organized live broadcasts from the Hotel Balmoral in Costa Rica to cover the First Central American and Caribbean Black Women's Encuentro, which took place later that month. Ana Sisnet, a Panamanian black woman, dedicated the program

...to black women's mothers and grandmothers, and all black women of the world who have given us their strength, their creativity and imagination, and their faith. They have contributed to our resistance and have inspired us to work for the future of the entire world....

From Nicaragua, Matilde Lindo came on the air to share the struggles of the black women on the Atlantic Coast of her country. "We exist, we are, and it is nice to be a part of humanity," she said.

From Belize and working with the Belize Organization for Women and Development (BOWAND), Ellen Annette Gentle came on the air to say, "We have to affirm our rights as black women. We work in housing to help low-income women to have their own homes; we also work for higher incomes."

From Limón, Costa Rica, FUSCAL member Barbara Johnson described the event as the First Central American Women's Encuentro. She talked about FUSCAL as a foundation that works toward the preservation of the black culture in Costa Rica.

Nancy Vargas interviewed Solange Pierre, a Haitian living in the Dominican Republic, about the results of the gathering: Following is Solange's impression:

One of the main achievements is that black women in Central America have formed their regional network. It can contribute to the linking and communication of black women in this region, and with other women in other parts of the world. Another achievement has been the debate about how women exercise power. We stated that we have to decentralize power within our institutions, at all levels. We have to diversify power so that we do not reproduce power issues.

Nancy asked Esperanza Miguel, from La Romana Province in the Dominican Republic, about the upcoming Fourth World Conference on Women in Beijing:

We have formed part of the local and regional process for the conference: dissemination of information, drafting our agenda, and so on. We have achieved the inclusion of black women's issues in the regional agenda.

Solange Pierre added her concern:

I ask how much a process such as this one where so many resources are spent... how much will it really have an effect on grassroots women's problems and needs? I am afraid that women of color might not have a real voice in China or in the agenda once the final conference takes place. We will share with other women in other regions, but how much we will really achieve beyond that is still to be seen.

Indeed, Solange was right. The Latin American and Caribbean official agenda for the Fourth World Conference on Women, drafted in Mar del Plata, Argentina, in September 1994 by the Economic Commission of Latin America and the Caribbean (CEPAL), recognized the "cultural plurality that comprises our region," but taking that issue to the global level would not be easy.

Jasmin Edding's experiences at FIRE had opened new possibilities for her network back in Germany. This is what she told us upon returning to her country:

Hello FIRE,

It's a while since I talked to you. I hope you are fine and healthy.

I know that you have been very busy all the time. Recently I met women from the radio here in Munich. It is a community radio and the women have twice a month 2 hours to be on air.... So far there are just 2 or 3 women who are doing the program and they are looking for women who want to do radio. So I met them and told them that I am interested in doing radio, but not by myself. I want to gather black women and migrant women and do our own thing. Now I look for women who are interested in doing radio. I know it is a lot of work and we might not do it on a regular basis, if we do it at all. If you have any hints or suggestions please don't hesitate to let me know. Did you send the interview already that I did with the German women? If possible I would like to have a copy if it is not too much effort.

So my dear, greet all the other women from FIRE. Take care. (How is your computer work doing?)

Looking forward to hearing from you.

Love and peace, Jasmin

The 25th of July of that year was a special Latin American and Caribbean Black Women's Day. Sergia Galvan, coordinator of the Latin American and Caribbean Black Women's Network, called FIRE live from the Dominican Republic:

Today we celebrate the Latin American and Caribbean Black Women's Day, which was declared as such at the First Latin American and Caribbean Black Women's Conference held in 1992. This day is very important for us because it allows us to render visibility to our reality and our daily life. It also allows us to affirm our ethnic identity, our gender identity, and our culture. It is an important day because with it we contribute to making effective the cultural diversity in our region, the diversity which is a source of strength and that empowers our struggle as black women in the women's movement. So we want to make a call to black women today to express our identity, to express our voices, and to fortify the links with all women—the solidarity and the support among women in our region.

Sergia also related the day to the Fourth World Conference on Women, which was held a little over a month later. She said, "We feel that it is an appropriate context to give visibility to the different identities of women throughout the world, especially of black women." She also shared how women were celebrating the day in her country with "a big drum festival... where through our ritual, we are expressing our identity."

South African Women
of All Backgrounds

FIRE's trip to South Africa in December 1994 was another instance of creating connections with traditionally invisible women across race and culture. Our visit was only a few months after the inauguration of a new government in South Africa that put an end to 40 years of legal apartheid and many more years of classical colonialism.

Black women, considered non-people during apartheid, raised their voices, strong in a new citizenship acquired through decades of struggle—a struggle that put its stamp on the Interim Constitution adopted on April 27, 1994. Today in South Africa, racial and gender discrimination have been banned by law.

However, because women there knew that an end to discrimination against them would be a monumental revolution that would transcend legal measures, they were organizing to find and hold their own voice in the middle of a complex transition. Tumy, a young South African who learned radio with FIRE, explained:

> There is a lot of confusion and excitement at the same time. Everybody is trying to get over what happened, and there are a lot of contradictions about that because we've got to forget the past and move on. But we really can't forget the past, because then we will repeat the same mistakes.... There are a lot of new things happening. I've been in South Africa the whole time. All the years that I have been here, I've only known one part of South Africa, but the whole of South Africa is open to me now. It's great that I can go everywhere, I can experience everything. Today, I am a radio woman, because I want my voice to be heard.

Tumy became a radio woman at a training workshop organized within the context of the first-ever Women's Health Conference in the new South Africa. Convened by the Women's Health Project at the University of Johannesburg December 1-4, the gathering was organized to draft a policy on women's health to present to the new government. The meeting brought together 350 women from all the provinces. One of the participants at the opening session set the tone for the conference when she said, "Women cannot have health until we have political rights."

The gathering was followed by a series of workshops, including one on radio. Tumy had volunteered to help FIRE do the training. Very quickly she learned to use the tape recorder and helped other participants interview each other, getting their voices on radio.

The interviews facilitated by the new radio woman ranged from testimonies to reports and assessments about the conference. In them, grassroots women, academics, health workers, nurses, doctors, and policymakers recorded their extraordinary voices of pain, hope, and struggle.

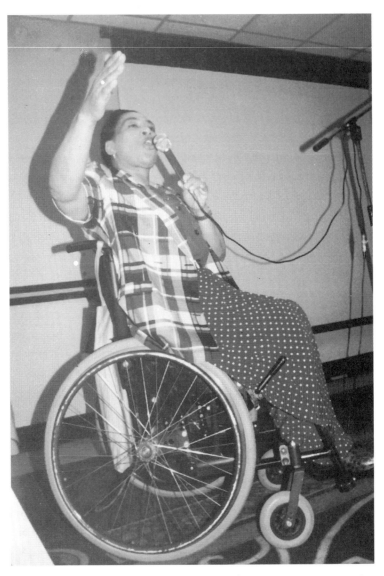

South African women's health concerns are heard worldwide via FIRE's live broadcasts from the 1994 Women's Health Conference in South Africa.

Mensy, one of the women interviewed, talked about the relationship between policies and action:

I'm from the Women's Network Project. I feel the way they did the policy in the past is that they never consulted the women or the people affected by this policy. That's one of my views.... For example, they had a good policy on free pregnancy coverage, but there were no facilities for it. Now one wonders what the policymakers will be doing about the implementation part of it, because if you introduce a policy, you have to think about building more hospitals and clinics and hire more nurses. Otherwise, the policy cannot be implemented accordingly. So I think that the issue of not involving women in policymaking is affecting us even today.

Women had both expectations and concerns about the new Reconstruction and Development Program (RDP). One of the rural women at the radio workshop expressed hers:

I want to develop our women in the Northern Transval (rural and South Africa) because no one comes to see what is happening there. All these RDPs end [up] at the urban areas. Media too. I try to organize women to come to the region. I also teach women to help themselves. I have attended [workshops for] training of skills like candlemaking and sewing, but there I am the only one who can train them. I want to encourage other women who have skills to come and help me.

Asked by an apprentice interviewer where she was going to get the funding for her skills training, she beamed with hope in the media as she answered, "That's why I asked you to interview me, because I want to be in the media so that the RDP can help me, and I'll also write to the other organizations to help me!"

Lucy, from Eastern Transval, described the developments at the conference:

...we are trying to get women in South Africa to unite, to talk about their problems, and hear what is happening in their regions. How did they solve the problems? In that way we are sharing that we must not be afraid of the problems. I am prepared to work hard here in South Africa.

Another participant came on the air to say:

My name is Ellen Dulley. I come from the Val Region. I work for Val Pottery Company. We are making pottery and are very advanced in the market. In the past we were having conference discussions speaking about our own problems of oppression and apartheid, but today we are discussing the problems of women [regardless] of color..., of language.... Men have to know that women are a-coming! That is the name of a song we sing at the union.

The Women's Health Conference became a place where women from different backgrounds learned from each other. Shenanz Sinemam, a medical student from Cape Town, voiced on FIRE that she had a very keen interest in women's affairs:

To me this conference has been simply wonderful because of the large variety of experiences that we are able to share for the first time as South Africans of all races and colors. That's simply beautiful because I never experienced that before... like listening to a lesbian woman telling me how she felt telling her family for the first time; like the experience of a rural woman telling me what it's like to sleep over at the well overnight because they can't get water. Those kinds of lessons are greater than any scientific paper.

In the intimate context of friends interviewing friends, some women gave their personal testimonies to each other. Elsie, a member of the Disabled People of South Africa, said that when she became disabled and went to the hospital, a doctor approached her asking her if she wanted him to do an operation to stop her from menstruating:

I refused because I did not want to have anything to do with operations. That saved me because the doctor did not explain fully the negative side and the disadvantages of such an operation. He was also unfair because I was newly disabled and could not make any clear decision. I was going through a trauma in my life. I would have also missed out the opportunity of having my own baby one day, if I wanted children. So I would have been denied the choice of parenthood.

Lesbians also shared their concerns on the air. For example, Beverly Titzin expressed these thoughts:

I want to tell you that I think that the South African government is not adequately addressing the issue of lesbians and AIDS.... Lesbians are not asking for special funding, but that any national fund that is [established] for AIDS should also address these issues. Lesbians must look at the kinds of sexual practices they engage in. I think that they must understand that their identity as lesbians does not exempt them from AIDS, but that their sexual practices can make the risk as viable for them as for anyone else.... I hope the government and all the lesbians hear this out there. We hope that all this that is being said over the radio will be incorporated [in research projects]. I hope that we can fight AIDS together.

Concerns about women's decision-making and the need to re-educate men were also raised on radio:

My name is Florence, a social worker by profession, but I work with women's affairs. Before I say anything else, I'd like to mention that though I am educated, I am a traditional woman. So I know how traditional customs retard the problem of women in South Africa. I would like to focus more on how traditions affect fertility among women. In the first place, women have to play a major role in fertility, but we have found out that there is nothing we can do without getting permission from our husbands, our in-laws, and everybody. What I say is that women do not have decision-making at all. I have noticed that women can achieve, they are able to organize themselves.... So what I am looking for is a strategy on how to include men in what women are actually doing. That is my concern.

Besides the radio training workshop, Feminist International Radio Endeavour did a live broadcast from South Africa. Women there got ready to have their voices travel through the telephone line to the radio station and on to listeners around the word. For Tumy, our newly recruited radio woman, this was an exciting event. "Imagine," she said, "putting South African women's voices in Central America. That's great!"

Cramped in one small bedroom of the hotel where the conference was taking place, more than 20 women watched with expectation as the equipment was being installed, and then they waited impatiently for the international phone call to come through. This is how I began the broadcast:

Welcome to Feminist International Radio Endeavour, FIRE, broadcasting live today from a new South Africa. Before I turn the microphone over to the women of this new nation, I want to share with you what it means for me to have come to this country. When I was a little girl I used to ask if my little island of Puerto Rico would ever stop being a colony, would ever be free. Once an uncle, fed up with my asking all the time, told me about a big country, the country of South Africa. He explained that its peoples were struggling to be a nation, but that it was very difficult. "Puerto Rico will never be free until South Africa is free—yet we will probably never get to see the liberation of South Africa in our lifetime," he told me. This year, South Africa has become a nation. I am still alive, and have had the privilege to come here to share with all these women....

Gail picked up after that, using a 10-second soundbite technique to give her message:

I just want to say hello to all our feminist sisters across the world and tell you about the wonderful poster that is here. It says: We South African women have fought for our liberation, and now we are here to fight for our rights. Thank you.

Some women had stated very clearly before the live broadcast that they were there to watch and did not want to come on the air, but the dynamics of the broadcast pulled them in spontaneously:

Hello, I am Karin speaking. I am a white South African girl. I can tell you that María has told us that this is an emotional night for her, but it is the same for all South Africans in this conference. To come together from all the different cultures in South Africa, as women who speak the same language. Even though we need some translation, we have come together to fight for all these policies that are so near to all our hearts. One of the things is the whole consultative process that took place before the meeting and is taking place here—the voices of women from the other cultures in the regions... the organizers really want to know what the grassroots women want to say, and they believe that is what should influence policy. It is a wonderful experience. Thank you.

My roommate at the hotel walked in to find dozens of women spread all over the place, taking turns speaking and listening to each other. "Imagine," she whispered, "our room has become a portable radio station!" She sat on her bed to wait for her own turn:

Hello, as you know we have had a lot of violence, especially concerning women. Women have had a lot of problems getting health care, getting shelter. I think it's time we stand up and help those women who did not have the chance. Now is the time, and we are prepared to help those women.

Today I attended a workshop on "Women, Development and Health." In this workshop we discussed housing, which is the most important thing here in South Africa. Many women do not have the right to ownership; only men. We also discussed health, which is the most important aspect. Most women so far, especially when they are pregnant, do not have enough health care; they do not have facilities. We are trying to make the government make a policy so we can help those women. Thank you very much.

Another guest spoke about the recent changes in her country:

Hello, I'm Mary speaking from South Africa. I can tell you that today, that this is another South Africa. Another South Africa in the sense that so many women can come together: Women of different colors and languages, speaking the same language—even we black women who could never speak out. This is the new South Africa and it's giving us hope. It's giving us hope because we can even speak to our sisters throughout the whole world. Imagine, here is María today, from Puerto Rico. I never thought I would ever meet a person from that area. Neither

365

Edited by Marika Sboros

Fiery feminist makes airwaves

Visiting Costa Rican broadcaster Maria Suarez predicts a bright future for local community radio and rural women fulfil their dream of setting up a radio station in their village. **BEATHUR BAKER** reports.

By liberating the airwaves, Costa Rican feminist broadcaster Maria Suarez of the Feminist International Radio Endeavour (FIRE), is getting women's voices heard throughout the world, albeit on predominantly male, international shortwave radio.

In South Africa for the national Women's Health Policy Conference last weekend, Suarez says she has always dreamt of coming to South Africa because of the political struggle in her native Puerto Rico — and more so now that this country is "free".

FIRE broadcasts twice daily for two hours on issues concerning women from a small location "surrounded by mountains" in Costa Rica, but the radio's endeavour draws responses from listeners around the world.

Suarez, a former educator and literacy trainer for 15 years, has been with the radio station since its inception in May last year, and has already covered several landmark global summits and conferences. Her goal, she says, is to give voices back to the voiceless.

With her trademark bag of compact broadcasting equipment, she travels wherever women invite FIRE to cover and broadcast their events.

The recent policy conference she attended, organised by the Women's Health Project, was the first of its kind to be held in South Africa. The aim was for women to come together and decide on what they want to see in future policy on women's reproductive rights and healthcare.

At the height of the three-day conference, held in Johannesburg, Suarez set up and broadcast live from her hotel room, which was packed with women from every corner of this country, eager to take part in FIRE's

Feminist broadcaster Maria Suarez ... setting the international shortwave frequency on fire with her message to women. PICTURE: ANTON HAMMERL

transmission.

Local women communicated, via her simple mixing board and telephone transmitter connection, with women half-way around the world.

Judging from the excitement and overwhelming response, Suarez says she sees radio becoming an accessible medium through which women can confidently raise their voices and improve their position in this country.

Those taking part say the experience of going on air live for

the first time was exhilarating, and the experience brought them confidence and inspiration that "we can do it too" — the message FIRE strives to promote universally.

But in her terminology, more simply, Suarez says the changing power of the airwaves is "the pure magic of radio". She says: "All FIRE does is help women realise the potential of radio as an intimate, one-to-one medium and provide or encourage them to explore the medium."

Suarez is excited about the

hands-on approach through which women are taking hold of their rights, a vital contribution to what Feminist Radio International sees as "the move by women in all parts of the world holding women's rights tribunals to break the silence and end the impunity surrounding violations of women's rights in all spheres of life".

Suarez says FIRE broadcasts on shortwave radio in 100 countries, and to an increasingly male audience. And next year, when it erects a facility in Can-

ada to bounce the signal back off the restrictive mountains surrounding the station, more countries, such as South Africa, will be able to tune in.

The station's secret to its growing popularity, says Suarez, is that it brings people live coverage of events in all parts of the world with few restrictions.

FIRE can broadcast to such a wide audience because of the co-operation it gets from women who tune in, says Suarez, and it keeps on top of issues through telephonic, written and faxed communication with international women's organisations.

She likens the growth of the radio station to that of the international women's movement, saying the world is on fire "wherever there are women".

Suarez encourages women to initiate and run their own broadcasting endeavours and programmes to have their voices heard in their countries and communities.

The station is part of Radio For Peace International and is funded by the United States Foundation for a Compassionate Society, which Suarez says is "dedicated to bringing women's values into reality and validating them as as a way to peace for all". It also sponsors other peace and social justice projects.

Suarez invites South African women to send their radio contributions on tape or in writing. FIRE accepts all formats — interviews, news, testimonies and stories — segments or completed programmes (of any length up to an hour) from outside contributors.

If possible, people should record their items with high-quality microphones to attain good audio levels which are important for shortwave radio.

FIRE can be contacted at Radio For Peace International, APDO 88, Santa Ana, Costa Rica. Tel: (506) 249-1821. Fax:(506) 249-1095

FIRE's presence in South Africa prompted this coverage of María Suárez and FIRE's broadcasts from the Women's Health Policy Conference.

did she think she would ever meet a person from South Africa, and here she is today. That's all we can say—thank you.

The last guest on the live broadcast was Barbara Klugman. Director of the Women's Health Project and one of the organizers of the conference, she was so tired that she had not joined the broadcast. But some women who had left the hotel room after they spoke on the air went after her, bringing her to the microphone.

It feels like a fantasy. The women are making it happen. It's just wonderful! I hope that people listening to this get a sense of what is happening here. We are drafting policy in a democratic process that has included women from all of the country. We have dealt with the hard-pressing issues such as environment and development, mental health, violence, aging, lesbian health, industrial health, nursing curriculum, legislation on abortion, sexually transmitted diseases, teenage pregnancy, contraception, pregnancy, and childbirth. In eighteen months, the Interim Constitution has to become a permanent one, and we are going to make sure women's concerns and needs are in it.

Our broadcast on March 7, 1996, was dedicated to women in South Africa, in the voice of Mignon, from a women's radio program on KAFR in the United States, produced and sent to FIRE by Diane Post. Mignon is a singer, songwriter, and anti-apartheid activist who lived in South Africa during apartheid and now lives in Australia:

The struggle has changed [in South Africa]. Now it is about building a country and everybody pulling together and creating a new South Africa. A lot of people do not really see the change yet, but the government has done an incredible job by setting up free medical service, helping people with jobs and housing, and the constant process of negotiations. During the last 10 years everybody drew up charters on what they wanted their country to be: A women's charter, a lesbian and gay charter, a workers' charter... and the government has taken them into consideration in drafting the Interim Constitution....

Women have always been the backbone of the struggle in South Africa. When you look at the struggle in Zimbabwe, women wanted their rights, and the men said come with us, take up guns and fight in the struggle, and we will do your liberation when we have the whole country's liberation. And they [the women] did that, and then when the war was over, they were put back into menial roles. But the women [in South Africa] are very powerful and have pushed through a lot of the sexism in the African tradition.

Women from Former
Socialist Countries

Women from the former socialist countries have also been underrepresented in media and in international events. Giving them a voice on FIRE has been our contribution to counteract this. From them we have learned, among many other things, that unless women organize to defend conquered rights, we can lose them. That has been the experience of women in many of the former socialist countries as revealed on FIRE's broadcasts.

Women from Russia

FIRE produced programs with Anastasia Podskaskya, the director of the Gender Studies Center in Moscow, about post-Beijing assessments by women in Russia.

Russian women today face unprecedented problems. A society in which women had vast opportunities for education and employment is trying to "democratize" itself and solve its economic problems by making women second-class citizens. There is increasing violence against women, brought about by market reform: Sexual harassment in the workplace, growing domestic violence, sexual exploitation of young women, street violence, growing domestic violence, unheard of violence against older women—with the objective of seizing their privatized homes. Then there are deepening problems of reproductive rights, particularly the limiting of access to medical assistance, including for childbirth and abortion.... We want our country to be accountable for its decisions at the Fourth World Conference on Women in China!

Women from Bosnia

Vesna Kusik from Zagreb in the former Yugoslavia spoke about the first women's conference in postwar Bosnia:

Because FIRE was not able to be there, we decided to send me here to Costa Rica to report about it! It was actually the First Conference of Bosnian Women, but it was very international. Participants included women from the former Yugoslavia, from Belgrade, from Macedonia, Women in Black, and women from the Philippines, India, the USA, and Europe. The purpose was to bring together Bosnian women, but the conference also brought together women of the world.

There were 400 women from Bosnia and 100 from other parts of the world. They decided to take the future into their hands and to overcome, as women, the political divisions, since women were not present in the peace negotiations nor in the declaration of war! These women have been the first to take a step toward unity. Women suffer war more, so when they survive, they are stronger than men. Establishing justice locally is very important, and that is why the conference was held—because peace was imposed, war was imposed, and justice did not seem to come about in the international court because there is no jurisdiction!

Women from Poland

Wanda Nowicka presented a testimony about reproductive rights in Poland at the NGO Forum of the UN Conference on Population and Development in 1994 in Cairo, Egypt. Wanda was one of the testifiers at the Cairo Hearing on Reproductive Health and Human Rights, she is a leading advocate for reproductive health in Poland, and founder of the Polish Federation of Woman and Family Planning.

I would like to testify before you on behalf of many Polish women who have suffered as a result of the anti-abortion law. I am sorry that none of them could come here to testify personally.

I have been working on the issue of reproductive rights for more than three years. The Federation for Women and Family Planning was established to keep abortion legal and also to prevent the consequences of the law we were sure would be introduced. The Federation runs a hotline for women, through which we give counseling on sexual and reproductive health and rights. This is how I was able to learn about these stories and present them to you.

Poland has had legal abortion, practically on demand, since 1956. For the majority of Polish women, restrictions to legal abortion were a phenomena of the past history that would never come back. Women in Poland took legal abortion for granted. Unfortunately, we were terribly wrong, and it is the irony of history that we lost our reproductive freedom in a time when the country regained independence from the communist system. Freedom for the country does not necessarily mean freedom for women.

The anti-abortion law was introduced in Poland in March, 1993, under very strong pressure from the Roman Catholic Church on authorities, on the medical community, and on the whole society. The anti-abortion law allows legal abortion in public hospitals only when a woman's life and health is threatened, when abortion is a result of rape or incest, or when a fetus is badly deformed. Doctors will be penalized up to two years in prison and lose their professional status if they perform abortions outside of the legal system. Many women have already suffered as a result of this law.

Grazyna, a woman of 35, has been blind since she was born. She is married to a disabled man. She has two children. She became pregnant again. She received two necessary prescriptions justifying a need for abortion from two different doctors, as the anti-abortion law demands, and she went to her district hospital. The director of her hospital refused to perform an abortion. He treated her with disrespect, telling her she should not have gone to her husband's bed if she was afraid of pregnancy. He also told her that he knows some families of blind people. They have many children, and they are all very happy.

Grazyna was completely broken. She knew best what having this baby would mean, and she realized that she and her husband could not afford another baby. She went from one doctor to another begging for help. They all agreed she should not have a baby, but none of them wanted to risk their professional careers. When she finally found a doctor who agreed to help her, she was desperate, near to committing suicide.

A similar story happened to a woman from Krakow who was raped. According to the Polish anti-abortion law, she could have a legal abortion. She got the necessary document from the police, but her district hospital denied her abortion. She tried all possible legal ways. It took her about a month to finally have an abortion in another public hospital. She probably would never have succeeded if the media had not gotten involved. They publicized the whole story and forced the medical authorities to obey the law. But many women do not have access to the media.

These two cases are examples of how the law is implemented. The practice of the law is much harder than the law itself. Many women who were raped have encountered many difficulties. One public prosecutor said to a woman, "You should have been more cautious with a man. You should have realized that a rape is hard to prove." Many raped women have just given up seeking legal abortion, not believing that they will truly be supported by the law enforcement institutions.

Legal abortion is not possible for the majority of unwanted pregnancies. Such women are desperate to find a solution. Some of them decide to go abroad, but that is not an easy way, either. I will quote you a letter we received from a woman in Krakow:

I started having sex at the age of 20, and because I was paralyzed by fear of getting pregnant, I used various contraceptive methods. But I became pregnant anyway. I was horrified. What was I to do? To give birth to the child was impossible for several reasons. This was the beginning of the most terrible period of my life, rushing from one doctor to another and begging them for help, of course with offers of appropriate payment. No one wanted to help me. My salvation came from an advertisement in the paper about abortions abroad. The amount I had to pay was astronomical by the standards of my and my boyfriend's income. We managed to find the money, but it was not the end of our problem, only the beginning.

Everything that happened afterwards was like a scene from a crime film. The meeting was arranged and a strange man picked me up in a car. We went off into the unknown. No one who has not actually been through such an experience can understand how much one can be afraid. I was handed over to doctors whose language I did not speak, and I had no idea what they were going to do with me. I was not even certain that I would wake up from the anesthetic. I believe that no one has the right to sentence me to such psychological and physical anxiety, but least of all, to such a level of sheer, mad, animal fear.

Many women cannot afford to go abroad or to pay a doctor in Poland. Some private doctors perform abortions illegally, but for an enormous amount of money. That is why such women use nonmedical methods. Doctors report that women come to hospitals as a result of self-induced abortion. The cervix is dilated with the aid of an enemator resulting in an idiopathic infection followed by miscarriage. This *procedure is dangerous for a woman. Some women inject themselves with soap or iodine, or perform irrigation using vinegar. Others, without medical advice, swallow various pills after having been told by someone that it might work. Women who have taken advantage of nonprofessional services often end up in the hospital for the "cleaning-up operation."*

There are also other victims of the law. At least six women were reported to have committed suicide as a result of unwanted pregnancy in 1993. Victims of the law also come from the medical profession. One woman doctor from Czestochowa performed an illegal abortion for a desperate woman who was six months pregnant. Something went wrong, the doctor took the woman to the hospital, and the case had to be reported to the police. Before the police came to the doctor, she committed suicide.

Why is a threat of unwanted pregnancy so dangerous in Poland? Although contraception is legal and theoretically available, in practice, as a result of high prices, lack of sex education in schools, little knowledge in society, and strong pressure from the Catholic church, it is not used by more than eight percent of the population. Women practicing the Catholic religion are often denied absolution at confession while using IUDs. The priests often criticize doctors who prescribe contraceptives; as a result, some doctors have stopped prescribing the pill.

There are doctors who deny contraception for religious or ideological reasons. This happened, for example, to a girl student. When she asked her doctor about contraception, the doctor told her that she should rather think about her studies, not about sex.

Another woman from Lublin experienced something she described in her letter to the Federation:

> *I would like to describe what happened to me. My case will show you best what kind of country we live in. Two women gynecologists work in a clinic for railroad workers where I go. One of them prescribed the pill for me. When I came back for a new prescription, my doctor was not there. The second doctor, to whom I was referred, refused to give me the prescription. She explained that she could not because it was against her beliefs. She asked me whether the Catholic church's teachings*

with respect to contraception were known to me. She also said that the pill equals abortion. After a sharp discussion, she threw me out of her office, without the prescription, of course. I received a prescription from the head of the clinic—the cardiologist.

Women in Poland have organized to struggle for the liberalization of the anti-abortion law. We supported the amendment to this law proposed by the Women's Parliamentary Group, which allows abortion for social reasons. This amendment was passed in the two Chambers of Polish Parliament last June. However, President Walesa vetoed the amendment in July. Last Friday, the Parliament voted in order to overturn the veto of the President. We needed two-thirds of the votes to be successful. Unfortunately, we lost. We had the majority, but it was not enough.

We feel so bad about losing and having to start the whole process from the very beginning. It will probably take years for us to win, but we are not going to stop. One day we will win.

Women's health is definitely a basic human right. Our health cannot be compromised. Neither the government nor the church has the right to endanger women's life and health. However, the process through which the policymakers will recognize this right of all women in the world might be long. I hope this hearing will shorten the process of retaining our basic human rights.

Women Seeking Peace in Their Nations

In El Salvador

Katerina Anfossi covered the 1992 El Salvador women's gathering, "One Step Forward Toward Constructing a New World." FIRE's participation provided the opportunity for us to grow professionally and personally, since the experience was a lesson about the development of a women's movement amidst a war and now in a hopeful new time of peace. The struggle of the women of El Salvador to survive and improve their quality of life has brought dignity to the human condition.

The Salvadoran women analyzed the process of negotiation toward peace in their country, concluding that women did not have adequate representation. This set the basis for their Mesa de Convergencia (Table of Convergence), that brought together all women's groups to develop their own agenda and platform of demands to negotiate with both the government and the revolutionary front, the FMLN.

A few months later, when the FMLN and the Salvadoran government were discussing the final draft of the peace agreements, FIRE received a call from FMLN Comandante Nidia Diaz—the only woman who was a delegate at the negotiations—calling from the UN where the last talks were taking place. She gave a report on the most recent news: there had been an agreement at three o'clock that morning. In her report on FIRE, Nidia gave credit to the role of women in the process toward a peaceful solution to the conflict in El Salvador:

Women have been at the forefront of this struggle together with the men. Today, once the Peace Treaties are signed, we want to be at the forefront of a process of reconciliation that recognizes that women should also be together with men in all areas of work that have to do with finding peaceful solutions in government, in political parties, in unions....

When the historical peace treaty was going to be signed in Mexico, FIRE was not able to be there. In order to cover it live for our audience, the staff brought a small television set to the RFPI studios, tuned into a local channel that was covering it live from Mexico, and talked on the shortwave program about what we saw. We described the scene, translating live most of the speeches given by the parties in conflict, and then playing Salvadoran women's voices about their expectations regarding the process.

In Germany

From giving voice to women from former Yugoslavia November 11-15, 1992, we took our microphones to Oberhausen, Germany, for the International Women's Peace Conference, convened by the International Women's Peace Archive. There, 26 women peace activists from Greenham Commons (a military base in England), Northern

Ireland, the former Yugoslavia, Kurdistan, the Netherlands, the United States, Ethiopia, Turkey, Latin America, Germany, and other countries discussed military disarmament, the closing of U.S. bases in Europe, refugee and displaced women, social impoverishment, racism, xenophobia, and maldevelopment. The meeting was convened to give women from the former Yugoslavia the opportunity to speak about the rapes and other violence against women that were taking place while most of the world and media ignored or purposely rendered it invisible.

"Yelka" a woman from that region talked about her experience of the war. She stood up and walked up and down among all of us as she told her story:

When I was a child, socialism came and all of a sudden I was told in school that what was needed was unity; that there were no nationalities—that we were all Yugoslav. I was also told that there were no ethnic-religious identities—Muslims, Christians, or Greek Orthodox— we were all Yugoslav. I was told that there were no particular languages; we had to speak one [language] to understand each other. I was then told that there is no such thing as men and women—we were all persons.

I am a Serbian, married to a Muslim, and living with our son in Croatia. When all hell broke loose here two years ago, I did not even know who I was. The worse it gets, the more I have to ask myself: Who am I?

The socialism we had was no answer, but what's going on now is no alternative, either. It gets worse. We have to put an end to all of it.

Besides taking part in the conference, the participants marched through the streets in protest against xenophobia, along with 300,000 others. An end to the increasing hatred and racism taking place in Germany and other parts of the world was the main demand. I described my experience on FIRE afterward:

It was my first time in Europe. Interviews with the women about their issues in Europe, and interviews with the marchers made me feel what political intuition had told me before. For the first time, I was able to see the "skinheads" come after some people. I felt no different from when I was in El Salvador during the war, and the army went after marchers for peace, scared and threatened.

375

It made me see, through the case of women in the former Yugoslavia and some investigation on the assassination of Petra Kelly of the Greens a few weeks before, that what is in crisis in this historical moment is not socialism, but capitalism. What has failed has been the models that people have used to counteract it—and socialism is one of them. But it is capitalism that is in crisis. What alternative do we have but to look into women's experiences, perspectives, and proposals? After all, women are the ones who have not been associated with the powers responsible for the mess and lack of perspective.

Special Coverage of Women with Disabilities

December 3, 1993, brought FIRE a special invitation to accompany people with disabilities who were going to march along San José's Central Avenue for International Day of Disabled Persons. They wanted to tell all of society that the "environment needs rehabilitation, and we need work, love and respect."

Women, men, and children with disabilities organized their slow and determined march, as the FIRE staff watched with our microphones closer to our hearts than to our mouths. As the marchers moved slowly

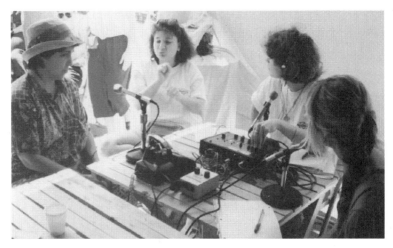

Signing over the airwaves—María Suárez, "Debbie," Jeanne Carstensen, and Debbie's interpreter (left to right) broadcast from FIRE's tent at the Fifth International Interdisciplinary Congress in Costa Rica, 1993.

with their canes, chairs, and helpers, the passersby, cab drivers, and motorcyclists became impatient. They honked their horns signaling the marchers to move faster and, in general, acted as if they owned the road.

We became angry—but "angry" is inadequate for describing our feelings. Indignation made us put away our microphones and form a security barrier on every crossroad as the marchers came to it, while we talked with the passersby about the issues raised by those with disabilities.

Many precedents of FIRE's involvement in supporting people with disabilities had characterized our coverage up until then. For example, at the Fifth Interdisciplinary Women's Congress at the beginning of that year, women with disabilities could not participate in many of the panels and forums due to the lack of access in the university's environment. FIRE's live broadcast tent opened its cloth walls, extended its microphones with extra cord, and women in wheelchairs, women who were blind, and their colleagues with hearing impairment were able to come on the air bringing their voices to the world.

I remember the moment when "Debbie," a woman who was deaf, came on the air for the first time on radio. She had approached me at a panel on women's human rights, talking to me through her translator in sign language: "Why can't we have a voice on this women's human rights issue? I want you to say it on your radio show, since no one mentioned it at the panel." She was angry. I was stunned. Immediately I told her that if she had been able to tell me with the support of her translator into sign language, she could also do it over the radio herself, with the same help. Next day she came on the air.

Her translator sat in front of the microphone, and Debbie's hands started flying. The mere sight of her excitement to be on shortwave made me lose touch with the technical controls, especially when she said to the audience:

As I am talking to you on radio, people of the world, I am becoming aware that perhaps anyone, even people with disabilities, can listen to me—except the ones like me. Deaf people cannot listen to radio, so this is a message for all, except my own: you have to understand and support us.

In August 1995, at the first International Symposium for Women with Disabilities, which was attended by more than 200 women prior to the NGO Forum in China, Jean Parker, Colorado Coordinator for the Cross Disabilities Center, interviewed Laura Hershey, writer, poet, and disabilities rights activist from Colorado in the USA. Laura was part of the 48-person delegation who attended the symposium.

LAURA: We spent the day outlining strategies for how to have the best impact at the NGO Forum in terms of raising the awareness of other attendees on disabled women's issues such as health care, education, employment, economic development, and access.

JEAN: What did the symposium suggest?

LAURA: In education, to provide access for girls for integrated equal education with nondisabled peers; in economic development and access, we are demanding real employment opportunities, not sheltered workshop type opportunities, and the importance of recognizing the impact of structural adjustment policies.... We were also advocating access to the NGO Forum, and there were many reactions from nondisabled women. It seemed as though it was the first time they actually paid attention and really heard us, perhaps because of the critical mass, vocal nature, and witnessing the barriers.

Laura recalled some of the interviews conducted with Robin Stevens, on Leadership Development Strategies for Women with Disabilities (30 women in the survey). One was Patrona Sandoval from Nicaragua, who had become disabled because of a "medical malfunction" during the birth of her child. She was told at the Disability Rights Organization in Nicaragua that their "agenda was for veterans" of the civil war. Patrona was motivated to overcome many obstacles to create her own network as she went door to door, to the isolated women with disabilities in their homes, to create an active 180-member organization.

Maria Ranfo from South Africa was, through her extensive activism and leadership, elected to the South African Parliament representing not only her geographic district, but also officially representing people with disabilities throughout South Africa. At the UN conference in Beijing, the South African delegation included a woman with a disability.

Senior Women

One of the many women interviewed by Katerina Anfossi, Debra Latham, and me at the 1991 Global Assembly of Women and the Environment was Alicia Pestalozzi, member of the Bunyan Foundation, which is dedicated to promoting elder women's needs and interests:

> *Young people do not listen to the elder. On the other hand, all of society thinks that all elder women need is to have access to their basic needs while they await dying. But there is a wealth of knowledge and wisdom that cannot die out for present generations. I think, upon talking here on FIRE, that people might listen to the elder on radio. I myself did radio in Italy when I was young. The wealth of material that could be collected is unimaginable.*

Since that time, FIRE has had on the air the Grandmothers of Plaza de Mayo in Argentina in their search for their two younger generations who had been *disappeared*; Grannies for Peace in Canada and the USA; and the Grandmothers of Europe who struggle against the presence of nuclear and military bases. FIRE has also had on the air native elders from Canada, the USA, and Latin America talking about their role in native communities.

Migrant Women

Migrant women workers have also been underrepresented, both in their countries of origin and in the lands where they travel in search of a job and a life. However, they have been represented in their own voices on FIRE.

Two such women on FIRE, who represent hundreds, were Gina Alunan, who presented the testimony of migrant worker Susan Paicano, and Teresita Cuizon, who related her own story. These testimonies were presented at the Tribunal on Accountability for Women's Human Rights at the NGO Forum in China in 1995. The tribunal, sponsored by eight NGOs and a UN specialized agency, was recorded by FIRE and broadcast in 1995.

> *I am Gina M. Alunan from the Philippines. I have worked for Filipino overseas migrants for the past 14 years. I was in Hong Kong from 1982 to 1986 working for Filipina domestic workers. From 1986 up to the*

present, I have been working for Philippine-based nongovernmental organizations doing support work for migrant workers who have suffered abuse and maltreatment while working overseas. I have talked to hundreds of Filipino migrant workers forced to leave behind their families because of the lack of better opportunities in their own country and who have suffered various forms of abuse.

I am also pleased to have with us today a Filipina migrant worker, Teresita Cuizon, who will be able to tell her own personal story and testify about her experiences as a migrant worker in the Middle East and now in the United Kingdom (UK). This will be her first time to speak before a huge crowd, but she feels she has to speak so the world will know. Teresita is a member of Waling-waling and works with Kalayaan and the Commission for Filipino Migrant Workers, all of which are nongovernmental groups campaigning for migrant workers' rights in the UK.

First, I will relate to you the story of Susan Paciano, who could not be here to testify. Her experiences typify the kind of horror stories and human rights violations that Filipina migrant women are commonly subjected to.

> My name is Susan Paciano. I am 39 years old, married, and a mother of five. I was born and grew up in Northern Mindanao. Both my husband and I come from peasant families. All our lives we have worked on our land to sustain the needs of our growing family, but life in the barrio was getting more difficult every day as we were faced with either drought or too much rain.
>
> I was recruited to work as a domestic helper in the Kingdom of Saudi Arabia. I had to pay U.S.$140 in placement fees plus 100 Saudi Ryals (U.S.$28) was to be deducted from my salary each month for the next six months. My contract stipulated a monthly salary of U.S.$200.
>
> On May 1, 1994, I departed for Saudi Arabia and worked there for nine months. My work as a domestic helper included cleaning the entire two-story house and taking care of my employer's five children. I woke up at around 4 or 5 o'clock in the morning and started working without having any breakfast.
>
> We had only one main meal a day, served at around 3 o'clock in the afternoon. All the food for the household was placed on the

table on a big plate. The first to eat were the male members of the family, followed by the female members, and only then could the servants and employees of the family eat whatever was left. I always felt hungry because I had to work very hard during the day.

My employers did not pay me on a monthly basis. I only received the equivalent of U.S.$100 in January 1995, and not U.S.$200 per month stipulated in my contract. I wanted to go home because I felt physically weak from lack of food, lack of sleep, and too much work, but my employer would not allow me to go. Because I could not finish my work on time, my employer constantly beat me and slapped me. I got weaker every day and eventually I was brought to the doctor and given some medicine. By then everything was hazy.

Finally, on January 28, 1995, my employer brought me to the airport. I was entrusted to an Arab man. He told me that he would not give me my passport and air ticket unless I had sex with him. I refused. He took hold of my arm and forced me to drink something. I cannot remember what happened after that, but I am sure that I was raped. I also do not know how I managed to return to the Philippines. My passport indicated that I arrived on January 31, 1995. Apparently, some Filipinos who were on the same plane that I took to Manila brought me to the mental institution, as I was not in my right mind anymore. They also contacted my family in Mindanao, who immediately came to Manila to see me.

On February 7, 1995, I was discharged form the hospital and brought to the Kalayaan Center for Migrant Workers for temporary shelter. Kalayaan is a nongovernmental organization that provides support services to Filipino migrant workers. I stayed there for two weeks with my husband. During this time, Kalayaan assisted me in retrieving my passport and air ticket, which were with the Filipinos who brought me to the hospital. They also facilitated my claim for medical and transportation assistance from the Philippine government, which took an eternity to process. During this time, too, I remembered the *inhumane and degrading experience that I went through at the hands of my employer. I cannot understand how a human being can do such things to another human being. I also could not understand why the Philippine government continues to allow its own citizens to be exploited and abused in another country. Can't the government provide us with decent jobs in the Philippines?*

I am now back with my family in our little barrio in Northern Mindanao. I have fully recovered, and I am in the best of health and receiving a lot of love and attention from my husband, children, and family. Life in the barrio is simple, and often it is difficult, but it is something I cherish now more than ever before.

I met Susan again in May of this year when I went to Mindanao to study the migration patterns of Filipinas coming from Mindanao. Physically, Susan looked totally different from the time when she was staying in our center. She had gained weight, her cheeks were not hollow anymore, there was a sparkle in her eyes, and she was able to talk animatedly about her experience. But once in a while, a tear or two would threaten to fall as she related the most difficult part of her life story as a migrant worker in Saudi Arabia. She vows never to leave her family again. She may have survived death, but she is scarred for life. Susan keeps in constant communication with Kalayaan. Susan may be lucky, as she has a loving family who understood and supported her all the way, but this is not the case for many of the women who have had similar experiences and receive no support from their families or the government.

Teresita Cuizon told her story:

My name is Teresita Cuizon. I am a 34 year-old widow with two children. I come from the Philippines. My husband died in April 1985. After his death, I had to take the responsibility of being a father and a mother to my children. I was working as a seamstress in the Philippines, and my salary was not enough to support my children anymore. My son was five years old and my daughter nearly four. I asked the help of

382

my sister-in-law, who was working as a chambermaid in the United Arab Emirates (UAE) University.

My sister-in-law recommended me as a domestic worker, and after a few weeks I had a job. She told me that my salary would be U.S.$400, but when I reached UAE, they just paid me 400 Dirham, which is equivalent to only U.S.$108. I complained to my sister-in-law, but they said to her that she had misunderstood them. We could not do anything because I was already there. They took my passport, and I never saw it again. They took me for a medical examination, even though I had already had one in the Philippines. They gave me medicine to clean my stomach. They said my stomach was dirty because I ate pork in the Philippines. They asked me to take a bath afterwards.

I had no time to eat or to wash my own clothes. There was no day off, not any time off at all. I could eat only when they finished, and I had to eat the leftover food. I could not use their plates, spoons, or glasses. Once they saw me using them, and they asked the chef to boil the utensils. I could not even use their toilet. They shouted at me if I spoke to anyone. It is hard to believe, but we are only animals to them and not human beings.

After two months, they took me to London. There was no room for me, so I slept on the floor. They told me to wash the flat, clean the carpet with soap, and wash and bleach all the curtains with my bare hands. My hand became allergic; it has cuts and it bled.

My boss tried to do bad things to me whenever I was alone. He would ask me to go to the guest house at 12 midnight and said, "I will be happy." I became afraid of him, but never mentioned this to his family. One night he was drunk and knocked on my door. When I opened it, he kissed and hugged me. I pushed him and said if he did not go out I would shout, so he left. He offered me a watch and money. One time he tried to convince me again. His wife saw us, but because she couldn't speak English, I had to call her daughter and tell her everything. I asked her to send me back home, but because I was hard working and had been very good to them, they didn't want to send me home, so I was transferred to work for their daughter.

In 1990, we went to London again. After a week, I asked them about my salary because my sister needed it for my children. They did not pay me for about six months, and my employer said she could not pay me because there was a problem in Kuwait (there was a war going on). She said there was a problem in the bank, too, but they still went shopping.

One day we went to Grosvenor Square Park, and I met an English lady named Eleanor. While the children were not looking, I told her about my difficulties with the family. She was very concerned about me. She tried to give me ten pounds, but I refused to take it because I was afraid my employer might see it and think I stole it from them. Eleanor gave me her telephone number in case I needed help.

After that day I was not allowed to go to the park anymore. Eleanor and the police helped me to get out of the house. I was very scared, but I still did not want to go back to my employers, even though they were trying to convince me to go back to them. People from the Commission for Filipino Migrant Workers came to help me. They were able to get me a solicitor to handle my case. Later on, I was able to find a job with a family whose daughter had cerebral palsy. My new employers also helped me try to change my visa.

Many people gave me the strength and confidence to carry on— I remember during the first few days after leaving my employer, I was very nervous every time the doorbell rang in the center, thinking that my employer had come to take me back.

I became a member of the organization of unauthorized domestic workers. We call ourselves Waling-waling after an exotic Philippine orchid that can only be found hidden in the mountains. The Waling-waling are very active in promoting and participating in the campaign of our partner organization, Kalayaan, which is working for justice for all unauthorized domestic workers. Our goal is to acquire our immigration and employment rights. We attend several training seminars to raise our awareness, and we meet regularly so that everyone is well informed. We hold a number of fund-raising and social events each year, including discos, trips, and picnics. The money raised from these activities is used to help members in need— those who have suffered a death in the family, the unemployed, someone who has an appeal or court hearing and must pay legal fees, those who have just left their employers and have nothing, and *those who are in the hospital. The Waling-waling also gives contributions to partner organizations and donations to fund-raising appeals in the UK and from their home countries.*

Over the years the Waling-waling has received a lot of support from the Commission for Filipino Migrant Workers and Kalayaan. The three organizations continue to work together in partnership to fight for the rights and welfare of unauthorized domestic workers. In Britain, such workers have no rights. We are tied to our employers in a form of modern-day slavery.

Lesbian Women

Lesbians have traditionally been underrepresented in media and in politics. It has been one of FIRE's objectives to make sure that they have a voice to the world. In 1995 we recorded and broadcast the first statement by a lesbian at a UN conference—Palesa Beverley Ditsie of South Africa speaking in support of lesbian concerns at the Fourth World Conference on Women:

It is a great honor to have the opportunity to address this distinguished body on behalf of the International Gay and Lesbian Human Rights Commission, the International Lesbian Information Service, the International Lesbian and Gay Association, and more than 50 other organizations. My name is Palesa Beverley Ditsie, and I am from Soweto, South Africa, where I have lived all my life and experienced both tremendous joy and pain within my community. I come from a country that has recently had an opportunity to start afresh—an opportunity to strive for a true democracy where the people govern and where emphasis is placed on the human rights of all people.

The Constitution of South Africa prohibits discrimination on the basis of race, gender, ethnic, or social origin, color, sexual orientation, age, disability, religion, conscience, belief, culture, or language. In his opening parliamentary speech in Cape Town on 9 April 1994, His Excellency Nelson Rolihlahla Mandela, State President of South Africa, received resounding applause when he declared that never again would anyone be discriminated against on the basis of sexual orientation.

The Universal Declaration of Human Rights recognizes the "inherent dignity and... the equal and inalienable rights of all members of the human family," and guarantees the protection of the fundamental rights and freedoms of all people, "without distinction of any kind, such as race, color, sex, language... or other status" (article 2). Yet every day, in countries around the world, lesbians suffer violence, harassment, and discrimination because of their sexual orientation. Their basic human rights—such as the right to life, to bodily integrity, to freedom of association and expression—are violated. Women who love women are fired from their jobs, forced into marriages, beaten and murdered in their homes and on the streets, and have their children taken away by hostile courts. Some commit suicide due to the isolation and stigma they experience within their families, religious institutions, and the broader community.

These and other abuses are documented in a recently released report by the International Gay and Lesbian Human Rights Commission on sexual orientation and women's human rights, as well as in reports by Amnesty International. Yet, the majority of these abuses have been difficult to document because—although lesbians exist everywhere in the world, including Africa—we have been marginalized and silenced and remain invisible in most of the world. In 1994, the United Nations Human Rights Committee declared that discrimination based on sexual orientation violates the right to nondiscrimination and the right to privacy guaranteed in the International Covenant of Civil and Political Rights. Several countries have passed legislation prohibiting discrimination based on sexual orientation.

If the Fourth World Conference on Women is to address the concerns of all women, it must similarly recognize that discrimination based on sexual orientation is a violation of basic human rights. Paragraphs 48 and 226 of the [draft] Platform for Action recognize that women face particular barriers in their lives because of many factors, including sexual orientation. However, the term "sexual orientation" is currently in brackets. If these words are omitted from the relevant paragraphs, the Platform for Action will stand as one more symbol of the discrimination that lesbians face and of the lack of recognition of our very existence.

No woman can determine the direction of her own life without the ability to determine her sexuality. Sexuality is an integral, deeply ingrained part of every human being's life and should not be subject to debate or coercion. Anyone who is truly committed to women's human rights must recognize that every woman has the right to determine her sexuality free of discrimination and oppression.

I urge you to make this a conference for all women, regardless of their sexual orientation, and to recognize in the Platform for Action that lesbian rights are women's rights and that women's rights are universal, inalienable, and indivisible human rights. I urge you to remove the brackets from sexual orientation. Thank you.

Lesbian women have always had an uncensored voice of FIRE.

Girls

Girls have been traditionally underrepresented except when they appear as victims of war crimes or domestic violence. FIRE has given girls a voice, a place, a space on the airwaves where they can frame their issues and visions. Girls from Nigeria, from the USA, from South Africa, from India, from Canada, and from Latin America have been featured on FIRE.

In some cases, they have not only been the voices, but also the producers, as is the case of Eugenia Bermudez Serrano from Panama, who was living in Costa Rica and who had been responsible for her own productions for FIRE from 1992 to 1994. In 1998 she was on the air again, in a talk given with her sister to U.S. students in Costa Rica. They spoke about their experience during the U.S. invasion of Panama in December 1989.

Eugenia was five years old at the time of the invasion of her country. Her sister, Mari Cruz, was two years old. Nine years later, they still remembered, but beyond remembering, they had their own ideas about how the damage could be "repaired." Eugenia shared her memory of the invasion:

In the Panama invasion, people didn't really seem to know what was happening, and that was the first and foremost source of concern. We could see the smoke outside the house. We could hear the helicopters. People were very nervous and started yelling. The people wanted to know why the helicopters were there and what was going on. I remember that my father embraced us and my twin sisters and told us not to be afraid, and not to speak, and not to move. Because the North Americans were racing around the block, nobody was allowed to move or to speak. It would be dangerous.

I also remember that my father put us under the bed because it was so dangerous. And the next day, I remember that we were in one part of the house and we didn't have any food. All the stores were closed and we needed something to eat, so he told us to stay put and not to move so he could go find us something to eat at the store in front of the house.

I remember that later we saw a military helicopter with machine guns pointing at the people. At that moment I had a lot of fear because as a girl at that time one could think that maybe it's a game, but when you see the people around you, you start to get scared.

It is extremely difficult to tell you this story. Some of the information that we have, we recovered afterward—for example, the psychological effects on the children. There are children in Panama who saw their houses destroyed by the bombs, children who saw how their parents were assassinated, how the military tanks went over the bodies of many people. Many people lost their homes and had to become refugees in the military bases. There were at least 4,000 people who were assassinated, and the U.S. government still says that it was 400. Many bodies were thrown into the ocean with bombs so there would be no evidence and so nobody would find them.

Mari Cruz's memory of the invasion was still vivid, even though she had been only two years old at the time:

We would hear the helicopters and the bombs, and the earth would shake with the explosion of the bombs. At night we could not go out, but not in the day either. The military were holding vigilance about some people that were fighting against them. It was a terrible

388

experience for children and adults. Many children were traumatized because they saw how their families were killed and how their houses were destroyed.

Eugenia spoke about the politics of the invasion:

Panama has been invaded by the U.S. more than 20 times in history. The only thing that I think I will never understand now or ever is why the U.S. government would not let us live on Christmas in peace and prosperity. Instead of bringing gifts, they brought bombs. While the rest of the world was celebrating Christmas, the United States was invading Panama. The military was testing their most sophisticated instruments, and I still ask myself, "Why did they want to invade such a small territory?"

I'm telling you so that you are aware of what really happened, because sometimes I have asked people from the U.S. if they know what happened in Panama and they say, "No." It is really ironic that you people who live in the U.S. are the ones who know the least about what is really going on in other parts of the world. The military that came to Panama were like the devil himself. Sometimes I ask myself, "What is the problem with the military people in the U.S.? Where do they hide their hearts?" No one can count the people they have killed in the world.

Asked by a participant what she hopes to see for Panama in the future, Eugenia's answer was:

That on December 31 in 1999, the Panama Canal will belong to the Panamanian people. There has been too much suffering, and I hope that when it is given back it will be given back in a peaceful way. With that, Panama can grow economically.

Traditionally underrepresented women will continue having a voice on FIRE's internet venue worldwide, for they are the silenced voices that speak agout the issues and experiences that make power structures uncomfortable. Those voices shake the very foundations of patriarchy.

CHAPTER 11

Nurturing the Spirit
of FIRE

Communication is the main artery that bonds people across countries. FIRE seems to embody the essence of communication to the people. Not only does it bring the ideas of the people in, but it actually brings the people in; this allows for the most diverse opinions and freedoms.

—Jessica Sanders, a language student
from the U.S. in Costa Rica

The world's first ongoing feminist international radio program was begun in 1991 and has been evolving, maturing, and developing ever since. We have met many challenges in building the organization of FIRE and overcoming logistical problems related to the technical and technological aspects of radio production. This chapter provides an in-depth and somewhat technical look at how FIRE met these challenges, both from our studios in Costa Rica and in remote locations.

Dynamics of Building the FIRE Team

In the beginning, RFPI, FIRE, and the Foundation for a Compassionate Society held weekly telephone conference calls. WINGS, the Foundation, Texas University Radio, Debra Latham (the director of RFPI), and FIRE's staff developed our agenda over the phone lines.

As we grew, we had to refine our dynamics as we built a team where each person would do all the tasks at hand: The programming, the controls, the networking, the writing, the activism, the gathering of testimonies, the laughing and the crying, the struggling in the face of injustice, and the celebrating of our strengths. We also decided to rotate tasks that required one person at a time: Coordinating meetings, drafting proposals, answering letters, and helping with domestic work around the station.

Major responsibilities were assigned: Katerina Anfossi and Nancy Vargas were responsible for the Spanish program; I had the English program, supported by Jeanne Carstensen when FIRE created a fourth, temporary, position, which she occupied from 1992 to 1994.

FIRE Summits: Building Community

Building the team we wanted was a process of assessment of past experiences, consideration of everyone's desires, and debate. We wanted a loose way of relating and working, where all could express their best efforts. We had come from different formal and nonformal organizations and institutions where there were some who "thought" and some who did the practical work. In some, there were some who "bossed," and others who had to do what the boss said. In most of them, hardly any collective reflection and search for consensus existed, and if it did, women were not in on the decision-making. Here we had a space where we had autonomy in building the project, and most of us were new at doing feminist radio. We were all feminist activists with different backgrounds of experience, age, nationalities, and kinds of links with the women's movement. We had a place where we all wanted to grow to our full potential.
—FIRE's first team summit,
reported in *Vista*, 1992

In order to tread the path with a collective perspective, FIRE organized a series of summits, starting in 1992. These summits were to be meetings held outside of the station, in one of our homes, with good lunch and coffee to make it through a whole day of going deep into issues that arose and needed profound sharing of thought, energy, feelings, crying, and anger.

During 1992, the staff held summits about issues such as negotiation, autonomy, and relationships with the University for Peace and the University of Global Communication, with RFPI, the Foundation for a Compassionate Society, the different expressions of the women's movement, and—most of all—relationships among ourselves. Thus, FIRE's personality could be affirmed while respecting and promoting the needs and interests of others.

We examined the issues of language and culture; we had a summit on global projections of FIRE; we had another on identity, diversity and commonalties. FIRE also held summits on the main issues at stake in the international agenda: The environment, human rights, reproductive and sexual rights, why the UN had called for a Fourth World Conference on women, and others.

That first full year, FIRE had the opportunity to cover important events in the women's movement. This was in addition to organizing and broadcasting tapes that kept coming in the mail, receiving on-the-air guests, turning written material into radio programs, learning the technical skills to edit live on the air, and connecting to international women's networks through letters, phone calls, electronic mail, faxes, and friends.

In 1993, some of our internal debates were centered on questions raised during the International Year of the Family. We also worked out how to denounce violators of human rights, while at the same time protecting our security in our participation at the Sixth Feminist Encuentro held in El Salvador.

Another issue we discussed was sources of funding, especially in light of the fact that the U.S. Agency for International Development (USAID) had selected Latin American women's groups and organizations as their target for funding for the Fourth World Conference on Women in 1995. After long debates, FIRE agreed not to request or accept funding from such an agency, at the same time refraining from judging those who did accept it. We valued the type of relationship we had with the Foundation for a Compassionate Society, and we decided to look for other sources with which the same open, nonconditional relationship could be established.

The issues of individuality and collectivity in decision-making, of expressing feelings, conflict resolution alternatives, North-South identity and priority, and even the nature of FIRE (Was it a collective? a team? a program?) all led to lengthy discussions among the staff.

Another topic of discussion was the balance between feminist activism and feminist communication in activities that FIRE covers; between protagonism and self-censorship; between balancing or prioritizing work with grassroots organizations and "experts." We also had to negotiate how to let FIRE be a professional space for women while also having a personal dimension.

In February of 1996, we dedicated ourselves to a special evaluation summit. This decision was prompted by a number of factors: The rapid expansion of FIRE in the midst of the global women's movement; the ever-growing expectations raised because of the experience of the FIRE-PLACE in China; the approaching fifth anniversary of FIRE on the air; the need to revise methods, organization, and radio formats; and the need to renew our individual and collective feminist commitments.

The evaluation revealed FIRE's renewed commitment to the organizational philosophy it had established from the start five years earlier: Collective direction of the project through deliberation and consultation; collective decision-making through consensus or majority; horizontality; equality; all staff members having all rights and methodologies; weekly meetings together with bilateral consultations and special summits; division of work; Spanish program producers and English program producers; and division of special tasks.

We also revisited the notion of individual responsibility in collectively assigned tasks. We again shared our objective of promoting a feminist perspective and providing a voice for women, with a special emphasis on those who have less of a voice than others, such as women of color, women with disabilities, lesbians, indigenous women, and grassroots women.

FIRE as Participatory Radio

In 1996, FIRE was the only permanent feminist international radio program in the world that gave a voice to ordinary women without censorship. By occupying this unique space, we were connecting women with women and men at home in more than 100 countries.

When women tune in to radio at home or at the workplace as they go about their daily tasks, and they are able to hear the thoughts, perspectives, and experiences of another woman, their feeling of isolation can be suspended and replaced with a feeling of connection and empowerment.

The intimacy of radio is like the intimacy of women talking to other women. Because, as women, we are in general, socialized to express our emotions more openly than men, and also to talk about them, the development of our oral skills carries with it a deeper level of intimacy. Too often, when women talk, we are first judged by how we look instead of by what we say. Radio is oral communication without visual images. It provides a safe format for sharing without fear of judgment about appearance or looks. Radio production in the hands of women is about communication without any fixed or predetermined format, which allows the free flow of ideas with feelings and of feelings with connections.

Participatory radio provides a space where women can create their own news, where they are inspired to re-create and promote their own viewpoint, without being confronted by the viewpoint of the interviewer and without feeling a need to be defensive. It is also a place where women can share their knowledge, and at the same time cry or laugh; where women can be subjective about their experience, where women can communicate their truth. Participatory radio shifts the power relationships for women.

FIRE broadcast live from most of the major international conferences throughout the first half of the 1990s, and also from local, national, and regional activities, actions, and events in many places of the world. We created a communications channel where people could learn of women's activities and perspectives on all issues.

Sometimes when women are together as activists—at a UN conference, at a local rally in the streets, in a gathering of five or five thousand women—they do not have the space or the opportunity to listen to themselves or to each other. Live radio broadcasting provides that opportunity to listen, thus bringing women together at yet another level.

Interactive Autonomy

From the beginning, FIRE decided *not* to become a formal network itself, but to become part of and work with existing networks. The reason for this decision was that the staff of FIRE believed that as a communication venue, FIRE could better articulate experiences, give women a voice on international media, and create news by joining with the efforts of others without duplicating the work of their organizations.

FIRE has been able to work hand-in-hand with most of the organizations and women's networks around the world since its creation. We have been able to do this by implementing the concept of *interactive autonomy* with everyone with whom FIRE has a direct relationship. Interactive autonomy does not mean marginalization, but on the contrary, it is a process of negotiation whereby each of the parties "puts on the table" its needs, interests, and objectives, and agrees to work cooperatively— offering different perspectives and directions—to provide solutions that are in the best interest of all, without sacrificing its main purpose.

Interactive autonomy does not mean that we can replace each other or merge with each other simply because we have the same needs, interests, and objectives. Rather, we must negotiate the role that each organization can play according to its identity and determine how to proceed in order that each group's goals are advanced or met. The secret is that each entity maintains its own identity. Although this methodology does not resolve power differences, it does help all parties recognize where they need each other within the power issues.

The concept of interactive autonomy applies to any kind of organization we relate to, be it the radio stations where we broadcast FIRE or the funding agencies that support us. On one side, the art of the whole matter is for everyone who directly relates to FIRE to know that they can influence the program, but that they cannot own it.

On the FIRE side, the art of interactive autonomy is to allow ourselves to be influenced without "selling" ourselves, and to act according to our objectives, remaining true to our purpose in the world of communication and in the women's movement so we can continue to influence others through our international feminist broadcasting.

Interactive autonomy in the communications process means that each interview is a two-way communication: Interviewer and interviewee both frame their comments and influence the direction of the interview.

Everyone belongs to FIRE and FIRE belongs to everybody!

Overcoming Technology's Psychological Barriers

From my experience in radio, I have discovered at least three layers to what I call *psychological barriers* in relationship to the radio controls, specifically the hardware technology. In describing what we are calling a gender construct, I want to emphasize that the following explanation does not apply to all men or to all women. There are men and women who have learned to go beyond the roles for which they have been socialized.

The first layer of the psychological barriers has to do with the fact that when we look at pictures of people working in radio around the world, we hardly ever see images of women working with the technical aspects of the productions.

The second layer has two parts. The first, is that most women have been socialized not to be interested in or to be motivated to explore the mechanics of how things work. The second is a result of the first. We, as women, very rarely develop the "male-oriented" mechanical and technological skills. In the socialization process women are trained to learn, at most, how to use equipment to provide service; men, in general, are trained to construct the equipment, to know how it works, to repair it, and therefore to control it.

Subjectively, this means that whenever we women find ourselves at the technical controls, we find ourselves thinking that we might not succeed, and that if we do it will be a miracle. On the other hand, most men, when they train women to do technical work, have the tendency to also believe that women will not succeed, and will even take a condescending attitude by beginning from scratch as if the Women do not know anything. Other men will start out with the specialized language that they know, thereby intimidating the women by making them feel that they don't have the background knowledge to learn the technology.

The third layer of psychological barriers results from the way in which we are conditioned not to have control of process in general. In radio it is not by chance that the controls are called *controls*, because whoever is in charge of that aspect of radio production determines who goes on the air, who does not, how long someone will be on the air, the rhythm of the program, and so on. That person is in a position to intimidate the person speaking into the microphone and influence what she is saying. Many women are intimidated about having this kind of control. Even when we are not intimidated by the technology, we are intimidated by the potential judgment of those who watch us operate the technical controls.

Throughout my years of producing FIRE, I have heard story after story of women who have been working in radio for 10, 15, or 20 years and who have never touched the technical controls: Women in the Philippines; women in Namibia; women in Canada, the U.S., Denmark, and Brazil. I have also heard story after story of women who have been responsible for the technical controls in broadcasting and who have had the men at the station sit and look at them through the glass—just to make them aware that they were being watched (controlled).

The staff of FIRE had the benefit of compassionate training on the controls, as we were trained by RFPI's only woman staff member, the director, Debra Latham. However, we have observed that the male staff members at RFPI have a less generous attitude when it comes to training women to operate the controls. Their tendency is to act as if they feel the women cannot handle the technology.

At FIRE, the technical controls are always in the hands of women.

Technology and Logistics of Building
the FIREPLACE in China

The logistical nightmare we experienced in Huairou, China in 1995 was not the first time in the five-year history of FIRE's live broadcasts from international conferences that we faced the challenges of remote live broadcasting. Vienna in 1993, Cairo in 1994, and Denmark in early 1995 had taught us that live broadcasting in the middle of the activities of the women's movement makes some people quite nervous. We always designed at least three alternatives when we set out to undertake a remote live broadcast.

Contingency Plans

Our best-case scenario for China was to have a glass booth at the Women's Alternative Media Action and Service Center (WAMASC) within the NGO Forum, with an exclusive international telephone line for the broadcasts.

Our second-choice alternative was to broadcast through one of the telephone lines from a hotel.

The third option was our worst-case scenario: FIRE would organize the daily four-hour radio programs, setting up three sets of loudspeakers throughout the WAMASC so that women could listen to the "internal circuit broadcasts" while we also recorded them on tape. One FIRE staff member would travel back to Costa Rica on September 6, taking the pre-recorded tapes back to be played internationally from the shortwave station. From September 8-16, the last eight days of the official UN conference, the international audience would have been able to listen to women's voices from the NGO Forum that had just ended.

A few months before the forum and conference, a joke about the alternative plans for FIRE's broadcasts began to go around the world. It first came out of the Kalmar meeting organized by the Swedish Institute for Further Education of Journalists. At that meeting, when FIRE presented its project and our three possible scenarios, one of the journalists smiled and commented:

Things seem very difficult for media in Beijing. What will FIRE do if it does not get a phone line at all, no place to set up the broadcasts, and no ticket to travel back to Costa Rica on time before the conference is over?

We answered, "We're bringing loudspeakers." Everyone laughed. From that day on, word had it that FIRE was so determined to broadcast, that it was going to bring a huge loudspeaker to "mouth" the programs in the streets of China if it had no alternative.

Fail-Safe Equipment

The simplicity and flexibility of our technology also has made it possible for us to deal with whatever situation we find ourselves in as we travel around the world. The night before the first live broadcast from the WAMASC, Amelia from the Fiji Islands came running into the hotel where one of FIRE's staff was staying:

I've been told that the electricity at the center has been cut off. If that is so, we will not be able to broadcast from the FIREPLACE! What will we do?

We had taken into consideration the fact that electricity can go off any time, for any reason, anywhere. We were able to reassure her:

Sleep in peace tonight, Amelia, FIRE will burn tomorrow anyway. All of its equipment is battery-run! Let's work on the electricity issue tomorrow, for all else that will be set in motion at that center.

Indeed, the microphones, mixing boards, telephone interfaces, and tape recorders we use are all small, lightweight, and relatively inexpensive. They are also easy to learn to operate.

The Funding Hurdles

For our trip to China, we bought some of our equipment in Costa Rica because it was less expensive there; other pieces came from the USA. That shopping trip—like many of FIRE's travels—was paid for with frequent flyer miles, and thanks to the solidarity of a member of the RFPI board who lives in Miami, there were no expenses for room and board.

Very early in the process, and even before FIRE had the money to travel, we had made our round-trip reservations from Costa Rica to China for the best fare possible.

FIRE maximized available funds in other ways too. By making sure we had a direct international telephone line to China so calls could be made from Costa Rica to China and not vice versa, we cut the cost of calls by more than 50 percent. By arranging with RFPI's staff in Costa Rica to make those feed calls from 2:00 a.m. to 6:00 a.m. Costa Rica time, we used the reduced night rates for four hours per day. FIRE's broadcasts from Radio China International while we were at the official conference took place from 8:00 to 10:00 p.m. in China so we could still benefit from reduced rates (in Costa Rica, it was 6:00 to 8:00 a.m., premium calling hours).

A live broadcast testing of the international phone communications systems between Costa Rica and China before the conference also gave FIRE the confidence that the FIREPLACE would work. Joan Boyle, member of the RFPI International Advisory Board and exchange student in China, organized a live broadcast with women in that country just before the forum and conference.

Funding for our coverage of the Fourth World Conference on Women and the parallel NGO Forum came from many sources. The Inter-American Human Rights Institute funded one of FIRE's staff members through the European Community. The NGO Forum Organizing Committee funded another staff member's plane fare to China with the part of their budget for bringing plenary presenters to Beijing. Translation, transcriptions, and the summary book were funded by the Caritas Tides Foundation. Other funders for the conference were Sisterfund, the UN Population Fund, and the continued support from the Foundation for a Compassionate Society.

FIRE's Awards

FIRE's first five years on the air had followed a path of struggles and successes, and others recognized our achievements along the way. At its February 1995 symposium, "Women and Media: Access to Expression and Decision-Making", UNESCO selected two FIRE productions for awards that would be presented at the FWCW.

One was the four-cassette series: "A Radio Tribunal on Violations of Women's Human Rights," based on the radio tribunal with the same name, organized by FIRE together with the program, "Women, Justice and Gender, of ILANUD—Latin American Institute for The Prevention of Delinquency. This tribunal was part of the Fourth Latin American and Caribbean Feminist Encuentro held in El Salvador in 1993. The cassette series includes the testimonies of 19 women from the region.

Another of FIRE's radio productions, "History of Gender in Central America," was selected for a UNESCO award. The program relates the feminist perspectives of women from the region, gathered during the First Central American Women's Conference: "New Women, A New Power", held in Nicaragua in 1992.

The Women's International News Gathering Service (WINGS) also selected FIRE for 1995 awards. According to WINGS producer, Frieda Werden, the Katherine Davenport Award was given to FIRE:

...for the innovative role it played during the United Nations Population and Development Conference (ICPD), held in Cairo, September, 1994, in support of the successful efforts of the international women's movement to influence the Agenda and Plan of Action of the Conference.

The award is named after feminist journalist Katherine Davenport from the United States, considered a pioneer in radio "by and about women" in her country dating from the 1960's until 1992, when she died. She was co-founder and producer of WINGS.

The Peacepower Foundation gave FIRE the Amigas Award in 1994 and 1995, which reads as follows:

For all of the time you spent thinking, dreaming, planning and creating ways to make your world a better place to live. For all the times you thought you were just an everyday, ordinary person, but somehow you pushed beyond what you had been told you could accomplish. For all the times you have spoken up for what you believe in. For the financial risks you have taken. For the inner courage you manage to rely on even when you don't think you have any courage.

For keeping a sense of humor, even when things look bad. For bringing hope to us all because of your commitment.

FIRE's awards continued to come in as Radio for Peace International in Costa Rica and Earth Communications in the USA gave FIRE its 1996 award for "the excellent live coverage of the IV UN Conference on Women, China, 1995."

Again, in 1997, Radio for Peace International and Earth Communications gave FIRE permanent staff members, Katerina Anfossi and me, the 1997 award "for loyalty to the development of the radio station."

Chapter 12

FIRE's Anniversaries

On May 1 of every year, FIRE has held a live call-in show in celebration of our anniversary. Letters and e-mail messages also come in from our listeners around the world for this occasion. Following are some of the anniversary messages we have received.

1992

> *May 1, 1992, was FIRE's first anniversary on the air: We were so afraid that no one would call that we started calling friends to come on the air. It was funny, because the first two or three people we called so they could talk to us on the air said that they had never, ever received a call from a radio station. As soon as we released the phone line, telephone calls poured in from Costa Rica, the USA, and Nicaragua from many supporters and women who have participated in the FIRE program.*
>
> —FIRE's Memories, 1992

Charlotte Walters, from the USA and living in Costa Rica, was first to call. She had listened to FIRE since it began and had also collected tapes for us.

Gabriela Echandi from the Foundation Ser y Crecer in Costa Rica, a foundation that supports incest victims, called to say, "It is important for us to share our projects and visions through shortwave feminist radio."

Zaira Carvajal from the Women's Studies Institute at the University of Heredia in Costa Rica called to say that FIRE "is an important contribution in the process of building the women's movement in the country, the Central American region, and the world."

Mae Brenes, a Costa Rican writer said that FIRE "is a space for women to communicate with the rest of the world."

Rose Mary Madden from Costa Rica was just returning from the CLADEM General Assembly in Brazil. She told us that FIRE is "one of the best projects in the region because it allows women an alternative for voicing their views." She also congratulated FIRE for the role we played in accompanying the Central American feminist movement in the organization of the Feminist Encuentro in El Salvador.

Pat Howell, a film and video producer told us. "Women from Latin America have been very isolated so far, and FIRE gives them a voice to connect."

Katherine Coberg, a U.S. lawyer from the American Civil Liberties Union told us, "I worked on the abortion case that was presented last week in the Supreme Court, challenging Pennsylvania state's restrictions on abortion. I think being able to talk about it on FIRE is great."

Frieda Werden from WINGS said that shortwave's global outreach is very necessary and that is the reason WINGS sends their tapes to us and listens to FIRE in Kansas City.

Argentina from the Matagalpa Women's Collective—who also does radio—said that we will always be connected, and that it was great to talk on the air for FIRE's first anniversary.

Laura Guzmán, director of the women's project at the Inter-American Institute for Human Rights said that she wanted "to point out that the space you have created was a felt necessity, because women feel the support in your efforts to get women's rights recognized as human rights."

Sally Jacques, FIRE correspondent at the Foundation for a Compassionate Society, said, "It is moving to listen to so many other women on FIRE talking about similar issues that we all share. Radio is essential for connection among women."

From UNIFEM in New York, Roxana Carrillo called to say that they follow our work closely, and that it is great to have access to media that focuses on women's perspectives on development, violence against women, and health issues as human rights issues.

Maralisse Hood from the USA, but who was actually living between Costa Rica and Guatemala, talked about the type of organization that FIRE is trying to build: "Your mission is ambitious, that of offering a space for women around the world from this little place called Costa Rica. It's a new experience."

Graham Russell, a Canadian human rights lawyer from the Central American Human Rights Commission (CODEHUCA), said, "Women's human rights are everyone's issue, and this message is out on FIRE."

Roxana Arroyo, also from CODEHUCA, said, "FIRE has opened a new awareness about women's feelings, because our feelings go out over shortwave."

Rhonda Copelon, human rights lawyer at the CUNY Law School in New York, said that at this point, "a world without FIRE would have less light."

FIRE celebrates its first anniversary with music from the Costaricanall-women's group, Claroscuro.

1993

On FIRE's second anniversary, a very special tape came over the phone line. It was Xiomara Fortuna, Sergia Galvan, and Ochi Curiel from the Dominican Republic with a show they had produced for FIRE's Anniversary:

NARRATOR: This FIRE has broken the "air-meter." Why? Because, besides having women's voices on the air, they are teaching women to "get the air out of patriarchy." They have also broken the "wave-meter" because they have reached shortwave, long wave, skinny waves, fat waves.... And now an intimate moment...

Control: Music

NARRATOR: FIRE is a space that represents women marked by silence; it is a space that turns silenced rebellions into mornings of hurricanes, of utopia, dreams, and hopes. It is like an ocean blue where the future for women is turned into many colors; a voice that announces and builds new horizons for women. It is like a drum that invites struggle. It is a conga [Afro-Caribbean drum] that calls the fire goddess. It is a mirror that reflects the life and subjectivity of women; a siren that denounces violence and oppression, that shouts strength for all.

Control: Song by Xiomara and Ochi

Fempress also celebrated FIRE's anniversary with an article about our two years on the air:

The need for women to have access to media is obvious when you look at most written press, or listen to TV and radio programs. Even though the number of women in media has expanded considerably since the end of the Decade of Women, the numbers are still small.... For centuries, there has been an effort to remove women from history... but women have lives, and their lives, through multiple forms of resistance, have never been silenced. One of the new forms of resistance is finding a voice on radio. FIRE is one of those voices. This is why its second anniversary is a celebration of the tenacity and creativity of women around the world who express their voices on FIRE.

1994

Three full years on the air! This time we had guests to celebrate our anniversary on the air with us in the studio. In addition, we had prepared a special tape on which we gathered words from different contexts of friends around the world who could not come or call, but who had been with us all year long. This is what they wanted to say to us on our third anniversary:

I hope FIRE continues with us forever. It has such important relevance because radio is the means through which women learn. You chose a great mechanism for women.
> —Ana María Brasileiro, UNIFEM for
> Latin America and the Caribbean

The following is from Vivian Stromberg, director of MADRE in the USA:

To FIRE: Thousands of thanks for weaving a fabric of voices of women from all around the world. Women's voices have always been very strong but have not been heard, largely because media is controlled and our questioning voices have been a threat because of the power our voices have.

Fortunately we are not easily quieted, and fortunately we have courageous people in all aspects of our work. The independent media that functions around the world is heard through that courage. FIRE is an excellent representative of the possibilities that can be created as we create our own media networks, as we try to bring our voices into mainstream media. Media outlets like FIRE allow that, and help us increase the impact of our work, desires, dreams, and strength as we connect one with the other around the world.

We received the following message from Olga Amparo Sánchez, who works with Corporación Casa Mujer in Colombia:

This program that you are building is a strength for those of us who are beginning to get into radio. For example, you helped me buy equipment and taught me how to use it as we are starting to do radio in Colombia. I feel more confident....

Anne Walker, Director of the International Women's Tribune Center, added, "I cannot imagine a world without FIRE."

Ana María Pizarro from the Nicaraguan Women's Health Network said:

It is very revolutionary that women have international shortwave access and that we can use it to get to so many places around the world. In Nicaragua we have access to Radio Mujer and space in others. The Women's Health Network of Nicaragua will always be supporting you.

Donna Sullivan of the Human Rights Law Group in the USA had this message for us:

I know that women all around the world share the gratitude that I feel, and the pleasure of looking forward to the future. I saw the work that FIRE did in Vienna at the Human Rights UN Conference, and that work is essential to making human rights work for women. In that process of transforming the human rights system so that it is responsive to women's lives and women's realities, you brought women's voices into the public arena so that those in power had to acknowledge it. I'm looking forward to Beijing and FIRE's presence there. It will be of critical importance in having the information in advance and in Beijing, in bringing women's experiences forward and making their voices heard.

Thais Corral of the Brazilian organization Falla Mujer, CEMINA, told us:

I am part of the group that produces Falla Mujer in Brazil. We are strong believers in radio in the hands of women. Our program was also born with the idea of bringing out women's voices. The international exchange is very important. With the new technological developments in media, radio seems insignificant, but women know better; we know it is accessible to us as women.

Our other special guests joined us in the studio. One of them was Alda Facio—Latin American and Caribbean women's candidate for the UN Special Rapporteur on Violence Against Women—and also a FIRE correspondent in many activities. Another guest was Carmen Costop and her three children, all Mayan Guatemalan refugees in Costa Rica. Also joining us was Ana Virginia Duarte, testifier at FIRE's first radio tribunal on the air that year, and also head of the Women's Human Rights Project at the Central American Human Rights Commission (CODEHUCA). Her program set forth the campaign for signatures to get the OAS to sign the convention about violence. Also present was all the staff including Olga Reyes from Spain, who then filled the fourth rotating position.

We shared our feelings about what FIRE meant to us, we celebrated Katerina's pregnancy, and we cried over Carmen's pain in separation from her ex-husband, her land, and her people. Carmen had this message for us:

I thank FIRE because it has taught me that life does not end, even as hard as it may get sometimes. There are many women who have not been exposed to this perspective, and therefore do not have a chance. Kata has taught me how to get out of my difficult situation as a woman. Thanks to FIRE, and keep it up.

1995

FIRE's anniversary on May 1, 1995, was marked by an immense mobilization through radio and electronic media. The combination was not by chance. FIRE was testing the effectiveness of the link between shortwave radio and electronic communications... and it worked. The day of our anniversary FIRE had women call because they read about the call-in show through the following e-mail announcement we had posted:

Subject: FIRE's anniversary—May, 1, 1995

May 1st is FIRE's 4th Anniversary on the air. We want to celebrate it by receiving live calls from you that day. Call us collect at the following phone number: (506) 249-1821. Or/and fax us your messages: (506) 249-1095, or through our e-mail. We will receive calls between 10:00-12:00 in the morning and 6:00-8:00 at night ,Costa Rica time. Remember: call on May 1st!...

In its four years of existence, we have learned that the strength of our endeavor is the product of our global connections. Let's show those connections live on the air this next May 1st. Call us collect to celebrate with us.

Kata, María, and Nancy—FIRE

E-mail responses were quick to come:

Date: Mon, 24 Apr 1995 12:27:42—0700
Subject: Re: FIRE's Anniversary—May 1, 1995
María, Nancy, Kata
Feminist International Radio, Costa Rica

Dear Women,

Congratulations for these four years of uninterrupted broadcasting on the air. This celebration concerns all of us who are committed to doing information and communication. The presence of FIRE is an inspiration and stimulus for the Latin American Women's Movement. We hope FIRE will grow and be present in all the corners of our continent. A warm embrace.

In sisterhood,

The women of ISIS International (Chile)

Date: Thu, 27 Apr 1995 11:49:44—0800
From: SKYE WARD
Subject: Greetings of solidarity from California April 27, 1995

Dear Sistahs:
Greetings and Respect!

I am sending this letter of solidarity to all the warrior women in Costa Rica. Please know that other sistahs here in the states are inspired by your attempts to organize, and positive healing energy is sent to you. As many of you may be aware... we womenfolk are under siege.

Date: Thu, 27 Apr 1995 18:31:41—0400
Subject: Greetings

This is important work you are doing. I am glad to know that there are sistahs out there willing to teach us how to take full advantage of this technology. Let me know how I can help you. I have been toying with the idea of getting a ham radio license. Your work inspires me further in that direction!!

Joy Alice

Lincoln, Nebraska, USA
Date: Mon, 1 May 1995 12:28:42—0700 (PDT)
Subject: Your anniversary

Dear María, Nancy, and Katerina:

Many congratulations on your anniversary. Hope that in the coming years you continue to provide such a warm and wonderful space for women's voices from all over the world.

P.S. I will try to call you live this evening. I look forward to our international collaboration on the Voices of Women for Beijing tape project. Lots of love.

Date: Mon, 1 May 1995 09:17:48—0700
Subject: Greetings to FIRE Radio

This is Technomama in Austin, Texas, United States, sending a warm embrace in celebration of the fourth anniversary of the Feminist International Radio Endeavour FIRE. Wherever you are in the world (or in cyberspace), I always feel close to Katerina, María, and Nancy. It's almost as if all of the women are part of a big international family. Thank you, in particular, as a woman of color, for everything you have done to inspire and support us by bringing our diversity of voices to all the corners of the Mother Earth. Dear sisters, we count on being able to congratulate you again in four more decades. Wishing you well,...

Foundation for a Compassionate Society

Subject: RE: FIRE's anniversary

María: Bravo. We're on line!

Just in case I don't get through on the telephone, I am e-mailing to congratulate the FIRE team—Katerina, Nancy, and María and everyone else for another splendid year. Congratulations too on your well-deserved awards from WINGS and UNESCO. You help us to understand what

411

women are doing and what is being done to us around the world. It is very critical for all of us that you are there, making the connections.

Many of us here in the U.S. are stunned by the revelations about and, even more so, by the coddling reactions to right-wing militia groups, which we see as dangerous, fascist groups that are targeting all minorities, including women and lesbians and gays. It is important that we connect these developments to the fundamentalist attacks on women in Algeria and other parts of the world and the Vatican's global attack on women in respect to the Beijing Women's Conference.

I also have some good news to report. We received last week the special report on the Inter-American Commission of Human Rights on the situation of Human Rights in Haiti. The report was about violations by the illegal regime and the problem of demilitarization thereafter. Our program, the International Women's Human Rights Law Clinic, together with two NY-based Haitian women's groups, several of the clinical programs at Harvard Law School, MADRE and the Center for Human Rights Legal Action in Washington, DC, filed a petition with the Inter-American Commission in order to call attention [to the fact that] you are there, making the connections.

Many of us here in the U.S. are stunned by the role of sexual violence against women in the repression of Haiti. We all filed it because, at that time, it was impossible for Haitian women living in Haiti to do so. We asked the commission to document the rape and sexual abuse of women and to recognize this rape as a form of torture under the American Convention. This is a very important development for Haitian women and for the human rights of women everywhere. This says loudly and clearly that rape is among the most egregious of human rights violations. It makes it much harder to ignore or bury it and, by recognizing that rape is one of the most traumatizing and terrible forms of abuse, it contributes to vindicating women's suffering and restoring their self-esteem or wholeness.

Many thanks and much love to you all.

Rhonda Copelon, Director of IWHR
International Women's Human Rights Law Clinic

Others messages came to us via fax:

April 18, 1995
Lima, Perú

Dear María and Friends of FIRE,

Congratulations—Congratulations—Congratulations—
Congratulations—

We are very happy for your awards from UNESCO and WINGS. You really deserve it. FIRE has become a model to follow for all of us who believe in a strong voice for the women of the world.

FIRE International is really the radio broadcast for all of us, and we want to be able to be in direct contact, station to station.

An enormous hug for all the women at the Feminist International Radio Endeavour and an enormous kiss from me. I love you and hope to see you soon.

Mariella Sala,
Coordinadora del Collectivo Radial Feminista del Perú

April 26, 1995
ISIS Manila, Philippines

"These are the very early mornings that Queen Isis sings; we sing to the beautiful young women who are here." [adapted Spanish birthday song]. Congratulations Feminist International Radio Endeavour! Sending a warm hello and congratulations from all your sisters in Manila. Sending our support for your struggle for the development of a world in which women and men are able to enjoy peace, justice, and liberty. Forward sisters!

Lynn Lee, Deputy Director
ISIS, Manila, Philippines

Date: Mon, 1 May 1995 09:17:48—0700
Subject: Greetings to FIRE Radio

Dear Friends,

The Women's Media Circle Foundation in the Philippines, producers of Womanwatch, and other radio and TV programs about women, send you our best wishes and congratulations. We'd like to visit you

413

one day and see how we can cooperate as a partner in radio wave activism on the other side of the Pacific in the near future. Mabuhay— Viva!

Anna Leah Sarabia

May 1, 1995
Interkonexiones
To: Katerina, María and Nancy, FIRE
From: Women Creating Communication Spaces, Interkonexiones

Dear Women of FIRE:

On this special day for you and for all of us we want to reach you through our thoughts, our emotions, and our words. Congratulations. Continue opening venues, or better yet, let us continue to open venues together.

Here in Freiburg, Germany, we find ourselves working to build, with hope, a program of exchange between Latin America and Europe. Our organization has, within its limited capacity, decided to contribute a little grain of sand to achieve a different communication, to give women a voice directly, to change the stereotypes of women, to get to know each other better, and to extend our hands from one continent to the other. We send our warm greetings from this side of the world.

Birgit, Christiane, and Carmen

May 2, 1995

Dear Friends, Women:

I am on my way to Germany and thinking about the inspiring and motivating time I spent with you. I hope FIRE will continue the wonderful work for many, many more years.

Congratulations on your Anniversary.

I'm looking forward to seeing all again.

Love and peace, many hugs,

Jasmin

May 1, 1995

To: Kata, María, and Nancy

Here's to FIRE for a Happy 4th Anniversary—keeping the fire burning. We hoped to hear your voices when we called about 20 minutes ago. María had wrapped up the show by then, so here's what we wanted to say:

Thank You FIRE and thank you for working so hard to get women's voices heard.

A happy 4th, and to the 5th, 6th, 7th, 8th, 9th, and 10th and many more that will follow.

Much love from all the women at Gender and Development Program, APDC, the Women and Media for Asia Pacific, Development Alternatives with Women for a New Era (DAWN), and the Asian Network for Women and International Migration.

Nareson Souffer, Coordinator
Meena Shirdas, WMNAP
Bee Yee, Program Officer

May 1, 1995

Dear María,

Thanks for your invitation to speak on your Fourth Anniversary of shortwave broadcasting. I will call at around 10 a.m. and 6 p.m., Costa Rica time. This is 4:00 a.m. and 10 p.m. Australian time, so I hope I am awake for the first one. Speak to you soon.

Regards, Karen James

May 1, 1995

Dear María, Nancy, and Katerina:

Many congratulations on your anniversary. Hope that in the coming years you continue to provide such a warm and wonderful space for women's voices from all over the world.

P.S. I will try to call you live this evening. Look forward to our international collaboration on the Voices of Women for the Beijing tape project. Lots of love.

Dorothy Kidd

May 1, 1995

Congratulations and Happy Fourth Anniversary to FIRE. "Keep the flames burning for women around the world!" Thinking of you today.

Burnadette and your sisters in the Islands of the South Pacific

May 1, 1995

Happy Anniversary!

Everyone at SIPAM wishes everyone at FIRE that this fourth celebration brings you as a major gift many, many more years of the creative, successful, and active life as you have had so far.

May 1, 1995

Dear Friends at FIRE,

From South America, Chile, receive all the best energy from the Goddesses, as always.

In this year of 1995, may our objectives be met and in a positive way with good results for all the women in the world.

In the name of all the women of the Caribbean, and especially from Santo Domingo, we are sending miles of hugs accompanied by the rhythm of the black drums and blood.

In Feminist Sisterhood,
Ochy Curiel

May 1, 1995

Wishing you a Happy May 1st and Happy Anniversary. In these days when evil spirits are manifesting themselves, we wanted to communicate on this Anniversary words of advice that were expressed by Eleanor Roosevelt in 1956, when she said the following:

"You cannot take this personally, you cannot hold a grudge. We have to finish each day of work, we cannot lose hope, we have to rise once and many times, even after we have been defeated, find responses by discussing... until you find a response to each argument. Women who are willing to play a leadership role have to say the truth even if they

are attacked for it. Each woman in her political life must develop a skin as hard as that of the rhinoceros to be able to deal with the present times."
Blanche Weissen Cook and Clare Coss

Other friends came, even the next day, traveling by car to the radio station, to celebrate FIRE's anniversary. Juan Pablo Arias Azofifa from Costa Rica and Paula Wilkies from the USA and a resident in Costa Rica, came to talk about the meaning of FIRE for them:

FIRE seems to cover the topics that affect the women and children of the world: Health, projects, and environment during the Earth Summit where it seemed the Women's Tent did more than anyone else....

Asked about which FIRE program has impacted her the most during her four years of listening, Paula said:

The coverage of the Rio Conference was very important... the recent coverage of the Social Development Summit also, because it brought the voices of very young girls who got involved in it.

1996

On May 1, 1996, we celebrated FIRE's Fifth Anniversary on the shortwave frequencies of RFPI. FIRE received many letters and phone calls from listeners and organized a gathering of some of our closest feminist friends and supporters (both female and male) in Costa Rica that day. Following are excerpts from some of the letters:

Dear Compañeras,
Happy Birthday #5 to Radio FIRE! Keep up the excellent work. You're right on the cutting edge of grassroots, participatory radio. Greetings to you from Silver Springs, Maryland, in the Washington, DC, metropolitan area. We send all of you a warm Puerto Rican embrace.
Erica Martinez Atabei, Producer,
WRLD Radio/International
Channel 30 in Fairfax, Virginia, Washington, DC

Queridas Compañeras de FIRE:

Today, May 1, 1996, International Workers Day, is also your anniversary of five years on the air—five years of FIRE's uninterrupted commitment in the defense and portrayal of the rights and demands of women. Our best wishes so that you may continue making a contribution in communications toward a better world. Muchísimas felicidades y un gran abrazo.

Elizabeth Salguero
Secretaria Ejecutiva, RED-ADA, Bolivia

Dear FIRE women:

We've been warming ourselves with your FIRE for the last couple of years. Let us all together keep flourishing into the next 500 years. Together we will light up the world.

Hugs and best wishes to all of you.

Vesna, Cathrine and BaBes [listeners in Croatia]

Sylvia Charsoodian, co-editor of *Wavelengths*, a women's shortwave monitoring magazine, wrote:

Many thanks for the past five years of feminist views, and hoping for many more years to come. As you know, we at Wavelengths *take note as much as we can of the times when radio stations emphasize women's impact on the news.... We enjoy listening to your station's positive reporting on women in the news!*

Later in the day, Nina Allen, Sylvia's co-editor, called to say:

I wanted to call [earlier], but what other women were saying was so interesting, that I kept listening and did not want to interrupt by calling! We began Wavelengths *because women who listen to shortwave are practically invisible, while men [listeners] seem to be very active in this activity. Yet there are many women who listen to shortwave who want to know other women who also find this activity very meaningful.*

Other messages continued to pour in from all parts of the world:

Thanks for the several years of broadcasts that we have listened to. We have really enjoyed your diverse programming.
                    —Konrad and Sharon, Boca Raton, Florida, USA

The English and Spanish sections of Radio Netherlands send greetings and best birthday wishes to FIRE on the occasion of your fifth anniversary. May you have many more successful years promoting the thoughts and voices of women in the interest of peace.
                    —Ginger da Silva, producer at Radio Netherlands

Yours is a marvelous effort. Congratulations, and we hope you have many more birthdays.
                    —from Telemanita, a video collective in Mexico

FIRE has been an inspiration to us, as we have seen your success in such a short time—so much so that you have inspired us to really consider building a radio [station] here in Asia.
                    —ISIS International, the Philippines

We missed your May 1 anniversary call-in but wanted to e-mail our congratulations on your first five years. When Human Rights Watch first founded a Women's Rights Project, FIRE was one of the few places where we knew that human rights abuse against women would be covered and that the voices of women who suffer and combat such abuse would be heard. Over the years, FIRE has become a key resource for HRW and many others in the field of women's human rights. FIRE is a crucial medium for connecting women to one another the world over in a global movement for fundamental social change. Congratulations and thanks.
                    —The Staff of the Human Rights Watch
                    Women's Rights Project

I was with you [in spirit] on your anniversary, although I could not call you because I was doing a radio workshop with a faraway population in Colombia. Thus, a "long wave" embrace, just as you do on the FIRE shortwaves!

—María Victoria Polanco, vice president of AMARC

The first call-in show began at 10:00 a.m. and ran until noon. The Spanish show opened with a presentation by Katerina, who began thanking all those who had made FIRE possible. Just as she was about to name them, FIRE received the first call.

Ana Ines Bolanos, a young Costa Rican student of journalism called from Heredia—two hours away from the radio station—to say that she was listening to the anniversary show and wanted to congratulate FIRE:

We have been trained by you, and that has been a great support to the new generation [of radio women] in the country.... We finally decided to open an experimental radio program on a local station where we will begin producing on the 15th of May, and we want FIRE to be there as our first guests on our first program.

One of her colleagues, Ivania, also called during the morning show to wish us well and to invite Katerina to be on their first radio show.

Another call came from Nancy Vargas, a former producer of FIRE, who had left in February to undertake national grassroots radio work. She was currently the vice-director of a national rural women's radio network that FIRE had worked with throughout our first five years. Nancy told us:

Chicas, congratulations for the immense efforts that have been undertaken by you and so many women around the world. Just as you, I am currently working on weaving among women the types of networks we need to forge changes in society. We need to keep connected to international networks, and continue giving grassroots women a voice on shortwave!

Frances Chavarria, member of the RFPI International Advisory Board and of the Global Women's Network, called from San José:

I am very grateful for the work that FIRE does with women in the world, and especially for having given women a voice. Thank you. You do beautiful work.

Luisa Cruz called from Piura, Perú, in the second largest desert of Latin America. She is producer of a rural women's radio program in her region.

I am an industrial engineer but I have been doing radio for the past ten years because of the role it plays in reaching women. To you all, and to the listeners in Latin America and the Caribbean, congratulations. We need to build our dreams. FIRE is doing just that. In this time of globalization of information, we need alternative voices and programs like FIRE.

Alda Facio, a Costa Rican feminist lawyer and coordinator of a women's program of the United Nations, also called to wish FIRE well, "Women have to be thankful to FIRE for giving us a voice."

Another Costa Rican feminist lawyer, Ana Elena Badilla from the Arias Foundation for Human Development, called to say:

FIRE has made an important contribution here in Costa Rica and also around the whole world, and it has been a very important venue to let people know the advances that women have had—which are things that are not portrayed in other media. You have all worked to do that, and we will always support you.

Milagro Rojas, a Costa Rican feminist from The United Nations Institute for the Prevention of Delinquency, also called to celebrate FIRE's anniversary, saying, "You come, you go, and nothing holds you back. Thank you FIRE!"

Julio Cesar Rodriguez from Chiriqui, Panama called to say, "This is the first time I have been able to listen to you, although I have listened to RFPI. I am happy to talk to you."

FIRE received a call from Daniel Hernandez in Guatemala City. He told us that he began listening to us during the live broadcasts from the Fourth World Conference on Women because someone told him that there was going to be a feminist radio program that would broadcast live:

I was very excited when I tuned into your station and heard you from Beijing. I am happy to come in contact with your perspective, one that I respect and admire. You have an effect on the minds of many people.

Misambu, a student at Friends World College and collaborator with FIRE during March and April 1996, joined us on the broadcast:

Congratulations to all women and men in the world who are spreading the word and consciousness of the women's movement. Thanks for the support. It has been wonderful for me to be here at FIRE. It has opened my mind, and when I leave I will keep it going. So, thanks FIRE, for giving me your FIRE.

Genevieve Vaughan, from the Foundation for a Compassionate Society, called with a special message. Several other women, also from the Foundation, were waiting with her to come on the air. Genevieve talked about her vision for re-creating justice in the world:

I was born into a family that has a lot of resources, and I realized that there is so much injustice on the planet, so many people suffering, that it seemed to me that there was a need for people who have the resources to use them for changing the injustices and the social structures. That re-creates justice. Feminism can clear out the privileging mechanism that is ingrained in privileging one gender over the other, a mechanism that has gone into class, race, and among countries. I care a lot about media programs because they provide a way for women to speak the truth to a large audience. They break through monolith and rock. We have done several media programs. One is FIRE, which is a success internationally and locally.

Katerina thanked Genevieve on the air for giving us the opportunity to build the FIRE radio program.

Journalists from WINGS, Carol Stall and Frieda Werden, also came on the air to congratulate us. Carol is a freelance writer working with

WINGS on a health survey related to the effects of nuclear waste. She said that she wanted to come to Costa Rica to work on the case of the women banana workers. She had first read about their struggle in the Internet article by FIRE from the First Costa Rican Tribunal on Violations of Women's Human Rights and had gotten in touch with the lawyer who had refused to take up the women's cases. Frieda said she was so proud of FIRE's work that she wanted to burst:

> *I remember when you were just a gleam in Genevieve Vaughan's eye! We laid a little bit of groundwork and you have built an elephant out of it. FIRE has a huge visibility throughout the global women's movement and has done so much to advance women's cause and to communicate it.*

After the morning call-in show, FIRE's staff went down the hill from the station to a luncheon party that had been organized at Katerina's house. More than 40 people—the feminists closest to FIRE, RFPI staff, and friends—had gathered for a "close contact" celebration of FIRE's anniversary. After a beautiful reunion, FIRE's staff climbed the hill back to RFPI's studios to prepare for the 6:00 to 8:00 p.m. call-in show.

The first caller was Paca Cruz, a Costa Rican feminist painter-artist who is part of the women's movement, who told us, "I want to congratulate you on the air, on your fifth anniversary. I am proud because of the great work you do."

Ana Elena Obando, a Costa Rican feminist lawyer, walked into the studio to share the call-in show with us and to say, "These women have built this with their hands, and we Costa Ricans feel proud of you and all women who have made this possible."

Another call came from Tim Hendel in Alabama in the U.S. A strong supporter of FIRE and a member of the RFPI International Advisory Board, he told the audience that he had supported FIRE by collecting shortwave radios and sending them to FIRE to distribute among women in the world. Tim talked about his participation in a very progressive church in Alabama, where he planned to give a talk about RFPI and FIRE, and to teach people how to tune in to shortwave.

The next caller was Panamanian Mario Bolaños from Panama City. At age 75, he said, "I listen to you every day here.... Your program is very enjoyable."

FIRE pointed out that it has been thanks to the Foundation for a Compassionate Society, the support of RFPI, the strength of the women's movement, and the commitment of its staff that the program has been possible. FIRE also reminded the audience that the call-in show and the gathering of feminists and supporters had been made possible by a contribution from the Caritas Fund of the Tides Foundation.

The next call to come in was from Cuba. Orlando Orama, a Cuban journalist, reported that more than two million Cubans marched though the streets that morning for the first of May celebration of International Workers Day. Vivian, his wife, also came on the air with, "Congratulations on behalf of Cuban women. Keep it going."

From Valparaiso, Chile, FIRE received a call from Margarita Plaza, producer of a women's radio program at community radio station Radio Placeres:

I wanted to congratulate you on behalf of all Latin American women who are making efforts to build popular radio alternatives here in Chile. Good waves, and good luck to you!... I will write to you so that we can exchange more programs.

Gustavo called from Chimaltenango, Guatemala. He said that he had heard FIRE that night and ran to a street phone to call us:

This is the first time I heard you, and I was so thrilled that I ran to call. I like it! Give me your address so that I can write to you regularly. I am very excited!

Debra Latham, general manager of RFPI and a former producer of FIRE, called from her house in Ciudad Colón. She was excited to share with FIRE's listeners that after five years what she values most is both what FIRE has become and also what she has learned from the women who have come on the air.

The first caller on the English program that night was Sophy Ly from Senegal, coordinator of the World Association of Community Radio Broadcasters (AMARC). She had just come back from a radio meeting in Nigeria, a conference on deregulation of the airwaves:

People want independent radio. Many women were eager to know about AMARC and about FIRE, and to know about international radio experiences happening in other places. AMARC is now working at the international level. I hope we can celebrate at least another 50 years together.

Ariane Bertoulie, coordinator of the AMARC Women's Network, called next from Canada. She talked about the special project, "Starting Points," that she is working on, for which AMARC will produce a series of tapes about the Beijing Platform for Action. The purpose of the tapes is to make it possible for a wide range of women to learn about the Platform for Action though radio, and, she said, "FIREPLACE broadcast tapes have a special place in the production. Thank you!"

Melba Jiménez, a producer for RFPI in Spanish, called from Ciudad Colón, only a few miles away from the station to say, "Happy Birthday to FIRE, and I hope you continue the good work."

Katerina and I related some of the history and origins of FIRE in order to give our listeners credit for their share FIRE's accomplishments:

It was 1991 when we began, and sometimes it seems that it was yesterday. Other times it seems that it was ages ago. So many voices, so many experiences, and such broad support keeps us going. Thanks to all! It is also your anniversary.

Jean Parker, coordinator of the Colorado Cross-Disabilities Coalition, also called. She is one of the women Tim Hendel taught to tune in to FIRE and RFPI. Jean—who, like Tim, is blind—produces Disability Radio Worldwide for RFPI.

I want to let the audience know that FIRE has been a very, very positive forum for women with disabilities and has been very supportive in providing space for women with disabilities to bring our issues to the forefront and to assist us in making public the issues that affect women with disabilities, and in particular the issues at the Beijing conference. We appreciate that! I hope you have many more years of the excellent program you produce.

FIRE ended the broadcast by thanking all the women who had been a part of FIRE during the last five years: Nancy Vargas, Jeanne Carstensen, Olga Rey, Firuseh Shokoo, Jasmin Edding, Ana Sisnett; also Evelyn, Michelle, Susana, Misambu, Amber, and many other volunteers.

1997

The first live call on FIRE's sixth anniversary, May 1, 1997, came from Genevieve Vaughan, only half a minute after we started the program. "Congratulations, FIRE. I will not keep the line busy, so that you can hear from others. I just want to thank you," she told us.

Visitors came to the radio station to talk with us live about FIRE's birthday. One of these was Ana Elena Obando, and another was Debra Cedeño, a Latina architect from the USA. Ana Elena spoke about the important role FIRE plays in the lives of many women:

First of all, congratulations to Katerina and María. The effort you have put into this program throughout the years is very important for the Costa Rican women's movement, because FIRE has taken our voices to other latitudes. For me, I feel that I am part of this radio program because it is always open to our voices, and to our emotions. It is a place where you can come and feel comfortable, and talk, and be heard.

We can also talk about what is happening in Costa Rica. It is very difficult in Costa Rica, and in many other parts of the world, for women to have a voice in media and really express what happens to them. Women's issues are not taken seriously by media. FIRE is the only one here where we can talk about those issues the way we need to. It is not an easy area for women.

Debra shared her vision about FIRE:

First of all, I think that the primary source for the world as far as women's issues are concerned has to be women themselves. But not only women's issues! The main role of FIRE is the outreach throughout the world. It is not easy to just go to a radio station and say, "I have this issue." Women are very often ignored.

What has impressed me the most about the history of FIRE is how a few women can come together, have a passion for radio, and open it to all women. Live broadcasts are just too much! You make even the smallest women's meeting international, and it has the same value as a big global conference.

I was also impressed with the story of Paulina Diáz Navas, because she learned from FIRE's live broadcasts information she could use for her own needs. We do not have to fly to have our voices heard; we just get on the phone.

Lynn Rosolli and Phillys Turril, two women from San Francisco presently living in Costa Rica, were among those who came to the studio to celebrate FIRE's seventh anniversary. Phillys told us:

What brought me to Latin America was that I wanted to explore it because of the people and the wildlife. The way of life here is so much healthier! Before I came here I lived in the USA. I was a nurse, but I'm divorced from it now. I want change. Maybe it is the midlife crisis. I was very much impacted by the culture here: First by the solidarity of the campesino people, and then by their hospitality, because they take you to their house even if they do not know you. That is why I am here!

About FIRE, she said that she has been a feminist in the USA. However, she felt that feminism in the USA was too conflict-oriented, so she embraced it only from a distance. She continued:

I thought that one person could not do much. How wrong I was! I have learned from the FIRE women, because they have done so much, and what they do is very proactive! I come from an abusive father, so in my younger years, if I had had access to anything like FIRE, it would have been a life saver. I felt very alone, yet in listening to FIRE, we can know that we are not alone.

Lynn also had an anniversary message for our listeners:

I came to Costa Rica from California. I felt I was reaching a dead end in my life, so I was looking for a richer style of life. We had traveled to

Latin America before and decided to come and spend some time to get to know the lifestyle better. I wanted what I saw when I first came—a change from the materialistic lifestyle to a more human-based and family- and community-based life.

It is amazing what Kata, María, Gen, and women around the world have done to make this program happen. It is an important tool for women because it reaches people in far away places, people who do not have access to other sources of information about women. It empowers women and gives us hope. It tells us that we can really change our lives. I was very moved when I heard on FIRE the testimony of a woman banana worker here. It was a case about how the pesticides affected her and her family. Yet, the damage is not recognized scientifically, so they do not get indemnification. They have organized to counteract that.

Richard McCarthy called from Alabama in the U.S. to wish FIRE a happy birthday, and to say, "I enjoy FIRE very much, thank you for your voices."

Sally Luther and John Newmeier from the USA and members of the board of RFPI also called. John told us, "I want to tell the FIRE women that we really like what you do. We want to wish you the best for the future! Hasta la vista!"

Norberto Cubieses, who was listening to FIRE the night of our anniversary, called from Argentina:

It was a month ago when I discovered the FIRE program on shortwave. I even wrote you a letter 15 days ago, because I was so excited about your program! I love your program, and I told you in my letter that I produce a program in Radio La Colifata, which is the only radio that is broadcast from within a psychiatric hospital. The patients there are the producers of the programs! I commented to you that there are two women who are interns, and they do radio and love to communicate with the rest of the world.

Debra Latham brought a chocolate cake to the studio to congratulate FIRE on its anniversary. She reminded the audience about earlier times when we had produced programs in a little studio at the University for Peace, and everyone had to be quiet when we were calling on the air. "We have all come a long way," she said.

FIRE thanked the Global Fund for Women for the grant to be able to translate FIRE's book into English. FIRE also thanked the United Nations World Health Organization for its grant to FIRE to prepare a Reception Report about FIRE's listenership. We also expressed our thanks for the grant from the Embassy of the Netherlands, because it made FIRE's presence and the live broadcasts from the Seventh International Women's Health Conference possible.

1998

On May 1, 1998, FIRE celebrated its seventh anniversary! We dedicated the day to the memory of Bella Abzug, who had died in March. FIRE played a program with Bella's last speech at the United Nations, and we had called listeners to ask them to write rather than call us that day. Letters came from all parts of the world:

Congratulations on your 7th Anniversary. The FIRE ladies have done a lot of good work to get this far. Sorry that FIRE is not on the air as much as it used to be. But I'm sure that you welcome the rest. Please keep up the excellent work!
—Richard McCarthy, Alabama, USA

Un saludo gigantesco de Boston Massachusetts para las compañeras y audiencia de FIRE. La labor de enlace y diálogo que uds. proporcionan al mundo realmente es de celebrar. En estos momentos de globalización y privatización, nos dan iluminación, información y la bendita inspiración que necesitamos todas para confrontar las bestias tercas que nos rodean. Sabiendo que uds. están alla en ese rincon de la planeta nos da animo y energía aqui en esta esquinita. Mil gracias por los caminos que uds. van abriendo y los lazos que estan tejiendo entre el sur y el norte. [Translation: A thousand thanks for the roads you have opened and the connections you weave between north and south.]
—Valerie Miller

Congratulations to FIRE for surviving and even thriving in the face of globalization, which has created even more challenges for alternative forms of media. Thank you for providing such a critical "voice for the voiceless," who unfortunately grow in number every day with globalization. You are a fine example of what Bella Abzug fought for all those years on behalf of women and all oppressed groups worldwide. Keep up the great work!!

—Margie Thompson, Associate Professor & Director,
University of Denver Masters in International and
Intercultural Communications

From: Susana Woodward

Hola! Saludos desde Duluth, Minnesota.

Muchas felicidades!! On behalf of the Latina, Chicana students at the University of Minnesota-Duluth, I want to thank you for a wonderful experience. It was wonderful to listen to these young women's voices. You left a very strong message at our campus and you touched a lot of women in this part of the world. FIRE, muchas felicidades y gracias por transmitir y conectarnos con mujeres de todo el mundo.

Adelante!!

Susana

Dear FIRE,

Your visit was truly inspiring!

I have been shopping for a shortwave radio and not having any luck in Duluth. I did find a mail order place that has several choices, so now I am learning about these radios so I'll know what I need to buy.

The week following your visit, I was doing a two-day training for women to facilitate a process of change for battered women's groups. One of the other trainers and I developed a piece called Interactive Autonomy. It was a two-hour exercise where we took women through a process of examining our differences and recognizing how they impact our work as well as enrich our work, helping women recognize the responsibility to make room for all women at the table. We also included a piece on looking at the invisible forces that control the power.

Vicky Ibanez

Date: Mon, 27 Apr 1998 17:49:09 EDT
Subject: Happy Anniversary!!!

Dearest María and FIRE Sisters,

I send you my heartfelt congratulations on the seventh birthday of Feminist International Radio Endeavour—one of the most respected and loved, as well as crucial, creative, practical, and valuable alternative institutions in the entire global Women's Movement. What you have built over the past seven years is simply amazing in its effectiveness. Indeed, I cannot imagine global feminism without the active presence of FIRE—and I feel certain that FIRE will continue to rise, blazing new pathways for all of us and keeping our spirits and souls warm. Bless you for all you do on behalf of giving voice to women all over the world.

In respectful, loving, global sisterhood,
Robin Morgan

Date: Mon, 4 May 1998 14:16:53 +0800
Subject: FIRE anniversary
From: IWRAW

I am so sorry I was not able to send you a message of congratulations in time. I was in Mongolia. I know it is late, but on behalf of IWRAW Asia Pacific I would still like to send FIRE our warmest congratulations, appreciation, and good wishes. FIRE has given voice to women all over the world. I will never forget the daily broadcast you did during the Vienna Conference on Human Rights, uniting women worldwide and keeping their agenda alive in the midst of the tensions of the intergovernmental negotiations.
Warm wishes to you once more.
Shanthi Dairiam, Kuala Lumpur, Malaysia

Date: Sun, 26 Apr 1998 22:38:26 PDT
Subject: Re: from fire
From: Dalya Massachi

Congrats on your 7th anniversary! FIRE is one-of-a-kind, against all odds. Here's to another 7 years and beyond....

From: Joyce Kramer

Congratulations! It is a real pleasure to be invited to join the party and celebrate FIRE's seventh anniversary on the air. I just returned from the International Women's Solidarity Conference in Cuba attended by 3,000 women from 79 countries. Most were Third-World and indigenous women who were there to express their rage about the forces of the modern world capitalist system which are polarizing the world economy, marginalizing local economies, and are especially harmful to the health and well-being of low-income women and children.

While attending this conference, I was ever more grateful that FIRE is giving such women voice around the world. I had opportunity to tell the women congregated there to "tune in" to FIRE, and the frequencies will be included in the final printed proceedings of the conference. I want to close by personally thanking the producers of FIRE for bringing women's voices of courage and hope into our lives and hearts.

Joyce Kramer, Ph.D., Professor, Department of Social Work
University of Minnesota Duluth, USA

Queridas FIRE,

Felicidades en su aniversario. Mas adelante durante este mes voy a hacer una larga carta de lo que FIRE ha significado para las mujeres Latinoamericanas en radio. Espero la lean al aire, y que cumplan muchos mas junto a nosotras! [Translation: *Congratulations on your anniversary. Later this month I will write a long letter about what FIRE has meant to Latin American women in radio....*]

—María Victoria Polanco, vice president of AMARC

Congratulations on your 7th anniversary, and for the creation of the new FIRE organization in Costa Rica.

—Genevieve Vaughan

We also had anniversary calls from two AC FIRE board members—Ana Arroba and Ana Elena Obando, who could not come on the air: In addition, Ligia Martín, Costa Rica's Ombudswoman, could not come on the air, but she called to wish us well.

At every one of FIRE's anniversaries we expressed special thanks to Genevieve Vaughan of the Foundation for a Compassionate Society. We thanked her for having given us the opportunity to make a contribution to bringing feminist perspectives to international media. We continue to work together in building stable feminist projects, which are so central to peace and justice in the world!

Over the years, we have learned a lot about women's media, we have accompanied the global women's movement through many international conferences, and we have helped women find and amplify their own voices. Our links with women's networks worldwide, in joint efforts throughout the decade, have strengthened our role in network support and communication. We have also grown as feminists and have enriched and strengthened each other. FIRE grew right along with us.

We were starting to light an eternal flame in the hearts and minds of people everywhere—that women can speak for ourselves, and in so doing can illuminate the world because women bring new, previously unheard perspectives to all issues. However, feminists never rest on their laurels, but are always thinking about the future. As Gina Vargas said at the Latin American and Caribbean Women's tent in Huairou, China, during the NGO Forum:

The hours stolen from the time to sleep, so that we can build our dreams; the lost lover and the new ones discovered here; the ruptures and the complicities constructed. It was thousands of us present there, and it is thousands of us, the ones that take part in this continuity.

Fatima Aloo of the Tanzania Media Women's Association agreed, saying, "When we dream together, reality begins to happen."

That is a good description of FIRE's vision for the future. FIRE needs to build on women's dreams from its place of power and effectiveness. May those dreams continue to keep the FIRE burning!

CHAPTER 13

Reception Report Study

*I will never forget the daily broadcast you made during the Vienna
Conference on Human Rights uniting the women worldwide and
keeping their agenda alive in the midst of the tensions of the inter-
governmental negotiations....*

—Letter from Shanthi Dairiam,
Kuala Lumpur, Malaysia.

In 1995, FIRE began working on a Reception Report Study. We
wanted to systematize some of the empirical data that we had been
collecting though the hundreds of letters (in Spanish and in English)
from men and women listeners throughout our first years on the air
on shortwave radio broadcasting.

The radio station that broadcast FIRE did not have any research
about its listenership, nor did it have any assessment based on
empirical data.

We wanted to know about our listenership for ourselves, and we wanted to know based on a quality study.

Our readings in search of studies about reception specifically in the world of shortwave radio made it evident that perhaps such research did not exist in international broadcasting—anywhere in the world. In 1993, FIRE had written to *Passport to World Band Radio*, the number one book that monitors shortwave. We asked for information regarding any such studies. Marie Lamb, of PWBR, responded that they did not know of any.

It also appeared that feminists had not done this kind of study either. In our extensive exchange with women in radio around the globe, and in our readings, we had not come across any initiative that had studied the listeners' response—male and female—to feminist women's radio programs.

Many studies of reception had been done in the region, including those published by some of the outstanding scholars from Latin America who had developed theories about the reception of radio, such as Alfaro, Fuenzalida, Hermosillo, and Matta during the '80s. There had also been studies by Casullo, Gomiz, Martín, Barbero, Roncagliolo, and others, who had elaborated theories of communications and also had reported very interesting and groundbreaking data about radio listeners. To our knowledge, however, none had studied the response to feminist radio programs as such. Thus, we found there was no existing information concerning our pressing questions! We had to undertake our own study to answer them.

We wanted to know why men and women listen to feminist programming, to discover what they do with the information presented in our programs, to find out if the intimacy of radio has any specific impact on the fact that so many of the letters of support we had received were from men.

We already knew well the impact FIRE was having in the women's movement, because other women involved in the movement were also voices on FIRE. However, we had very little systematic information about our impact on listeners, beyond their gratifying response whenever we called for them to act upon an urgent case (for example, the case of Paulina Díaz Navas—see Chapter 3); their response to our call for urgent action just before the Feminist Encuentro in El Salvador (see Chapter 4); or their response when FIRE staff were denied our visas to go to China for the Fourth World Conference on Women (see Chapter 7).

We also wanted to know whether people who listen to our programs also use the information in their own lives. If they do, how do they use it?

Focus of the Study

We narrowed our broader questions for the study down to three: (1) Location of our listeners, (2) gender of our listeners, and (3) whether our feminist orientation was a factor in listener support.

1. *Exactly where in the world was FIRE being heard? We knew empirically that our radio station could reach 100 countries, but we wanted to know where people listened to FIRE in particular. We also wanted to know, percentage-wise, from which countries we got more letters, and others where listener response was less frequent.*

   According to the preliminary report of the study, the 600 letters sent directly to FIRE or sent to the radio station about FIRE between 1991 and 1997 came from 43 countries. The highest percentage of letters—28.7%—came from the United States, and Cuba was second with 25.9%. Next highest was the United Kingdom with 5.2%, then Mexico with 3.7%, and Japan with 3.2%.

2. *We also wanted gender-desegregated data about the listeners who wrote, because we were under the impression (from reading the letters) that there were more letters from men than from women.*

   The draft report showed that 73% of the letters received by FIRE came from men and 27% came from women! The study states that men write more letters to stations than do women. Indeed, there is evidence about this in some of the letters from men to FIRE, where they say they listen to the program with their wives while they do home tasks. In two of the letters the women wrote a note and also signed the husband's letters to FIRE. One woman added a note to her husband's letter saying she would like to write, but finds no time to do so.

3. *Another issue we wanted to find out about stemmed from the fact that FIRE was the only systematic program at the station (meaning that it was broadcast without interruption since May 1, 1991) that was produced by Latin American and Caribbean feminists, and the only program that was produced in two languages: Spanish and English.*

   Does this factor have any influence on our listenership? Do they like the themes and focus, considering that most of the other programming during those years at the station was produced by males from the United States, and that all of the programming in Spanish other than FIRE was also produced by a Latin American male?

Some of the preliminary conclusions by the researcher demonstrate that 80.7% of the listeners who wrote listened to the program because they liked it; 19.3% listened to it because they listened to shortwave radio in general! According to the author of the investigation this is an expression of the "loyalty of the listeners to this feminist program."

How the Study Was Funded and Organized

In the quest for answers to some of these questions, FIRE designed and presented a project proposal for the funding of the research. The UN World Health Organization, specifically the Special Program for Research and Training in Tropical Diseases, granted FIRE the funds for the study. FIRE had worked with the WHO as advisor to their project, Radio Cum Pictorial for Women's Health Education in Africa (see Chapter 8). In funding FIRE's research, the WHO was interested in knowing the extent of the reach of FIRE's program as a possible venue for their own educational programs in women's health.

We selected journalist Norma Valle Ferrer from Puerto Rico to conduct the research. She was an established radio journalist, academic, and research specialist at the University of Puerto Rico, and producer of Agenda de Hoy at Radio Universidad de Puerto Rico. FIRE chose her to head the study because she was a Latin American and Caribbean woman and because she was a scholar in radio research and production.

Her hypothesis for the study was that:

...listeners of radio, specifically the shortwave audience, listen to FIRE in Spanish and in English because FIRE is feminist. They (the listeners) perform a mediation between their own concepts and information, and the ones they receive on FIRE, and use it in their public and daily life.

She stated that if this hypotheses is proved to be true, the results will have an impact on the theory of gender, on the theory of communications, and on the relationship between both, especially if the word "feminist" and the ideological and cultural construction it represents proves not to intimidate the listeners! "This research," she said, "is part of the profound debate taking place within the women's movement, and within the discipline of mass communications."

Methodology

The methodology of the study combined quantitative and qualitative methods. It was designed by Valle, herself. She had searched for similar studies in the world of shortwave, and she did not find any, demonstrating the unique nature of her study.

Her study included in-depth interviews, questionnaires with open and closed questions for listeners, analysis of listeners' letters, systematization of the data in letters, and a focus group composed of feminists in Costa Rica who listened to FIRE.

The in-depth interviews were with Katerina Anfossi and me, as founding staff of FIRE; with Debra Latham, founder and director of RFPI; and with James Latham, board member and station engineer

A database was created from the more than 4,000 reception reports received by the station from 1991 through the first half of 1997. Of these, the ones that mentioned FIRE's radio program were studied. The database also included information from letters received directly by FIRE during those same years. These amounted to more than 600 letters!

According to Norma Valle's preliminary report in early 1999, "the highest percentage (29.6%) of the total of letters received by FIRE during those years came in 1995 when the UN World Conference on Women and the NGO Forum took place in China. Among other activities, FIRE organized 52 hours of live broadcast that year and received the most letters for a single activity.

The frequency of letters were as follows: 7.8% of the total of letters came in 1991; 9.2% in 1992; 10.9% in 1993; 18.1% in 1994; 29.6% in 1995; 16.7% in 1996, and 7.8% in the first half of 1997. Some of these letters are reprinted later in this chapter. Many are quoted in earlier chapters of this book.

A questionnaire was sent to the listeners who wrote to FIRE in the 18 months from the beginning of 1996 through the first half of 1997; 125 men and women from 20 countries had written during that time span. Of the total, 94 wrote though regular mail, and 31 wrote though e-mail. Listeners wrote from Cuba, the USA, Mexico, Panama, Spain, Angola, Argentina, Colombia, Denmark, Japan, Finland, Ecuador, Guatemala, Uruguay, El Salvador, Perú, the UK, Italy, Germany, and Costa Rica.

The questionnaire was accompanied by the following letter from the producers of FIRE, explaining the purpose of the study:

August 28, 1997

Dear friend of FIRE:

Hello from Costa Rica! For several years now, we have been considering the idea of getting to know our audience better.

Professor Norma Valle, an expert in communications research, is conducting an in-depth study of our audience. She has designed a questionnaire that we include with this letter. Since you have written to us, we hope you might be willing to share with us some of your ideas about radio and about FIRE.

We would really appreciate it if you fill out the questionnaire and return it to us as soon as possible. We are also including a self-addressed envelope.

It is very important for us to hear from you.

> *Cordially yours,*
> *María Suárez and Katerina Anfossi, Producers*

The questionnaire that accompanied the letter contained questions about listeners' interests, ages, gender, times when they listened, what they did with information they heard on FIRE, and assessment of the role of FIRE in shortwave broadcasting. The responses were incorporated in the database, and the information was analyzed and interpreted along with the other data.

Some of the closed questions were the following:

13) When you do not listen to FIRE, it is mainly because:

_____ *problems with signal* _____ *poor audio quality*

_____ *topic is not interesting* _____ *disagree ideologically*

_____ *it's a repeat* _____ *hours are not convenient*

_____ *other* _____

14) How did you learn of FIRE?

_____ *exploring the short wave band*

_____ *somebody recommended it*

_____ *read an article*

_____ *other* _____

15) Why do you listen to FIRE? (You can check more than one.)

_____ *company* _____ *information*

_____ *entertainment* _____ *opinion*

_____ *personal advise*

_____ *because it's feminist*

_____ *because it's progressive*

_____ *because it has a Latin American perspective*

_____ *other*_____

16) Which programs do you prefer? (You may check more than one.)

_____ *interviews* _____ *musical selections*

_____ *news from different countries*

_____ *live transmissions*

_____ *other* _____

The questionnaire also included the following three open questions:

1. *How is FIRE like other programs; how is it different?*

2. *What do you do with the material (information, opinion, advice) that you receive from FIRE? Do you integrate it into your daily life? Explain.*

3. *Do you think it is important that women do radio; that is, produce, own, work with radio with a gender perspective? Explain.*

Responses

Sixty-four persons responded and sent back the questionnaire. This amounts to 51%, which is considered highly satisfactory. Generally, in this kind of study, a 30% response is considered good!

Responses came from Cuba, the USA, Spain, Mexico, Panama, Colombia, Denmark, Argentina, Angola, Japan, Finland, Ecuador, Guatemala, Uruguay, El Salvador, Perú, the United Kingdom, Italy, Germany, and Costa Rica.

Analysis of Listeners' Letters

Some of the most outstanding pieces analyzed by Valle include those quoted below.

I listened a first time, but now I want to listen to it more and more.
—Marcos Pastega, 25-year-old lawyer,
Italy, June 1991

I also thought that the programs about Nobel Peace Prize winner Rigoberta Menchú were interesting. I have been listening to you for a long time, and I like the human rights programs.
—Jorge Raúl Ocegueda, Mexico, November 1992

I think the programming is good. But what has amazed me is FIRE, because it is strange to find a shortwave program especially for women. I think it must be the only one at the present moment.
—Miguel Midonno, Argentina, 1992

The program caught my attention especially because of the updated topic and content about violence against women, abuse, and racism—shameful facts that must disappear so that women can achieve equality toward their ever more-recognized right to develop their capacities.
—Fabian Espino, student, Mexico, January 1993

If anyone wanted to really be informed about what was happening in Cairo [UN World Conference on Population and Development] there was no other more effective media than RFPI and its FIRE program, both in English and in Spanish... you were the eyes and ears of each of us who were not there.
—Jacqueline Espinoza, Panama, 1994

FIRE programs are better every day, and I feel your strong voices that make echoes in our hearts and minds, moving us to want to form part of the women's movement that works to change the world, and stop being simple observers and receptors of the transformations.
—Jacqueline Espinoza, Panama, 1994

...about your programs I have to say that although they are addressed mainly to females, I think that the issues dealt with are relevant to all of the family, particularly the men who oftentimes are the ones responsible for most of the problems women have.
—Ramón Gonzalez Martinez, Cuba, 1994

I think your programming is spectacular. Women like you who defend our rights on a daily basis should be sitting on a throne.
—Aymara Santoya Reyes, planning specialist, Cuba

Your voices trespassed the walls of our homes, the offices, the schools, and the streets.
—María José Silveira, Portugal, writing
during the Beijing broadcasts

...what a joy to have tuned in to FIRE! Here I am, working with campesino women. Thanks for the work you do, because it nurtures our desire to continue living and working for a just society for women.
—María Elena, political organizer, Chiapas, Mexico, 1995

Focus Group

A focus group composed of feminists in Costa Rica who listen to FIRE also formed part of the study. Seven women, among them human rights activists, communicators, lawyers, and journalists, came together to talk with each other and with Norma Valle about different issues regarding their participation in FIRE, and why and how they listen to it. What they do with the information they get on FIRE was also a topic of the dialogue.

According to Valle's preliminary findings, all of the women stated that radio for them is "primarily information, in second place entertainment, and thirdly it is company."

About the characteristics of FIRE that make it different from other radio programs, Ana Duarte said, "FIRE is the first radio that I have found that is more spontaneous, richer, less formal."

Mitzi Stark said, "In FIRE I can listen to women's voices from all over the world."

About what they do with the information they gather from FIRE, the women stated that they use it in their lives. Ana Elena Obando said she uses it in her own training workshops; Ana Duarte said that she uses the information from FIRE for her articles in her human rights organization.

More Letters from Listeners

The complete results of the Reception Report Study by Norma Valle will be published by FIRE as a separate volume. Meanwhile, through reading some of the letters sent to us by listeners throughout the years, you can also assess the impact FIRE has had on our listening audience.

1991

This is my first time hearing your broadcast, and I fully support your view that violence against women must end. I believe that this type of program is long overdue and urge you to continue your broadcasts. It was informative, and addressed a critical issue sensitively but without sensationalism. Good program! I am a black African American woman and have been listening to shortwave radio as a hobby for about 15 years!

—Evelyn Hampton, Chicago, USA

I enjoyed listening to the program featuring the problem of women being used and abused sexually and being battered. I found the program to be very interesting and very informative. Even though the program I listened to was a women's magazine show, I think it was a topic that would have mass appeal, be it male or female listeners.

—Patrick Traver, Canada

I really liked the program. I think that it is very positive to recognize all the rights and values that women have. This is the first time I've heard FIRE, but be assured it will not be the last....

—Luis Angel Vargas, Panama

1992

I have decided to write to you after many months of thinking about it, or I should say, after many month of paying attention to your program, which I think is very informative and interesting! It is atypical in shortwave.

—Eduardo Moya, DXer, Portoviejo, Ecuador

[I] congratulate you for the tireless work you do in the promotion of the rights of women. I know that yours is a long struggle, but I am sure it will render success....

—Manuel Rodiguez Gonzales, Cuba

It is such a pleasure to know that such an honest, informed and sensitive broadcaster exists in this "modern" world. Many of the current international religious broadcasts are truly frightening....

—Steve Martin, California, USA

1993

I just wanted to convey that I admire FIRE very much and I listen as often as propagation in our waning Cycle 22 [type of radio receiver] allows and, of course, as time permits a working mother of two beautiful daughters! I still have the photograph that FIRE sent me of the staff and the business card, both of which are framed and continue to rest on my dresser as one of my most prized "QSLs!" As you are aware, I am an avid shortwave listener!

—Cathy Zylka, New York, USA

I listened to your program, and I have no words with which to express what I feel. I feel ashamed about how women's rights are savagely violated.

—Cesar Medina Sanpedro, Spain

I found your broadcast most interesting. I have been listening to the women's congress program with female guest speakers from all around the world, and I am very impressed with your unique program material.

—Paul Newton, Australia

1994

It is about time there was a radio program on the women's perspective. I made a tape of this program I heard for my wife. It was about women at the Global Forum in Rio de Janeiro.

—Dwayne Scurlock, Georgia, USA

My favorite program is FIRE, which I listen to regularly. It must be a tremendous job to put up a whole hour every day... thanks for doing such an excellent job.

—Grace Moulton, Florida, USA, in a letter to RFPI

My position regarding feminism is very positive. I myself feel the issues because I am a blind man, and because of it I also feel discrimination, prejudices, etc. But of course, throughout my life I have also felt great solidarity... please do a program about blind women in Latin America, because to be blind, and to be a woman... the difficulties are double!

—Joaquín Lagatixa, Portugal

I listen to your program all the time, and I am very interested in all the issues you raise in it, because you portray the problems women face in our continent, and also that we are not just waiting, but on the contrary, are struggling to find solutions!

—Savina Romero Gonzalez, Cuba

1995

Some time ago after the conference I heard about FIRE over the radio when an interview with its producers was broadcast. She told about FIRE's experience at the NGO Women's Conference trying to set up the FIRE-PLACE in Beijing. At the same time the regular broadcast frequency was given as 7.385 on the 41 band. Could you please let me know the time you broadcast and if this frequency is correct. I live in California. I was so impressed with the work you are doing and hope to be able to locate you at last on the shortwave. Looking forward to hearing from you.

—Alice Kawash

1996

...it was good to hear Bella Abzug sounding so enthusiastic and positive. She has always been one of my favorites, her and Barbara Jordan. I think it's that voice of hers. Anyway, I also liked your biography in the last Vista. *I am curious as to how you learned about FIRE and Radio for Peace and how you became part of FIRE's staff. Also, how possible would it be for me to get a copy of the horseback ecotour? I was also interested in the tapes about the women's tribunal. Are they available for purchase? Anyway, I look forward to hearing back from you soon. I will also be asking for some advice from you about how to do interviews and so forth at conferences. I have some opportunities coming up and would like to make the most of them.*

—Jean Parker, Colorado Cross Disabilities Coalition.

I have been faithfully listening to your shortwave station and have finally discovered your WWW page! I enjoy the Far Right Radio Review program. I also like Counterspin, Hightower's comments (wish his segment was longer), and Food Not Bombs. My wife likes the feminist programming (FIRE). My wife and I are expecting our first child in April. I am wondering if anyone from the La Leche League is interested in producing a program on breastfeeding on FIRE. It is really strange as to how much you get bombarded with formula company propaganda for just registering at the hospital! We hear you regularly very well on 7485 khz. Keep up the good work.

—Konrad and Sharon, Boca Raton, Florida, USA

Reception report: I have heard with excellent reception your broadcast of today. Time: 0100-0120 UTC. 7385 khz. SINPO: 54434. Date: 2/14/96. Program in English. Subject: campaign against proliferation of land mines on FIRE. Please acknowledge via e-mail.

—Guillermo A. Iacobucci

1997

I find FIRE to be very informative and interesting. Today's discussion on NAFTA and APEC was most enlightening.

—Nicholas Peter, New Jersey, USA

This evening we enjoyed FIRE with a commentary about breast cancer and nuclear waste, particularly important to me. My sister recently battled breast cancer and the nuclear power plant in the nearby town is being dismantled!

—John Cases, USA

I know that male domination of women and women's rights is an ongoing battle in the USA, but at least it is out in the open arena. Here in Asia, women equal property. Please direct some program at this, because you can be heard in Japan.

—Jason Glavy, Japan

1998

I find [FIRE programs] very instructive and educational for the millions of women in the world who live in oppressive conditions.... Enclosed is a poem by José Martí called "Girl from Guatemala" for you to read on the air.

—Anarda María García , Cuba

Cyberspace Broadcasting:

Broadcasting in cyberspace has been no different for FIRE in terms of listener response. Although these broadcasts started in the middle of 1998 and we thought it would take years to build a listenership, the fact is that FIRE has already received an outstanding number of letters from our cyberaudience! A Reception Study of these broadcasts might also show interesting trends about feminist radio in cyberspace! As in radio, the Internet is an intimate medium of communication.

Letters have come from India, Sweden, the USA, Canada, Costa Rica, Mexico, Guatemala, India, Ecuador, Nicaragua, the Philippines, and other countries around the world.

One of the most interesting e-mails that FIRE has received came from a female police officer in the USA:

I found your web site while I was looking for information on Costa Rican TV and newspapers... your mention on working to end violence against women on a global level was very compelling.

She then asked us to help her in a domestic violence case of a Tico living in the USA, by finding information about him in Costa Rica.

The radio program coordinator of Comunicación e Información de la Mujer (CIMAC) in Mexico, Loursed Barboza, wrote to say that she also wanted us to help her download the sound files from the FIRE web site.

Frieda Werden from WINGS did download and rebroadcast FIRE on the 8th of March, 1999, and she wrote to let FIRE know, "You are on the air right now!"

"This is just great!" said Genevieve Vaughan after listening to FIRE on the web.

Its just great to listen to FIRE in the Internet. Fantastic! You women have given us a gift toward the future: New ways of connecting among us.
—Dorothy Kidd

We are here in Oakland, California, and we've been listening to the web site, it's fabulous! Your work is amplifying 20-fold and is inspiring our work here. Thank you! Thank you!
—Lisa Rudaman, National Radio Project Women's Desk

It was a great pleasure for me to navigate your FIRE site and be able to experience the commitment that you have to justice... the content is so very interesting, and one feels like you take us to a radio booth. There is news in it that we hardly ever hear in the media in Costa Rica.

—Victor Zuñiga, computer programer, Costa Rica

Juan, a Chilean living in Sweden, wrote after he heard FIRE's Internet report, "The Pinochet Case Seen Through the Eyes of Women." He shared his own testimony about having been a prisoner in the Stadium in Chile during the dictatorship:

Really, I feel we will never finish knowing about the atrocities committed.... I am very happy to see there are so many people who can contribute with a grain of truth.... I was detained in Los Alamos, in London Street prison, and then the Stadium.

Netcasting seems to be mainly about networking! New audiences, new venues, and new fires seem to open toward the new millennium.

APPENDICES

The current state of the world is the result of a system that attributes no value to peace. It pays no heed to the preservation of national resources, or to the labor of the majority of its inhabitants, or to their unpaid work, not to mention their maintenance and care. This system cannot respond to values it refuses to recognize.
—Marilyn Waring, New Zealand, author of *If Women Counted.* Quoted in WEDO press release, Miami, Florida, USA, November 1991

APPENDIX I. JUNE 1992

United Nations Conference on Environment and Development (UNCED and Earth Summit): Rio de Janeiro, Brazil

The Action Agenda 21 that was adopted by UN member states at the Earth Summit included a section entitled, "Global Action for Women Towards Sustainable and Equitable Development of Agenda 21." This section was a treatment of the ways environmental issues affect women, and how women can affect environmental issues.

The section, together with other parts of the document that mention the role of women, is considered a major achievement by women themselves, in their effort to influence the Summit.

According to Bella Abzug of the International Policy Action Committee (IPAC)—a coalition that organized thousands of women to lobby the U.N. Summit:

When we went to monitor the first PrepCom toward the summit in August 1990 in New York, the first draft document did not even mention women once! Women's NGOs and women State delegates raised the issue that unless the concerns of women from a gender perspective be brought into the document, there would be trouble. We organized the November 1991 Women's Congress for a Healthy Planet to bring that perspective into the process so that, by the second PrepCom in March, women had organized a strong women's caucus that actively lobbied delegates of the Summit.

—FIRE, 1992

According to Anita Anand for Women's Feature Service:

The final document adopted by the United Nations recognizes the work of the UN Decade for Women, and the groundwork laid by the Forward Looking Strategies, which is the official document that was adopted after the Women's Decade. This enabled a framework in which gender intervention found its place, in policy and in practice. National machineries, grassroots organizations, academic and research institutes all together have enabled the success of the women's lobby... many lessons have been learned, and one is that for women to be active participants in development at all levels, they need to be mainstreamed into development.

APPENDIX II. JUNE 1993

United Nations Conference on
Human Rights: Vienna, Austria

The Vienna Declaration affirms that women's rights are human rights, and that violence against women must be eradicated. It clarifies the indivisibility and universality of human rights, and the predominance of rights over culture and religion. It also calls for the creation of a Special Rapporteur on Violence Against Women, a Special Protocol to the Convention on the Elimination of All Forms of Discrimination Against Women (CEDAW), the consideration and approval of a UN Declaration on Violence Against Women, and other measures regarding the rights of girl children and women's human rights education.

Vienna was a stepping stone toward mainstreaming women's rights. However, as at the Earth Summit in Rio de Janeiro, the events surrounding the conference showed invisible forces at play. Challenging these forces is a task that remains for us.

This conference had no land in between the Rights Place for Women and the Official Conference. Both were held in the United Nations Building, with one floor in between (the official conference was, of course, on top). But hierarchy from top down was not what separated both meetings; it was the security doors that had to be passed every day to be able to move from one forum to the other: Security doors—selective control of people—at a conference on human rights! "Security" was to decide who could sit in and listen, and who couldn't. "Security" was to decide when NGOs could come in and monitor the states, and when they could not.

Indeed, "security" was selective to protect only the official conference. A prime example was Emma Hilario. A Peruvian woman and one of the 33 testifiers at the Global Tribunal on Violations of Women's Human Rights, she came to give her testimony as a survivor of a death threat by the Shining Path terrorist organization in her country. A few hours later, while walking through the UN building where the Conference and NGO Forum were taking place, she was followed by members of the Shining Path. She was confronted with more oral death threats from seven terrorists present at the NGO Forum as we were taking her back to her hotel.

There was no security for her. The women who were with her had to get her safely out of the situation. Eventually, and as a result of pressure by the women, the Austrian authorities provided body guards for Emma. The UN kept their security police only at the entrance of the official meeting.

However, security officers did come down once to The Rights Place for Women: "We were told that the women have an illegal radio station installed here, and that is not allowed in the UN building," one of them said to a woman activist who was there at the time. The "illegal" radio was the mixing board, telephone, microphones, and interface with which Katerina Anfossi, Jeanne Carstensen, and I were broadcasting live on FIRE. They looked at it and decided nothing was illegal. But security had come to control the "legality" of NGO activities.

Also coming out of the 1993 UN conference in Vienna, the Feminist Video Collective produced a video entitled *Breaking Frontiers*. With the financial support of the International Cooperation office of the Netherlands Embassy in Costa Rica and UNIFEM, it focuses on the role that tribunals can play in the struggle for women's human rights.

Another production was a legal interpretation of the testimonies, produced by Roxana Arroyo, a Costa Rican feminist human rights lawyer. The video has been presented to the recently named Special Rapporteur on Violence Against Women and Human Rights Working Groups at the United Nations to help them reconceptualize human rights to include what happens to women during the course of their lives.

Appendix III. September 1993

Funding of Women's Networks Working Meeting, The Hague, Netherlands: "When Cinderella Designs Her Own Shoes"

A very broad venue for networking was expanded in Vienna. From September 17-19, 1993, 18 women from different international women's networks gathered in the Netherlands to share new criteria for instruments for evaluation of networks and to challenge the traditional criteria used by many funding agencies that have supported these networks' activities, but have had a hard time understanding and accepting what the networks and their dynamics are all about.

The following networks were present at the working meeting:

- Center for Human Rights and Legal Aid, Bangladesh
- Center for Population and Family Health, USA
- Center for Women's Global Leadership, USA
- CHANGE, the United Kingdom
- CLADEM, Argentina

- FIRE
- Flora Tristan, Perú
- ISIS, Philippines
- ISIS-WICCE, Switzerland
- Women Living Under Muslim Laws, Pakistan and France
- Women's Feature Service, India.
- Women's Global Network on Reproductive Rights, Holland

NOVIB, one of the funding agencies, responded to the need of these networks to share criteria. It financed the meeting convened by Women Living Under Muslim Laws because NOVIB, itself, has felt the urgency stemming from the women's networks they support, and has had to respond to it in their concept of establishing partnership relations.

Issues such as the nature of women's networks to facilitate linkages and make connections; to have fluid not-so-formal structures to collaborate and provide coordination of effort and solidarity; autonomy; the problems women have with language taken from business and war and applied to evaluation of our work, such as: *impact, product,* and *marketing projections* were discussed extensively. When time came to talk about partner relationships between donors and women's networks, someone raised the issue that too often donor agencies try to impose their own agendas on the women's groups they sponsor. Spontaneously, a Pakistani yelled:

Oh, I know. That has a name: The Cinderella Syndrome. You know— Whose shoe will fit on my foot?!

Under the title, "When Cinderella Designs Her Own Shoes", I reported the following on FIRE, after having played some of the participants' voices:

NARRATOR: As a participant at the workshop, I want to leave you listeners with some food for thought about some facts of life. Evaluators can also take them if they want—if they want to interact with some level of parity upon relating to women's networks, I mean. Here they are...

Control: *Music*

NARRATOR: "Accountability of time" cannot be the measure of evaluation. When it comes to women, if you go by time spent, you measure the precision of your watch—just that. And you might also find out that clocks were not made for and by women to keep our time. If they did, instead of 12 numbers, they would probably have twenty, and a day's time, instead of 24 hours, would probably have at least 35. We would be the queens of universal nonstandard time!

Control: Music

NARRATOR: FEEDBACK cannot be the measure of IMPACT. What feedback many times measures, when it comes to women's networks, is the BACKLASH women get when we organize and act on our own behalf. OUTREACH is what we want, and it too often does not act like a boomerang coming back, but rather takes the form of ripples, like pebbles on a pond. The more the ripples grow, the more they move away, making it impossible to trace them back to the source. And then many pebbles on a pond, creating many ripples on the water, all of a sudden become a moving turmoil that shakes everything around. And when evaluators see that, they say its an expression of the impact, and they want to stop it, analyze its parts, trace it back... when precisely what characterizes it is its movement, and that it cannot be traced back to any particular origin because it is the whole that makes it shake everything around. Let yourself be moved by it... that different tide is what we might need in life!

Control: Music

NARRATOR: IMPACT has its own road that no one controls, and we belong to networks, precisely because we don't want to control or be controlled.

Control: Music

NARRATOR: STRATEGIES might not be the word for what we do and why. I can tell you that what I think women do in networks is ACT with INTENT. It stems from needs that we have and actions that we have identified to move toward the fulfillment of those needs in life. Who has time to try to understand that? To evaluate might then be to give women back their own value.

Control: Music

NARRATOR: AND women do have a political agenda that is ours by right. Who's willing to share its viability. That's what "partners" would be all about!

Control: Music

NARRATOR: CINDERELLA has walked barefoot for 5,000 years, and, indeed, she wants to skip the accountability of time, because if she doesn't, at 12 o'clock she's turned into a pumpkin. Nothing against pumpkins, it's just that what women want is to be taken into account for what we are. Cinderella also wants to wear a shoe. One that she designs and builds to fit her needs in life. She wants to trace her path with instruments for a better life.

Control: Sound effects of steps

NARRATOR: WARNING—Cinderella's path will take you through a road not yet traced by history. Her story is different, so she traces a different path. Are you willing to come? If so, please take your old shoes off. Walk barefoot for a while. You might begin to understand.

Appendix IV. October 1993

Sixth Encuentro of Latin American and Caribbean Feminists: San Salvador, El Salvador

Three weeks before the encuentro, the Central American Organizing Committee received anonymous threats stating that if the encuentro took place in El Salvador as planned, actions would be taken against the organizer and the hotels where the event was to be held. The message was clear to all. History, and recent facts in that country, spoke of more than 75,000 dead, most of whom had received such threats before they were killed. The international women's movement, human rights organizations, and feminists throughout the world undertook a global solidarity campaign demanding that the Salvadoran government guarantee the right of assembly under secure conditions, and demanding respect of all human rights.

FIRE undertook a special campaign through an urgent action to stop political persecution of feminists, sent through WOMANET at the Women's International Tribune Center. In less that six days we had received 14 letters of support from women in all parts of the world:

- Central American Human Rights Commission, Costa Rica
- Center for Human Rights and Legal Aid in Pakistan

- Collective of Solidarity with Mothers and Abducted Children, France
- Feminist Collective, France
- Flora Tristan, Perú
- International Lesbian Information Center, Denmark
- Latin American Institute for Alternative Legal Services from Latin America
- North South Institute, Canada
- Professional Women Workers Union
- Tree Mom, Holland
- Tribune Center in New York
- Young Women Christian Association in Switzerland
- Women Living Under Muslim Laws
- Voils Secours Violence-Help, Switzerland

The broad campaign of hundreds of letters of support did not stop repressive actions in El Salvador, however. The first 60 feminists who arrived "en mass" by air on October 29, a day before the encuentro, had their passports with their Salvadoran visas illegally "retained" by immigration officials. From 4:00 p.m. until 8:00 p.m., the feminists waited at the airport. Officers told them their names had to be "verified on a special list to determine whether or not they could enter the country."

At 8p.m. all the women in the airport were allowed to attend the encuentro. Four women from Cuba, however, had not even boarded their plane in Mexico because the Salvadoran Embassy there refused to give them visas despite a campaign that had been undertaken on their behalf. This was strongly denounced at the encuentro, both at the Tribunal on Violations of Women's Human Rights, and in a special activity of solidarity with the people of Cuba.

Against this background, the encuentro began on Sunday, October 30, in one of the biggest hotels on an isolated beach 60 kilometers from the capital city. Every day from 9a.m. until 11p.m. the encuentro was patrolled by the blue helmets of the United Nations.

At the tribunal held at the conference, Sara Lovera of Mexico denounced the retention of the documents of 65 feminists who arrived at the El Salvador International Airport to attend the Sixth Feminist Conference, calling it an "act of political repression... with the intention of inhibiting our free expression and participation."

Appendix V. September 1994

International Conference on Population and Development: Cairo, Egypt

W omen won a great deal in Cairo, including stonewalling the Vatican and other fundamentalist forces. The Program for Action approved by consensus reflects a new philosophy and contains action proposals that go far beyond family planning as a demographic fix. Human rights, the participation of women, broad definitions of reproductive and sexual health, and the need for education, equality and empowerment of women are now official goals and not just proposals of the Women's Caucus.

The relationship between the environment, lack of development and power, and unsustainable patterns of production and consumption of countries of the North and of the Southern elites was finally acknowledged. The conference also recognized that:

> ...*human beings are at the center of sustainable development and that the right to development is a universal and inalienable right, and an integral part of fundamental human rights...*

It also acknowledged the following principle:

Advancing gender equality and equity and the empowerment of women, and the elimination of all kinds of violence against women, and ensuring women's ability to control their own fertility are cornerstones of population and development-related programs.

Nancy Vargas and I also announced in Cairo that the vast majority of states had reached consensus on paragraph 825 in the Final Action Plan, agreeing on language that recognizes abortion as a women's health issue, with the statement, "This shows that women have been very effective."

I later wrote the following observation about the significance of women's activities in Cairo in the international struggle for women's development and rights:

In the history of the feminist and women's movements, "Cairo," our shorthand for the ICPD (International Conference on Population and Development), has become a shining example of the organized action of women in one of the most controversial UN conferences, in terms of the subjects under debate and the forces in dispute, ever held. Our success is undeniable. Today's feminist movement was somehow able to suffuse the Program of Action for the next 20 years with a women's reproductive rights and sexual and reproductive health perspective. The philosophy of the Program for Action approved by the ICPD broke with the traditional view of women as mere instruments for reducing fertility. It enables women to claim their rights and full participation in society.

The Program for Action stipulates that its recommendations are to be adopted in accordance with national legislation but this obstacle is not new. As always, it is up to us to ensure that States undertake its implementation, independent of whether they signed with reservations or without. These are international guidelines. And that is why these issues must be taken up in Mar del Plata (Argentina) on the way to Beijing (the site of the last Preparatory Committee meeting of Latin America and the Caribbean).

The Latin American and Caribbean Women's Health Network has proposed a resolution to link Cairo and Beijing by requiring governments and international organizations attending the FWCW to report on implementation of ICPD accords. The network also proposes broadening these agreements to include recognition of sexual rights, which were not approved in the ICPD program.

Cairo was a triumph for women, but it didn't cover everything. Discussions about the development paradigm were postponed for the U.N. World Conference on Social Development (in Copenhagen, Denmark, March 1995). Women's position in Cairo was that we cannot achieve self-determination without changing the conditions imposed by oppressive development models.

Globalization

Cairo was significant in other ways, as well. We became actors there at a critical juncture in contemporary history, at a time when the globalization of the world economy, of extreme political hegemony and of patrilineal ideologies joined forces against our interests and needs.

The feminist movement awoke to the effects of globalization a long time ago, when it decided to put itself on the global agenda at every opportunity. I don't know if it was political intuition or 20-20 vision, but we now know we cannot abandon the international arena to the routes outlined by the governments and the invisible powers (the International Monetary Fund, World Bank, fundamentalists, mainstream media, armed forces, Mafia, etc.) that do not sit at the United Nations.

Their collusion in globalization has put us in a situation where every shot fired against the people of Chiapas and their resistance to free trade agreements wounds us all; where every boat of Haitians sinking in the Caribbean, and every Haitian woman raped, shatters our hopes of peace and well-being; where the failure of any Cuban woman to obtain the comprehensive health care she is legally entitled to, put all of us under the blockade of our own energy in the fight for self-determination.

Parallel Is Not Enough.

Ten years ago in Nairobi, we learned to organize and act parallel to the official 1985 "Decade for Women" World Conference in an NGO Forum that definitely made an impact.

But when we view the "equality, development and peace" platform of Nairobi in today's context of globalization, we realize that, no matter how remote or focalized, nothing that occurs is without immediate repercussions for all of us.

Today, under the assault of patrilineal globalization, we have learned that we must be everywhere: In our own parallel forums and in their conferences (the governmental ones).

If we want to make an impact, we must make our presence felt in all spheres of power. Otherwise, governments forget about us. Their connections and global commitments to the World Bank and the IMF, to multinationals, to military and commercial powers, to fundamentalists and the rest, give them amnesia. "Out of Sight, Out of Mind," as the saying goes.

Feminist analyses since Nairobi have shown us that if we do not decide, as a movement, to be involved in all aspects of international politics, it will be our fate to drown with every Haitian raft, to be humiliated with every woman raped, to die from every bullet in Chiapas and to submit to every blockade.

Historically excluded from the United Nations, the feminist and women's movements resolved to gain access to power by attending meetings and putting themselves on the agenda in the international arenas where global issues are being discussed.

Since Nairobi, feminist and women's organizations from the South have broadened our presence in the places where international politics are discussed. We have also put our stamp on feminist agendas throughout the world. One of the ways to counteract globalization is by incorporating articulated diversity. That is why we Latin American and Caribbean women are involved in all these processes.

Our success at Cairo was influenced by women's experiences at the 1993 World Conference on Human Rights in Vienna, where we put an end to the forced disappearance of women from the international human rights agenda by affirming women's human rights and reconceptualizing existing rights by including violence against women.

Cairo also benefited from women's participation in Rio de Janeiro (at the 1992 UN Conference on Environment and Development, UNCED). Women there declared that our bodies are our first environment, from whence springs the gender perspective we bring with us to every other conference.

This brings us back to the ICPD, the most controversial conference in the history of the UN. In Cairo, women were the targets of much of the debate over control of reproduction and sexuality and the ways these are related to population and development.

In Cairo, women threw off the veils of Islam and María and revealed the importance of their leadership and the need to place women at the center of the agenda. The conclusion was that as long as women are denied the right to make decisions about their own bodies, we cannot begin to talk about development.

In none of these conferences were we offered a place on the agenda. Our presence in each and every one was achieved through day-to-day community, local, national and regional organizing, the result and extension of women's historical struggles.

Today these struggles are being waged in this new context of extreme globalization. Nairobi gave us the well-known slogan: "Think Globally, Act Locally." Our new experiences suggest a new slogan: "Think Diversity, Act Globally."

Building on the Past

...The worst thing we could do would be to view women's experiences in a strictly linear way. Cairo synthesized and updated the achievements of Nairobi and went on to surpass what Nairobi was able to accomplish at that time.

Cairo brought the agenda up-to-date in one area crucial to women: Our place as subjects of social policies that affect our reproductive and sexual rights and comprehensive health.

Our experiences have taught us that we must transform Beijing from a conference about women into a conference with a women's gender perspective that will make international organizations, states and civil society responsible for answering to the interests and needs of women.

In Mar del Plata, a woman attending our first panel discussion on these conferences summed up our position quite aptly: "In this world," she noted, "there are not only rights; there are also responsibilities." Although she might have meant something else, she is right. We are in the process of making governments responsible for what they have failed to do for women: Approve our rights, recognize our gender perspective and provide the necessary resources for our development.

—María Suárez, *Mujeres en Acción*, ISIS, Chile, 1995

468

Appendix VI. March 1995

UN Conference on Social Development
(Social Summit): Copenhagen, Denmark

Heavy debates—especially in reference to the relation between social development and economic growth—characterized the final Preparatory Committee meeting held in August 1994 in New York, USA. After the first week of debates, the new text presented at the official meeting had no reference to international instruments, did not accurately reflect the role of women in social development, and did not address the effects of globalization of world markets and trade liberalization.

Indignation was felt among NGOs, especially women's NGOs. The Women's Caucus at that point presented a revised document toward the Summit, which contained our main views about the issues at stake.

In relation to poverty, it stated the following:

We affirm that poverty eradication requires the provision of social and economic security, ensuring that women throughout their life cycle have access to basic needs and services, including productive services, and that labor practices which discriminate against women are removed.

To achieve poverty eradication, governments must: Reconstruct an economic system to eliminate inequities inherent in the global market economy now supported by international financial institutions and trade agreements; ensure the participation of individuals and community-based organizations, particularly women's groups, in the analysis, design, implementation and evaluation of policies and programs; make changes in the financial system and legal structure and overall economic environment to increase access to financial services by low-income women entrepreneurs and producers. The indicators must also include sexual and reproductive rights to guarantee women's full social participation.

In the area of productive employment and the reduction of unemployment, the Women's Caucus stated that it strongly objects to the deletion of key issues from the original draft Program of Action, and reiterated our position as follows:

...reconstruct an economic system which eliminates joblessness, underemployment, poverty, forced labor and gender bias. Reconceptualize productive employment in terms of its social usefulness, safety, adequate remuneration and non-exploitative nature, recognizing both wage and self-employment. Reaffirm and recognize the broader concept of work that affirms women's work, paid and unpaid, in the community, the informal economy, and the domestic sphere. Enforce the International Code of Conduct and international standards to protect workers' security, safety, well-being, and right to organize. Redirect financial resources to low-income women entrepreneurs and producers through women-managed, women-centered institutions in order to generate employment and contribute to poverty reduction. Reduce military spending and convert jobs held by those in the military-dependent industries to employment that will create jobs in essential industries to improve the quality of life. Recognize that the alleviation of youth unemployment requires special gender-sensitive attention to the transition of young women and men from school to living wage work, year-round youth employment programs, educational upgrading, training, job placement, and apprenticeships.

On the topic of social integration, the Women's Caucus document stated:

> ...*social integration is social participation. Political, social and economic participation in society belongs to all individuals, communities, races and ethnicities by right....*

> ...*social integration promotes and protects human rights and creates the social and economic conditions which make it possible to act upon these rights.*

Following is a list of other important points contained in the document:

- States are called to sign and ratify the document, without reservation; to enforce CEDAW and the Covenant of Economic, Social and Cultural Rights; and to enact legislation to promote and protect women's human rights, particularly the eradication of violence against women of all ages: Children, adolescents, and adults.

- "...women's full realization in social participation relies on the integration of sexual and reproductive rights into the social-economic development process." Policies must be developed to combat the traditional inferior status of girls and women, and to educate society on the benefits of improvement of that status.

- Human security means "access to well-being, which is sustainable social and economic development without discrimination based on gender, age, race, class, ethnicity, sexual orientation, religion or other social and political factors."

- Military budgets must be reduced—a minimum of three percent annual reduction in military spending over the next decade to be directed toward the creation of "nationwide community-based trust funds to finance more community enterprises, especially women's initiatives, which have sustained rural communities."

- Power and responsibility must be transferred to people at the community level "so that they have decision-making authority over the distribution of resources." Accountability, transparency, participation, and equity should be established as guide mechanisms to secure monitoring, evaluation and accountability for what is done and not done.

- International financial institutions must be held accountable. "It is essential that the Bretton Woods Institutions are accountable to the United Nations and to the communities they impact." There should be a 50 percent representation of women in all accountability processes. "A new development paradigm must focus on the primacy of people and their environment," recognizing that "women have the strongest stake in this paradigm," and thus, they must have a central role in the analysis, design, implementation, and evaluation of policies and programs.

- The chapter entitled "An Enabling Environment" states that the official document:

    ...must recognize that "globalization" of the world markets and trade liberalization have taken place within economic structures that have allowed the accumulation and concentration of wealth in transnational corporations and social elites; as a result, poverty has increased and deprivation has fallen most heavily on women, children, and the elderly.

- There should be redistribution of power and resources among nations, within nations, between women and men, and among all social sectors; establishment of mechanisms to hold corporations responsible and accountable to an International Code of Conduct; reinforcement of international human rights and ILO Conventions, particularly those protecting the work of women and children from economic exploitation; focus on debt reduction and cancellation and the establishment of mechanisms to support the work of women and the interests of the least developed nations; and the use of social impact assessments to monitor the impact of the new trade agreements on people and social sectors.

- New policies and appropriate infrastructure must be created to reverse and mitigate the adverse social and environmental effects from current structural adjustment programs and trade policies. National governments and financial institutions must design macroeconomic policies explicitly in service of social goals and programs and refuse to subordinate the imperatives of social reproduction to those of economic production. A favorable political environment includes the establishment of transparent, participatory, and accountable structures nationally and internationally for the development of social policies, and women should have 50 percent representation in those structures. Such a political environment would also guarantee gender-based analysis of all institutions, policies, and practices. It would strengthen and streamline the UN's role in linking political, economic, and social factors for sustainable development, expand the role of UNIFEM, and ensure that the Bretton Woods Institutions are accountable to the UN in its coordination of sustainable human development.

- In relation to the implementation of the Program of Action that would come out of the Social Summit, the Women's Caucus stated:

> ..all government policy should give specific attention to the impact on women and recognize the central role that women play in social and economic development. It calls for the adoption of national strategies with specific actions and deadlines by national governments for achieving key commitments in international agreements related to social policies. The strategy should be developed in full consultation with NGOs and civil society and monitored by an independent national commission that should report annually to national government and an international commission that monitors the Summit outcomes. Terms of trade should be fair, democratically negotiated and not harmful to the social development of communities and nations.

- Bretton Woods Institutions and emerging World Trade Organizations should report and be accountable to the UN bodies responsible for the overall economic, social, and cultural policy, in partnership with civil society. The objective of this change is to ensure that economic policy and its implementation serve global sustainable social development objectives. Twenty percent of allocations of national budget and 20 percent of the international cooperation should be assigned to social development, and these percentages should escalate to 60 percent by the year 2000.
- There should be active promotion of the role of women and advancement of the status of women in participation in decision-making, and the recognition and promotion of the inherent rights

of indigenous peoples for self-determination with their full and effective participation ensured.

One of the critical issues of the conference was a proposal that called on the World Bank and the International Monetary Fund to become accountable to the United Nations system. As of now the Bretton Woods Institutions, created in 1944, are "specialized agencies" within the United Nations. Both institutions negotiated their "independence" from the UN system in 1947, even though the delegates of Norway, the then-Soviet Union, and Venezuela stated that the agreements violated some articles of the UN Charter.

Today, these institutions have decision-making power about macroeconomic policies that goes beyond the functions that specialized agencies should have. In principle, it is the Social Economic Council of the UN that should make global recommendations to be decided by the General Assembly.

A Women's Caucus Letter drafted on February 15, 1995, just before the Copenhagen Summit, outlined some of our critical issues:

We support a call for measuring and valuing unwaged work and reflecting this in national accounting systems such as in satellite accounts of the Gross National Product. We also support "equal remuneration for men and women for work of equal value" along with the core labor standards of the ILO (International Labor Organization) conventions. We support the definition of terms related to reproductive and sexual health care and services and the family in its various forms as agreed to in the ICPD. We support the priority of universal human rights and international obligations over national or cultural sovereignty; ratification of human rights instruments; economic, social and cultural rights; rights to self-government, territorial integrity and freedom from coercion; right to development as a human right and integral part of fundamental human rights; rights of refugees, migrants and their families. We support people-centered sustainable development and are very concerned with contradictory references to "sustained economic growth."

At minimum, compromise language should be used which links "sustained economic growth" to Agenda 21 or the broader concept of sustainable development "*in the context of sustainable development*" *as formulated at ICPD. We support the reduction or cancellation of "all types of debt" including multilateral debt (owed to the international financial institutions). Unfortunately, our position to review and redesign structural adjustment policies and develop new economic policies and programs that are socially responsible and nondiscriminatory was not adopted. Within the constraints of the bracketed language. We support the language, "ensuring that structural adjustment programs are so designed as to minimize the negative impact of structural adjustment and economic transformation" and call for the deletion of paragraph 11b calling for "an enabling environment that attracts foreign and domestic direct investment, encourages savings, induces the return of flight capital and promotes the full participation by the private sector, including nongovernmental organizations, in the growth and development process. We support steps toward establishing coordination and accountability between the Bretton Woods Institutions and the United Nations. We support all calls for "new and additional resources" including international taxation. We support the 20-20 concept for "countries to give higher priority to basic social services by allocating, at least, 20 percent of ODA and 20 percent of national budget, respectively, to priority social programs. We support the language on "conversion of defense industries."*

The Southern-based women's network DAWN issued a comprehensive statement at the Summit:

DAWN welcomes the opportunity provided by the Summit to put forward its vision and recommendation for the construction of new models of social advancement which are equitable, participatory, holistic, and sustainable; processes which respond to the basic principles of human rights, and accommodate and give wider representation to a broad spectrum of social formations... DAWN firmly believes that the eradication of poverty and unemployment, or assuring social integration, cannot be achieved without a fundamental shift in the thinking and direction of the global political economy and its management. The Summit should be able to pave the way for a new development paradigm which focuses on the primacy of peoples and which corrects imbalances in the allocation of power and resources to different social groups.... An agenda for more equitable gender and social relations requires eradicating the power structures that maintain women's subordination in all social spheres—personal, cultural, familial, economic, social and political—that maintain discriminatory institutions and practices and justify inequality in terms of social and economic resources. It also means recognizing that such domination is the means of appropriating women's personhood, sexuality, work and services in the domestic, market and public spheres, maintaining an unequal burden of labor and responsibility in our societies. The Summit is to ensure that all forms of discrimination against women are eradicated and that governments commit themselves to achieving this in the shortest term.

DAWN's proposals called for the following:

A program of debt alleviation, which includes cancellation of the foreign debt repayments from the most affected countries—particularly multilateral debt in Africa—and restructuring and rescheduling in other poverty-stricken countries on the condition that resources are directed at eradicating poverty and to promoting social reconstruction; an international Code of Financial Conduct, restructuring conditions under which countries receive financial aid, which should ensure a redistribution of the cost of adjustments away from the poor and vulnerable to other sectors of society; a special fund for targeted poverty alleviation programs with low-interest loans for the poorest countries; a strong and global commitment for demilitarization, including a ban on the sales of weapons to global hot spots; diversion of a minimum of three percent annually from military spending to human development investment; an emergency fund to protect low-income countries from negative terms of trade or other stocks; a global gender-equity social development fund financed by taxing international speculative financial flows; removal of barriers to resource flows to small producers, especially low-income, self-employed women; increased investment in support of social capital formation; a comprehensive plan of land reform which ensures the equitable distribution of good land; a code of conduct for national, multinational, and transnational corporations to ensure social responsibility and the protection of workers' rights; a reorganized UN system, which brings in the Bretton Woods Institutions, aiming at increased effectiveness and accountability in fostering social equity and human development.

Among the special ongoing activities of the 180-Day Global Campaign to support positive change in women's lives was The DAWN Campaign Against Poverty, which had the following goals:

...to broaden and deepen the issues of poverty and human rights by linking them together, to make visible the catastrophic impact of economic fascism in the lives of women and the poor; to galvanize and reshape world opinion so as to establish as a non-negotiable ethic the fundamental human right of all people not to have their lives traded for profits; and to enable the building of solidarity among women and the poor so they can know they do not suffer in isolation or silence.

Another document coming out of the 180-Day Global Campaign was the Pledge To Gender Justice. This pledge was drafted by a working group of nongovernmental organizations in preparation for the Linkage Caucus to be convened at the Preparatory Committee meeting for the Fourth World Conference on Women, from March 15 to April 4, 1995. However, it was actually launched in Copenhagen on March 8, 1995. It stated:

To achieve full equality, citizenship, and human rights for women and sustainable development in the world, governments and the United Nations must not only adopt the Platform for Action, an Agenda for Equality, but commit to implementing and enforcing their agreements....

In Nairobi, women outlined a comprehensive plan of Forward-Looking Strategies for the Advancement of Women to the Year 2000. In Rio, women were recognized as managers of natural resources and the moving force for sustainable development. In Vienna, women's rights were acknowledged as universal, inalienable, and indivisible human rights. In Cairo, women's health, empowerment, and reproductive rights were placed at the center of population-related development policies. In Copenhagen, the political, economic, and social empowerment of women were recognized as key to eradicating poverty, unemployment, and social disintegration. But too many of these promises remain unfulfilled.

The pledge outlines commitments for the creating of mechanisms of accountability, allocation of resources, and reinforcement of commitments. It also delineates commitments by governments to meet with women to determine national plans regarding women's needs and commitments unto which they have signed in previous conferences. It also states commitments that the UN should make, among which are gender balance in positions at the UN, integration of a gender perspective into all programs, and strengthening of UN institutions that have as a mandate the empowerment of women. In the pledge, civil society commits itself to inform and mobilize, and to monitor and hold the UN and member states accountable for their commitments and to periodically review and submit progress reports to the appropriate bodies.

Earlier during the 180-Day Global Campaign, WEDO announced the following examples of actions planned all around the world for September 6 to mark the end of the 180-Day Campaign:

- *Bangladesh*—Rally for Women's Empowerment and Equality in Dhaka. Ishrat Shamim, Center for Women and Children Studies.

- *Canada*—Tent city: 24-hour Women's Tent City in Toronto on the grounds of the Ontario Legislature Building, organized by the National Action Committee on the Status of Women, Southern Ontario Region.

  Celebration in Halifax with guest speakers and performances, music by Raging Grannies, and water ceremonies. During this event, messages from Nova Scotia delegates would be sent to the Beijing conference.

- *Cameroon*—In Yaounde, Media and Community Teach-In on the conference and campaign results.

- *China*—Morning rally and celebration to launch the many actions and events of the day and to mark the culmination of the 180-Day Campaign. Thousands of women and men gathered at the

Kuumba Stage in Huairou for a morning celebration. Emphasizing respect for the diversity of *all* women, and the need for action and commitment at the conference in Beijing, activists wore ribbons and buttons calling on governments and civil society to commit to all of our Earth's daughters.

Speakers and performers included the following: Bella Abzug, WEDO (USA); Afifa Dirani Arsanios, Sisterhood Is Global Institute (Lebanon); Raimunda Gómez da Silva (Brazil); Douvaouissa Aissa Hanadi, LEWCE (Cameroon); Mangala Kiranjit, Nepal National 180-Days Committee; Wangari Maathai, Greenbelt Movement (Kenya); Chief Bisi Ogunleye, COWAN/NARWA (Nigeria); Vidya Rao (India); Sunera Thobani, NAC (Canada); and Sweet Honey in the Rock (USA).

Activities in China also included Girls' Day at the official conference in Beijing. This day of panels, forums, and activities had been coordinated by UNICEF (Misrak Elias/Sree Guruaja, UNICEF Day of Solidarity for Filipina "Comfort Women," with demands to end rape in war and military sexual slavery).

- *Colombia*—March for Women's Equality to give voice to women's struggles in Colombia and to unite with women around the world (Sara Gómez Acevedo, Fundación Diálogo Mujer/Camino a Beijing).

- *El Salvador*—Meeting of indigenous and peasant women and men in Sonsonate to discuss the rights of women, including implications of the FWCW for local issues.

- *Ghana*—Women's Rights and Sustainable Development forum and panel discussion in Accra.

- *India*—Festival of Women's Videos in New Delhi, highlighting key issues of the conference: Women's economic empowerment and political participation and rights.

- *Nepal*—Rally for Women's Rights and Peace March in Janakpur; also an "appreciation of girls" ceremony and a fast for those in poverty.

- *The Netherlands*—Flowers & Postcards Action, in Amstelveen. Women would deliver flowers to heads of women's organizations, while others would distribute postcards in shopping centers and other public places asking women to send postcards to their friends with the slogan, "People of All Nations, Please Be Wise, Look at the World Through Women's Eyes."

- *United States of America*—Call for Economic Justice. Leaders of major U.S. women's organizations hold a press briefing in Washington, DC, on economic justice for women, and they request a meeting with President Clinton and Congressional leaders.

In addition to the preceding activities, women and men planned other actions for women's equality in countries of every region of the world, including Barbados, Egypt, Gabon, Israel, Italy, Jamaica, Kenya, Norway, South Africa, and Uruguay.

Meanwhile at the NGO Forum, a very heated process of debate, conflict, and final negotiation had to be undertaken by women in the face of an alternative NGO Declaration drafted and announced by some NGOs at the forum on March 10, 1995.

Women were not the only ones who expressed differences with the declaration that had already been distributed and signed by some 370 NGOs. Some NGOs accused the NGO drafting committee of supporting commitments of some NGOs in earlier processes, and not representing the NGOs present at Copenhagen. Others stated that the declaration was even more conservative than the one that was being discussed at the official summit, and women complained that it had no gender perspective.

At an NGO press conference held on March 10, many women journalists complained that the original document did not include a gender perspective. Representing FIRE, I asked the NGO press conference conveners to give the floor to Peggy Antrobus from DAWN, a women's representative who was not sitting at the table of presenters who were all men, except for one woman. Peggy explained that the second draft was weak, but through a process of negotiation and hard work by the women, the final version was:

...very much improved, at least in regards to women, as it has a whole section on households and recognizes the relationship between gender and development.

Women were finally able to incorporate gender language into the alternative document, as demonstrated by the following excerpt from the declaration:

We expected that the Social Summit would address the structural causes of poverty, unemployment, and social disintegration, as well as environmental degradation, and would place people at the center of the development process. These include not only economic, political, and social causes, but also the cultural structures of gender inequity....

Conflict also rose out of women's request for a chapter of recommendations and demands that dealt with the household level, not only with national and international concerns. These issues finally made it into the declaration in the following statement of recommendations:

AT THE HOUSEHOLD LEVEL: The new vision of development requires the transformation of gender relations, in which women are equal participants in the decision-making process; women and men must share responsibility for the care of children, the elderly, and people with disabilities; domestic violence in all its forms must not be tolerated; women must be guaranteed sexual and reproductive choice and health; and children's rights should be respected and enhanced.

The final summit declaration contains strategies to face some, but not all, of the most pressing social and economic calamities faced in the world today. It produced few significant new commitments to provide additional funds by rich countries, although the unilateral commitments by some governments were positively valued: Pakistan announced an $8 billion program aimed at social programs, Austria announced a $100 million dollar debt cancellation program, and France endorsed the "Tobin Tax"—a speculative transfer tax for development. The 20-20 formula remained as a voluntary choice for governments, although it has become an important international parameter to assess governments' commitments since it was adopted at the Cairo Conference on Population and Development.

The declaration, a 110-page document, contains 10 commitments regarding the core issues of the summit. It is more of a map for the creation of just societies on the planet: It calls for a clear commitment by the international community to eradicate absolute poverty; for social responsibility for economic programs, for the recognition of women's unremunerated work, and for the imperative of people's empowerment in the designing and implementing of social development policies. One commitment calls for the promotion of full respect of human dignity and the achievement of equality between women and men. Another calls for an improved and strengthened framework for all levels of cooperation for social development.

Appendix VII. September 1995

UN Fourth World Conference on
Women (FWCW): Beijing, China

Regional PREPCOM:
Mar del Plata, Argentina

At the Regional Preparatory Committee Meeting for Latin America and the Caribbean in Mar del Plata, Argentina, women negotiated the section of the official draft entitled, "Acknowledging the Cultural Plurality in the Region" in order to have it recognize the following obstacles:

- The exclusion or marginalization of some groups of people in the decision-making process, based on cultural and ethnic factors, and the double marginalization of women in this respect.

- The exclusion of some people from overall participation in the political process, as well as from the social, political, and economic benefits of development.

At the same time the draft document recognized achievements:

- The development of women's organizations that portray women's own culture and ethnicity and defend their rights to participation.

- Broader space given to women's events worldwide—such as the Decade of Cultural Development, the Year of Indigenous Peoples, and the Social Development Summit—recognizing and strengthening the visibility of women's organizations.

- The beginning of recognition of the contribution of women to culture throughout history.

Following are some of the guidelines adopted in the official text:

- Promote cultural equity and respect of cultural diversity so as to stimulate visible and equitable participation of women and men of all ethnic and cultural groups at the regional and national level.

- Recognize and value cultural plurality of women, and satisfy their needs in relation to gender equity, respecting their cultural diversity and identity.

- Grant sexual education to women and men beginning at early ages to promote sensitivity and knowledge of human sexuality, gender equity, and cultural diversity.

- Give visibility to the negative impact that sexism, prevailing in structures and family relations, has on women.

- Favor a positive value of the integration of women in the public sphere, and of men in the private sphere.

- Motivate families, the educational system, and all social organizations that intervene in the construction and transmission of culture to assign equal value to cultural differences, and to respect gender equity in all forms of cultural expressions.

- Promote participation and initiatives of women in artistic and cultural expressions, particularly those that counteract violence against women.

- Stimulate the cultural arts of women, ensuring women's participation in the processes of creation and in contests, programs, and activities in the cultural domain.

- Promote participation of women in the decision-making levels of public institutions, national and intergovernmental, that regulate and finance cultural and artistic programs.

- Eliminate sexist expressions from language, and contribute to the creation of a discourse that expresses the reality of women.

- Revise all educational curricula and materials to eliminate discriminatory expressions, replacing them with others that respect gender equity and cultural diversity; promote training of teachers in that respect.

- Stimulate information networks among women and homologous organizations that promote gender issues by fomenting and supporting their initiatives toward cultural changes.

The following statement is from Chapter I of the draft, which deals with equality, democracy, and citizenship:

Racism as an ideological construct that sustains the domination of one sector of the population over another is one of the fundamental impediments to a sustainable development of nonwhite sectors in the Latin American and Caribbean population, which makes up the greater part of our continent.

...The full participation of women means eliminating the social, political, legal and cultural obstacles that obstruct the complete experience of citizenship and participation in it; nor must we forget the persistent colonialist, sexist and racist cultural practices in all our countries.

The proposals and recommendations from the Mar del Plata PREPCOM include a call to governments, nongovernmental organizations, and women's movements to "develop greater sensitivity toward black..." and other identities and calls for desegregation of ethnic data in health programs, vigilance about media's negative and discriminatory images (of black women and other identities), elimination of racist stereotypes in texts in schools, fluid integration of minority organizations in communications networks "to defend and affirm their members' cultural values, promote their instruction and interaction, consolidate the objectives and advance them in leadership roles."

The document also points out the violence provoked by racism, the way in which violence against women takes on particular characteristics due to racial considerations, and calls for studies and plans of action that will eradicate and prevent the specific violence suffered by women, including those who are black.

According to WEDO, the Platform for Action aproved 12 ctitical areas of concern, which are presented below.

1. Poverty

   Strategic Objective: To enable women to overcome poverty.

   Actions to be taken:

   • Gender-sensitive economic policies: Assess poverty and gender implications of macroeconomic policies, i.e. structural adjustment programs. Financial institutions should study their effect on the poor and develop gender-sensitive policies. Quantify and value women's unpaid work. Reflect those contributions in the Gross National Product.

   • Target policies and programs to poor women: Increase education, training, and health investments. Introduce women-friendly credit systems, promote self-help organizations, and assist households headed by females.

   • Help rural women overcome poverty: Provide rural women with access to land and other productive resources, and to credit and extension services.

   • Address the needs of migrant women workers and displaced women: Provide legal protection of their rights as workers.

2. Education

   Strategic Objective: To ensure women's access to quality education and training.

   Actions to be taken:

   • Achieve education for all: Remove gender disparities in education policies; provide education and training to all.

   • Bridge the gap in education between developing and developed countries: In the South, provide the same quality education and training as in the North.

   • Prevent girls from dropping out of formal education: Enable girls/young women to stay in school to the highest level.

- Prepare women for the 21st century: Encourage women and girls to enter new fields of study; broaden their career options and facilitate their re-entry into the labor market.

- Participatory decisionmaking: Elect more women to the boards and committees of schools and higher education authorities. Encourage and support research by and on women.

- Gender-sensitive education and research: Remove social stereotypes from curricula, textbooks, and teacher training programs.

3. Health

Strategic Objective: To increase women's full access to appropriate, affordable and quality health care.

Action to be taken:

- Deliver affordable and accessible health care for all: Adopt a comprehensive, integrated, and adequately funded health service model for women that emphasizes health promotion and disease prevention.

- Reproductive health and rights: Meet the target of reducing infant and maternal mortality by 50 percent. Bridge the gap in qualitative and quantitative care between developed and developing countries.

- Governments should provide adequate funding for reproductive health and family planning programs.

- Develop gender-sensitive programs to combat HIV/AIDS.

- Research: Encourage and support research on prevention, treatment, and health care systems related to diseases and conditions that have specific effects on women. Involve health workers in gender-sensitive research and training.

4. Violence Against Women

Strategic Objective: To eliminate violence against women.

Actions to be taken:

- Address the root causes of violence against women: Study and publicize links between gender-based violence and male power, privilege, and control, and their effects on relationships between men and women.

- Integrated eradication measures: Adopt national legislation in accordance with the Declaration on the Elimination of Violence Against Women.

- Train the judiciary, police and health professionals to enhance their sensitivity and ensure fair treatment of women who are targets of violence.

- Increase recruitment of women to the police forces and encourage women into the judiciary.

- Provide legal and social assistance. Adopt special measures to protect women in vulnerable situations.

- Stop sex trafficking and forced prostitution. Design special measures for medical and psychological care.

5. Effects of Armed Conflict

   Strategic Objective: To increase the participation of women in conflict resolution, and protect women in armed and other conflicts.

   Actions to be taken:
   - Bring more women into the peace process: Countries and the UN should aim for gender parity in peace negotiations and conflict resolution. Women should be involved in peacekeeping efforts in both civilian and military roles.

   - Recognize, reinforce and utilize women's roles and expertise as counselor, peacekeeper, educator, therapist, and caregiver in the society at large.

6. Economic Structures and Policies

   Strategic Objective: To promote women's economic self-reliance and control over economic resources.

   Actions to be taken:
   - Secure economic rights for women: Eliminate all laws and regulations that discriminate against women in economic activities.

   - Put in place employment programs that target women; guarantee loans for women entrepreneurs; and provide training in nontraditional areas of work.

- Give women access to resources, employment and appropriate working conditions, market and trade: Implement the principle of equal pay for work of equal value by the year 2000.

- Create a flexible supportive workplace: Create a work environment that allows women to participate in economic activities and that gives both women and men flexible time for family and economic responsibilities.

7. Inequality in Decisionmaking
   Strategic Objective: Strengthen factors that promote the full and active participation of women in power structures and decisionmaking.

   Actions to be taken:
   - Ensure the training of women to become decisionmakers.

   - Revise educational materials to reflect women's equality, rights, and actual contributions to decisionmaking.

   - Design training programs aimed at equipping women to participate in management and decisionmaking.

   - Establish leadership training structures at the community level.

   - Promote the sharing of decisionmaking in the family a the norm.

   - Provide equal access, participation and opportunity in all career sectors.

   - Pass laws that give women equal opportunity in the public and private sectors.

8. Gender Equality
   Strategic Objective: Integrate gender equity dimensions into policy, program planning and implementation.

   Actions to be taken:
   - Generate and disseminate gender-disaggregated data and information for planning and evaluation.

   - Increase the collection of gender-specific statistics and indicators and develop new indicators that show the gender dimension of policies and programs.

- Strengthen national machinery at the highest political level of governments, with adequate staff, resources, and financial autonomy, and establish links with other national machinery and with the UN system.

- Governments should develop tools for gender analysis and require government officials to apply these tools in developing policies and programs.

9. Women's Human Rights

Strategic Objective: Apply and enforce information norms and standards to safeguard full enjoyment of human rights by women.

Actions to be taken:

- Make international instruments effective: All human rights bodies should include the status of women and the human rights of women in their deliberations and findings, and use gender-specific data. The High Commissioner for Human Rights should monitor the extent to which human rights mechanisms identify violations and to which women are ensured their human rights.

- Improve cooperation between the Commission on the Status of Women and the Commission on Human Rights.

- Ratify human rights conventions, especially the Committee to End Discrimination Against Women (CEDAW) so universal ratification is achieved by the year 2000.

- Implement international norms and national practice: Enact laws and develop public policies in keeping with international conventions—including CEDAW—and the Declaration on the Elimination of Violence Against Women.

- Achieve legal literacy: Establish information campaigns and national training programs on women's rights under existing legal systems.

10. Media

Strategic Objective: Enhance the role of traditional and modern communications media to promote awareness of equality between women and men.

Actions to be Taken:

- Guarantee the access of women to information and participation in the media: Governments should guarantee the rights of all people to communicate, disseminate, and exchange information, and to ensure access by women to information and to the media on an equal basis with men.

- Support and encourage NGOs to develop information material based on national experience.

- Guarantee more balanced participation of women in government-owned media at the decisionmaking level.

- Eliminate gender stereotyping in the media: Encourage a more positive presentation of women in the mass media through studies, awareness campaigns and other forms of self-regulation by media institutions, including advertising associations.

- National machineries for women should promote measures toward a more positive image of women.

- Accurately portray the diverse and changing social and economic roles of women in society.

11. Environment

    Strategic Objective: Promote women's contribution to managing and safeguarding the environment.

    Actions to be taken:

    - Involve women in programs for sustainable development: Increase the proportion of women at the levels of decisionmaking, planning, technical management, and control of environmental degradation.

    - Eliminate constitutional and legal obstacles to women's full participation in sustainable development and public life by the year 2000.

    - Disseminate gender-relevant knowledge: Promote the enhanced value of women's roles though education.

    - Develop environmentally sound technology in consultation with women.

- Develop programs of consumer awareness to promote sustainable patterns of consumption, especially in industrialized countries.

12. Girl Child

Strategic Objective: Promote the survival, development, and protection of the girl child.

Actions to Be Taken:

- Eliminate all forms of discrimination against the girl child: Implement the UN Convention on the Rights of the Child.

- Eliminate negative cultural attitudes and practices against girls: Remove educational barriers and develop programs that enable girls to develop self-esteem. Promote positive images of girls and boys in the media.

- Eliminate discrimination against girls in education, skills development, and training: Ensure universal and equal access to primary, secondary, and higher education by the year 2005.

- Eliminate discrimination in health and nutrition: Design quality health-care programs for girls and training programs for health planners on girls' special needs.

- Eliminate the economic exploitation of child labor and protect young women at work: Define a minimum age for child employment and ensure adequate work conditions, social security, and continuous training and education.

- Eradicate violence against girls: Pass laws to protect girls and young women against all forms of violence.

PREPCOM III: New York, USA, March 1995

The last PREPCOM toward the Fourth World Conference on Women took place from March 15 to April 4, 1995, at the UN Headquarters in New York City, USA.

Tension about many issues became apparent very soon, as more than 400 NGOs who had requested UN accreditation for the official conference still had not received an answer. Catholics for Free Choice was one such organization, as well as some women's human rights, Tibetan refugee, and Taiwanese NGOs.

Many governments at the time—including the government of Costa Rica—were refusing to negotiate with the local women's movement to have NGO representation in their official delegations. Many funding agencies—USAID, among many others—were not meeting their commitments to fund women's representatives at the conference.

The tensions escalated when, just after the PREPCOM, the Chinese Organizing Committee announced a change of venue for the NGO Forum. In addition to the many obstacles they were facing at all levels, all of a sudden, women were not even sure they would be able to participate effectively at the Fourth World Conference on Women. The proposed venue was Huairou—about 40 miles away from the site of the official UN Women's Conference at Beijing.

The Draft Platform for Action itself left a lot to be desired. Most of the debates at the final PREPCOM were focused on defending gains made by women at previous UN conferences, such as those that referred to reproductive and sexual health and women's human rights. On the other hand, the issues about macroeconomic development paradigms ignored at the Social Development Summit were also absent from the Beijing Draft Platform for Action.

The road to China at that point was marked by many tough experiences. There were so many obstacles at once that women believed none was by chance. The story of how the global women's movement organized and developed strategies to deflect the counter-offensive against its gains will one day have to be systematized for the sake of history. Not all has been said, not all has been acknowledged, not all has been reckoned with, but the fact is that in the long run women made it to Beijing and back, and were able to influence the conference's agenda.

Another on-site visit to China had been undertaken by delegates of the Women's Human Rights Caucus for the Fourth World Conference on Women. Among them were Florence Butewa from WILDAF, Lourdes Sajour from the AWHRC, Charlotte Bunch from the CWGL, and Roxana Carillo from UNIFEM. They issued a report, and the CWGL recommended its acceptance on the venue.

The outcome of the struggles that arose at the New York PREPCOM came about only a few weeks before the NGO Forum and the conference in China. The Chinese Organizing Committee had to negotiate with the NGOs, and the UN had to get involved. The results of the negotiations were that the Chinese Organizing Committee and the Facilitating Committee agreed to hold the NGO Forum in Huairou, China, by then a "different site from the one we originally saw in Huairou last April" (IWTC, Global Faxnet #16).

The faxnet outlines the commitments agreed to, as reported by Irene Santiago, Executive Director of the NGO Forum:

> [There will also be] a satellite site in Beijing near the UN World Conference site... which will enable NGOs to be close to the UN site... [In addition to] the Beijing Recreational Center, which will be the base for accredited NGOs to lobby the World Conference. [There has been] an acceptance of all registered participants. All registered participants will be granted visas, facilities for all activities in Huairou, choices of hotels either in Beijing or Huairou, transportation and [provision of telephone lines] as many IDD lines as needed for the press and NGOs.

What would effectively happen in China was not clear, but as of this decision, women worldwide knew there would be an NGO Forum, and they knew where it would be. Many celebrated the achievements of the negotiations, and many remained concerned about the results, especially considering that there were no mechanisms agreed to concerning what would happen if the commitments were not met.

DAWN Strategy Meeting:
Barbados, May 1995

The change of venue was still a hot issue during the Barbados meeting in May 1995, where women from Africa, Asia, Latin America, and the Caribbean met to plan for Beijing. The DAWN Strategy Meeting that met between May 15 and 16 in Barbados had as its objectives to:

> ...assess preparations for the Fourth World Conference on Women and the NGO Forum as a whole, and specifically the results of PREPCOM III, and evaluate the state of the Draft Program for Action. It also aimed at formulating strategies toward mobilizing the women's

movement and its potential allies, lobbying governments and the UN system, and influencing media.

Also, according to DAWN:

...the meeting had been hastily arranged in the context of the disappointment and frustration experienced at PREPCOM III in New York over substantive and procedural issues in the preparations for the FWCW.

Participants were members of DAWN from countries throughout the South, and also some networks. Among them was FIRE, WEDO, CAFRA, IWTC, subregional focal points, and the Latin American Focal Point toward the World Conference and NGO Forum.

After the meeting, DAWN drafted strategies related to action—building, lobby work, focus on issues included in the Draft Platform and issues that were not in the draft platform, and media strategies, alliances, and actions. They also held a press conference at which women from the Southern countries spoke about the change of venue, and what they felt needed to be done. Panelists were Virginia Vargas, Coordinator of the Latin American and Caribbean NGOs, Bene Mandunagu from Nigeria, Devake Jane from India, and others. Peggy Antrobus, Secretary General of DAWN, spoke first.

All of these women are from countries of the G-77. The Fourth World Conference on Women is very important to women and people who have grown in organization, yet have experienced a deterioration in people's social and economic conditions, and a rise of fundamentalism. We want to secure our gains and move toward the next century. The international women's movement has intervened very successfully in the international conferences. Yet we have had to face increasing obstacles on the road to Beijing. The change of venue of the NGO Forum is an expression of the obstacles. It is unacceptable to many women and to the NGO Forum organizers who have requested the UN to intervene to look for an adequate site. We are asking the G-77 countries to support the request of the Facilitating Committee.

On May 10 the NGO Facilitating Committee voted to reject the Huairou site for the NGO Forum in Beijing. The committee wrote a letter to UN Secretary General, Mr. Boutrous Boutrous-Ghali requesting his intervention, thus taking responsibility to ensure that the NGO site is adequate, accessible, and in close proximity to the governmental conference, and that NGOs have substantial access to the governmental conference.

Following is the text of the NGO Forum Committee's letter to the UN Secretary-General:

Dear Mr. Boutrous Boutrous-Ghali:

On behalf of the NGO Forum on Women, I ask your support in our negotiations for an appropriate site in Beijing. As you are aware, the NGOs, as of this late date, have not agreed upon a site for their August-September Forum. A delegation from the NGO Forum went to Beijing from April 24 to 28, 1995 to visit possible sites.

The report has met with deep disappointment from the global community of women and the larger international community. There is distress and anger, and it is mounting.... The distance between the UN Conference and the NGO Forum will seriously compromise the concern stated in CSW Resolution 36/8, which "emphasizes the importance of close proximity between the Forum and the Fourth World Conference on Women." I may also point out that this is not an issue of NGO access to the UN Conference alone. It is a matter of the governments' access to the Forum as well, since the Forum has traditionally been the source of some of the most far-reaching and groundbreaking ideas on development...

Women have participated effectively in all of the past UN conferences and the regional preparatory meetings for the Fourth World Conference on Women. It is the interconnectedness and interdependence of the UN and NGO meetings that we must continue to support and reinforce. We acknowledge the role you and member states have played in helping to make this possible.

Mr. Secretary General, we know that your action on this matter will enable us to find a solution that meets the concerns of the UN, our Chinese hosts, and the global community of the NGOs.... We are prepared to work with you in true partnership... Indeed, how can we have a celebration if the UN Conference in Beijing serves to disenfranchise the representatives of half of humanity? With kind regards,

Sincerely yours,
Khunying Supatra Masdit, Convener

At the same time, the International Women's Tribune Center, the Latin American and Caribbean Focal Point, and other caucuses issued letters asking women around the world to write to the Secretary General in support of their efforts to negotiate the site and conditions for the NGO Forum. More than 2,000 faxes were delivered within five days. The response to calls for letters to the UN from around the world was overwhelming for the Secretary General. He finally decided to send a delegate to China to be in the negotiations between the Chinese Organizing Committee and the Facilitating Committee.

In the meantime, a group of Third-World women visited China upon invitation from the All-China Women's Federation. The delegation of the Third World Network to Beijing during the period of May 9–16, 1995, consisted of the following persons:

- Evelyne Hong, Third World Network, Penang, Malaysia
- Mr. Ooi Kim Aun, Third World Network, Consumer Association of Penang, Malaysia; fluent in Mandarin
- Vicky Tauli-Corpuz, Convener, Asian Indigenous Women's Network, Philippines
- Liza Largoza-Maza, Secretary General, Gabriela, Philippines
- Rose Mensah-Kutin, Third World Network, Ghana Dzodzi Tsikaba, ISODEC, Gender Unit, Third World Network, Ghana, Africa
- María Hamlin Zuniga, International People's Health Council, Nicaragua

The report of their visit follows:

During our stay we were able to discuss critical issues with high-level members of the All-China Women's Federation, the Chinese Society for Human Rights Studies, the State Family Planning Commission, the China Women Judges Association, the Huairou Scenic Area officials, and with the Dongzhimin Chinese Medical Hospital.... We met at great length with Madame Wang Shuxin, vice-president of the All-China Women's Federation—ACWF, vice-president of the Chinese People's Association for Peace and Disarmament, and Member of the Standing Committee of the Eighth People's Congress. We also conversed with Madame Huang Qizao, vice-chair of the Chinese Organizing Committee for the Fourth World Conference on Women and the Director of the NGO Forum Committee.

We expressed our concerns about the Fourth World Conference on Women and particularly about the NGO Forum site and accommodations, as well as the registration procedures. The discussion with Madame Wang clarified the following points:

1. The Chinese have been collaborating with the NGO Facilitating Committee in New York for two years.

2. China has the responsibility for provision of the venue site, as well as logistics and arrangements for the conference and receptions. Meeting rooms, exhibit areas, the press center, shopping areas, and snack bars are to be arranged by the hosts.

3. All participants must register with the Facilitating Committee in NY. In October 1994, the Facilitating Committee and the Chinese NGO Committee reached an agreement on 20,000 foreign guests and several thousand Chinese NGO representatives. There are other international conferences in China in September. This NGO Forum will be much larger than previous NGO Forums. However, the Chinese are willing to accommodate additional participants. They did not indicate how many. Hotel reservations: Many of the forms received by the hotel service in China do not provide adequate information. Madame Wang suggested that all persons make reservations in China and with the NY Facilitating Committee in order to avoid unsatisfactory situations. The original hotel reservation form was for Beijing city hotels only. A new form is being published to include the Huairou hotels and residence halls. (It was not available when we left May 16).

According to Madame Wang, the Chinese government has NO responsibility for the selection of the participants. That is the responsibility of the NY convener. Only the convener will send out confirmation of registration, and China will send out hotel confirmations. China will NOT apply censorship against groups and individuals. All types of groups are welcome to come to Beijing.... Our delegation visited the Huairou Scenic Tourist Area on Friday, May 12.

Last month the working group of the NGO Facilitating Committee made a visit to China. Lots of resource requirements were being made in the original center. The same have to be provided in the new area. Actually there are bigger spaces in the new area. Over 30 hotels and residential buildings exist in Huairou. One hotel will be the core of the forum. Kinders, nurseries, a business center, press center, and accreditation center are being prepared. In the Official Report by Madame Supatra Masdit, convener of the NGO Forum, she stated clearly the information related to the facilities in Huairou. Since the visit of the NY NGO Forum Delegation, construction and remodeling is taking place on a 24-hour basis. Sanitation and toilet facilities are being augmented as requested. Original arrangements for booths, exhibits, shopping centers, and direct-dial telephone services are being installed for NGO's and the press at this time.

Huairou is a key environmental protection area. The air and water are of good quality. A shortcoming is the distance from downtown Beijing. It is about 45 minutes by bus from the official conference site. The government will provide continual shuttle buses. Those NGOs with consultative status to participate in the official conference will be provided with a function hall near the official conference.

Another difficulty is the provision of facilities for disabled persons. We emphasized our concern and the importance of resolving this problem in a dignified manner. Our hosts assured us they would do everything possible to respond to this concern.

Our delegation concludes that the Huairou Scenic Tourist Site is adequate for the NGO Forum, especially given the fact that the forum will take place before the official conference, and there will be only three days of overlapping activities.

Our delegation is requesting that women use their energies to work together for the success of the NGO Forum and the Fourth World Conference on Women.

We request that the NY Facilitating Committee clarify to the women of the world the previous arrangements made with China in terms of responsibility for the selection and notification of participants, the number of participants that will be selected by the Facilitating Committee, and the scheduling of events for the NGO Forum.

The Chinese government, and in particular Chinese women, are working to provide visitors with the possibility of meeting in conditions that are adequate and will permit our discussions to take place without difficulties and according to the demands being made by the Facilitating Committee.

Sisters, let us organize ourselves around the important issues relating to the Official Document and the Plan of Action, to ensure the success of this important Fourth World Conference on Women.

Many discrepancies became evident throughout those months prior to the final negotiation and in the face of the decision of the Facilitating Committee to accept the venue after the Chinese Organizing Committee agreed to abide by some critical criteria. Some of the discrepancies remained. However, women were relieved to know that they finally had some sense of certainty about the fact that the Forum would take place, that there was a place for it to happen, and that the Chinese Organizing Committee had agreed to some basic criteria presented by the Facilitating Committee on behalf of women.

Women's Rights as Human Rights and the Fourth World Conference on Women

The United Nations Fourth World Conference on Women produced some positive results and achievements, but it also left some matters still to be resolved and overcome.

Among the positive results is one that has to do with the affirmation of the recognition that women's rights are human rights. This was not new, considering that the United Nations recognized that at the World

Conference held in Vienna in 1993. However, the fact remained that the Vatican and other fundamentalists wanted to backtrack from it by promoting a narrow definition of universality of human rights to include only those human rights that are already in the traditional international definitions of human rights.

Women's rights as human rights would have been watered down if the Vatican's position had been adopted. Women celebrated that this did not happen. However, doubt continues as to how the accords and resolutions reached at the Fourth World Conference will be implemented to positively impact women's day-to-day lives, and especially how they can be translated into compliance with human rights.

APPENDIX VIII.   MARCH 1996

*Commission on the Status of
Women: New York, USA*

The UN Committee on the Status of Women was preparing to meet in New York from March 11-22. Media was one of the issues to be discussed at the Beijing followup meeting, as described in the following article by the International Women's Tribune Center:

WHAT CAME OUT OF THE COMMISSION ON THE STATUS OF WOMEN?

Meeting for the first time since the Beijing meetings, the CSW held dialogues with three panels of experts on poverty, women and the media, and child and dependent care, including the sharing of responsibilities between men and women.

Women and the Media: The CSW reconfirmed the importance of free expression, and debated the need for women's full enjoyment of such expression, along with equal access to the media, balanced and diverse portrayals of women, and media information aimed at eliminating violence against women. It said that human rights instruments must be applied in a way which took into account the systemic nature of discrimination against women.

The CSW urged noncoercive self-regulation and voluntary guidelines to eliminate gender-biased programming and to encourage nonstereotypical gender images. It said that governments should raise awareness of the media's role in promoting nonstereotyped images of women and men and in eliminating violent images. Media professionals should be encouraged to exchange information on voluntary guidelines for a gender-balanced portrayal of women and men.

It also encouraged women's equal participation in management, programming, education, and training, including through affirmative action and equal opportunity policies, so as to achieve gender balance in the media. The CSW noted that NGOs play an important role in media education, research, consumer advocacy and monitoring. It encouraged media networks to commit to gender equality and urged governments to review existing media policies to integrate a gender perspective. It also called for the strengthening of women's role in global communications networks and a reduction of barriers to their involvement in global information technologies.

—IWTC, Global Faxnet

It must be noted that the Mexican delegation opposed the adoption of a clear recommendation for the adoption of an Optional Protocol to the Convention on the Elimination of All Forms of Discrimination Against Women. The Optional Protocol is considered by women to be one of the most important achievements of the FWCW and the Vienna Conference on Human Rights in 1993. It would give women the ability to present cases about discrimination and to hold governments accountable for the violations. The Optional Protocol was finally adopted by the United Nations in 1999.

Three topics formed part of the agenda of the CSW: Poverty, media, and shared responsibilities. The objective of the discussion was to draft resolutions of recommendations to the United Nations Economic and Social Council. The governments promoted backtracking in each one of these issues in relation to what is in the Platform for Action. The NGOs worked intensely to convince them to respect the commitments acquired in the Beijing Platform.

In the discussion about poverty, the controversial issue was the one related to resources for implementation of the Platform for Action. The

CSW arrived at the same recommendation that had already been reached: Provision of new and additional resources at all levels, national and international.

In regard to media, the controversial issue, again, was that of stereotypes that affect the image of women and the regulation of media vs. freedom of expression. The CSW arrived at an agreement that recommends self-regulating mechanisms.

On the topic of shared responsibilities, the most controversial issue was the part that governments play in promoting the excess burden that is carried by women. Also discussed was the responsibility of civil society. There was no backtracking from Beijing in this area either.

Glossary

ABANTU — Advice, Consulting, Information, Training, Institutional Development, Networking and Management for Sustainable Development

AC FIRE — Feminist Interactive Radio Communications Association; FIRE became a part of this legal nongovernmental organization, which was formed in Costa Rica in 1998.

ADEFRA — German Black Women's Network

AFP — French Press Agency

ALAI — Latin American Information Agency

AMARC — World Association of Community Broadcasting

APC — Association for Progressive Communications

APDC — Asian and Pacific Development Center

APEC — Asia Pacific Economic Forum

BBC — British Broadcasting Company

BOWAND — Belize Organization for Women and Development

CAFRA — Caribbean Feminist Research Association

CALANDRIA — Peruvian Women in Communication

CEDAW — Committee to End Discrimination Against Women

CEFEMINA — Feminist Center for Information and Action, Costa Rica

CEMINA — Center for Women's Projects, Brazil

CEPAL — Economic Commission of Latin America and the Caribbean

CEPIA — Citizens, Studies, Information and Action

CIM — Inter-American Committee for Women

CIMAC — Mexican Women's News Agency

CIMUJER — Women's Center for Legal Advocacy, El Salvador

CLADEM — Latin American Committee for Women's Rights

COC — Chinese Organizing Committee

CODEHUCA — Central American Human Rights Commission

CONAVIGUA — National Committee of Widows of Guatemala

CSW — Commission on the Status of Women

CUNY — City University of New York

DANIDA — Dutch International Cooperation Program

DAWN — Developing Alternatives with Women for a New Era

DHRE — The People's Decade of Human Rights Education

ECOSOC — United Nations Economic and Social Council

FALN — Puerto Rican Independence Movement Armed Forces for National Liberation

FEDIM — Federation of Cuban Women

Fempress — major Latin American and Caribbean magazine

FIRE — Feminist International Radio Endeavour

FLS — Forward Looking Strategies for the Advancement of Women to the Year 2000

FMLN — Farabundo Martí for the Liberation of El Salvador

FOJO — Swedish Institute for Further Education of Journalists

FRRR — Far Right Radio Review

FUSCAL — Costa Rican Foundation for the Promotion of People of Color

FWCW — United Nations Fourth World Conference on Women, Beijing, China, September 1995

FZLN — Zapatista Freedom Liberation Army

G-77 — Group of Third-World Countries and China

GYF — Global Youth Forum

HIVOS — International Humanist Institute for Cooperation via Development

HRW — Human Rights Watch

ICADS — Central American Institute for Development Studies

ICDCW — Institute for Community Development and Communications by Women

ICPD — International Conference on Population and Development *(add place and date)*

IFJ — International Federation of Journalists

IIDH — Inter-American Human Rights Institute

ILANUD — Latin American Institute for the Prevention of Delinquency

ILO — International Labor Organization

ILSA — Latin American Legal Services Institute

IRAW — International Rights Action Watch

IRRRAG — International Reproductive Rights Research Action Group

ISDN — digital phone line

ISIS — Women's International Communication Service

IWTC — International Women's Tribune Center

KULU — Women in Development (Denmark)

LANETA — Internet server, Mexico

MADRE — Women's NGO, USA

NGO — nongovernmental organization

NOW — National Organization of Women

OAS — Organization of American States

OXFAM — NGO for development, UK

PANOS Institute — Information and Communication for Sustainable Development, UK

PARLACEN — Central American Parliament

PREPCOM — preparatory meeting to a world conference

RCNA — Radio Caribbean News Agency

RDP — Reconstruction and Development Program

RED ADA — Women's Communication Network, Bolivia

RFPI — Radio for Peace International

RIF — Radio Internacional Feminista (Spanish name for FIRE)

RSMLAC — Latin American and Caribbean Women's Health Network

SEM — Women's Feature Service

SIPAM — Integrated Health Service for Women

SOA — School of the Americas

TAMWA — Tanzania Women's Media Collective

UCR — University of Costa Rica

UN — United Nations

UNCED — United Nations Conference on Environment and Development

UNEP — United Nations Environmental Program

UNESCO — United Nations Education, Science and Culture Organization

UNIFEM — United Nations Development Fund for Women

UPAZ — University for Peace in San José, Costa Rica

USAID — U.S. Agency for International Development

Vista — bulletin of Radio for Peace International

WACC — World Association for Christian Communication

WAMASC — Women's Alternative Media Action Service Center

WATC — Women's Affairs Technical Committee

WATER — Women's media organization, Austin, Texas, USA

WEDO — Women's Environmental and Development Organization

WHO — World Health Organization

WILPF — Women's International League for Peace and Freedom

WINGS — Women's International News Gathering Service

WLUML — Women Living Under Muslim Laws

Womnet — information network created by the International Women's Tribune Center

WOW — Wider Opportunities for Women

WPA — Women's Political Agenda

WTN — National Women's Television Network, Canada